"India's transformations will have great impact on Asian and global politics in the decades to come. This volume insightfully scrutinizes their diverse dimensions to highlight the promise and the pitfalls that mark India's ascent on the world stage."

Ashley J. Tellis, *Tata Chair for Strategic Affairs, Carnegie Endowment for International Peace*

"India's emergence from an aspirational power to a rising power is occurring in the middle of major global, regional and domestic changes. Here is a well-thought out set of papers capturing the opportunities and constraints that India is facing in its long-held aspiration for great power status and wider influence in the international system."

T.V. Paul, *James McGill Professor of International Relations, Department of Political Science, McGill University, Canada*

"brings together scholarship to reflect deeply on the significant and current issues facing a globalizing India. *Global India* is an easy read, and its coverage and topicality will render it invaluable for students and researchers alike."

Rahul Mukherji, *Professor and Chair, Modern Politics of South Asia, South Asia Institute, Heidelberg University*

Global India

India's anticipated rise to prominence in what has been termed the 'Asian 21st century' will have a significant impact upon geopolitics in the coming decades. As India's stature continues to increase across Asia and the world, appreciating which interests and principles structure the country's international interaction has never been more important. Central to these dynamics is how India's identity – and the longstanding values, principles and practices underpinning it – acts as the paramount factor that deeply structures the conduct of its international affairs. Acknowledging this centrality, this edited volume uses this factor as its foremost theme of analysis through which to understand and analyse India's most important regional, great power and diplomatic interactions. Not only providing a mechanism better to appreciate the historical foundations of these relationships, the focus on identity is also necessary to appreciate how the Hindu nationalism of the ruling Bharatiya Janata Party (BJP) under the leadership of Narendra Modi is now permeating Indian diplomacy. For the BJP, the pursuit – and attainment – of global influence and heightened status is the driving imperative of the BJP with regard to India's contemporary international affairs.

Chris Ogden is Senior Lecturer/Associate Professor in Asian Affairs at the University of St Andrews, where he researches contemporary great power politics, foreign policy and national security dynamics across South and East Asia. His most recent book is *The Authoritarian Century: China's Rise and the Demise of the Liberal International Order* (Bristol University Press, 2022). https://chris-ogden.org/.

Europa Country Perspectives

The *Europa Country Perspectives* series, from Routledge, examines a wide range of contemporary political, economic, developmental and social issues from areas around the world. Complementing the *Europa Regional Surveys of the World series*, *Europa Country Perspectives* is a valuable resource for academics, students, researchers, policymakers, business people and anyone with an interest in current world affairs.

While the *Europa World Year Book* and its associated Regional Surveys inform on and analyse contemporary economic, political and social developments at the national and regional level, Country Perspectives provide in-depth, country-specific volumes written or edited by specialists in their field, delving into a country's particular situation. Volumes in the series are not constrained by any particular template, but may explore a country's recent political, economic, international relations, social, defence, or other issues in order to increase understanding.

Barcelona, the Left and the Independence Movement in Catalonia
Richard Gillespie

The Taiwan Issue
Problems and Prospects
Edited by Benjamin Schreer and Andrew T. H. Tan

Facets of Security in the United Arab Emirates
Edited by William Guéraiche and Kristian Alexander

Disappearances in Mexico
From the 'Dirty War' to the 'War on Drugs'
Edited by Silvana Mandolessi and Katia Olalde

Electoral Politics in Sri Lanka
Presidential Elections, Manipulation and Democracy
S. I. Keethaponcalan

Global India
The Pursuit of Influence and Status
Edited by Chris Ogden

For more information about this series, please visit: www.routledge.com/Europa-Country-Perspectives/book-series/ECP.

Global India

The Pursuit of Influence and Status

**Edited by
Chris Ogden**

Routledge
Taylor & Francis Group

ESSAIR

LONDON AND NEW YORK

Designed cover image: © Shutterstock

First published 2023
by Routledge
4 Park Square, Milton Park, Abingdon, Oxon OX14 4RN

and by Routledge
605 Third Avenue, New York, NY 10158

Routledge is an imprint of the Taylor & Francis Group, an informa business

British Library Cataloguing in Publication Data
A catalogue record for this book is available from the British Library

ISBN: 978-1-032-24401-3 (hbk)
ISBN: 978-1-032-42161-2 (pbk)
ISBN: 978-1-003-30513-2 (ebk)

DOI: 10.4324/9781003305132

Typeset in Times New Roman
by Taylor & Francis Books

For Erin

Contents

Illustrations

Figures

Tables

Contributors

Maneesh Arora is Assistant Professor of Political Science at Wellesley College, Massachusetts. He received his PhD from the University of California, Irvine in 2019 and his M.Ed from Boston University in 2014. He specializes in race and ethnicity politics and public opinion, and is an affiliated researcher with the Taubman Center at Brown University and Sciences Po in Aix-en-Provence.

Astha Chadha is a Japanese Government MEXT PhD scholar at Ritsumeikan Asia Pacific University and a researcher at the University's Center for Democracy Promotion. Her research is focused on India-Japan relations, the role of religion in international relations, security and defence analyses of regional powers in the Indo-Pacific, South Asian rivalries and conflict resolution.

Aleksandra Jaskólska is Assistant Professor in the Faculty of Political Science and International Studies at the University of Warsaw. Her research interests include the role of domestic actors in shaping Indian foreign policy, political systems in countries of South Asia, regional parties in India, cultural diversity in South Asia and demographic challenges faced by South Asia. She is also involved in the activities of the Centre for Contemporary India Research and Studies, University of Warsaw.

Vedant Mehra is Lecturer in International Studies at Leiden University. He holds a Master of Science in International Relations and Diplomacy from Leiden University and a Bachelor of Arts in Political Science from the University of Delhi. Vedant's teaching and research interests concern comparative politics, diplomacy and security policy, with a focus on South Asia.

Agnieszka Nitza-Makowska is Assistant Professor and supervisor of Asian Studies at the Collegium Civitas, Warsaw. Her work focuses on soft power, environmental diplomacy, South Asia and its relations with China. Her most recent project investigates environmental diplomacy as a soft power instrument.

Aayushi Liana Shah is Junior Lecturer of Security Studies at the Faculty of Governance and Global Affairs of Leiden University. Her research interests include state diplomacy, South Asian and Indian foreign policy, conflict negotiations, crisis communication and critical approaches to security. Aayushi is also involved in designing and developing serious games on themes such as international conflict and crisis negotiations.

Parama Sinha Palit is Adjunct Senior Fellow in the Rajaratnam School of International Studies (RSIS) at Nanyang Technological University, Singapore. She specializes in foreign policy, diplomacy and international relations, and is the author of *Analyzing China's Soft Power Strategy and Comparative Indian Initiatives* (Sage, 2017). Her forthcoming book concerns *New Media and Public Diplomacy: Political Communication in India, the United States and China* (Routledge).

Vishwesh Sundar is a Lecturer on the BSc International Relations and Organisations programme at Leiden University. He holds an Advanced Master degree in International Relations and Diplomacy from Leiden University. His research specializes in migration and remittances and he has authored several articles on the topic.

Chirayu Thakkar is a Doctoral Candidate jointly with the National University of Singapore and King's College London. He has also been a Visiting Fellow with the Stimson Center, Washington DC. He has published in *International Affairs, Contemporary South Asia*, and outlets such as *Foreign Policy, National Interest* and *War on the Rocks*.

Christian Wagner is Senior Fellow at the German Institute for International and Security Affairs (SWP), Berlin. His main areas of interest are India, South Asia and the Indo-Pacific with a special focus on domestic politics, foreign policy and security issues. For more information, see www.swp-berlin.org/en/researcher/christian-wagner.

Stephen P. Westcott is Assistant Professor in the Department of Geopolitics and International Relations at the Manipal Academy of Higher Education. His research focuses on South Asian border disputes and Indo-Pacific geopolitics. He is the author of *Armed Coexistence: The Dynamics of the Intractable Sino-Indian Border Dispute* (Palgrave Macmillan, 2022).

Aleksei Zakharov is a Research Fellow in the School of International Affairs at the Higher School of Economics National Research University, Moscow. He also works as a Research Fellow at the Institute of Oriental Studies of the Russian Academy of Sciences. His area of research revolves around India's foreign policy, Russia–India and India–US relations, as well as the overall geopolitics of South Asia and the Indo-Pacific.

Chris Ogden is Senior Lecturer/Associate Professor in Asian Affairs at the University of St Andrews, where he researches contemporary great power politics, foreign policy and national security dynamics across South Asia and East Asia. His most recent book is *The Authoritarian Century: China's Rise and the Demise of the Liberal International Order* (Bristol University Press, 2022). https://chris-ogden.org/.

Sara Perlangeli is an Independent Researcher. She most recently completed an MPhil in Modern South Asian Studies at the University of Oxford.

Teesta Prakash is a Research Associate for the Southeast Asia program at the Lowy Institute, Sydney. Her research focus is on aid and development finance in the Indo-Pacific region. Additionally, she writes on Indian foreign policy towards Southeast Asia and the Pacific region.

Shubha Kamala Prasad is Assistant Professor of International Relations at the Hertie School, Berlin. Her research examines domestic sources of foreign policy, spanning sub-state conflict to diaspora mobilization. Her prior work experience includes organizing Track II Dialogues between India and Pakistan.

Nomita Prithviraj is Lecturer in Security Studies at Leiden University. She holds an Advanced Master degree in International Relations and Diplomacy from Leiden University. Her research interests relate in conflict resolution, negotiation, diplomacy and peace building.

Miriam Prys-Hansen is a Lead Research Fellow and Head of Research Programme 4: 'Global Orders and Foreign Policy' at the German Institute for Global and Area Studies (GIGA). She has published on global and regional environmental politics, the global climate regime, and the BRICS, as well as regionalism and regional institutions with a regional expertise on South Asia. For more information, see www.giga-hamburg.de/de/da s-giga/team/prys-hansen-miriam.

Sara Sadhwani is Assistant Professor of politics at Pomona College and a visiting scholar at the Bill Lane Center for the West at Stanford University. Her research examines elections, representation, and public opinion with a focus on Asian American and Latino voting behaviour. Prior to academia, she worked for nearly a decade advocating for the rights of immigrants at social justice organizations in Los Angeles.

Yoichiro Sato is Professor at the Ritsumeikan Asia Pacific University and is the Dean of the Department and the Graduate School of Asia Pacific Studies. His most recent major works include *Regional Institutions, Geopolitics and Economics in the Asia Pacific* (co-edited with Steve Rothman and Utpal Vyas, Routledge, 2017), and *Identity, Culture and Memory in Japanese Foreign Policy* (co-edited with Michal Kolmaš, Peter Lang, 2021).

Preface

The European Scholars of South Asian International Relations (ESSAIR) was founded in 2018, with an initial Steering Committee consisting of Chris Ogden, Raphaëlle Khan, Nicolas Blarel, Arndt Michael and Hannes Ebert. Its core aim is to establish an annual forum in Europe dedicated to scholars working on the international relations of South Asia, at which established academics and policy experts, emerging scholars and current postgraduate students can meet to discuss, exchange and synthesize their ideas. The first of these conferences took place in 2020, with annual iterations thereafter. This edited book brings together a selection of thirteen exceptional papers that were first presented at ESSAIR 2020 and ESSAIR 2021, by nineteen innovative scholars of South Asian affairs.

The contributions to this volume further reflect ESSAIR's goal of actively embracing a plurality of cutting-edge theoretical perspectives for the study of South Asia under the wide aegis of international relations (IR) and history, including political science, security studies, foreign policy, IR theory, comparative politics and institutionalism. They also underline how South Asia's contemporary rise to prominence will considerably impact upon geopolitics in the coming decades, and how it will be a dynamic central to the widely anticipated – and leading – role that Asia will play in international politics in the twenty-first century. Within an ever more interdependent and globalizing world, appreciating South Asia's politics and international relations has thus never been of such significance.

For more information about ESSAIR, please visit https://essair.org/.

Chris Ogden, Edinburgh, July 2022

Abbreviations

AAGC	Asia Africa Growth Corridor
AAP	Aam Admi Party
ADB	Asia Development Bank
AEP	Act East Policy
AIIB	Asian Infrastructure Investment Bank
AJK	Azad Jammu and Kashmir
ASEAN	Association of South East Asian States
BBIN	Bangladesh, Bhutan, India, Nepal Initiative
BIMSTEC	Bay of Bengal Initiative for Multi-Sectoral Technical and Economic Cooperation
BJP	Bharatiya Janata Party
BRI	Belt and Road Initiative
BRICS	Brazil, Russia, India, China, South Africa grouping
CAA	Citizenship Amendment Act
CHOGM	Commonwealth Heads of Government Meeting
CPEC	China Pakistan Economic Corridor
EAEU	Eurasian Economic Union
EU	European Union
FDI	foreign direct investment
FIPIC	Forum for India-Pacific Islands Cooperation
FOIP	Free and Open Indo Pacific
FONOP	Freedom of Navigation Operations
Hindutva	Hindu-ness
ICCR	Indian Council for Cultural Relations
IFS	Indian Foreign Service
INC	Indian National Congress
IPCC	Intergovernmental Panel on Climate Change
ISA	International Solar Alliance
ISRO	Indian Space Research Organisation
ITEC	Indian Technical and Economic Cooperation
J&K	Jammu and Kashmir
JWG	Joint Working Group
LAC	Line of Actual Control

LoC	Line of Control
MEA	Ministry of External Affairs
MoU	memorandums of understanding
MSR	Maritime Silk Road
MTCR	Missile Technology Control Regime
NAM	Non-Aligned Movement
NATO	North Atlantic Treaty Organization
NGO	non-governmental organization
NRI	Non-Resident Indian
NWS	nuclear weapons states
OCI	Overseas Citizen of India
ODA	Official Development Assistance
P5	permanent 5 members of the UNSC
PIC	Pacific Island Countries
PIF	Pacific Island Forum
RSS	Rashtriya Swayamsevak Sangh
SAARC	South Asia Association for Regional Cooperation
SAGAR	Security and Growth for All in the Region
SCO	Shanghai Cooperation Organisation
SII	Serum Institute of India
SLOC	sea lines of communication
SRM	Special Representative Mechanism
TERLS	Thumba Equatorial Rocket Launching Station
UK	United Kingdom
UNFCCC	United Nations Framework Convention on Climate Change
UNGA	United Nations General Assembly
UNSC	United National Security Council
UPA	United Progressive Alliance
US	United States
WHO	World Health Organization
WTO	World Trade Organization

Introduction

A Rising and Assertive India

Chris Ogden

India's contemporary rise to prominence will significantly impact upon geo-politics in the coming decades and is a key pillar of the widely anticipated Asian twenty-first century. As India's stature continues to increase, appreciating which interests and principles structure her international interaction has never been of greater importance. Focusing upon the state's present-day emergence as an economic, military and now diplomatic powerhouse, this edited book rigorously and informatively sets out the core – and wide-ranging – elements, relationships and challenges essential to understanding this rise. These factors crucially relate not only to consolidating India's pre-eminence within South Asia – as the foundation of its great power claims – but also how it interacts with the world's other great powers in the guise of China, Japan, Russia, France and the United States (US), and how New Delhi is able to articulate its global vision on the world stage. Prestige, rivalry and leadership permeate these interactions, especially as India asserts its influence and interests concerning issues ranging from the functioning of trade in South Asia, reacting to religious intolerance and conceiving of the Indian Ocean Region to climate policy, foreign aid and managing the ongoing Covid-19 pandemic. India's future stature in global affairs will vitally depend on how it deals with these and other concerns.

Central to these dynamics is how India's identity – and the longstanding values, principles and practices underpinning it – acts as the paramount factor that deeply structures the conduct of its international affairs. Acknowledging this centrality, this volume uses this factor as its foremost theme of analysis through which to more fully understand New Delhi's most important regional, great power and diplomatic interactions. Not only providing a mechanism to better appreciate the historical foundations of these relationships, the focus upon identity is also necessary to appreciate how the Hindu nationalism of the Bharatiya Janata Party (BJP) under the leadership of Narendra Modi is now permeating Indian diplomacy. For more than any other political entity in India, the pursuit – and attainment – of significant global influence and heightened status is the driving imperative of the BJP concerning India's contemporary international affairs. It is the keystone upon which New Delhi's economic, strategic, cultural, military and territorial

DOI: 10.4324/9781003305132-1

interests now rest, and is the central contention and analytical assertion permeating all the chapters of this volume considering the core dynamics of *Global India*.

Locating Identity

At their heart, India's global relations are driven by the values, principles and practices of the state's national identity, as determined by its major political parties and leaders. Such an identity is this volume's essential analytical 'lens' through which India's global relations will be explored, and which rests upon its history, memory and experience. Moreover, identity is argued to shape foreign policy as it 'forms the basis of interests' (Chacko, 2012: 13), as well as the ways in which other states are perceived as potentially cooperative partners or as prospective disruptive threats. Identities are thus crucial determinants of interaction that are exogenous to the international environment and act as mechanisms that do 'not establish clear policy options ... (but instead) offer a general vision and direction' (Björkdahl, 2002: 22). Focusing on identity acts as a guiding and orientating device through which a state's foreign policy proclivities can be better situated and understood. As per constructivist accounts in international relations – 'non-material structures affect what actors see as the realm of possibility: how they think that they should act; what the perceived limitations on their actions are, and what strategies they can imagine, let alone entertain, to achieve their objectives' (Reus-Smit, 2013: 226).

An identity-based form of analysis also underpins the *inter*-national aspect of global affairs, whereby 'reciprocal interaction ... create(s) and instantiate(s) the relatively enduring social structures in terms of which we define our identities and interests' (Wendt, 1992: 406). Such exchanges point to the importance of *intersubjectivity* and the *co-constitution* of identity and interests, which are dependent not only upon India's identity but how that identity interacts with, relates to and eventually coalesces – or not – with the identity and interests of other states. Such an exchange highlights how 'the producer of the identity is not in control of what it ultimately means to others' (Hopf, 1998: 175). Through this innate search for similarity and difference, the 'constitution of identity is achieved through the inscription of boundaries' (Campbell, 1992: 8), allowing a state to define itself against others. At times this is positive, for instance when India pursues economic or strategic goals that are shared by other key international stakeholders. At other times, it is negative, for example when it seeks to define itself (the '*self*') against negative experiences such as its colonial subjugation, or by explaining its identity versus '*others*' who are seen as enemies (such as Pakistan). Such a process aids the definition – and justification – of a state's identity and its ongoing construction.

In these ways, 'normative or ideational structures are as important as material structures' (Reus-Smit, 2013: 224). They also give meaning to material factors in international relations, whereby the formative building blocks of identity – primarily *history, memory* and *experience* – allow us to better comprehend the importance given to such factors. Using identity also lets us to focus explicitly upon what India regards as important in its global interactions. Crucially, such an emphasis permits our analysis to highlight *the role of internal factors* in the delineation of Indian foreign policy, whereby its domestic structure is of importance. By extension – through analysing New Delhi's key bilateral and regional relations – we can also pinpoint which interests other states regard as being important, and more decisively where these perspectives converge and diverge with India's. Such convergence and divergence are not limited to India's external relations but are also apparent internally between its dominant political groupings, in the guise of the Indian National Congress (INC) and the BJP. These groupings provide competing '"images of the world" ... (that) serve as switches determining the tracks on which the dynamism of interests kept (a state's) actions moving' (Weber quoted in Morgenthau, 2006: 11).

As Zerubavel notes, history 'constitutes one of the most important mechanisms by which ... (a state) constructs a collective identity' (Zerubavel, 1995: 214). Encompassing many of the key mechanisms intrinsic to identity formation, history is innately co-constitutive, incorporates repeated interactions between actors and provides context to these exchanges. Moreover, an appreciation of history provides the basis for understanding any 'distinct posture or orientation of the Self toward the Other' (Wendt, 1999: 258), as based upon a set of 'socially shared beliefs' (Alexandrov, 2003: 34). Due to its impact upon identity formation, the past has the capacity to affect the present but also the future of a state's foreign policy. It also acts as a repository to be used in the creation and sustenance of particular narratives about a state, and its past experience and future ambitions. Such narratives have the power to create 'good stories, gripping drama, believable (though not necessarily 'true') historical accounts ... (and) to locate the experience in time and place' (Bruner, 1986: 12). The use of such dominant accounts of the past thus serve to give meaning to a state's contemporary behaviour and decisions, and are ways in which identities are simultaneously created, maintained and propagated. Crucially, historical narratives are 'not simply imposed by the outside observer but rather are constructed by the participants themselves' (Barnett, 1999: 12) and in a media-driven age, 'the state which tells a better story prevails' (Khanna & Moorthy, 2017: 300).

India's Domestic Political Sources

India's national identity is primarily 'rooted in Indian history' (Dixit, 2004: 22). In the last decade, the basis of this identity has undergone a major shift as the ascendancy of the BJP to power under Narendra Modi, and their significant success in national elections in 2014 and 2019, has successfully challenged – and to a degree, superseded – the politics of the INC. Such a shift has seen the emergence of a more assertive and confident India, which when combined with the state's ever-increasing economic and military prowess, has translated into a more visible, determined and vocal foreign policy style. It has also opened up new possibilities for the conduct of India's international affairs, as states across South Asia, the Indo-Pacific and the world adjust not only to a more powerful India but also the resultant fluctuating power balances within global politics as a whole. Interaction, defining self and other and historical narratives underline these identities.

Under the INC, India gained independence in 1947 as a materially weak state yet driven by a desire to return to its pre-colonial status as a top-ranking great power in global affairs. As such, Nehru believed that 'India is going to be and is bound to be a big country that counts in world affairs' (Nehru, 1949: 216). Cognisant of both India's situation and its ambitions, he and others deployed a strategy of *moralpolitik* through 'the aggressive use of morality to advance national interests' (Karnad, 2002: 3). This approach was based upon a combination of values and pragmatism that also used historical discourses from ancient sources such as the *Mahabharata* to help construct India's contemporary identity. In particular, and despite being written around 900 BC, the *Mahabharata* was regarded as 'an irrefutable testimony to the greatness of India: its literary greatness, its spiritual greatness, its human greatness' (Bose & Jalal, 1998: 48). Thus, by providing a certain uniqueness to its perceived role on global affairs, India sought 'to bring about a more spiritual, tolerant and moral world order' (Dixit, 2004: 22). The identity that early leaders helped create rested upon a self / other dynamic that sought to 'conjure up the idea of a morally superior India professing scruples, having ethical bearings and offering a war-weary world an alternative path to peace and reconciliation' (Karnad, 2002: 1).

In these ways, 'a distinctive view of India's past allowed them [India's leaders] to shape their vision of India's future' (Cohen, 2001: 26). Underpinning this vision – and again reflecting India's relative material limitations versus other states in the international system – were key principles relating to non-violence (*ahimsa*), economic self-reliance (*swadeshi*), complete independence (*purna swaraj*), non-alignment and positive neutralism. In the divisive Cold War world, non-alignment championed 'principles of sovereignty, territorial integrity and political independence of states, the rights of peoples to self-determination and non-intervention in matters which are essentially within the jurisdiction of states' (Strydom, 2007: 5). Ultimately, 'the memories of colonial rule contributed to a political culture which privileged the concept of national autonomy' (Ganguly & Pardesi, 2009: 5) and the avoidance of acrimonious alliances (Adeney & Wyatt, 2010: 219). Domestically, the INC pursued a form of politics that was inclusive and tolerant of all religious factions, promoted plurality and equality and was anti-communal in that it did not privilege any one group over another (Ogden, 2014: 21–29).

The INC's interpretation of the past was not the only narrative informing India's political identity and thus how this identity impacts upon India's foreign policy proclivities. An alternative non-secular and religious-cultural view is held by the BJP whose focus upon *Hindutva* ('Hindu-ness') emphasizes 'a political community united by geographical origin, racial connection and a shared culture based on Sanskritic languages and common laws and rites' (Corbridge et al., 2013: 180) – a triptych of Hindus, Hindi and Hindustan. This narrative constructs India being first and foremost a Hindu state, and Hindus as representing the original community of India (Commuri, 2009). Contrary to the plurality and anti-communal outlook of the INC, some groups (such as Muslims and Christians) are perceived as intruders and are expected 'to demonstrate their loyalty to India and also recognize that India was (and is) primarily a Hindu civilization' (Varshney, 1991: 1001). Moreover, this majoritarian viewpoint sees India as being a state that 'will help build a more harmonious world order' (Bajpai, 2003: 250). Overall, the BJP can be argued to employ 'religious, allusive, militant, masculine, and anti-Muslim' (Guha, 2007: 635) rhetoric, which accelerated under Narendra Modi as India's Prime Minister since 2014. Such determining traits were in many ways the inverse of those held by the INC, and it is this volume's focus upon national identity, its formation across time and the influence of history and experience upon it, that will allow us to trace these changes and continuities.

Pursuing Influence and Status

Despite the clear differences between the INC and the BJP in terms of their political outlooks, both parties have displayed a remarkable consistency in terms of India's core foreign policy goals – the pursuit of influence and status. Central to this overlap is 'a consensus of ensuring India's emergence as a great power that is fully autonomous, influential and respected in the global comity of nations' (Ogden, 2011: 3). Such a vision of India can be regarded as the 'classic, underlying and timeless core in Indian foreign-policy' (Chaulia, 2002: 221), which is undeniable to those in the INC, BJP or beyond. A major part of this worldview is a narrative of victimhood, whereby the 'humiliations of imperialism and colonialism created a desire to gain prestige in the international system' (Miller, 2013: 31). Noting the touchstone of British imperialism as an essential 'other' to overcome so as to realize India's true 'self' identity, Miller notes a 'consciousness of past exploitation and perceived continued mistreatment' (Miller, 2013: 25) that is used to stimulate a sense of national pride and a need to re-find past glories and status. It is for this reason that Nehru pertinently noted the desire among the independence movement 'to revitalise India; ... through action and self-imposed suffering and sacrifice ... would we recharge the battery of India's spirit and waken her from her long slumber' (Nehru, 1989: 56).

In these ways, the INC's *moralpolitik* thus initially allowed for the peaceful and diplomatic expression of these yearnings, and Nehru would later note that 'if we have attained some respect in the eyes of other states in the world, it is because we have spoken with some sense of responsibility, with some sense of, not condemning, but trying to win over the people' (quoted in Kennedy, 2012: 201). With their emergence as a political competitor to the INC in the 1990s, and their eventual attainment of a majority in India's national elections in 2014 and 2019, the BJP added a strain of assertiveness and self-confidence in their heightening of India's global influence and status. Through an evident 'tone shift' (Ogden, 2018) and greater pragmatism, the BJP promoted an 'India First' policy through Modi's 'renewed energy, vigour, and planning in India's engagement with the rest of the world' (MEA, 2016). Modi's extensive foreign travel in his first term also emphasized 'his trademark style of wooing and sweeping the world off its feet ... [it] is a charm offensive ... to position India as a major power whose time to shine on the world stage has finally come after decades of disappointment' (Chaulia, 2016: 18). Overall, Modi has sought to make India a *vishwaguru* ('teacher of the world'), via the core belief that "nothing is better appreciated and better guaranteed to create respect ... in the world than a country that stands up for itself" (Karnad quoted in Sardesai & Thomas, 2016: 19).

Underpinning this approach has been a continued embrace of economic liberalization and (some of the benefits of) globalization, so as to maximize India's development and modernization aims. Although again differing in tone compared with the INC, the BJP is displaying deep continuities from previous governments and sees these aims as central to informing and strengthening its influence and status in global affairs. Modi's 'Make in India' campaign thus seeks to promote economic development by fostering global investment flows. It also underlines a focus on 'modernisation, not westernisation' (Modi quoted in ANI, 2013) and an India more 'favourably inclined toward Asianism as an alternative to the American capitalist model' (Jaffrelot, 2003: 45), which thus protects longstanding foreign policy aims concerning sovereignty and autonomy. India is also endeavouring to create a stable environment in which it can continue to prosper, with Modi declaring that 'in a world that is full of fault lines and rifts, we need to build a shared future' (quoted in Chainey, 2018), which is bolstered by ever-greater Indian visibility in international institutions. Intrinsic to such a vision is having a more equitable world, whereby 'India does not want to be simply co-opted into the existing international order that is controlled by the west. It must find its due place in it and be in a position to change the rules rather than simply adhere to existing ones' (Sibal quoted in Wojczewski, 2019: 196). By doing so, India's influence and status will become truly commensurate with that of a great power in international affairs, which will confirm the true arrival of *Global India*.

Structure and Chapter Outlines

Via a primary analytical emphasis upon the role of India's national identity, including its historical foundations and ongoing evolution over time, this volume's Chapters thus dissect and interrogate the most vital aspects of India's regional and global relations. Integral to their collective analysis are: (a) the role of history, memory and experience; (b) the intersubjectivity and co-constitution of identity based upon conceptions of 'self' and 'other'; and (c) the designation of fluid elements of continuity and change within both Indian foreign policy and the domestic political actors guiding its formation and delivery.

From this basis, Part I, concerning 'Consolidating Pre-eminence in South Asia', begins with Chapter 1 by Christian Wagner, which considers how India's regional environment in South Asia is evolving. Influenced by a more influential China, as well as a decoupling of India-Pakistan relations, he shows that New Delhi is being increasingly forced to shift its strategic attention to the Indo-Pacific in order to re-gain influence. Chapter 2 by Agnieszka Nitza-Makowska then deliberates on how ever-closer economic linkages between Pakistan and China are further altering the way in which India interacts with its region. In particular, she reveals how New Delhi's regional and global standing is being undermined by such links and the ways in which India is having to respond. In turn, Chapter 3 by Parama Sinha Palit analyses evidence of increasing digital religious intolerance in India and Bangladesh. She finds that such intolerance is frequently being exacerbated by the BJP's *Hindutva* identity and is now shaping India's public diplomacy. To conclude Part I, in Chapter 4 Sara Perlangeli investigates how Hindu nationalist accounts envisage the wider Indian Ocean. She uncovers how these narratives entail elements of India's commonality, leadership and status within the region, but also aspects of threat and fear.

In Part II, regarding 'Deepening Great Power Relations', Chapter 5 by Stephen P. Westcott then looks at India-China relations through the prism of their ongoing territorial disputes. He highlights key themes relating to India's – as well as China's – attempts to protect their regional and global prestige, which is hampering progress in negotiations. Chapter 6 by Astha Chadha and Yoichiro Sato next examines India's growing strategic convergence with Japan. Unearthing significant synergies concerning economic and military cooperation in the Indo-Pacific, as well a common partner in the US, New Delhi's relations with Tokyo are also being influenced by an ever more powerful China. Continuing the theme of India's growing strategic value and significance in contemporary geopolitics, Chapter 7 by Aleksei Zakharov scrutinizes the evolution of France and Russia's interaction with India. He discovers the increasing importance that both states place upon having better ties with New Delhi, especially from a military perspective, as well as India's need for foreign partners to boost her global influence. Part II ends with Chapter 8, in which Chirayu Thakkar unveils the complexities behind India–US relations. He ascertains how despite growing strategic convergence in many areas, New Delhi is not completely assimilating itself to US interests, and instead aims to maintain its autonomous status.

Part III, 'Articulating a Diplomatic Vision', begins with Chapter 9 by Aayushi Liana Shah, Nomita Prithviraj, Vedant Mehra and Vishwesh Sundar, who cogitate upon the role of paradiplomacy in India's international affairs. Showcasing the multiple values and principles influencing the nature of India's modern diplomacy, it confirms the influence of globalization and sub-national identities upon New Delhi's global interactions. In turn, Chapter 10 by Miriam Prys-Hansen focuses upon the interplay of narratives and identities upon how New Delhi conceives of its climate policy. She asserts differences between the current BJP and previous INC regimes, and how India's strategy is influenced by identity, as well as a search for global leadership. Chapter 11 by Teesta Prakash then ruminates on India's growing use of foreign aid in the Pacific region. In particular, she emphasizes New Delhi's growing strategic competition with Beijing, as India seeks to balance China's influence in the region. Next, Chapter 12 by Shubha Kamala Prasad, Maneesh Arora and Sara Sadhwani deliberates on how the normalization of Hindutva sentiments within India are impacting the Indian diaspora in the US. They determine that identity, religion and geography are all crucial variants in this interplay and are influencing external political preferences. Finally, Chapter 13 by Aleksandra Jaskólska then studies the impact and political opportunities that Covid-19 has had for Indian diplomacy. She relates how India's domestic and international responses to the pandemic have had a varied – if at times, negative – impact upon New Delhi's pursuit of status and influence, and lays bare a state whose material shortcomings, especially vis-à-vis China, may hamper this quest.

Pulling together the findings from each of these chapters, the 'Conclusions' chapter by Chris Ogden seeks to pinpoint the various common themes structuring New Delhi's contemporary international relations. In unison, the interweaving of these strands confirms the importance of identity in India's global diplomacy, the ongoing need to gain further power and prestige on the world stage and the ever-increasing importance that all states – in particular the international system's great powers – place on enhancing their ties with India. This latter point especially underscores the primacy of India – as well as its strategic necessity – in our understanding of current and future international relations, and confirms how the reality of *Global India* will shape and transform modern geopolitics.

References

Adeney, Katherine and Andrew Wyatt (2010) *Contemporary India* (Basingstoke: Palgrave Macmillan).
Alexandrov, Maxym (2003) 'The Concept of State Identity in International Relations: A Theoretical Analysis', *Journal of International Development and Cooperation*, 10 (1): 33–46.
ANI (2013) 'India Needs Modernisation, Not Westernisation: Narendra Modi', *DNA India*, 14 July. Available at www.dnaindia.com/india/report-india-needs-modernisa tion-not-westernisation-narendra-modi-1860977 [last accessed 7 April 2018].
Bajpai, Kanti (2003) 'Indian Conceptions of Order and Justice: Nehruvian, Gandhian, Hindutva, and Neo-Liberal', in Rosemary Foot, John Lewis Gaddis and

Andrew Hurrell (eds.), *Order and Justice in International Relations* (Oxford: Oxford UP), pp. 236–261.

Barnett, Michael (1999) 'Culture, Strategy and Foreign Policy Change: Israel's Road to Oslo', *European Journal of International Relations*, 5 (1): 5–36.

Björkdahl, Annika (2002) 'Norms in International Relations: Some Conceptual and Methodological Reflections', *Cambridge Review of International Affairs*, 15 (1): 9–23.

Bose, Sugata, and Ayesha Jalal (1998) *Modern South Asia: History, Culture, Political Economy* (London: Routledge).

Bruner, Jerome (1986) *Actual Minds, Possible Worlds* (Cambridge, MA: Harvard UP).

Campbell, David (1992) *Writing Security: United States Foreign Policy and the Politics of Identity* (Minneapolis, MN: University of Minnesota Press).

Chacko, Priya (2012) *Indian Foreign Policy: The Politics of Postcolonial Identity from 1947 to 2004* (New York: Routledge).

Chainey, Ross (2018) 'Narendra Modi: These Are The 3 Greatest Threats to Civilization'. Available at www.weforum.org/agenda/2018/01/narendra-modi-davos-these-are-the-3-greatest-threats-to-civilization/ [last accessed 3 March 2018].

Chaulia, Sreeram (2002) 'The BJP, India's Foreign Policy and the "Realist Alternative" to the Nehruvian Tradition', *International Politics*, 39 (2): 215–234.

Chaulia, Sreeram (2016) *Modi Doctrine: The Foreign Policy of India's Prime Minister* (New Delhi: Bloomsbury).

Cohen, Stephen P. (2001) *India: Emerging Power* (Washington, DC: Brookings Institution Press).

Commuri, Gitika (2009) 'The Relevance of National Identity Narratives in Shaping Foreign Policy: The Case of India-Pakistan', *Journal of South Asian Development*, 4 (2): 161–202.

Corbridge, Stuart, John Harris and Craig Jeffrey (2013) *India Today: Economy, Politics & Society* (Cambridge: Polity Press).

Dixit, J. N. (2004) *Makers of India's Foreign Policy* (New Delhi: HarperCollins).

Ganguly, Sumit, and Manjeet S. Pardesi (2009) 'Explaining Sixty Years of India's Foreign Policy', *India Review*, 8 (1): 4–19.

Guha, Ramachandra (2007) *India After Gandhi: The History of the World's Largest Democracy* (New Delhi: Macmillan).

Hopf, Ted (1998) 'The Promise of Constructivism in International Relations Theory', *International Security*, 23 (1): 171–200.

Jaffrelot, Christophe (2003) 'India's Look East Policy: An Asianist Strategy in Perspective', *India Review*, 2 (2): 35–68.

Jain, B. M. (2008) *Global Power: India's Foreign Policy, 1947–2006* (Lanham, MD: Lexington).

Karnad, Bharat (2002) *Nuclear Weapons and Indian Security* (New Delhi: Macmillan).

Kennedy, Andrew B. (2012) *The International Ambitions of Mao and Nehru – National Efficacy Beliefs and the Making of Foreign Policy* (Cambridge: Cambridge UP).

Khanna, Shrey, and P. Moorthy (2017) 'Analysing India's Soft Power Functioning in the Twenty-first Century: Possibilities and Challenges', *India Quarterly*, 73 (3): 292–311.

MEA (2016) *Ministry of External Affairs, Annual Report 2015–16* (New Delhi: Policy Planning and Research Division, Ministry of External Affairs).

Miller, Manjari Chatterjee (2013) *Wronged by Empire: Post-Imperial Ideology and Foreign Policy in India and China* (Stanford, CA: Stanford UP).

Morgenthau, Hans J. (2006) *Politics Among Nations* (New York: McGraw-Hill).

Nehru, Jawaharlal (1949) 'Non-Alignment With Blocs', in *Jawaharlal Nehru's Speeches*, volume 1 (Delhi: Publications Division, Government of India), pp. 216–218.

Nehru, Jawaharlal (1989) *The Discovery of India* (New York: Oxford UP).

Ogden, Chris (2011) 'International "Aspirations" of a Rising Power', in David Scott (ed.), *Handbook of India's International Relations* (London: Routledge), pp. 3–13.

Ogden, Chris (2014) *Hindu Nationalism and the Evolution of Contemporary Indian Security: Portents of Power* (Delhi: Oxford UP).

Ogden, Chris (2018) 'Tone Shift: India's Dominant Foreign Policy Aims Under Modi', *Indian Politics and Policy*, 1 (1): 3–23.

Reus-Smit, Christian (2013) 'Constructivism', in Scott Burchill and Andrew Linklater (eds.), *Theories of International Relations* (Basingstoke: Palgrave Macmillan), pp. 217–240.

Sardesai, D. R., and Raju C. G. Thomas (2016) *Nuclear India in the Twenty-First Century* (London: Palgrave Macmillan).

Strydom, Hennie (2007) 'The Non-Alignment Movement and the Reform of International Relations', *Max Planck Yearbook of United Nations Law*, 11: 1–46.

Varshney, Ashutosh (1991) 'India, Pakistan, and Kashmir: Antinomies of Nationalism', *Asian Survey*, 31 (11): 997–1019.

Wendt, Alexander (1992) 'Anarchy is what States Make of It: The Social Construction of Power Politics', *International Organization*, 46 (2): 391–425.

Wendt, Alexander (1999) *Social Theory of International Politics* (Cambridge: Cambridge UP).

Wojczewski, Thorsten (2019) 'Identity and World Order in India's Post-Cold War Foreign Policy Discourse', *Third World Quarterly*, 40 (1): 180–198.

Zerubavel, Yael (1995) *Roots: Collective Memory and the Making of Israeli National Tradition* (Chicago, IL: University of Chicago Press).

Part I

Consolidating Pre-eminence in South Asia

1 India's New Regional Environment

South Asia 2.0

Christian Wagner

The rise of states in the international system is often linked with their pre-dominance over their immediate neighbourhood (Mearsheimer, 2001). (Neo-) realist approaches would highlight aspects like economic power and military dominance by which states try to pursue their national interests vis-à-vis other countries (Waltz, 1979). In contrast, (liberal) institutional approaches would also emphasize the ability of states to provide public goods for instance through regional institutions, generous trade agreements, and connectivity designs in order to exert influence (Keohane, 2012). These different theoretical approaches are mirrored in the debate on India as a 'regional power' or a 'regional hegemon' in South Asia (Sen Gupta, 1975; Mohan, 2022). India has a long history of political, diplomatic, economic, military, cultural, open, and clandestine interventions in its neighbouring countries, with successes and failures. Its neighbours have used different strategies in order to follow, support, neutralize, or resist India's initiatives.

The chapter argues that South Asia is undergoing a fundamental change that will have far reaching repercussions on India's relations with its neighbours. This transformation has been triggered by different processes on the global, the regional and the national level. Some of these developments have been initiated by India, while some have been initiated by other states to which India has had to react. Collectively, these changes may lead to what could be referred to as *South Asia 2.0*. So far, South Asia may not have been a perfect place for India's regional ambitions but there are many indications that South Asia 2.0 will most likely be a much more difficult regional environment for India. However, India's weakened position in the region does not necessarily imply that this will have negative consequences on its international rise and ambitions. The gap between a weakened regional status and India's growing international status, for instance in global governance fora, indicates the conceptual weaknesses of existing theoretical approaches. From this basis, it seems that the concept of rising states in the twenty-first century may need a different theoretical approach within which the regional and the international levels are not necessarily linked any longer. This may also challenge aspects of India's foreign policy identity which has traditionally linked its international power aspirations with a leading role in the region.

DOI: 10.4324/9781003305132-3

In order to elaborate these arguments, the first part of this chapter will look at the creation of the concept of South Asia. The focus here will be on the evolution of historical descriptions and the different internal and external developments that shaped the idea of a distinct region after the period of decolonization in 1947. The second part will then look at recent changes on the different levels that shape the contours of South Asia 2.0. Globally, the emphasis will be on the rise of China and the impact of its Belt and Road Initiative (BRI) on South Asia. On the regional level, the focus will be on the growing estrangement between India and Pakistan since 2016. On the national level, the rise of religious nationalism that can be observed in many parts of South Asia is undermining traditional forms of cultural syncretism.

The Creation of South Asia

The geographical landmass that is known as the Indian subcontinent has seen various denominations. Historically, this part of the world has been referred to as 'India' by Greek and Latin authors or as 'Hindustan' by Persian scholars (Clémentin-Ojha, 2014: 1). The terminology was derived from the Indus River and was adopted in European maps which referred to the subcontinent as 'Hindostan' and/or 'India' (Schwartzberg, 1992: 51–52). Sanskrit texts from the subcontinent like the Puranas also used the term 'Bharat'. In turn, the political development of the region was mostly shaped by power struggles between regional kingdoms. Hence, a political order encompassing the whole area of the subcontinent has always remained the exception not the rule. Some dynasties have been able to establish an empire, for instance the Mauryas in the third century BC or Moghul emperors like Akbar in the sixteenth century.

The arrival of the European powers in the late fifteenth century changed the political landscape. 'British-India' which developed since the mid-eighteenth century consisted of a mixture of direct and indirect rule with the colonial administration and more than 500 princely states. During the anti-colonial struggle, the concept of an Indian civilization was formulated in order to underline its equivalence with the Western civilization. The idea of the Indian civilization was derived from religious texts and was related to a social order (Bhattacharya, 2012), while the concept of the Indian civilization consisted of different variants (Hoeber Rudolph, 2010). In this context, Indian nationalist writers started to link the term 'Bharat' with concepts of ethnicity and territory thereby establishing a new interpretation of the term (Clémentin-Ojha, 2014: 4). The development of the concept of *Hindutva*, which was formulated by V. D. Savarkar and M. S. Golwalkar during the 1920s and 1930s, also initiated a debate about 'Greater India' that highlighted the influence of Indian culture to regions like Southeast Asia (Raghavan, 2018). At the time of independence different names like 'Bharat, India, Al-Hind and Hindustan coexisted to designate the Indian subcontinent' (Clémentin-Ojha, 2014: 2).

External Drivers: The Cold War and the Development of Area Studies in the United States

The creation of 'South Asia' as a new and distinct conceptual notion only came after the decolonization of British India in 1947. It seems to have been driven mostly by external factors rather than by initiatives emanating from within the region. In the context of the Cold War, area study centres were established at American universities in order to provide better knowledge on the growing number of newly independent states. South Asian studies were themselves fostered by different developments (Brown, 1964; Patterson, 1998). As such, philanthropic foundations like Carnegie provided financial support for universities like Pennsylvania in 1948, and later for Cornell, while in 1951 a report of a joint committee from American Council of Learned Societies and the Social Science Research Council was published, entitled 'Southern Asia Studies in the United States: A Survey and Plan'. As a result, the US government instituted language fellowship programmes for the region. In the 1950s, the Rockefeller and Ford Foundation also started their first programmes for Indian and South Asian studies.

In 1957, South Asia became a sub-region of Asian studies with the newly established Association for Asian Studies (Patterson, 1998: 29). In this period, area studies centres were also established under the National Defence Education Act of 1958. Although federal funding changed in later years, multiple universities were able to use federal financial support to establish a continuing research tradition on South Asia (Patterson, 1998: 33–34). Research on South Asia received a further boost with the amendment of Public Law 480. Since the 1950s, the United States had shipped food-grains to India to avoid famine which had been paid in Indian currency but with the amendment of Public Law 480, the Library of Congress was able to use the Indian currency of the American administration for educational and research purposes. Similar programmes were established with Pakistan, Nepal, and Sri Lanka which led to a massive increase of library resources on South Asia in the United States (Patterson, 1998: 30).

Internal Drivers: Regionalism and Foreign Policy in South Asia

Compared to the developments in the United States, there was hardly any initiatives from within South Asia to promote regional cooperation. After the decolonization of India, Pakistan, and Sri Lanka in 1947/48 all countries in the subcontinent faced similar challenges with regard to their economic and social development. One of the earliest attempts was the 'Colombo Plan for Co-operative Economic Development in South and South-East Asia' which was initiated by the Commonwealth and started in 1951. India's development cooperation with neighbouring countries further intensified when the Indian Technical and Economic Cooperation (ITEC) program was launched in 1964.

But in this early period, India's approach to its neighbourhood was mostly shaped by its bilateral security interests rather than by the provision of regional public goods. The friendship treaties with Bhutan (1949), Nepal (1950), and Sikkim (1950) strengthened India's pre-eminence in these countries and allowed New Delhi to pursue its security interests in the Himalayas vis-à-vis China. On the global level, Jawaharlal Nehru, India's first prime minister, underlined India's international ambitions often with reference to its civilization, its history and traditions in a liberal interpretation (Nehru, 1961: 21, 39). With regard to India's regional environment, Nehru was a strong protagonist of Asian solidarity but he did not conceptualize of the neighbouring region as being 'South Asia' (Nehru, 1961).

Prime Minister Indira Gandhi continued India's bilateral approach towards its neighbourhood. The 'Indira Doctrine' underlined India's self-image as a regional power after the defeat of Pakistan and the creation of Bangladesh in 1971 (Hagerty, 1991). This self-conception laid the foundation for India's interventions in Sri Lanka and the Maldives in the 1980s. As a counterweight to India's regional ambitions, Bangladesh launched the idea of closer regional cooperation in 1977 (Michael, 2013). These negotiations led to the first summit of the heads of states in Dhaka and the creation of the South Asia Association for Regional Cooperation (SAARC) in December 1985.[1] Despite numerous activities and support from international agencies, SAARC has never been able to become a successful regional organization. The most obvious indicator is the number of summits held. Initially, the idea had been to have annual summits, but the political tensions mostly between India and Pakistan have led to a postponement several times. Hence, in the 31-year period between 1985 and 2015, SAARC had only 18 summits.

India's approach towards the region changed fundamentally in the 1990s. In 1996, foreign Minister I. K. Gujral highlighted the principle of non-reciprocity of India's relations with its neighbours, signalling a renunciation of the Indira Doctrine. The change was eventually initiated both through economic liberalization since 1991, which required more regional cooperation, and policy failures like the military intervention in Sri Lanka between 1987 and 1990. At the SAARC summit in 2007, Prime Minister Manmohan Singh laid out his vision of regional connectivity, stating that 'connectivity – physical, economic and of the mind, enabling us to use fully our geographical and resource endowments, has historically been the key to our region's peace and prosperity. South Asia has flourished most when connected to itself and the rest of the world' (quoted in Ministry of External Affairs, 2007). India also provided special regulations for less developed neighbours to increase economic collaboration but Indian governments lacked resources and capacities to provide regional public goods in a substantive manner.

What Constitutes South Asia?

The brief overview shows that in contrast to regional initiatives, external drivers seem to have been more important and effective in shaping the notion of 'South Asia'. In contrast to historical notions like 'India', 'Hindustan', or 'Bharat', the terminology of 'South Asia' also included the recognition of the post-colonial state system that developed in the subcontinent after 1947. Until the mid-2010s South Asia could be described by several characteristics. First, from an outside perspective, the region was mostly equated with the rivalry between India and Pakistan and its negative implications like the Kashmir conflict, the danger of nuclear escalation and terrorism (Cohen, 2013; Ganguly, 2002; Paul, 2009). From India's perspective, South Asia was for most of the time after 1947 an additional set of bilateral relationships rather than a strategy for providing regional public goods. In these ways, South Asia was a difficult neighbourhood politically, and bilateral relations remained dependent on domestic political constellations. Changes of government, be it by elections or by coups, could also have far reaching repercussions as India experienced – for instance – in its relations with Bangladesh, Nepal, Sri Lanka, and the Maldives.

Second, economically, South Asia was still shaped by the paradox of being one of the fastest growing regions on the one hand, but also being the poorest in global comparison on the other hand. Intra-regional trade had improved over the decades but only by minimal margins, and in the 1980s was estimated to be around 3%. In 2015 South Asia was still the least integrated region in the Asia-Pacific with an intra-regional trade of only 6% (UNESCAP, 2018: 1). Despite its claim as a regional power, India mostly lacked resources and capacities to provide public goods for its neighbours in a long-term perspective. Moreover, the lack of complementarity did not create incentives for closer regional economic collaboration.

Finally, on both the societal and cultural level, South Asia became famous for its 'unity in diversity'. This highlighted the syncretic traditions that have emerged from the intermingling of different religious belief systems and societal structures over the centuries. One of the most famous examples are the Sufis who have combined local traditions from Islam and Hinduism. But these traditions could not prevent a variety of distributive conflicts over resources, rights and identity, culminating partly in civil wars like for instance in East Pakistan, Sri Lanka and Nepal.

The Contours of South Asia 2.0

Different developments on the global, regional, and national level may have long term repercussions on the concept of South Asia and India's relations towards its neighbours. On the global level, the main driver is China's rise and the implications of the BRI in South Asia. And on the regional level, it is the process of decoupling between India and Pakistan, which can be observed since 2016. On the national level, rising nationalism and authoritarianism in many countries may strengthen national identities at the cost of religious and linguistic pluralism. These developments may also resonate in the foreign relations with other countries. In India, nationalist Hindu groups and parts of the ruling Bharatiya Janata Party (BJP) have supported the idea of Nepal as a Hindu state which was opposed by many centre and leftist parties in the Himalaya state. In Sri Lanka, extremist Buddhist groups and parties have often been critical vis-à-vis India's engagement. In their view, New Delhi was perceived as a representative of the Tamil minority whose demands for more autonomy were seen as a threat to the religious unity of the country.

The Global Dimension: The Impact of the BRI in South Asia

Few other regions have been so deeply affected by China's BRI than South Asia, in both positive and negative ways. On the positive side, for many South Asian countries the BRI offers a large and welcome investment which helped to improve national infrastructures. Pakistan, which is one of China's few strategic partners, has received the largest investment. The China Pakistan Economic Corridor (CPEC) is projected to have received around $60 billion for various infrastructure and energy projects (Economic Times, 2021), however the actual figures and many project details are not very transparent, which has created various controversies between the government and the opposition parties. Sri Lanka was a case that received a lot of international attention in the BRI debate, whereby because of its massive investment, China became Sri Lanka's single largest lender, holding 12% of the country's total debt (Roy Chaudhury, 2019). Sri Lanka was also the first country in the region where Chinese investments faced criticism after the change of government in 2015. In 2017 the Sri Lankan government had to enter into a treaty of 99 years to hand over the port of Hambantota that had been built with Chinese investment.

During his visit to Bangladesh in 2016, President Xi announced future investments of $24 billion in the country, and the Indian think tank Gateway House estimated that China has already committed $31 billion for various infrastructure projects (Mahmud, 2019). In Nepal, China became the largest investor in the Himalayan country for the first time in 2014, with China's development assistance being $38 million in 2014/15, which was far larger than India's $22 million (Bhatia et al., 2016). In September 2018, China and Nepal also agreed on a 'Trade and Transit Protocol' that allowed the landlocked Himalayan country access to Chinese sea and dry ports. This has reduced Nepal's dependence on land access only through India. In response, governments in New Delhi have used border blockades various times in order to put pressure on Kathmandu. On the negative side, the adverse impact of BRI investments like rising debts levels, the lack of transparency or the unclear outcome for local employment have also triggered controversial debates in many South Asian countries.

From the Chinese perspective, regarding the response to its connectivity designs, South Asia seems to represent extreme opposites. On the positive side, the CPEC is the single largest project of the BRI. Moreover, Pakistan's strategic importance has increased because it is one of the few countries in which China's maritime and land belt connectivity projects meet. On the negative side, India is the most important country in Asia that constantly refuses to participate in the BRI. India's main and unique criticism is that the CPEC runs through Kashmir, which is claimed by New Delhi as Indian territory. Moreover, India has also criticized the lack of transparency in the BRI projects and the dangers of rising debt for recipient countries (Indian Express, 2021).

BRI investments after 2013 have also shifted the regional geopolitical matrix in favour of China. But one would be mistaken to argue that India lost its influence in South Asia only because of the BRI. China had already invested in the region and had expanded its ties with India's neighbours long before the BRI. Moreover, India's neighbours have a long tradition of playing the 'China card' in order to balance India's influence. As a result, the BRI may have just strengthened a process that has already long been there in South Asia. For the smaller states, China is politically a neutral partner compared to India, because there are hardly any major bilateral issues. Economically, China is more attractive than India and the BRI has increased this economic attractiveness (Wagner, 2016). Furthermore, the constellation between India and its neighbours has been conducive to China's increasing weight in South Asia.

What are the potential implications of the BRI for the conception of South Asia? On the positive side one can argue that infrastructure investment will contribute to enhance economic growth in the mid- to long-term perspective. Better economic development may also foster more regional cooperation, thereby strengthening – at least indirectly – institutions like SAARC. On the negative side, one can argue that Chinese investment will further strengthen the bilateral economic relations (i.e. trade flows) between China and the recipient countries. However, the integration of South Asian economies into Chinese value and supply chains will not provide incentives for closer regional cooperation with India. Moreover, large Chinese investments will shape the norms and technical standards used in South Asian economies to which Indian companies might then have to comply in the long term, which would reduce India's influence in this regard. As such, the BRI may not create new incentives to increase the low levels of intra-regional trade. These developments will therefore undermine the process of regionalism and will further weaken the concept of South Asia.

The Regional Dimension

The first factor to consider here is the de-coupling of India–Pakistan relations, which is often used in South Asia as a synonym for the India–Pakistan relationship. Although the main issues, such as the lingering conflict over Kashmir remains, 'de-coupling' rather than 'rapprochement' seems to have become the dominant trend in bilateral relations since 2016. Leading up to this trend, when Indian Prime Minister Modi took power in 2014, he invited all neighbouring countries to attend the inauguration of his government. Moreover, Modi propagated a 'Neighbourhood First' policy, and his surprise visit to Pakistan in December 2015 seemed to open a new era of bilateral relations. The Pathankot attack in early January 2016 however appeared to sabotage Modi's attempt for a rapprochement with Islamabad similar to the Kargil War in 1999. But even after the attack Pakistan continued its cooperation and offered its support to India (Syed, 2016).

The break in bilateral relationships became obvious after the Uri attack in September 2016. Militarily, India reacted with surgical strikes against terrorist camps across the Line of Control. Such military operations seemed to have happened in the past as well but it was the first time that the Indian government made them public. Diplomatically, India withdrew from the scheduled SAARC summit in Islamabad in October of that year and was supported by other SAARC members. Moreover, India used the BRICS (Brazil, Russia, India, China, South Africa) summit in Goa in October 2016 to extend the Bay of Bengal Initiative for Multi-Sectoral Technical and Economic Cooperation (BIMSTEC) and invited Afghanistan and the Maldives, which were officially not members of the grouping. This was an obvious attempt to create a 'SAARC Minus One' format. Since then, the Modi government has put more efforts in the revitalization of BIMSTEC rather than on SAARC. India also became less inclined towards any form of dialogue and insisted that talks with Pakistan would only be possible again once terrorism had ended.

The new Pakistan Prime minister Imran Khan, who took power in summer 2018, tried again to set up a dialogue with India. But his attempts failed in 2019 after the terrorist attack in Pulwama in February 2019, which was claimed by the Pakistan based group Jaish-e-Mohammed, and which led to India attacking alleged terrorist camps in Balakot in the Pakistan province of Khyber Pakhtunkhwa. In contrast to previous retaliatory measures, the Balakot air raid included a strong message, because for the first time India attacked Pakistan territory directly in peace time. Moreover, the Indian government decided to withdraw Pakistan's Most Favoured Nations status and imposed a custom duty of 200% on all goods from Pakistan entering India (Dawn, 2019). This was mainly a symbolic measure because Pakistan had never replicated this status to India.

In August 2019, the Indian decision to withdraw the special status of Jammu and Kashmir and bifurcate the state into two Union territories provoked sharp reactions from Pakistan. As part of Pakistan's diplomatic activities against India's decision, Khan also took back his offers for talks (Masood & Abi-Habib, 2019). The opening of the Kartarpur corridor for Sikh pilgrims from Pakistan in November 2019 then created new hopes for the resumption of the dialogue, however these did not materialize (Basu, 2019). Overall, since 2016, there has been an obvious decoupling of the bilateral relationship. The decoupling is probably least problematic in the economic field because the official trade has always been lower compared to the informal trade via third countries. It is more evident in the political field where both sides have substantiated their mutual accusations over '-Kashmir' and 'terrorism'. The composite dialogue between 2004 and 2008 that had brought substantial improvement in the bilateral relationship and even a workable solution for Kashmir also become somewhat of a distant dream.

The second factor in the regional dimension is that of sub-regional cooperation, whereby South Asia has also seen a variety of new and revived regional and sub-regional initiatives in recent years. As already mentioned, the revitalization of BIMSTEC was closely linked to the deterioration of the India–Pakistan relations after 2016. Since then, India has started various initiatives in the context of BIMSTEC but progress so far is hampered by a lack of resources (Xavier, 2018). In turn, the Bangladesh, Bhutan, India, Nepal (BBIN) Initiative has its origins in the SAARC process and aims to make regional cooperation more effective with the creation of sub-regional formats. The main outcome so far is the 'BBIN Motor Vehicles Agreement' that was signed in 2015. The original idea was to have a similar agreement on the SAARC level but this failed because of differences with Pakistan. In 2017, Bhutan backed out of the agreement, and until 2019 the three other states have still not implemented the agreement which aims to improve road connectivity and transport corridors (Chatterjee & Ganguly, 2020). Another sub-regional format in the SAARC context is the maritime cooperation between India, Sri Lanka and the Maldives that started in 2012 (Radhakrishnan, 2012).

As a new development, China has also started various initiatives for regional institutions with a series of tri- and multilateral dialogues with South Asian countries. In 2017, Beijing established a dialogue format with Afghanistan and Pakistan aiming at bringing Afghanistan closer to the BRI and discussing common security challenges (Siddiqui, 2019). In summer 2020, India and China faced a serious crisis after transgression of the Line of Actual Control in Ladakh/Aksai Chin. In June, a clash between the two armies in the Galwan valley left 20 Indian soldiers and an unknown number of Chinese soldiers dead. The incident also undermined the rapprochement between the two countries that had started with Rajiv Gandhi's visit to China in 1988. In long negotiations both sides had signed six agreements in order to establish a status quo along the LAC (Kumar, 2020). Following the crisis with India, China started to intensify its dialogue with India's neighbours and held a joint meeting with Afghanistan, Nepal and Pakistan to encourage the South Asian countries to 'step up cooperation for regional peace and security, and work together to curb the coronavirus' (Elmer, 2020).

The fight against the Covid-19 pandemic has helped China intensify its links with South Asia and to open another chapter in Sino-Indian rivalry in South Asia (Haidar, 2020; Malhotra, 2020). In particular, China used the pandemic to revitalize its Health Silk Road project, which was devised as far back as 2015. South Asian countries like Bangladesh, the Maldives, Nepal, Pakistan, and Sri Lanka have also benefitted from Chinese medical support in the guise of testing kits, personal protective equipment and other medical supplies. Inadequate public health systems in most South Asian countries all offer China a perfect foot in the door in the post-Covid era through investments in health infrastructure (Pal & Bhatia, 2020: 2). In November 2020, China also staged a meeting with Pakistan, Bangladesh, Nepal, and Sri Lanka 'to build up a "political consensus" in efforts to contain the Covid-19 pandemic and boost economic development' (Roche, 2020). In reaction to the pandemic, India has also sent medical supplies and medical teams to all of its SAARC partners except Pakistan. Moreover, the Indian government revitalized SAARC and initiated a Covid-19 Emergency Fund to which all members, except Pakistan, contributed more than US $18 million (Bhattacherjee, 2020).

These initiatives underline that China prefers traditionally bi- or mini-lateral formats over regional institutions. They also indicate that China is willing to intensify the dialogue with like-minded countries in South Asia on its own conditions. Hence, India will no longer be the largest and most resourceful player when it comes to regional initiatives. It should also not be overlooked that India has been hit much harder economically by the pandemic than China. India suffered the largest economic contraction among the emerging economies when its gross domestic product (GDP) fell by more than seven per cent in the fiscal year 2021 (Wire, 2021). Thus, the gap in national power already existing between India and China will widen as a result of the pandemic. This will also affect the geopolitical matrix in South Asia, which will be further tilted against India.

Even before the pandemic, India had reacted to China's growing presence in the region. As such, the government in New Delhi had initiated new forms of collaboration with external powers in South Asia, for instance with the US, as well as Japan in Sri Lanka and Afghanistan. This is an interesting departure from India's traditional South Asian policy, which has for many long years been critical of any engagement on the part of external powers in the region. However, China's growing presence in the region may also pose new challenges for South Asian countries in their policies to balance New Delhi and Beijing. Chinese investments are much greater and affect more parts of state and society, and China offers attractive benefits for national elites, for instance with regard to scholarships and higher education. Chinese investments in the public health sector also reach large portions of the population. These factors allow one to predict that China's presence in the respective countries will be more prominent over time, which will also make it more difficult to balance Chinese power through relations with countries like India.

The National Dimension: The Rise of Nationalism

South Asia is often referred to as a 'civilizational entity' (Khilnani, 1997: 6), underpinned by commonalities linked to common social and cultural practices that range from common religious practices to similar marriage patterns and eating habits. They have been formed in the cultural encounters that have crossed the boundaries and territories of the post-colonial nation state. In its modern characteristic, tea, cricket and Bollywood are often referred to as common cultural symbols of South Asia (Mohammad-Arif, 2014). But the debate about culture as unifying factor also implies an ambivalence because the emphasis on pluralism and diversity is also seen as part of this cultural heritage. Attempts to homogenize cultural traditions into an imagined dominant identity have often led to severe conflicts. One example are the various conflicts over the national language in many South Asian countries after 1947. In India, the three-language formula put an end to the controversy over the national language in the 1960s. But the BJP has brought up again the issue as part of their policy for a stronger cultural unification of India (Wire, 2022). In Pakistan and Sri Lanka, the language question was the starting point for violent conflicts that paved the way for civil war. The idea of South Asia being a cultural entity may come under pressure with the rise of nationalist ideologies and populist leaders. The Indian Prime Minister Narendra Modi and the Pakistani Prime Minister Imran Khan have promised to respectively build a 'New (Naya) India' and a 'New (Naya) Pakistan'. The election of President Mahinda Rajapakse in Sri Lanka in 2005 and of his brother Gotabaya Rajapakse in 2019 and the autocratic tendencies of Sheik Hasina in Bangladesh may also indicate a new phase for 'hybrid' democracies in South Asia in which pluralism and dissent may be less accepted.

The debate has gained new importance in India after Modi and the BJP were re-elected in 2019. The ideological foundation of the BJP and organizations like the Rashtriya Swayamsevak Sangh (RSS) is the concept of Hindu-ness (*Hindutva*). The protagonists of *Hindutva* like V. D. Savarkar and M. S. Golwalkar have always emphasized the idea of national unity. For Savarkar the Hindu nation rested on the commonality of land, blood and culture (Vijayan, 2015), while Golwalkar emphasized the unity of geography, race, religion, culture and language that formed the basis for his idea of Hindu-ness (Golwalkar, 1939: 60). Both highlighted the glory of a past Hindu nation whose achievements had been destroyed with the invasion of foreigners like the Muslims and later the British. The concept of *Hindutva* itself is a variety of ethnic nationalism that has its roots in fascist movements in the 1920s and 1930s in Europe, yet even among Hindu nationalist groups there is no consensus and no common definition of what *Hindutva* should be. For instance, the RSS has modernized its agenda and also aims to include Muslims and Christians into its organization. However, the smallest common denominator seems to be a concept of 'nationalist patriotism' (Andersen & Damle, 2018) that is linked to culture.

It should not be overlooked that these ideas gained a strong democratic legitimacy as the Modi government achieved two consecutive election victories with an absolute majority. But the enforcement of 'cultural unity' in a diverse society like India will be accompanied by serious domestic conflicts. The abolition of the traditional Muslim divorce (Triple Talaq), the bifurcation of the state of Jammu and Kashmir into two Union territories, and the verdict of the Supreme Court over the temple/mosque dispute in Ayodhya in 2019 indicate that privileges for religious minorities that have been a cornerstone of India's democracy after 1947 will no longer have the same place in Modi's new India. Moreover, it has often been pointed out that the concept of *Hindutva* includes a populist and autocratic dimension, as it pretends to represent 'the people'. The increase of sedition charges indicate that the public space for free speech is shrinking. In 2021, India occupied rank 142 of the Freedom of Press Index (Nair, 2021). In the same year, India has also seen the highest numbers of internet shutdowns in the world (Chakravarti, 2021).

Hindutva is first and foremost a domestic project that aims to unify Indian society. But ethnic nationalisms often have a transnational dimension that challenges the boundaries of the nation-state. Examples from South Asia would be for instance the Pashtuns in Afghanistan and Pakistan, and the controversy between Bangladeshi versus Bengali nationalism. In the *Hindutva* discourse the transnational claim is part of the debate on *Akhand Bharat* or 'undivided India'. Key protagonists such as Deendayal Upadhyaya have always included the territory of Pakistan as part of *Akhand Bharat* and have therefore demanded the reunification of the two states. Interestingly, he did not pursue similar claims with regard to Nepal or Sri Lanka because he viewed these countries as closer to Indian culture (Bhishikar, 1991: 157–159). Hence, protagonists of *Hindutva* have argued the case for replacing the notion of 'South Asia' with 'India' and then to use 'Bharat' instead of the Indian Union (Clémentin-Ojha, 2014). However, in the *Hindutva* discourse, 'Bharat' describes an imagined territory that is not congruent with the present state system that shapes South Asia.

Prospects: India in South Asia 2.0

There are many indications that the concept of South Asia that developed after the decolonization in 1947/48 is undergoing a fundamental change which will also affect India's policies towards its neighbours. The concept of South Asia owed its existence more to external developments like the strategic imperatives of US foreign policy and the creation of area studies rather than to developments in the region. A distinct regional identity started to shape the region only after the mid-1980s with the creation of SAARC. But regionalism remained weak and South Asia's international image was mainly shaped by negative factors, for instance being a region of 'chronic instability' and having a low level of economic integration.

For India, South Asia has always been a difficult neighbourhood with regard to its own regional ambitions. The emergence of South Asia 2.0 will create new challenges for India. First, on the global level, South Asia 2.0 will be shaped by an increased rivalry between India and China and no longer between India and Pakistan. After the border incursions in summer 2020, it became clear that India and China have divergent perceptions on the issue. New Delhi sees the border question as a bilateral problem whereas Beijing has started to perceive it as a part of its geopolitical rivalry with the US in the Indo-Pacific. Second, on the regional level, India has decoupled its relations with Pakistan and has fostered new regional initiatives like BIMSTEC or BBIN. But China has also become increasingly active in setting up its own regional dialogues. As a result, on the regional level, South Asia may no longer have one institutional structure like SAARC but may be characterized by different sub-regional formats headed by India or by China. As China is economically more powerful than India, it has more resources to provide regional public goods for instance via its Health Silk Road. Finally, on the national level, the tendency towards more nationalist and authoritarian governments in the region may foster greater cultural homogeneity that will diminish diversity and forms of religious syncretism. While Indian governments have been used to collaborate with authoritarian regimes in its neighbourhood, the presence of nationalism in multi-ethnic societies may create new bilateral conflicts. The implementation of the Citizenship Amendment Act of 2019 could also have repercussions on the relations with Bangladesh if the government in New Delhi were to try to send back persons without proper Indian citizenship (Khasru, 2018).

The emerging contours of South Asia 2.0 further indicate that India will be faced with a much more difficult regional environment. Indian governments have already reacted and have intensified their collaboration with other powers like the US, Japan and the United Kingdom in the region. On the global level, South Asia 2.0 may not necessarily restrict India's rise. South Asia 2.0 can also be an interesting test case to show the limits of traditional theories that have linked the rise of a state with its regional predominance. This may also affect India's foreign policy identity which has often taken for granted that the country is the dominant power in South Asia. It seems that this debate has to be revisited in the twenty-first century with India and its region as an interesting test case.

Acknowledgements

The author would like the participants of the first conference of the European Scholars of South Asian International Relations (ESSAIR) 2020 for their valuable comments and questions on an earlier draft.

Note

1 The founding members of SAARC were Bangladesh, Bhutan, India, the Maldives, Nepal, Pakistan and Sri Lanka. Afghanistan joined SAARC in 2007.

References

Andersen, Walter K.; Damle, Shridhar D. (2018) *The RSS: A View to the Inside* (New Delhi: Penguin).

Basu, Nayanima (2019) 'How Kartarpur Corridor Talks Went on Despite India–Pakistan Tension, Diplomatic Roadblocks', *The Print*, 6 November. Available at https://theprint.in/theprint-essential/kartarpur-talks-went-on-despite-India–Pakistan-tension/316008 [last accessed 6 November 2019].

Bhatia, Rajiv; van Deutekom, Joost; Lee, Lina; Kulkarni, Kunal (2016) 'Chinese Investments in Nepal', 16 September. Available at www.gatewayhouse.in/chinese-investments-nepal-2/ [last accessed 17 September 2016].

Bhattacharya, Sabyasachi (2012) *Talking Back: The Idea of Civilization in the Indian Nationalist Discourse* (Oxford: Oxford University Press).

Bhattacherjee, Kallol (2020) 'Will Modi's COVID-19 Fund Initiative Revive SAARC?', *The Hindu*, 20 March. Available at www.thehindu.com/opinion/op-ed/will-modis-covid-19-fund-initiative-revive-saarc/article31111318.ece [last accessed 20 March 2020].

Bhishikar, C. P. (1991) *Pandit Deendayal Upadhyaya: Ideology and Perception. Part V, Concept of the Rashtra* (New Delhi: Suruchi Prakashan).

Brown, W. Norman (1964) 'South Asia Studies: A History', *The Annals of the American Academy of Political and Social Science*, 356: 54–62.

Chakravarti, Ankita (2021) 'India Saw Highest Number of Internet Shutdowns in the World in 2020', *India Today*, 4 March. Available at www.indiatoday.in/technology/news/story/india-saw-highest-number-of-internet-shutdowns-in-the-world-in-2020-1775608-2021-03-04 [last accessed 25 March 2022].

Chatterjee, Bipul; Ganguly, Arnab (2020) 'Time to Implement the BBIN Motor Vehicles Agreement', *The Economic Times*, 12 February. Available at https://economictimes.indiatimes.com/blogs/et-commentary/time-to-implement-the-bbin-motor-vehicles-agreement/ [last accessed 12 February 2020].

Clémentin-Ojha, Catherine (2014) '"India, that is Bharat …": One Country, Two Names', *South Asia Multidisciplinary Academic Journal*, 10. Available at http://journals.openedition.org/samaj/3717 [last accessed 8. January 2020].

Cohen, Stephen P. (2013) *Shooting for a Century: The India–Pakistan Conundrum* (Washington, DC: Brookings Institution Press).

Dawn (2019) 'India Withdraws Most Favoured Nation Status for Pakistan', 15 February. Available at www.dawn.com/news/1463999/india-withdraws-most-favoured-nation-status-for-pakistan [last accessed 15 February 2019].

Economic Times (2021) 'China Asks Pakistan to Create Enabling Conditions for its Investors in CPEC Projects'. Available at https://economictimes.indiatimes.com/news/international/world-news/china-asks-pakistan-to-create-enabling-conditions-for-its-investors-in-cpec-projects/articleshow/87760187.cms?from=mdr [last accessed 25 March 2022].

Elmer, Keegan (2020) 'China Holds Meeting with Pakistan, Nepal and Afghanistan as Tensions Simmer with India', *South China Morning Post*, 30 July. Available at www.scmp.com/news/china/diplomacy/article/3095028/china-holds-meeting-pakistan-nepal-and-afghanistan-tensions [last accessed 26 November 2020].

Ganguly, Sumit (2002) *Conflict Unending: India–Pakistan Tensions since 1947* (Oxford: Oxford University Press).

Golwalkar, M. S. (1939) *We – or Our Nationhood Defined* (Nagpur: Bharat Publications).

Hagerty, Devin T. (1991), 'India's Regional Security Doctrine', *Asian Survey*, 31 (4): 351–363.

Haidar, Suhasini (2020) 'Aid Offers from India, China Galore', *The Hindu*, 14 June. Available at www.thehindu.com/news/national/aid-offers-from-india-china-galore/a rticle31828030.ece [last accessed 14 June 2020].

Hoeber Rudolph, Susanne (2010) 'Four Variants of Indian Civilization', in Peter J. Katzenstein (ed.), *Civilisations in World Politics* (London: Routledge), pp. 137–156.

Indian Express (2021) 'Jaishankar on China's BRI: "Connectivity Initiatives Must Respect Sovereignty, Territorial Integrity"', 26 November. Available at https://indianexpress. com/article/india/india-china-belt-and-road-initiative-sco-meeting-7641433/ [last accessed 25 March 2022].

Keohane, Robert O. (2012) 'Twenty Years of Institutional Liberalism', *International Relations*, 26 (2): 125–138.

Khasru, Syed Munir (2018) 'The Spectre of Deportation', *The Hindu*, 17 December. Available at www.thehindu.com/opinion/op-ed/the-spectre-of-deportation/article25 758775.ece [last accessed 17 December 2018].

Khilnani, Sunil (1997) *The Idea of India* (New York: Farrar, Straus, Giroux).

Kumar, Shri Gaurav (2020) *India-China Border Agreements* (New Delhi: United Service Institution).

Mahmud, Arshad (2019) 'Chinese Investment in Bangladesh Comes with Risks', *The Asia Times*, 17 July. Available at www.asiatimes.com/2019/07/article/chinese-investm ent-in-bangladesh-has-sometimes-violent-implications/ [last accessed 17 July 2019].

Malhotra, Jyoti (2020) 'Covid Has Brought Back Chinese Whispers in Sri Lanka, Nepal: Is India Listening?', *The Print*, 5 May. Available at https://theprint.in/op inion/global-print/covid-has-brought-back-chinese-whispers-in-sri-lanka-nepal-is-in dia-listening/414468/ [last accessed 5 May 2020].

Masood, Salman; Abi-Habib, Maria (2019) 'Pakistan Leader Vents Frustration at India: "No Point in Talking to Them"', *The New York Times*, 21 August. Available at www.nytimes.com/2019/08/21/world/asia/India–Pakistan-kashmir-imran-khan. html [last accessed 21 August 2019].

Mearsheimer, John (2001) *The Tragedy of Great Power Politics* (New York: Norton).

Michael, Arndt (2013) *India's Foreign Policy and Regional Multilateralism* (Basingstoke: Palgrave Macmillan).

Ministry of External Affairs (2007) 'Address by Prime Minister Dr Manmohan Singh to the 14th SAARC Summit, 3 April, (New Delhi)'. Available at www.mea.gov.in/ Speeches-Statements.htm?dtl/1852/Address [last accessed 9 November 2021].

Mohammad-Arif, Aminah (2014) 'Introduction: Imaginations and Constructions of South Asia: An Enchanting Abstraction?', *South Asia Multidisciplinary Academic Journal*, 10. Available at http://journals.openedition.org/samaj/3800 [last accessed 18 February 2020].

Mohan, Raja C. (2022) 'India and South Asia: The Elusive Sphere of Influence', *ISAS Insights*, 6 January. Available at www.isas.nus.edu.sg/papers/india-and-sou th-asia-the-elusive-sphere-of-influence/ [last accessed 24 March 2022].

Nair, Sobhana K. (2021) 'India Again Placed at 142nd Rank in Press Freedom', *The Hindu*, 21 April. Available at www.thehindu.com/news/national/india-again-placed-a t-142nd-rank-in-press-freedom/article34377079.ece [last accessed 21 April 2021].

Nehru, Jawaharlal (1961) *India's Foreign Policy: Selected Speeches, September 1946 – April 1961* (New Delhi: The Publications Division, Ministry of Information and Broadcasting).

Pal, Deep; Bhatia, Rahul (2020) *The BRI in Post-Coronavirus South Asia* (New Delhi: Carnegie Endowment for International Peace).

Patterson, Maureen L. P. (1998) 'Institutional Base for the Study of South Asia in the United States and the Role of the American Institute of Indian Studies', in Joseph W. Elder; Edward C. Dimock; Ainslie T. Embree (eds), *India's Worlds and US Scholars, 1947–1997* (New Delhi: Manohar, American Institute of Indian Studies), pp. 17–108.

Paul, T. V. (2009) *The India–Pakistan Conflict: An Enduring Rivalry* (Cambridge: Cambridge University Press).

Radhakrishnan, R. K. (2012) 'India, Sri Lanka, Maldives to Sign Agreement on Maritime Cooperation', *The Hindu*, 15 December. Available at www.thehindu.com/news/international/india-sri-lanka-maldives-to-sign-agreement-on-maritime-cooperation/article4203041.ece [last accessed 15 December 2012].

Raghavan, T. C. A. (2018) 'Temptations of a Greater India: The Legacy of an Ambitious Project in History', *Open*, 8 March. Available at https://openthemagazine.com/essay/temptations-of-a-greater-india [last accessed 14 December 2020].

Roche, Elizabeth (2020) 'India, China Flex Muscle to Gain Supremacy in Post-Covid South Asia', *Mint*, 13 November. Available at www.livemint.com/news/world/india-china-flex-muscle-to-gain-supremacy-in-post-covid-south-asia-11605256955535.html [last accessed 13 November 2020].

Roy Chaudhury, Dipanjan (2019) 'Chinese Investments in Sri Lanka Compromises Colombo's Sovereignty', *The Economic Times*, 26 December. Available at https://economictimes.indiatimes.com/news/defence/chinese-investments-in-sri-lanka-compromises-colombos-sovereignty/articleshow/72975247.cms [last accessed 28 December 2019].

Schwartzberg, Joseph E. (1992) *A Historical Atlas of South Asia* (Oxford: Oxford University Press).

Sen Gupta, Bhabani (1975) 'Waiting for India: India's Role as a Regional Power', *Journal of International Affairs*, 29 (2): 171–184.

Siddiqui, Naveed (2019) 'Trilateral Dialogue: Pakistan, China, Afghanistan Agree on "Enhancing Counterterrorism Cooperation"', *Dawn*, 8 September. Available at www.dawn.com/news/1504054 [last accessed 26 November 2020].

Syed, Baqir Sajjad (2016) 'FO Offers Cooperation to Delhi Over Terrorism', *Dawn*, 3 January. Available at www.dawn.com/news/1230407/fo-offers-cooperation-to-delhi-over-terrorism [last accessed 3 January 2016].

UNESCAP (2018) *Unlocking the Potential of Regional Economic Cooperation and Integration in South Asia: Potential, Challenges and the Way Forward* (New Delhi: United Nations).

Vijayan, Suchitra (2015) 'Rewriting the Nation State', *The Hindu*, 17 March. Available at www.thehindu.com/opinion/op-ed/rewriting-the-nation-state/article7000179.ece [last accessed 17 March 2015].

Wagner, Christian (2016) 'The Role of India and China in South Asia', *Strategic Analysis*, 40 (4): 307–320.

Waltz, Kenneth N. (1979) *Theory of International Politics* (Reading, MA: Addison-Wesley Publishing Company).

Wire (2021) 'COVID's Bitter Pill: India's GDP Contracts 7.3% In FY'21'. Available at https://thewire.in/economy/covid-bitter-pill-india-gdp-contracts-7-3-percent-fiscal-year-21 [last accessed 25 March 2021].

Wire (2022) 'Indians From Different States Should Communicate With Each Other in Hindi: Amit Shah'. Available at https://thewire.in/politics/indians-from-different-states-should-communicate-with-each-other-in-hindi-amit-shah, [last accessed 8 April 2022].

Xavier, Constantino (2018) *Bridging the Bay of Bengal: Toward a Stronger BIMSTEC* (New Delhi: Carnegie Endowment for International Peace).

2 India and the China–Pakistan Economic Corridor

Agnieszka Nitza-Makowska

Announced in 2013 and since then dubbed a game-changer, the China–Pakistan Economic Corridor (CPEC) is a multifaceted project that has the potential to significantly influence South Asia's turbulent environment. In particular, while tightening Islamabad's cooperation with Beijing, the CPEC may eventually bring significant shifts within the India–China–Pakistan strategic triangle. By augmenting China's presence in South Asia to an unprecedented extent and extending across the disputed territories of Pakistan-administered Kashmir, the project directly challenges India's standing in the region. Moreover, the development of the grand Belt and Road Initiative (BRI), with the CPEC as its pilot component, seems to be on a collision course with the determination of India's ruling Bharatiya Janata Party (BJP) to pursue and attain significant global influence and heightened status for the Indian state. This ambition has become an integral element of India's desired identity in the world order and the paramount factor in structuring the conduct of its international affairs. Consequently, the inroads made by Beijing under the BRI in South Asia and beyond oblige New Delhi to reassesses its strategic priorities and approaches.

This chapter contributes to this topic by analysing the narratives surrounding the CPEC in India, the ways in which it is transforming the Indian state's relationship with Pakistan, and India's regional and global standing as an emerging great power. The chapter also sheds light on how the two all-weather friends, as China and Pakistan refer to each other, want India to be perceived in Pakistan and beyond South Asia. It draws on English-language publications by Indian and Pakistani think tanks and research institutes, triangulated with primary sources such as policy documents, public opinion polls, media publications, and semi-structured interviews with opinion shapers, including academics, journalists and other civil society representatives conducted online in April–May and October–December 2021. These interviews involved six individuals from India and Pakistan, all referred to here as interviewees and identified in the 'Interviewees' section at the end of this chapter.

DOI: 10.4324/9781003305132-4

Narratives, Identity and the CPEC

While the CPEC's physical infrastructure, which is still under construction, affects dynamics at the domestic, inter-state and global levels (Kuszewska and Nitza-Makowska, 2020: 224), the narratives that policy makers, media outlets, and civil society representatives produce also merit study. Notably, these narratives expose the sharp contrasts in perceptions of the CPEC between stakeholders within India and Pakistan. These differences rest largely upon the history of the bilateral relations of the two South Asian arch-rivals and their triangular dynamics with China, as well as questions related to whether and how these states construct their identities vis-à-vis each other.

Such a focus upon history and identity is especially important for India. The popular belief behind the state's independence struggle that 'India had something unique to offer to the world, and that its age, rich history, size and talents entitled it to a major role in it' (Parekh, 2006: 3) has been broadly shared by subsequent ruling elites since the state's inception in 1947. Recently, Ram Madhav, National Secretary-General of the BJP, highlighted the link between India's rich heritage and the conduct of its foreign affairs, noting that 'India's strong point is its culture and civilisation. We are increasing our engagement with other countries and the global community based on our cultural thinking and civilisational ethos' (quoted in Xavier, 2020: 11). Thorsten Wojczewski (2019: 181–182) argues that in the post-Nehruvian discourse, this kind of belief took shape through a notion of Indian Exceptionalism according to which the state represents a 'unique symbol of tolerance, pluralism and peaceful co-existence … [with] the moral capacity for leadership in global politics' (Wojczewski, 2019: 191). Indeed, the way India constitutes itself in international affairs via connectivity strategies, including, among others, its engagements with Japan and Iran as well as its 'Neighbourhood First' policy umbrella for South Asia, suggests the state's desire to prove these capacities in numerous areas such as defensive security, research and innovation, and environment and climate change. Highlighting India's values and practices underpinning these multifaceted strategies, New Delhi claims that 'connectivity initiatives must be based on universally recognised international norms, good governance, rule of law, openness, transparency and equality. Connectivity initiatives must follow principles of … balanced ecological and environmental protection and pre-servation standards; transparent assessment of project costs; and skill and technology transfer' (Ministry of External Affairs, 2017).

Core components of India's 'exceptional' identity were constructed in relation to its rough neighbourhood represented primarily by Pakistan and China. For almost its entire existence, in othering the Muslim state of Paki-stan, India has emphasized its own secularity (Pasha, 1992), notably in the Kashmir dispute. As Mona Bhan argues, 'going back to partition in 1947, India wanted to hold on to Kashmir because Kashmir legitimised India's secular identity' (Big Q, 2019). However, laws reflecting the BJP's Hindu nationalism (beef bans, a discriminatory citizenship law) have distanced India from its traditional secularism (Jaffrelot, 2017). Such developments therefore weakened its deployment of the secularism card against Pakistan and beyond in foreign affairs, to the extent that it has been played at all in the CPEC context. The leading Indian narrative sees the project as China-orchestrated and serving Beijing's interests, which include destabilizing India, rather than as a tool to extend Muslim interests in South Asia.

In othering autocratic China, and particularly discussing Beijing's global ambitions and modes of cooperation through the BRI, stakeholders in India often refer to New Delhi's espousal of principles commonly associated with democracy and the corresponding values, such as civil liberties and human rights, in order to draw contrasts with autocratic China. Although the BJP's overall domestic performance (with respect to, for example, the laws mentioned above, restrictions on foreign funding for non-governmental organizations (NGOs), or the tightening alignment between the party and the judicial leadership) has caused a democratic decline and an erosion of freedoms, as marked by India's recent downgrade to 'partly free' status in the Freedom Index (Freedom House, 2021), such narratives remain prevalent, especially in the context of the CPEC's impact on local communities in Pakistan-administered Kashmir and Baluchistan.

China's Post-2013 In-roads into South Asia

Except for India and Bhutan, all the South Asian states (Pakistan and Afghanistan in 2013, the Maldives in 2014, Nepal and Sri Lanka in 2017, and Bangladesh in 2019) have signed memorandums of understanding (MoUs) establishing cooperation with China under the BRI, which has now been joined by over 140 countries worldwide. While Beijing initially included the Bangladesh–China–India–Myanmar Economic Corridor in its grand infrastructure strategy, in the face of New Delhi's reticence to fully commit (Marchang, 2021) and little progress, that particular project fell off the list of 35 corridors presented at the Second 'Belt and Road Forum' in April 2019.

Mainstream discourse among foreign policy experts and academics in India supports the state's absence from the BRI, perceiving it as an ephemeral project surrounded by a lack of transparency. Resonating with this consensus, observers have argued that 'India should ignore the BRI.... BRI will not be successful unless India joins it. India does not want to be part of this game' (Interviewee 2, 2021). Indeed, joining an initiative unilaterally orchestrated by China would undermine India's ambitions to become 'a self-assured player of the big league' (C3S, 2017). Accordingly, after the Second 'Belt and Road Forum' M.R. Sivaraman, from the Chennai Centre for China Studies argued that 'had Modi gone to the BRI summit, he would have been the equivalent of Turkmenistan paying obeisance to the mighty Xi in his palace' (C3S, 2017). Without receiving much attention, some limited voices in India have argued that it should reconsider its position vis-à-vis the BRI.

One Interviewee for this project mentions such voices but – along with two other interlocutors from India – agrees with New Delhi's definitive rejection of the CPEC because it is a BRI specific component (Interviewees 1–3, 2021).

Although Beijing denies any hegemonic ambitions, the BRI is also often seen as a vehicle for 'the Chinese plan to build a new world order' (Maçães, 2019: 9). The CPEC, as the BRI's pilot project, comprises a 3,000-kilometre network of highways, railways, and oil and gas pipelines to link Gwadar in Baluchistan with China's Xinjiang. This unprecedented investment of over US$62 billion by one Asian state in another has multiple possible implications, including a bolstered role and reputation for China as a provider of international investments and driver of development as well as a heavier Chinese socio-economic and military footprint on Pakistan and a transformed security landscape (Kuszewska & Nitza-Makowska, 2021). Consequently, the project is sure to test Beijing's capacity to introduce its own order on a regional scale. However, given India's contestation of the CPEC and the generally turbulent environment in South Asia, China may well fail this test. As Indian Interviewee 1 noted in reference to South Asia's regional dynamics; 'you never know how the CPEC is going to work' (Interviewee 1, 2021). Accordingly, the Long-Term Plan for the CPEC (CPEC, 2017: 7), serving as the official roadmap for the project, and recognizes the following conditions; that 'the geopolitical environment is inherently unstable in South Asia, … [and that] the mix of international, regional, national and extremist factors might cause disruptive activities, threatening the security of the CPEC building'.

The two main South Asian states, India and Pakistan, are the source of the sharpest contrasts in the region, perceiving China's inroads through the prisms of rivalry and win–win cooperation, respectively. They are further differentiated by the amount of attention given to the CPEC by their governments, media and experts. Viewed in Pakistan as a game-changer, the project has garnered vast attention in that country, but from India's perspective, it is one of many factors for foreign policy making. Indeed, the Indian informants interviewed for this chapter claim that the project is rarely debated – and that this is especially true among local media. As Indian Interviewee 1 notes, 'in Kolkata, we have had no discussion in local media on the CPEC in last 6–7 months' (Interviewee 1, 2021).

Consistent with New Delhi's position towards the CPEC, the share of the Indian public with a favourable view of China decreased from 35% in 2013 to 23% in 2019 (Pew Research Center, n.d.), making India one of the countries with the least positive perceptions of this state worldwide. Additionally, only 20% of Indian respondents agreed that China's growing economy benefits their country, while 61% expressed the opposite opinion (Pew Research Center, 2019). Even more Indians (73%) admitted to holding a negative view of Beijing's military might (Pew Research Center, 2019). While India's discourse paints the CPEC more as a corridor of power than as a mere economic project, this investment is seen as a harmful vehicle for coupling the economic and military aspects of China's performance. This perception was shared by the Indian interviewees in this chapter, who see the CPEC as 'an irritating instrument' (Interviewees 1–3) to extend China's influence.

In contrast to Indians, Pakistanis seem to be among the greatest China enthusiasts globally, with one survey finding the share of the public holding a favourable view of China to be 78% in 2014 and 85% in 2015 (Pew Research Center, n.d.). Consistent with this, the CPEC has drawn considerable enthusiasm in Pakistan. In 2018, 65% of Pakistani respondents believed that this project was beneficial for their country, and 87% said the economy would be very or somewhat positively affected by the project (Gallup, 2019). Interestingly, Pakistani interviewees for this chapter, even while objecting to the CPEC and attributing its popularity, like Interviewee 4, to Pakistanis' 'brainwashing' (Interviewee 4, 2021) by Beijing, still refer to China as 'our friend' (Interviewees 4–6, 2021). Indeed, a wave of CPEC criticism has been on a modest rise in Pakistan and appeared among the interviewees in this chapter; for instance, Interviewee 4 comperes Beijing's inroads under the project's umbrella to a foreign invasion (Interviewee 4, 2021). Yasir Masood (2018), an academic currently associated with the CPEC Centre of Excellence, comments of these tendencies; 'it is most unfortunate that some Pakistani opinion-makers have been deceived by propaganda and are hand in glove with Indian-driven designs of portraying CPEC as a fiction or a failure'.

This dichotomy in prevailing attitudes corresponds to how India and Pakistan perceive each other in the CPEC context. In particular, emerging in India's process of othering the militaristic hybrid regime in Pakistan and autocratic China, key components of India's identity such as adherence to democratic values and pluralism underpin how New Delhi perceives the impact of CPEC-related developments on Pakistan's state and society. India's stakeholders promulgate a narrative positing Pakistan as a casualty of the great power conflict that the project advances, with Pakistan's status in international dynamics downgraded to being China's proxy or vassal state (C3S, 2017). Indeed, in their perception, Pakistan has fallen into a model patron–client relationship with China, characterized by discrepancies in power and influence between the parties and unequal access to benefits. In line with Islamabad's demotion in regional affairs to Beijing's client, 'the long-standing paradigm of Pakistan centrality in India's security outlook … (has) become outdated' (Singh et al., 2021: 4), with a corresponding shift in focus to Pakistan's patron in Beijing. However, there are other reasons for this position that are not directly related to CPEC, including China's opposition to India's membership in the Nuclear Suppliers Group and support for Pakistan's interests in Jammu and Kashmir (such as via its joint disapproval of the bifurcation of Jammu and Kashmir into two union territories in August 2019). In addition, the CPEC is not the only context in which India–Pakistan dynamics play out. An Indian interviewee for this chapter argued that New Delhi perceives its troubled nuclear fellow through the prism of

Pakistani domestic extremism and cross-border terrorism. As he recognizes, 'India has not sent any signals [of] the CPEC becoming an irritant between India and Pakistan. India has a different issue with Pakistan, which is cross-border terrorism. And in this context Pakistan is seen as a major obstacle for India's rise' (Interviewee 2, 2021).

The CPEC-enthusiast narrative in Pakistan presents India as the greatest opponent and saboteur of the project. According to this narrative, and in order to cripple the CPEC, New Delhi designed a dedicated cell of the Research and Analysis Wing (its foreign intelligence agency) at a cost of $500 million (Masood, 2018) and strengthened its collaboration with local insurgents in Baluchistan (Ali et al., 2019; Khetran, 2017: 120), the fragile epicentre of the project. According to General Zubair Mehmud Hayat, former Chairman of the Joint Chiefs of Staff Committee, because of this type of collaboration with Baluch separatists, 'India [has] become an extremist country from being a secular one' (Khan, 2017).

Moreover, a leading narrative in Pakistan considers India's objection to the project harmful to the region and beyond. Namely, some see this opposition as another manifestation of a hegemonic Indian stance that has already damaged South Asia's regional integration (Malik, 2017). Offering the 'most lucrative economic and commercial package to address centuries-old economic worries of the regional states' (Malik, 2017), Beijing is presented as a better partner in business and politics than New Delhi. In this context, Zamir Akram (Institute of Strategic Studies, 2020), the United Nations ambassador in Pakistan, refers to Nepal, which, he argues, has been bullied by India with blockades, resulting in shortages of basic commodities, but which has been granted the 800 km Lhasa–Kathmandu highway by China. Additionally, this narrative tends to emphasize New Delhi's rejection of the BRI as a driver of Indian isolation in international affairs.

Unlike the CPEC discourse among Pakistani stakeholders, the Long-Term Plan for the CPEC itself does not mention India directly. However, aligning with the prevailing narrative among them, it suggests benefits for Pakistan's neighbouring countries and beyond. As such, the Long-Term Plan (CPEC, 2017: 9) posits that the CPEC will elevate 'the status of South Asian and Central Asian countries in [the] labor division of [the] global economy … [and promote] regional economic integration through stable trade growth, international economic and technological cooperation and personnel exchange'.

New Delhi Reassesses its Strategic Priorities and Approaches

By undermining New Delhi's ambitions to become a new great power, the CPEC has garnered vast criticism in India. Darshana M. Baruah argues:

New Delhi is worried that Chinese-funded infrastructure projects may: (1) run afoul of accepted international standards and norms; (2)

undermine Indian sovereignty claims on disputed border territories and other security interests, especially vis-à-vis China and Pakistan; and (3) grant China greater geopolitical influence and undue economic and diplomatic leverage over the policymaking decisions of India's neighbors in ways that disadvantage India.

(Baruah, 2018: 13)

Reflecting these concerns, the prevailing narrative in Indian media outlets, think thanks and university research institutes on the CPEC focuses upon:

- disputed areas in Kashmir, particularly the violation of India's territorial sovereignty by the project developments in Gilgit-Baltistan and Azad Jammu and Kashmir (AJK), as well as the neglect of local and universal norms, including human rights, civil liberties and environmental standards;
- Baluchistan, namely the role of Gwadar Port, as a potential Chinese naval base, that would expand the state's maritime capabilities and elevate its position in the Indian Ocean Region; and, as in the Kashmiri case, the neglect of norms and standards; and
- New Delhi's attempts to build alliances to counter Beijing's influence in South Asia and beyond, with a particular focus among Indian academics on mini-lateral groupings, in contrast with the cooperation mode under the BRI.

Each of these factors will now be discussed in turn.

The Kashmir Dispute and India's Rejection of the BRI

Vali Nasr has argued that 'the centrality of the Kashmir conflict to Pakistan and India's enduring rivalry has less to do with the geostrategic or economic significance of the small province, and more with the symbolic value that it holds for dominant perceptions of national identity in the two countries' (Nasr, 2005: 179). Extending across the disputed areas of Gilgit-Baltistan and AJK, the CPEC has not only enforced these territories' symbolic meaning but also endowed them with a multidimensional strategic weight. Among the numerous projects under the CPEC umbrella, the following involve Pakistan-administered Kashmir: (1) the Kohala and (2) Azad Pattan hydropower projects on Jhelum River; (3) the Mirpur–Muzaffarabad–Mansehra road between AJK and Khyber Pakhtunkhwa; (4) the Mirpur industrial zone; (5) the Gilgit–Shandur road and (6) the realignment of the Thakot–Raikot section of the Karakoram Highway linking Gilgit-Baltistan and Khyber Pakhtunkhwa; (7) the cross-border fibre optic cable (Khunjrab–Rawalpindi) between Gilgit-Baltistan, Khyber Pakhtunkhwa and Punjab; and (8) the Moqpondass Special Economic Zone (see http://cpec.gov.pk).

In India's prevailing narrative, this infrastructure build-up is a violation of the state's territorial sovereignty. Considering Pakistan-occupied Kashmir, as they refer to the disputed areas as being part of India, the Indian interviewees in this chapter arguably shared this perception (Interviewees 1–3, 2021). As Narendra Modi said at the Shanghai Cooperation Organisation Summit in June 2018 and has repeated on many other occasions, 'India … cannot accept a project that ignores its core concern on sovereignty and territorial integrity' (PTI, 2018). Looking at the BRI through such a prism, New Delhi may contest it without openly admitting its potential to prevent the arrival of *Global India*. In this regard, the CPEC-related infrastructure build-up aligns with an expansion of China's military footprint in the disputed areas. Experts from the Centre for Asian Strategic Studies – India, a New Delhi-based think tank, argue that 'China has long been known to have inducted more than 4,000 troops of the PLA disguised as technicians and labourers to create deep tunnels along the course of (the) economic corridor' (CASS-India, 2017) in Gilgit-Baltistan. Furthermore, according to Arun Sahgal from the Delhi Policy Group, the coupling of the exercise of Beijing's economic and military instruments under the CPEC has turned Pakistan-occupied Kashmir into China-occupied Kashmir (DPG, 2016). This perception leads to further marginalization of Pakistan in India's foreign affairs, particularly at the expense of China rising as a major threat against the arrival of *Global India*.

New Delhi will also lose its legal grounds to undermine CPEC-related developments, particularly in Gilgit-Baltistan, after the upgrade of the region's constitutional status to Pakistani province. Indeed, on 1 November 2020, Islamabad announced such a decision, and subsequently, on 9 March 2021, Gilgit-Baltistan's legislative assembly 'unanimously adopted a resolution to make the region an interim province of (Pakistan)' (Hussain, 2021). This formal absorption is meant to be completed by an amendment to Pakistan's constitution. Such a scenario may have some positive implications for the Kashmir dispute, for instance through the meeting of local demand for more political participation and investments. However, Indian stakeholders view such outcomes through the prism of their narrative about the negative consequences of Pakistani–Chinese collaboration, including an increase in human rights and environmental standards violations by the Chinese. From the Indian perspective, as long as Gilgit-Baltistan is subject to CPEC infrastructure developments, local needs will be entirely neglected. For instance, experts from CASS-India argue that 'the opposition [of the people of Gilgit-Baltistan] to the economic corridor will be crushed without compunction' (CASS-India, 2017). Further, they refer to ire 'against the Chinese for leaving the locals out of the economic benefits of the Karakoram Highway and the emerging economic corridor' (CASS-India, 2017). This perception resonates with reporting by the *Times of India* on the superior position of Chinese mining companies over local ones and forceful land acquisitions in the area (Times of India, 2021). Business Standard (ANI, 2017) has also interviewed European experts about similar practices related to CPEC developments. Yoana Barakova, from the Amsterdam-based European

Foundation for South Asian Studies, admitted that Gilgit-Baltistan is likely to be excluded from the project's high financial profits and will suffer from its numerous negative environmental impacts (ANI, 2017). In the context of these impacts, the *Economic Times* characterizes the CPEC Bunji and Bhasha dam projects as instruments for expropriating Gilgit-Baltistan's water resources for Punjab province (Economic Times, 2017).

Gwadar and India's Traditional Cooperation Routes in the Indian Ocean Region

Following the Kashmir issue, the development and militarization of Gwadar Port in Pakistan's Baluchistan and its potential contribution to China's maritime capabilities in the Indian Ocean Region are the second most significant CPEC-related concerns in New Delhi. Investments in this port – a precious pearl in the (in)famous string of strategic assets around India – along with other Maritime Silk Road (MSR) projects pursued under the BRI umbrella, require New Delhi 'to beef up its own asymmetric capabilities … (by) leveraging its geographical advantages' (DPG, 2016). Due to these advantages, India's absence from the MSR projects will prevent them from working effectively regardless of China's financial strength, according to Sundeep Kumar (2017) of C3S. With these distinct capacities, India and China are each simultaneously attempting to restore their maritime trade and cooperation routes in the Indian Ocean Region, where their traditional spheres of interests overlap.

In June 2014, less than a year after Beijing announced its MSR, with Gwadar and the Melaka Gateway, Kyaukpyu and Hambantota as its key ports, India launched its Project Mausam (Monsoon). While this initiative can be seen as a direct answer to the MSR (Haldar, 2018), according to official sources in New Delhi, it differs significantly from Beijing's infrastructure build-up in the region. Spearheaded by India's Ministry of Culture, Project Mausam 'aims to re-connect and re-establish communications between countries of the Indian Ocean world, which would lead to an enhanced understanding of cultural values and concerns' (Government of India, 2014). By March 2021, 39 countries were invited to join the project, among them Bangladesh, Saudi Arabia, Indonesia, Oman, Singapore, Malaysia, the United Arab Emirates, and Myanmar, which are also hosts of significant hubs along the MSR. Through this initiative, albeit low-profile in comparison to China's physical connectivity investments, India seeks to win hearts and minds in the Indian Ocean Region in its own way. The effectiveness of this approach depends on numerous conditions, including recipient states' desire and absorption capacity for non-material connectivity projects of the Mausam variety.

Referring to the CPEC exclusively, China's full control over Gwadar Port, which was leased for 40 years in 2017 to the China Overseas Port Holding Company, is key to the strategic functioning of this corridor, according to R.

S. Vasan (2017) of the C4S. Notably, he emphasizes this facility's role in ensuring China's energy security. Indeed, within the overall CPEC and BRI infrastructure, this strategically situated hub will grant China an alternative energy supply route to bypass the Malacca Strait chokepoint. However, the Indian foreign policy think tank The Gateway House observe that these capacities may be undermined by: (1) drinking water shortages in Gwadar region, which limit the development of the city and port; (2) Baluchistan's fragile security situation resulting from a long-standing insurgency targeting both Pakistani and Chinese individuals; and (3) high logistical costs of moving oil and other goods between Gwadar and China's main economic centres, primarily resulting from the additional geographical distance of some 2,000 kilometres from the China–Pakistan border to areas more populated and prosperous than Tibet and Qinghai, such as Sichuan and Yunnan (Bhandari & Agarwal, 2018). As a consequence of these challenges, Bhandari and Agarwal expect Gwadar Port to serve primarily as a Chinese naval base.

Regardless of their intended purpose, China's moves in Pakistani Baluchistan have catalysed Indian engagements in Iran's Chabahar Port, only 172 kilometres away from Gwadar. In May 2016, India signed an agreement with Iran to affirm a $500 million investment in this hub, seen as a strategic gateway to Afghanistan and Central Asia. However, relative to China's role in the arrangements over Gwadar, India's footprint in Chabahar is lighter, with no control ceded over the Iranian port. While the different character of the two bilateral engagements may result from the gap in capacities between fragile Pakistan and Iran, a rising middle power unwilling to reduce itself to serving as another state's proxy, it also demonstrates the difference between India and China as investment providers.

The bilateral India–Iran deal was followed by the trilateral Chabahar Agreement among the two states and Afghanistan to launch a land transit-and-trade corridor stretching from Chabahar to Kabul. Officially, the three parties designed the International Transport and Transit Corridor to optimize the cost and time of moving goods and people, ensure related safety standards and facilitate their own access to international markets (Chabahar Agreement, 2016). Narendra Modi expressed his hopes for this corridor by saying, 'we want to link with the world. [The] agreement … can alter the course of history of the region' (Hindustan Times, 2016). However, the smooth development of the corridor and Chabahar have been largely undermined by (1) Afghanistan's declining security situation, especially since the Taliban took over in August 2021, and (2) a possible collision in the trajectories of New Delhi's engagements with Tehran and Washington, which made headlines in the Indian media after some sources over-hastily announced India's withdrawal from the Chabahar–Zahedan Railway project in July 2020. The declaration by India's ambassador to Tehran, Gaddam Dharmendra, that 'Americans cannot tell us what to do' (quoted in Hindustan Times, 2020) put an end to these speculations. While the fact that the

United States (US) exempted the Chabahar port from sanctions could well be a valid reason for India's engagement, Dharmendra used the opportunity to accent New Delhi's standing in regional and international affairs through observations that India would not simply comply with the great powers' interests.

Moreover, as in the case of CPEC-related developments in Pakistan-administered Kashmir, Indian stakeholders emphasize that local and international norms and standards are being violated in Baluchistan where the project's infrastructure is under construction. Gopalaswami Parthasarathy, a former diplomat, mentions the exploitation of the provinces' natural resources by Chinese mining companies; 'Pakistan is China's gold mine!' (Parthasarathy, 2021) he exclaims. In addition, Indian media outlets are eager to publish opinion pieces by Baluch activists depicting declines in standards of living in the Gwadar region and even, in extreme cases, violations of human rights and civil liberties. As such, Hakeem Baloch, president of the Baloch National Movement UK, claims:

> [T]o ensure the safety of the Chinese megaprojects, Pakistani military personnel have forced locals to migrate; the migrations have resulted in huge displacements in and outside of Balochistan. Innumerable little villages and hamlets have been burnt into ashes by Pakistani forces with the blessings of China to pave way for the CPEC.
>
> (Baloch, 2021)

Moreover, Baloch emphasizes the massive militarization of Gwadar, whereby 'there is such a high number of security forces personnel that it outnumbers the civilians. Technical vehicles of the Pakistani military patrol the town 24/7 and all entry and exit routes of the town have very strict security checkpoints, where everyone is checked and questioned individually' (Baloch, 2021). Indeed, removal of some of these checkpoints was one of 19 demands formulated during local protests in Gwadar that erupted in November 2021. The main triggers for these protests were water and electricity shortages and concerns over Chinese trawlers' illegal activities threatening the income source of Baluchistan's largely fishery-dependent coastal communities (Kartha, 2021). Interestingly, in the context of the CPEC's local impacts, the Indian and Pakistani interviewees in this chapter emphasize that the project primarily, if not exclusively, benefits particular sections of Pakistani society, such as the security establishment, as pointed out by Indian Interviewee 1, which is incomparably more privileged than the protesters in Baluchistan and elsewhere in the country (Interviewees 1–6, 2021).

Hundreds of BRI MoUs versus Indian Mini-Lateralism

New Delhi's capacity to build alliances to balance the strengthened China–Pakistan all-weather friendship under the CPEC, and China's inroads beyond South Asia, are other oft-discussed topics in Indian discourse. As such, Haldar observes that 'India is engaged in various bilateral as well as multilateral commitments, which give it an enough leverage to function on its own without having to bother about China's policies' (Haldar, 2018: 8). Moreover, this narrative not only counters the image of India spread by Pakistani stakeholders as a lonely and abandoned power in regional and global affairs but also identifies the country as a key contributor and co-designer of the mini-lateral groupings trending in the Indo-Pacific. Bringing together the smallest possible number of states needed to achieve real international action, mini-lateral gatherings (Naím, 2009) offer a type of cooperation that contrasts with that under the BRI. In particular, China's mega strategy operates on the basis of countless individual MoUs between Beijing and foreign governments. Rajeswari Pillai Rajagopalan of India's Observer Research Foundation emphasizes New Delhi's commitments to mini-lateral cooperation (Rajagopalan, 2021). Further, she provides the examples of the country's trilateral security arrangements with the US and Japan (such as the Malabar naval exercise), the engagement with France and Australia agreed in 2020 to ensure an inclusive and rules-based Indo-Pacific, and the Quadrilateral Security Dialogue (Quad) involving the US, Japan and Australia. Not coincidently, while none of these groupings officially targets China, they do include major contestants of Beijing in the Indo-Pacific. To be seen as a power capable of reconfiguring regional and global affairs rather than an 'underachiever' (Volgy et al., 2011: 6) always one step behind China, India – while encouraging and participating in such groupings – should reach beyond this circle.

Among the above mini-lateral groupings, the Quad, initially founded in 2007 and reborn a decade later, has received the most attention. According to a joint statement of the involved parties released in 2021, called 'The Spirit of the Quad', the group aims to promote 'a free, open rules-based order, rooted in international law to advance security and prosperity and counter threats to both in the Indo-Pacific and beyond' (Spirit of the Quad, 2021). Lacking a complex formal agenda, the Quad has been recognized as a reaction to China's assertive behaviour in the Indo-Pacific, not only by Beijing – which has dubbed it the 'Asian NATO' or 'foam in the ocean' (quoted in Rai, 2018) – but also by policymakers, academics and media worldwide. Countering this perception, 'Indian officials have repeatedly emphasised that the Quad is not directed against any particular country' (Singh et al., 2021), as the experts from DPG point out. For instance, India's Minister for Foreign Affairs Subrahmanyam Jaishankar regularly highlights that New Delhi's 'interest in the Quad is not determined by the deterioration in Sino-Indian relations' (quoted in Singh et al., 2021). Accordingly, 'The Spirit of the Quad' does not mention China (Spirit of the Quad, 2021).

However, it makes frequent references to democracy in statements, such as 'we support the rule of law, freedom of navigation and overflight, peaceful resolution of disputes, democratic values, and territorial integrity … [and the

Quad] seeks to uphold peace and prosperity and strengthen democratic resilience, based on universal values' (Spirit of the Quad, 2021), all of which underline the differences in political values and regimes between Quad members and China. Indeed, as a key element of all four of its constituent states' identities, democracy has been projected as an essential principle underpinning Quad cooperation. For instance, echoing the words of Japan's Prime Minister Shinzo Abe, this gathering has often been referred to as the 'Asian Arc of Democracy' (Heydarian, 2020). On the one hand, this association allows India to claim its moral superiority over autocratic China. On the other hand, the claim itself may appear unfortunate and superficial, given India's current domestic political dynamics.

Conclusions: Can *Global India* Arrive Beyond the BRI?

The BRI and the CPEC are still under construction, and their full implications are unknown due to the lack of transparency typically surrounding China's business activities, the lack of a long-term vantage point from which to assess the impact of already completed projects, and the Covid-19 pandemic which has prevented on-site research activities and other investigations by independent parties. However, China's mega strategy has become a prism shaping the view of most elements of India's international strategy, such as its commitment to mini-lateral groupings in the Indo-Pacific, which to a significant extent are recognized as attempts to balance China's rise in the region. Though New Delhi denies having such a motivation, this prism may prevent the arrival of *Global India* that is India from being perceived as a great power capable of reconfigure regional and global affairs.

To change this, India is seeking to project itself as a superior and moral power vis-à-vis China – autocratic and notorious as it is for leaving a heavy carbon footprint wherever it treads – by emphasizing own adherence to human rights, civil liberties, and environmental standards. Notably, Indian stakeholders recognize that such norms and standards are violated in Pakistan-administered Kashmir and Baluchistan, where the CPEC infrastructure is being built. Moreover, democracy, as an element of Indian identity that China does not share, seems to be constitutive component of the Quad's character as well. New Delhi's response to the BRI, to a vast extent underpinned by its core values, which are, at the same time, distant from those of its adversaries in Beijing, suggests that since the project's launch, India's unique moral capacity for leadership in global politics has been significantly affected by the process of othering China. However – and paradoxically, from the perspective of the notion of Indian Exceptionalism – Beijing's 'offer', in the form of the BRI, appeared to be a unique and appealing one, at least to most South Asian states. To avoid falling short of its prospective great power designation, India needs to pave its own way, in alignment with its core values, to hearts and minds in its sphere of interest, for instance, by offering transparent cooperation modes respecting local norms and communities, especially those that the BRI has failed and will fail. If the leading narrative in India is right, there are likely to be (at least) a few of these.

Interviewees

- Interviewee 1 (2021). Indian academic and think tank expert in history, international relations and security studies based in Kolkata, 22 November [online].
- Interviewee 2 (2021). Indian academic specialised in international relations based in New Delhi, 4 December [online].
- Interviewee 3 (2021). Indian think tank expert in international relations and journalist based in Chennai, 8 December [online].
- Interviewee 4 (2021). Pakistani academic specialised in history and Pakistan studies based in Lahore, 20 May [online].
- Interviewee 5 (2021). Pakistani academic specialised in international relations and journalist based in Faisalabad, 11 May [online].
- Interviewee 6 (2021). Pakistani academic specialised in history and Pakistan studies based in Islamabad, 21 May [online].

References

Ali, Anwar, Shah, Bahadar, Rizwan, Muhammad and Ali, Muhammad (2019) 'Indian Factor in CPEC: Prospects and Challenges for Pakistan', *Pakistan Administrative Review* 3 (2): 61–73.

ANI (2017) 'CPEC Violating Rights of Gilgit-Baltistan Residents: European Think Tanks', *Business Standard*, 17 October. Available at www.business-standard.com/article/international/cpec-violating-rights-of-gilgit-baltistan-residents-european-think-tanks-117101700377_1.html [last accessed 20 December 2021].

Baloch, Hakeem (2021) 'Read about Gwadar, CPEC, the High-handedness of the Pakistani Forces and the Resistance against it by the Baloch People', *Opindia*, 23 October. Available at www.opindia.com/2021/10/gwadar-cpec-high-handedness-pakistani-forces-resistance-by-baloch-people/ [last accessed 20 December 2021].

Baruah, Darshana M. (2017) 'India's Answer to the Belt and Road: A Road Map for South Asia'. Available at https://carnegieendowment.org/filesWP_Darshana_Baruah_Belt_Road_FINAL.pdf [last accessed 20 December 2021].

Bhandari, Amit and Agarwal, Aashna (2018) 'Gwadar: Trade Hub or Military Asset?'. Available at www.gatewayhouse.in/cpec-gwadar-trade-or-military/ [last accessed 20 December 2021].

Big Q (2019) 'Q+A: Kashmir: What's Behind One of the Most Volatile Rivalries in the World?'. Available at: www.thebigq.org/2019/08/01/qa-kashmir-whats-behind-one-of-the-most-volatile-rivalries-in-the-world/ [last accessed 20 December 2021].

C3S (2017) 'C3S Dialogue: BRI Summit and CPEC'. Available at www.c3sindia.org/business-economics/c3s-discussion-bri-summit-and-cpec/ [last accessed 20 December 2021].

CASS-India (2017) 'Chinese Economic Corridor'. Available at www.cassindia.com/chinese-economic-corridor [last accessed 20 December 2021].

Chabahar Agreement (2016) 'The Chabahar Agreement'. Available at http://mea.gov.in/Portal/LegalTreatiesDoc/016P2941.pdf [last accessed 20 December 2021].

CPEC (2017) 'Long Term Plan for China–Pakistan Economic Corridor 2017–2030'. Available at www.pc.gov.pk/uploads/cpec/CPEC-LTP.pdf [last accessed 20 December 2021].

DPG (2016) 'India-China Relations: Bilateral and Regional Contexts'. Available at www.delhipolicygroup.org/uploads_dpg/event/files/seminar-on-india-china-relations-bilateral-and-regional-contexts-1009.pdf [last accessed 20 December 2021].

Economic Times (2017) 'China-Pakistan Water Pincer against India', *The Economic Times*, 16 May. Available at https://economictimes.indiatimes.com/news/politics-and-nation/china-pakistan-water-pincer-against-india-as-part-of-cpec-mega-dams-are-planned-in-gilgit-baltistan/articleshow/58693447.cms?from=mdr [last accessed 20 December 2021].

Freedom House (2021) 'Freedom in the World: India'. Available at https://freedomhouse.org/country/india/freedom-world/2021 [last accessed 20 December 2021].

Gallup (2019) 'Public Opinion Polling on China–Pakistan Economic Corridor'. Available at http://gallup.com.pk/wp-content/uploads/2019/09/Public-Opinion-Polling-on-China–Pakistan-Economic-Corridor-2.pdf [last accessed 20 December 2021].

Government of India (2014) 'Project "Mausam" Launched by Secretary, Ministry of Culture'. Available at https://pib.gov.in/newsite/PrintRelease.aspx?relid=105777 [last accessed 20 December 2021].

Haldar, Sayantan (2018) 'Mapping Substance in India's Counter-strategies to China's Emergent Belt and Road Initiative', *Indian Journal of Asian Affairs*, 31 (1–2): 75–90.

Heydarian, Richard Javad (2020) 'Quad Alliance Forms "Arc of Democracy" around China', *Asia Times*, 27 July. Available at https://asiatimes.com/2020/07/quad-alliance-forms-arc-of-democracy-around-china/ [last accessed 19 April 2022].

Hindustan Times (2016) 'India, Iran and Afghanistan Sign Chabahar Port Agreement', *Hindustan Times*, 24 May. Available at www.hindustantimes.com/india/india-iran-afghanistan-sign-chabahar-port-agreement/story-2EytbKZeo6zeCIpR8WSuAO.html [last accessed 20 December 2021].

Hindustan Times (2020) 'Americans Can't Tell Us What to Do on Chabahar: India Envoy', *Hindustan Times*, 25 July. Available at www.hindustantimes.com/india-news/americans-can-t-tell-us-what-to-do-on-chabahar-india-envoy/story-1wSnyO71OMfESKYbrc5IHM.html [last accessed 20 December 2021].

Hussain, Sajjad (2021) 'Gilgit-Baltistan Assembly Adopts Resolution Demanding Interim Provincial Status from Pakistan Govt', *Outlook India*, 9 March. Available at www.outlookindia.com/newsscroll/gilgitbaltistan-assembly-adopts-resolution-demanding-interim-provincial-status-from-pakistan-govt/2043563 [last accessed 20 December 2021].

Institute of Strategic Studies (2020) 'India's Aggressions Towards its Neighbours: A Threat to Regional Stability'. Available at https://issi.org.pk/wp-content/uploads/2020/06/Report_Webinar_June_12_2020.pdf, [last accessed 20 December 2021].

Jaffrelot, Christophe (2017) 'India's Democracy at 70: Toward a Hindu State?', *Journal of Democracy*, 28 (3): 52–63.

Kartha, Tara (2021) 'Imran Khan Is Embarrassed. Gwadar Protest Isn't just for Baloch Rights, but Politics Too', *The Print*, 13 December. Available at https://theprint.in/opinion/imran-khan-is-embarrassed-gwadar-protest-isnt-just-for-baloch-rights-but-politics-too/780584/ [last accessed 20 December 2021].

Khan, Omer Farooq (2017), 'Top Pak Army Man Says India Sabotaging CPEC', *The Times of India*, November 14. Available at https://timesofindia.indiatimes.com/world/pakistan/top-pak-army-man-says-india-sabotaging-cpec/articleshow/6164721 9.cms [last accessed 20 December 2021].

Khetran, Mir Sherbaz (2017) 'Indian Interference in Balochistan: Analysing the Evidence and Implications for Pakistan', *Strategic Studies* 37 (3): 112–125.

Kumar, Sundeep (2017) 'Why India's Decision to Not Endorse China's New Silk Road Project is Wise Foreign Policy'. Available at www.c3sindia.org/archives/why-indias-decision-to-not-endorse-chinas-new-silk-road-project-is-wise-foreign-policy-by-sundeep-kumar-s/ [last accessed 20 December 2021].

Kuszewska, Agnieszka and Nitza-Makowska, Agnieszka (2021) 'Multifaceted Aspects of Economic Corridors in the Context of Regional Security: The China–Pakistan Economic Corridor as a Stabilising and Destabilising Factor', *Journal of Asian Security and International Affairs*, 8 (2): 218–248.

Maçães, Bruno (2019) *Belt and Road: A Chinese World Order* (London: Hurst).

Malik, Ahmad Rashid (2017) 'India's Isolation on the Belt and Road Increases', *Pakistan Today*, 3 November. Available at https://issi.org.pk/wp-content/uploads/2017/11/Comment-India's_Isolation_on_the_Belt_and_Road_Increases.pdf [last accessed 20 December 2021].

Marchang, Reimeingam (2021) 'BCIM Economic Corridor an Integral Part of BRI for Regional Cooperation: Positioning India's North-East and Act East Policy', *Journal of Asian Security and International Affairs*, 8 (2), 249–269.

Masood, Yasir (2018) 'Why India Fear and Oppose CPEC?', *Times of Islamabad*, 8 August. Available at https://timesofislamabad.com/08-Aug-2018/why-india-fear-and-oppose-cpec [last accessed 20 December 2021].

Ministry of External Affairs (2017) 'Official Spokesperson's Response to a Query on Participation of India in OBOR/BRI Forum'. Available at https://mea.gov.in/media-briefings.htm?dtl/28463/Official+Spokespersons+response+to+a+query+on+participation+of+India+in+OBORBRI+Forum [last accessed 20 April 2022].

Naím, Moisés (2009) 'Minilateralism: The Magic Number to Get Real International Action', *Foreign Policy* (173): 135.

Nasr, Vali (2005) 'National Identities and the India-Pakistan Conflict', in T. V. Paul (ed.), *The India-Pakistan Conflict: An Enduring Rivalry* (Cambridge: Cambridge University Press), pp. 178–201.

Parekh, Bhikhu (2006) 'Defining India's Identity', *India International Centre Quarterly*, 33 (1): 1–15.

Parthasarathy, Gopalaswami (2021) 'Imran Khan's China Embrace', *The Tribune*, 7 January. Available at www.tribuneindia.com/news/comment/imran-khans-china-embrace-194722 [last accessed 20 December 2021].

Pasha, Mustapha Kamal (1992) 'Declining Hegemony: Kashmir, Secularism and Resurgent Islam', *Strategic Studies*, 15 (1): 25–40.

Pew Research Center (n.d). 'Opinion of China'. Available at www.pewresearch.org/global/database/indicator/24/country/in [last accessed 20 April 2022].

Pew Research Center (2019). 'Attitudes toward China'. Available at www.pewresearch.org/global/2019/12/05/attitudes-toward-china-2019/ [last accessed 20 April 2022].

PTI (2018) 'India Will Not Accept Project that Violates its Sovereignty: MEA on China's OBOR', *The Economic Times*, 5 April. Available at https://economictimes.indiatimes.com/news/defence/india-will-not-accept-project-that-violates-its-sovereig nty-mea-on-chinas-obor/articleshow/63632894.cms?from=mdr [last accessed 20 December 2021].

Rai, Ashok (2018) 'Quadrilateral Security Dialogue 2 (Quad 2.0) – a Credible Strategic Construct or Mere 'Foam in the Ocean'?', *Maritime Affairs: Journal of the National Maritime Foundation of India*, 14 (2): 138–148.

Rajagopalan, Rajeswari Pillai (2021) 'Explaining the Rise of Minilaterals in the Indo-Pacific'. Available at www.orfonline.org/wp-content/uploads/2021/09/ORF_IssueB rief_490_Minilaterals-IndoPacific.pdf [last accessed 20 December 2021].

Singh, Hemant Krishan, Sahgal, Arun and Sahu Ambuj (2021) 'The Quad's Present and Future: A Geostrategic Perspective from Delhi'. Available at www.delhipoli cygroup.org/uploads_dpg/publication_file/the-quads-present-and-future-a-geostrate gic-perspective-from-delhi-2779.pdf [last accessed 20 December 2021].

Spirit of the Quad (2021). 'Quad Leaders' Joint Statement: "The Spirit of the Quad"'. Available at www.whitehouse.gov/briefing-room/statements-releases/2021/03/12/qua d-leaders-joint-statement-the-spirit-of-the-quad [last accessed 20 December 2021].

Times of India (2021) 'Explained: What Pakistan's Gilgit-Baltistan Plan Means for India, China', *The Times of India*, 4 August. Available at https://timesofindia.india times.com/world/pakistan/explained-what-pakistans-gilgit-baltistan-plan-means-for -india-china/articleshow/85039940.cms [last accessed 20 December 2021].

Vasan, R. S. (2017) 'China–Pakistan Economic Corridor (CPEC): Questions Abound?'. Available at www.c3sindia.org/environment-health/China–Pakista n-economic-corridor-cpec-questions-abound-by-commodore-r-s-vasan-in-retd/ [last accessed 20 December 2021].

Volgy, Thomas J., Corbetta, Renato, Grant, Keith A. and Baird Ryan G. (2011) 'Major Power Status in International Politics', in Thomas J. Volgy, Renato Corbetta, Keith A. Grant and Ryan G. Baird (eds), *Major Powers and the Quest for Status in International Politics: Evolutionary Processes in World Politics* (New York: Palgrave Macmillan), pp. 1–26.

Wojczewski, Thorsten (2019) 'Identity and World Order in India's Post-Cold War Foreign Policy Discourse', *Third World Quarterly*, 40 (1): 180–198.

Xavier, Constantino (2020) 'Sambandh as Strategy: India's New Approach to Regional Connectivity'. Available at www.brookings.edu/wp-content/uploads/2020/01/ Sambandh-as-Strategy-India%E2%80%99s-New-Approach-to-Regional-Connectiv ity.pdf [last accessed 20 April 2022].

3 Digital Space and Religious Intolerance in South Asia

India and Bangladesh

Parama Sinha Palit

The digital space, dominated by social media platforms like Facebook, Twitter and Instagram, have indeed revolutionized global communication by placing the *public* within its network. By heralding free speech and facilitating access to unfiltered information, this new form of communication network has been applauded for ending the monopoly over information and extending the boundaries of democracy. Scholars like Shirky (2011) have emphasized the 'political power of social media' by listing several enabling tools available for political participation in the digital era. Social media, she argues, offers 'coordinating tools', helps to create 'shared awareness', and fosters 'horizontal communication' (Shirky, 2011).

However, these digital tools have equally exposed the dark underside of technology and democracy. In fact, several studies have been undertaken to correct the initial euphoria around social media-enabled transformative citizen activism, including downright criticism of 'slactivism' as a form of evacuating actual political energy (Morozov, 2011) involving very little commitment or effort, and focusing instead on the challenges posed by the internet-driven communication. The networked public, provided with alternative information sources, now pose as a new category of 'misinformed masses', capable of producing unverified information, while being heavily influenced by *disinformation*, predominantly religious in nature. Disinformation (*dezinformatsiya*), deliberately coined by the Russian leader Joseph Stalin, was an effort to make it sound French, and thereby emphasize its Western origin (Pacepa & Rychlak, 2013). It was subsequently borrowed and polished by the department of black propaganda of the KGB in the 1950s (Bittman, 1985).

Digitally-mediated propaganda, a new form of manipulation of the public perception, has only became more severe in the contemporary online space. By often targeting centre Parties and the mainstream press, movements and Parties on the radical Right, spread disinformation and fake news that can be traced to growing legitimacy problems in many democracies (Bennett & Livingston, 2018: 122). The complex media landscape consequently has created a dystopian cycle of narratives – causing an emergency in democratic societies including South Asia. With 448 million social media users in India (Datareportal, 2021a) and 45 million social media users in Bangladesh

DOI: 10.4324/9781003305132-5

(Datareportal, 2021b), this dimension of religion and associated tensions is acute in these two neighbouring states. Technology has similarly constrained the capacity of political actors to control the framing of events, while providing them with opportunities to control social media content. Empowered by technology, political actors are investing in new forms of communication for influence enhancement by using big data marketing, data surveillance and bot forces (Howard & Wooley, 2016). This chaotic media ecology has led several remedial accounts to emerge – raising pertinent questions about how social media is *transforming from a potential forum for radical empowerment of ordinary citizen voice to a propaganda tool of political authorities* (Howard & Wooley, 2016).

The networked public's navigation of complex diplomacy and foreign policy issues has further complicated the diplomacy realm, apart from impacting upon each modern state's global reputation. Post-independence, India's pursuit of multilateralism and peaceful co-existence had underscored its aspirations for peace and harmony while it struggled to secure global stability in an era of sharp ideological and military polarization. The 'idea of India' – espoused by Jawaharlal Nehru, India's first Prime Minister – was based on secularism and was also a celebration of Indian pluralism and its cultural diversity. Nehru's admiration for the 'other Asian civilizations' had significantly shaped India's diplomacy, making it one of the hallmarks of his foreign policy vision and diplomatic outreach (Tharoor, 2012).

Similarly, after Bangladesh was founded in 1972, its first President Mujibur Rahman, had also based his foreign policy on *mujibvada* – comprising key concepts of secularism, democracy, Bengali nationalism and socialism (Bharadwaj, 2003). Mujib had rejected Islamist politics to demonstrate his aversion to the two-nation theory – an ideology over which the Indian subcontinent was partitioned in 1947 (Fair, 2021). However, Bangladesh has not been able to avoid communal tensions and radicalization. The global technological revolution is now amplifying online hate and disinformation provoking mistrust and divisions between communities.

Rapid advancements in communication technology were expected to usher in a new era in diplomacy and stronger bilateral ties. A more democratic multiplicity of new, competing narratives and inclusive discourses was expected to thrive in the new communication landscape. However, the power of social media not only brought in its wake more communal disharmony, manipulation of public perceptions in line with narrow political interests but also a dip in India-Bangladesh bilateral relationships as well. Scholars have pointed out the emergence of a 'new India' – increasingly characterized by 'a new intellectual current, feeding nascent new narratives' and attempting to cast a 'self-conscious Indic stamp on the understanding of Indian history and culture, ancient and more recent' – in sharp contrast to the Nehruvian 'idea of India' (Dehejia, 2018). Similarly, Bangladesh has also been witnessing pronounced Islamic radicalism with ultra-intolerant anti-Hindu outfits gaining traction in politics (Mukharji, 2020).

This chapter examines the contemporary narratives around online religious campaigns and the targeting the minorities, which disrupts *relational* public diplomacy[1] between the two South Asian countries – India and Bangladesh. By promoting a wider 'fake news era', characterized by the disproportionate dissemination of radical messages, these two states are not only encouraging intolerance, but manipulating public perceptions as well. The chapter also investigates whether this social media-driven communication has inhibited conversations in open spaces while swamping local discourses with disinformation in the new contentious digital environment under the current leaderships of India and Bangladesh.

The Academic Discourse

A survey of the literature on religious intolerance, especially with regard to Muslims reveals that most of the literature is predominantly Western, and discusses its prevalence in Western states and societies (Brasset & Browning, 2018; Hayden, 2018; Manor, 2019). The corpus of texts containing the word *Muslim* also shows that such a population is being consistently framed as an ominous and deadly threat (Berntzen, 2018) with immigration being targeted as its main cause. In the digital domain, hashtags have played a critical role in marking and declaring identities in distinction to other groups and opinions, given their potential to create collective conversations in times of crisis, conflicts and controversies (Giglietto & Lee, 2017).

Hashtags like #anti-Muslim, #MuslimBan, #totalboycottofmuslims have become conspicuous online within pandemic-related disinformation campaigns, stoking Islamophobia and provoking global hate attacks against the Muslim community. A study by the Equality Labs, a South Asian digital human rights group, revealed that a 'Corona jihad' hashtag was used around 300,000 times between 29 March and 3 April 2020, and viewed by as many as 165 million people (Mahzam, 2020). There were similar other prominent hashtags such as #BioJihad, #Coronaterrorism, #MuslimsSpreadingCorona, which, when translated into local languages, gained phenomenal online traction (Mahzam, 2020) during the same period. In fact, compared to the past, the digital communicative revolution has rendered contemporary religious hatred more explicit, expressive, extreme and composite in nature.

States across the world are witnessing hate against their minorities with religious intolerance accentuating online falsehoods. India is no exception in this regard. In April 2017, according to a Pew Research Center analysis of 198 countries, India – a secular[2] and liberal democracy – was ranked fourth worst in the world in terms of religious tolerance with religion-related terror showing a major spike (Bhattacharya, 2017). In fact, both India – where Islam is the second largest religion after Hinduism – and Bangladesh together witnessed a major surge in minority violence after the onset of Covid-19 (Sinha Palit, 2020b: 101–102; Prothom Alo, 2020). Interestingly, unlike in the West, South Asia's anti-Muslim discourse is more a legacy of the Partition in

1947 – when British India was divided into India and Pakistan – than immigration.

While prejudices against Hindus are comparatively less pervasive, it is also conspicuously understudied. However, Hinduphobia is gradually gaining traction in Islamic countries like Bangladesh. There is little doubt that whether they be Islamists or the far-right extremists (i.e. right-wing political actors espousing politics supporting the view that certain social orders and hierarchies are inevitable, natural or normal and are supported by natural law, economics, or tradition), both share a notion of society based on exclusive identity and the demonization of different or foreign groups and worldviews (Fielitz et al., 2018: 15). There is no denying that a generalized abasement and stigmatization of entire groups of people also threatens the very foundations of democratic cultures and open societies (Fielitz et al., 2018: 15) both in India and Bangladesh, in a similar way to the West.[3]

Islamophobia/phobism and Hinduphobia/phobism: Origins, Opinions and Social Media

Before perusing the literature on Islamophobia and Hinduphobia, it is important to define our key terms. According to the Council of Europe – a leading international organization upholding democracy, human rights and rule of law – Islamophobia is defined as 'the fear of or prejudiced viewpoint towards Islam, Muslims and matters pertaining to them' (Wade, 2019: 21). The term *Islamophobia* may have been in circulation since, at least the beginning of the twentieth century, in a variety of languages (Lopez, 2011: 556–573), but post-1990s the term came to signify both unfounded hostility towards Islam and *fear* or *dislike* of all or most Muslims (Kallis, 2018). Interestingly, while Islamophobia assumes that a fear of Islam is natural and can be taken for granted, the use of the term *Islamophobism* – more relevant and pertinent in this context – presumes that this fear has been fabricated by those with a vested interest in producing and reproducing such a state of fear, or phobia (Kaya, 2019). There is no denying that *Islamophobism* has turned out to be a practical instrument of social control in the hands of the conservative political elite for ensuring compliance and subordination in an age of neoliberalism, that is essentializing ethnocultural and religious boundaries (Kaya, 2019).

When it comes to Islamophobia and its threats, its origins can be traced to Samuel Huntington, known for his celebrated work *The Clash of Civilizations* (Huntington, 1996). It was Huntington who generated the main ideological matrix of contemporary Islamophobia of which the central logic is the production of a new civilizational enemy (Mudde, 2015). Later its translation into French helped its spread to many European nations, with its analytical framework subsequently influencing the European political classes (Mudde, 2015). According to Huntington, it is *religion* that distinguishes different civilizations, and is decisive in differentiating cultures (Bouamama, 2018: 25).

In fact, the Western perception of Islam as a religion changed dramatically after the terrorist attacks in New York on 11 September 2001, popularly known as 9/11, acquiring a very different meaning and momentum – ideologically, politically, and in the social context (Allen, 2010: 83–84). The term was reinvented and revitalized as a potent exclusionary ideology upon which the radical Right redefined and narrowed the notion of 'us' in opposition to 'them', mixing race with culture, prejudice with rational arguments about integration, compatibility, and absorption capacity (Bunzl, 2005: 499–508) giving rise to *Islamophobism*.

Subsequently, a scholarly consensus emerged contending that, in the aftermath of the 9/11 attacks on the United States (US), the sustained intensity of media coverage of Islam and Muslims resulted in an almost universal awareness of the religion and its adherents, which further 'created a vicious cycle of growing extremism and entrenched social discontent, political polarization grounded in identity politics and a heightened fear of the "other"' (Perry, 2019: 10). Since then, the literature on the threat that Islam poses, its radicalism and extremism experienced in the Western states has proliferated (Bayrakli & Hafez, 2015; Berntzen, 2018; Bevelander & Wodak, 2019).

A significant amount of work has also focused on the far-right wing groups, concerning 'Radical Islamism and anti-Muslim racism, which manifest themselves in the form of far-right extremism and Right-wing populism exhibit a symbiotic relationship' (Fielitz et al., 2018) while sharing narratives focusing on three elements: the victimization of the 'in-group', the demonization of the 'out-group' and conspiracy theories about political elites and the media (Fielitz et al., 2018). Digital media has only perpetuated the divide between 'them' and 'us', as is highly evident in the South Asian context. In fact, the outbreak of the pandemic witnessed an avalanche of online conspiracy theories targeting the Muslims in India (Sinha Palit, 2020a) while religious misinformation (a non-deliberate attempt to spread information, distinct from agenda-driven disinformation) inundated Bangladesh's online space (Barua et al., 2020).

Though scholars like Mouffe (2009) have expressed reservations about the potential of new media (digital platforms consumed on laptops, cell phones, desktops and tablets), and the internet in particular, in encouraging the agonistic model because media practices tend to reinforce pre-existing ideas rather than eliciting confrontations with antithetical positions (Carpentier & Cammaerts, 2006: 964–975), the use of social media for spreading Islamophobia and hate crime[4] against Muslims and Islam has heightened, receiving strong academic attention (Evolvi 2019; Giglietto & Lee, 2017). In fact, scholars have drawn attention to homophily – 'the principle that a contact between similar people occurs at a higher rate than among dissimilar people' (McPherson et al., 2001: 416) – as hindering the insurgence of agonistic confrontations, facilitating the creation of polarized groups that reinforce their identities by selective exposure to like-minded users. It is further established that Twitter's homophily is often *emotion-based* (Ferrara & Yang, 2015) leading to political polarization since networked publics 'are mobilized and connected, identified, and potentially disconnected through expressions of sentiment' (Papacharissi, 2016: 5). Consequently, Twitter users – although exposed to high-level public discussions – are presented with a structure facilitating conversations with like-minded people rather than improving dialogue between different groups. Twitter is therefore regarded as being 'insufficient for reasoned discourse and debate, instead privileging haste and emotion' (Yardi & Boyd, 2010: 325).

The basic premise of Islamophobia – *fear* of the 'other' – is visible in Bangladesh where heightened anti-Hindu sentiment (or Hinduphobism) or Hinduphobia is dominating the digital space. More appropriately defined, the term signifies an 'aversion to Hindus or to Hinduism; cultural bias, possibly ethnically motivated, against Hindus, Hinduism or both' (Long, 2011). Interestingly, the 'anti-Hindu' idea has also been a rallying point for large sections of the Hindu Indian diaspora that have been aggrieved over creation of negative stereotypes of Hindu religious 'sympathizers'. Negative religious stereotypes tend to be exploited for manipulation and fabrication by many contemporary conservative leaderships – for example in Pakistan under former Prime Minister Imran Khan, and Turkey under President Tayyip Erdogan and their followers – to force a different conversation in which tolerance and accommodation are replaced with misunderstanding, misinterpretation and violence against minorities.

Although Hinduphobia as a realm of study is yet to draw attention similar to Islamophobia, some initial work has been done on the subject (Al-Zaman, 2019; Mohapatra & Sahoo, 2014; Resolve Network, 2018). Like elsewhere, social media has also been extensively deployed to target the Hindu minority in Bangladesh, which with a share of 8.5% in total population is the second largest minority group, followed by Buddhists who comprise 0.6% of the population, and are equally vulnerable to digital communalism and contempt (Al-Zaman, 2019: 68). However, scholarly work on the use of technology to spread hate against the Hindu population is rare. A few print articles and editorials do highlight recent social media-driven developments (BBC Bangla, 2017; Daily Star, 2021; Gumaste, 2020; Hasan, 2021; Prothom Alo, 2020) indicating that the contemporary digitized media landscape is indeed witnessing an enduring suppression and marginalization of religious minorities, both in physical society and in cyberspace, demanding an accommodation of the 'other'.

Right-Wing Politics and Social Media-Fed Religious Intolerance

Although the narrative on Islamophobia and Hinduphobia in India and Bangladesh has been more embedded in the psychology of the Partition (Gumaste, 2020; Venkatesh, 2019), as alluded to earlier, the rise of the Right-wing in India has perpetuated the anti-Islam discourse, converting the

narrative from Islamophobia to *Islamophobism* with radicalism and extremism defining India's political system. Since the election of the Bharatiya
Janata Party (BJP) in 2014 – long committed to *Hindutva* with autarkic
instincts (Mehta, 2019) – some scholars have identified Hindu nationalism as
a polarizing force (Gettleman et al., 2019). An increasing internet-fed communal tension, damaging India's global reputation, has also been visible
(Subramanian 2020). India has been specifically drawing global attention
because it has not only been 'inspirational' for the rest of the world given its
diverse culture and religion but also for its robust democracy. However, the
growth of the pro-Hindu brand of nationalism has gradually become more
acceptable in the mainstream discourse with several sections of the ordinary
public emboldened by its Hindu majoritarian narrative. Mediated by algorithms and bots, often inadvertently or otherwise, extreme content marked by
hate-driven speeches is being increasingly circulated, frequently followed by
acts of violence (Freedom House, 2021a). Related digital algorithms are also
driving the youth – the most rapidly expanding group of smartphone users in
India fuelled by the cheapest mobile data in the world (BBC, 2019) – and
others, to view videos glorifying violence, promoting conspiracy theories and
disinformation along religious line thereby stressing India's secular character
(OpIndia, 2020).

The continued salience of Hindu nationalism in contemporary India presents the paradox of transnational internet media technologies aiding a
staunchly chauvinistic nationalist ideology (Udupa, 2018) with a digitally
active public increasingly 'losing sight of the liberal components of modern
democracies' (Reinemann et al., 2017). With orthodox and polarizing agendas and actions generating violence, propelling discriminatory policies and
also stifling dissenting protests (Indian Express, 2019; Print, 2019), India's
status declined from Free to Partly Free (Freedom House, 2021a) in 2021.

Indian political leaders, in their own way, are contributing to the frenzy.
Many leaders in the so-called Hindi belt of North and Central India, cutting
across party lines, have begun highlighting Hindu credentials to keep voter
loyalties alive with direct interaction (Pal et al., 2016) and wooing the net-
savvy electorate who pose as *Hindutva* supporters. While the Indian Congress
is taking out *Parivartan yatras* ('tours to bring about change'), the Aam
Admi Party (AAP) has promised, that if voted to power, the Party would
make Uttarakhand the global spiritual capital of the Hindus (Naqvi, 2021).
Many fear that the scrapping of Article 370 of the Indian Constitution that
granted special status to Jammu and Kashmir in 2019, and the Citizenship
Amendment Act[5] could release a backlash that can create a 'South Asian
Ummah' (Muslim unity), extending from Khyber in Pakistan to Chittagong
in Bangladesh (Javaid, 2020).

Secularism as a core basic structure of the Constitution of India has been
under stress for quite some time. Since the early-1990s, secularism has been
radically altered, with 'recognition of India as a Hindu state', in which
secularism does not lie as the bedrock of the Constitution becoming

dominant even if it is 'entirely outside the document's aims and purposes' (Parthasarathy, 2018). In fact, it is interesting to point out here that B. R. Ambedkar – the 'father' of the Indian Constitution – had rejected the proposal to include the word 'secular' during the drafting of the Constitution because he felt secularism was inherent to the Constitution's structure (Shankaran 2015) and its addition could only complicate the notion.

Like India, Bangladesh is also witnessing a constant flow of online disinformation and misinformation, especially along religious lines, sowing discord and resulting in truth and reality being constantly contested. A new wave of 'religious revivalism' among Muslims is underway and the outcomes are evident concerning religious intolerance; radical groups prone to militancy; the promulgation of Islamic sentiments in social life; increasing numbers of madrasas, as well as the Islamization of education (Al-Zaman, 2019: 70). Many recent studies are highlighting the 'shifting trends in Islamic majoritarianism where blasphemy and atheism are deemed to have deadly implications' (Hasan, 2021). Ranked 'partly free' by the Freedom House (2021b) for persecuting its minorities, the Hindus and their houses of worship, Bangladesh's past has had a critical role to play in the current developments, with the seed of socio-political separation and animosity along religious line alienating it from India, both physically and psychologically.

After independence in 1947, the leadership in un-divided Pakistan not only cultivated an anti-India sentiment but made efforts to revive the 'Muslim identity'. While Sheikh Mujibur Rehman included *secularism* as one of the four core governing principles in the first Constitution of Bangladesh in 1972, it was later amended by subsequent leaderships. General Ziaur Rahman fortified the religious basis of the Constitution by deleting *secularism*, and adding an Islamic invocation above the preamble (5th Amendment, 1979). His successor, President Hussain Muhammad Ershad, while maintaining that 'the state religion of the Republic is Islam but other religions may be practiced in peace and harmony in the Republic' (8th Amendment, 1988) then made Islam the state religion by introducing Article 2A. In 2011, Prime Minister Sheikh Hasina restored *secularism* to the Constitution, while maintaining Islam as the state religion and making no changes to the preamble, retaining its religious invocation (15th Amendment). Despite the supporters of Hasina claiming that she has attempted to modernize Islam, backing it up with a more scientific temper, extremism against Hindus has been on the rise generating demands for radical outfits to be dealt with strongly (Mukharji, 2020)

These internal dynamics have increasingly influenced the ordinary Bangladeshi public perception, giving way to an anti-India sentiment (Al-Zaman, 2019), which subsequently has been converted into an anti-Hindu bias (Mukharji, 2020). Following this logic, India is largely perceived as a 'Hindu *rashtra*' by most Bengali Muslims – which is a thoroughly post-Partition legacy and thought-process (Gumaste, 2020). The demolition of the historical Babri Masjid in Uttar Pradesh in 1990 in India had set the stage for the increased alienation of Hindus, thereby shaping a more rabid anti-Hindu discourse in the country. The free and enormous flow of information facilitated by the mainstream traditional media (both print and television) that obliterated communication boundaries had also added to the discourse. Islamic extremists unleashed terror and attacked local Hindus after the demolition (Al-Zaman, 2019), furthermore shook Bangladesh's pluralist outlook. In contemporary networked India and Bangladesh, digital tools have perpetuated the hate linked to religion with majoritarian-dictated politics while impairing their public diplomacy practices.

Online Religious Intolerance and Public Diplomacy

Digital media is fast altering the relational dynamics between the state and the public, with the latter often challenging the state's legitimacy and authority (Zaharna & Uysal, 2016: 110). In fact, the public, by seizing upon the power of social media, have become parallel players in setting the trajectory of public diplomacy. In particular, Mark Leonard argues that public diplomacy 'should be about building relationships, starting from understanding other countries' needs, cultures, and peoples and then looking for areas to make common cause' (Leonard, 2002: 48). Unfortunately, the current social media ecosystem is bereft of such ideals, hurting bilateral relationships by their continuous flow of disinformation. While illiberal acts in India precipitated by Hindu nationalist sentiments intimidates Bangladesh, 'religious revivalism' in the latter also worries India. In fact, despite India-Bangladesh relations being otherwise robust,[6] they have faced notable challenges in the recent past due to rise of the *Hindutva* agenda, policies like the CAA and National Register of Citizens[7] and Bangladesh's efforts to revive its Muslim identity.

Hindutva-driven Islamophobia appears to have permeated into the Hindu mainstream in India (Waikar, 2018). The radical discourse against Islam and Muslims has also begun to touch a wider sympathetic mainstream audience, revealing a deeper penetration of strands of *Islamophobism* as a form of racial-cultural-religious prejudice magnified by security and cultural concerns. In all of these realms, the role of social media has been critical, with digital platforms playing a critical role in diffusing radical ideas against its minorities. For instance, during the assembly polls in India's north-eastern state of Assam in 2021, the Hindu right-wing ecosystem circulated a morphed video of Maulana Badruddin Ajmal, the chief of the All India United Democratic Front on social media, claiming that he was prodding the Muslims of Assam to vote for him with the purpose of setting up 'an Islamic nation' with the help of the Congress and not leave 'a single Hindu' without converting them to Islam (Wire, 2021).

Bangladesh's online space is equally responsible for spewing hate and rumours which are often India-specific. A Bangladeshi faculty member explained such a trend as follows:

there is a politics behind what kind of posts will agitate people the most. So, in Bangladesh, any social media posts that reflects attack or criticism of Islam gets very widely circulated and is capable of leading to catastrophes and mass violence. There are organisations and lobbies which are behind these posts who later identify minorities by tagging them or hacking their social media accounts to accuse them falsely. Conspiracies develop. Posts then rallies then violence.

(Quoted in Prothom Alo, 2020)

As an example of such a phenomenon, in October 2021, unrest was triggered by online rumours about the Quran being allegedly placed at the feet of the Hindu goddess Durga. Reports suggested that Muslim hard-liners had used social media to provoke the violence (Bhaumik, 2021). In the wake of the incident, violence against Hindus swept across Bangladesh, with temples targeted, homes attacked and several Hindus killed. The mayhem sparked international protests from Dhaka to London (Ganguly, 2021), once again highlighting how a domestic issue generates international attention. It also demonstrates how a large digital followership is capable of spreading messages via reactions through networks across borders. India's nationalist fervour, including that in parts of its diaspora, has also become globally noticeable and has added to the concern with 'the new trend of host countries noticing and taking action against Islamophobic social media activism by the Hindu diaspora' (Swain, 2020).

A new global culture of nationalism and 'emotional antagonism' diffused through social networks (Evolvi, 2019) is increasingly hurting relational public diplomacy between India and Bangladesh. Notwithstanding the challenges, the leaderships of both countries have been keen to diplomatically engage with each other. Hasina had invited Modi to attend the birth centenary of Sheikh Mujibur Rahman, along with the golden jubilee celebrations of the country's half-centenary, to mark 50 years of bilateral ties. Modi's visit to Bangladesh in April 2021 was his first foreign tour since the beginning of the pandemic, underscoring his intent to firm up his government's 'neighbourhood first' policy. However, the larger public diplomacy goal of the state visit ran into problems following protests in Dhaka and the violence that followed. These events are stark reminders of the challenges that lie ahead for durable diplomatic engagement.

Conclusion: The Ascendance of Online Religious Nationalism Shapes Contemporary Diplomacy

The contemporary online media environment is extremely complex and contentious, crafting and shaping a dystopian narrative, often leading to a form of 'crisis public diplomacy' (Zaharna, 2003). Social media, while emerging as the tool of deception, has also entailed simultaneous communication between multiple public domains in a highly visible, rapidly evolving and contested public arena, thereby also causing crisis in several democracies. Saving democracy, it is argued, is not about arming against fake news and disinformation – at least not primarily. It is instead, and perhaps more importantly, about creating genuine spaces for politics: that is, spaces for contestation, for political difference and for pluralism to thrive (Farkas & Schou, 2020). This chapter has tried to highlight this evolving paradox, while underlining how genuine online spaces are being leveraged for misleading and dividing the public along religious lines in India and Bangladesh.

While religious intolerance has emerged as a global national concern, India and Bangladesh – both traditionally recognized for communal harmony, pluralism, and as strong democracies – have come under heightened international scrutiny. Given their longstanding values and principles, including their traditional accommodation of other cultures and religions, their unregulated digital space has invited immense academic focus. With nationalism riding high on politics, the evolving political environment in both states has been increasingly being identified with communal clashes, hate and violence over the past few years. While efforts have been underway to tackle communally charged disinformation, a new form of citizen responsibility is also being called for since the development of multiple social networks has involved everybody in the new information process.

The adverse impact of disinformation on domestic communal relations, public order, and the larger context of national security, has been noted by both the South Asian countries. While India has blocked several Twitter, Facebook accounts and YouTube channels for spreading disinformation (Economic Times, 2022), Bangladesh had also shut down many social networking sites in an effort to contain fake news (Devnath, 2018). While governments must take stringent policies to contain online disinformation, tough censorships on digital media might perpetuate more controversial tendencies to 'control'. This is a challenge that new media regulations need to look at closely. While information and communication revolution has accelerated the digitalization of public diplomacy, it has equally made way for a volatile online space with the online public, often inadvertently or otherwise, constraining the government's public diplomacy efforts. Similarly, governments have also found the adoption of digital tools advantageous for imposing certain conversations in line with their ideologies. All of these developments are not only giving rise to a new conservative culture but also making crises a new norm in the practice of public diplomacy. The examples of India and Bangladesh are illustrative in this regard.

Notes

1 Political communication has gained enormous prominence with the shift in public diplomacy to a more *relational* orientation toward publics brought about in a new media-enabled political environment with advanced technologies emphasizing *participation* (Zaharna & Uysal, 2016).

2 India's secularism has been celebrated for decades for its emphasis on 'neutrality' between different religions as opposed to *prohibition* advocated by many Western countries (Sen, 2005).
3 Marine Le Pen of the Front National (FN) in France is an example of far-right politics in Europe with strongly polarizing impact.
4 Wolfe and Copeland (1994: 201) define hate crime as 'violence directed towards groups of people who generally are not valued by the majority society, who suffer discrimination in other arenas, who do not have full access to remedy social, political and economic injustice'.
5 The CAA amended the Citizenship Act (1955) in 2019 to allow Indian citizenship for Hindu, Sikh, Buddhist, Jain, Parsi and Christian religious minorities who fled from the neighbouring Muslim majority countries like Pakistan, Bangladesh and Afghanistan before December 2014 'due to religious persecution or fear of religious persecution'.
6 Bangladesh is India's biggest trade partner in South Asia with both countries having deep economic ties. People-to-people connectivity is high and has increased with new land transport connections, including fast trains.
7 The NRC is a register maintained by the Government of India containing names and certain relevant information for identification of Indian citizens of Assam, a northeast state which is also home to a large population of Bengali Muslims. The register was first prepared after the 1951 Census of India. In 2013, the Indian Supreme Court ordered its update. The final updated NRC for Assam was published in August 2019. There are concerns that several people currently living in Assam might not be found to be 'citizens' following the updating.

References

Al-Zaman, Sayeed (2019) 'Digital Disinformation and Communalism in Bangladesh', *China Media Research*, 15 (2). Available at www.chinamediaresearch.net [last accessed 20 May 2021].

Allen, Chris (2010) *Islamophobia* (Farnham: Ashgate).

Barua, Zapan, Barua Sajib, Aktar, Salma, Kabir, Najma, Li Mingze (2020) 'Effects of Misinformation on COVID-19 Individual Responses and Recommendations for Resilience of Disastrous Consequences of Misinformation', *ScienceDirect* 8, December 2020. Available at https://doi.org/10.1016/j.pdisas.2020.100119.

Bayrakli, Enes, Hafez, Farid (eds) (2015) 'European Islamophobia Report'. Available at www.islamophobiaeurope.com/reports/2015/en/EIR_2015.pdf [last accessed 28 May 2021].

BBC (2019) 'Mobile Data: Why India Has the World's Cheapest'. Available at www.bbc.com/news/world-asia-india-47537201 [last accessed April 2022].

BBC Bangla (2017) 'Social media ki mooldhara r gono madhdhom theke beshi shoktishaali hoe uthchche?' ['Is Social Media Becoming More Powerful than Mainstream Media?']. Available at www.bbc.com/bengali/news-38786844.amp [last accessed 27 March 2021].

Bennett, Lance W., Livingston, Steven (2018) 'The Disinformation Order: Disruptive Communication and the Decline of Democratic Institutions', *European Journal Communication*, 33 (2).

Berntzen, Erik Lars (2018) 'The Anti-Islamic Movement: Far Right and Liberal?'. Available at https://cadmus.eui.eu/handle/1814/51864 [last accessed 23 December 2021].

Bevelander, Pieter, Wodak, Ruth (2019) *Europe at Crossroads: Confronting Populist, Nationalist, and Global Challenges* (Sweden: Nordic Academic Press).

Bharadwaj, Sanjay (2003) 'Bangladesh's Foreign Policy vis a vis India'. Available at https://ciaotest.cc.columbia.edu/olj/sa/sa_apr03/sa_apr03bhs01.html [last accessed 21 April 2022].

Bhattacharya, Ananya (2017) 'India is the Fourth-Worst Country in the World for Religious Violence'. Available at https://qz.com/india/959802/india-is-the-fourth-worst-country-in-the-world-for-religious-violence/ [last accessed 20 November 2019].

Bhaumik, Subir (2021) 'Why Did Muslim Hardliners Attack Hindus in Bangladesh's Worst Bout of Communal Violence in Two Decades'. Available at www.scmp.com/week-asia/politics/article/3153016/why-did-muslims-attack-hindus-bangladeshs-worst-bout-communal [last accessed 22 April 2022].

Bittman, Ladislav (1985) *The KGB and Soviet Disinformation: An Insider's View* (London: Pergamon Press).

Bouamama, Said (2018) 'The Making of Contemporary Identity-Based Islamophobia', in *Countering the Islamophobia Industry* (Atlanta, GA: The Carter Center).

Brasset, James, Browning, Christopher (2018) 'Social Media Europe and the Rise of Comedy in Global Diplomacy'. Available at www.e-ir.info/2018/10/14/social-media-europe-and-the-rise-of-comedy-in-global-diplomacy/ [last accessed 23 May 2019].

Bunzl, Matti (2005) 'Between Anti-Semitism and Islamophobia: Some Thoughts on the New Europe', *American Ethnologist*, 32 (4). Available at www.jstor.org/stable/3805338 [last accessed 23 December 2021].

Carpentier, N., Cammaerts, B (2006) 'Hegemony, Democracy, Agonism and Journalism: An Interview with Chantal Mouffe', *Journalism Studies*, 7(6).

Daily Star (2021) 'Hefajat Supporters Attack Hindu Homes'. Available at www.thedailystar.net/backpage/news/hefajat-supporters-attack-hindu-homes-2062373 [last accessed 24 March 2021].

Datareportal (2021a) 'Digital 2021: India'. Available at https://datareportal.com/reports/digital-2021-india [last accessed 29 March 2021].

Datareportal (2021b) 'Digital 2021: Bangladesh'. Available at https://datareportal.com/reports/digital-2021-bangladesh [last accessed 29 March 2021].

Dehejia, Vivek (2018) 'From Nehru's "Idea of India" to Modi's "New India"'. Available at www.livemint.com/Opinion/17Gy2lnHnG8xRlLO6PTxcM/Opinion-From-Nehrus-idea-of-India-to-Modis-new-India.html [last accessed 20 April 2022].

Devnath, Arun (2018) 'Bangladesh's Fight against Fake News'. Available at www.thehindu.com/news/international/bangladeshs-fight-against-fake-news/article25807800.ece [last accessed 27 April 2022].

Economic Times (2022) 'Indian Government Blocks 16 YouTube "News" Channels'. Available at https://economictimes.indiatimes.com/tech/technology/indian-government-blocks-16-youtube-news-channels/articleshow/91076845.cms [last accessed 27 April 2022].

Evolvi, Giulia (2019) '#Islamexit: Inter-group Antagonism on Twitter', *Information, Communication & Society*, 22 (3). Available at www.tandfonline.com/doi/full/10.1080/1369118X.2017.1388427 [last accessed 14 May 2021].

Fair, C. Christine (2021) 'Bangladesh at 50: Hard Democratic Realities, Unfulfilled Secular Promises'. Available at www.firstpost.com/world/bangladesh-at-50-hard-democratic-realities-unfulfilled-secular-promises-10232211.html [last accessed 23 April 2022].

Farkas, Johan, Schou, Jannick (2020) *Post-Truth, Fake News and Democracy* (New York: Routledge).

Ferrara, Emilio, Yang, Zeyao (2015) 'Measuring Emotional Contagion on Social Media'. Available at https://journals.plos.org/plosone/article?id=10.1371/journal.pone.0142390 [last accessed 7 June 2021].

Fielitz, Maik, Ebner, Julia, Guhl, Jakob, Jena, Quent, Matthias (2018) 'Loving Hate: Anti-Muslim Extremism, Radical Islamism, and the Spiral of Polarization'. Available at https://resolvenet.org/research/loving-hate-anti-muslim-extremism-radical-islamism-and-spiral-polarisation [last accessed 16 May 2021].

Freedom House (2021a) 'India'. Available at https://freedomhouse.org/country/india/freedom-world/2021 [last accessed 5 June 2021].

Freedom House (2021b) 'Bangladesh'. Available at https://freedomhouse.org/country/bangladesh/freedom-world/2021 [last accessed 5 June 2021].

Ganguly, Sumit (2021) 'Bangladesh's Deadly Identity Crisis', *Foreign Policy*. Available at https://foreignpolicy.com/2021/10/29/bangladesh-communal-violence-hindu-muslim-identity-crisis/ [last accessed 22 November 2021].

Gettleman, Jeffrey, Schultz, Kai, Raj, Suhasini, Kumar, Hari (2019) 'Under Modi, a Hindu Nationalist Surge Further Divided India'. Available at www.nytimes.com/2019/04/11/world/asia/modi-india-elections.html [last accessed 1 June 2020].

Giglietto, F., Lee, Y (2017) 'A Hashtag Worth a Thousand Words: Discursive Strategies Around #JeNeSuisPasCharlie After the 2015 Charlie Hebdo Shooting', *Social Media + Society*, 3(1). Available at https://doi.org/10.1177/2056305116686992 [last accessed 13 May 2021].

Gumaste, Vivek (2020) 'There May Be No Hindus Left in Bangladesh in 30 Years'. Available at www.sundayguardianlive.com/opinion/may-no-hindus-left-bangladesh-30-years [last accessed 24 March 2021].

Hasan, Mubashar (2021) 'Minorities Under Attack in Bangladesh'. Available at www.lowyinstitute.org/the-interpreter/minorities-under-attack-bangladesh [last accessed 22 April 2022].

Hayden, Craig (2018) 'Digital Diplomacy', in Gordon Martel (ed.), *The Encyclopedia of Diplomacy* (Chichester: John Wiley & Sons).

Howard, P., Wooley, S. C. (2016) 'Political Communication, Computational Propaganda, and Autonomous Agents – Introduction', *International Journal of Communication* 10: 4882–4890.

Huntington, P. Samuel (1996) *The Clash of Civilizations* (New York: Penguin Books).

Indian Express (2019) 'Denied Permission to Protest Abrogation of Article 370, Activists Seek Support Online'. Available at https://indianexpress.com/article/cities/ahmedabad/denied-permission-to-protest-abrogation-of-article-370-activists-seek-support-online-6061503/ [last accessed 22 April 2022].

Javaid, Azaan (2020) 'Scrapping Article 370 was 'Marital Rape', Assault on Faith of J&K, Says PDP's Naeem Akhtar'. Available at https://theprint.in/india/scrapping-article-370-was-marital-rape-assault-on-faith-of-jk-says-pdps-naeem-akhtar/469152/ [last accessed 15 June 2021].

Kallis, Aristotle (2018) 'The Radical Right and Islamophobia', in *The Oxford Handbook of the Radical Right* (Oxford: Oxford University Press).

Kaya, Ayhan (2019) 'Populism as a Neo-liberal Form of Governability: Resorting to Heritage, Culture and Past'. Available at www.researchgate.net/deref/http%3A%2F%2Fwww.solvatech.com.cy%2Fbooks%2Febook_COHERE_ipad_2018.pdf [last accessed 23 December 2021].

Leonard, Mark (2002) *Public Diplomacy* (London: Foreign Policy Centre).

Long, Jefferey (2011) *Historical Dictionary of Hinduism* (New York: Scarecrow Press).

Lopez, Fernando Bravo (2011) 'Towards a Definition of Islamophobia: Approximations of the Early Twentieth Century', *Ethnic and Racial Studies* 34 (3).

Mahzam, Remy (2020) 'Disinformation: The Spreading of Islamophobia'. Available at www.rsis.edu.sg/rsis-publication/icpvtr/global-health-security-covid-19-and-its-impacts-disinformation-the-spreading-of-islamophobia/#.XrzBx2V3bVp [last accessed 4 May 2020].

Manor, Ian (2019) *The Digitalization of Public Diplomacy* (Basingstoke: Palgrave Macmillan).

McPherson, M., Smith-Lovin, L., Cook, J. M (2001) 'Birds of a Feather: Homophily in Social Networks', *Annual Review of Sociology*, 27(1). Available at https://doi.org/10.1146/annurev.soc.27.1.415 [last accessed 14 May 2021].

Mehta, Gautam (2019) 'Hindu Nationalism and the BJP's Economic Record'. Available at https://carnegieendowment.org/2019/04/04/hindu-nationalism-and-bjp-s-economic-record-pub-78720 [last accessed 30 July 2020].

Mohapatra, Atanu, Sahoo, Chandra Prakash (2014) 'Violence against Minority Hindus in Bangladesh: An Analysis'. Available at www.vifindia.org/article/2014/july/30/violence-against-minority-hindus-in-bangladesh-an-analysis [last accessed 29 May 2021].

Morozov, Evgeny (2011) *The Net Delusion: The Dark Side of Internet Freedom* (New York: Public Affairs).

Mouffe, C. (2009) 'Democratic Politics and Agonistic Pluralism'. http://consellodacultura.gal/mediateca/extras/texto_chantal_mouffe_eng.pdf [last accessed 7 June 2021].

Mudde, C. (2015) 'The Problem with Populism'. Available at www.theguardian.com/commentisfree/2015/feb/17/problem-populism-syriza-podemos-dark-side-europe [last accessed 10 June 2021].

Mukharji, Shantanu (2020) 'Is Islamic Radicalism on the Rise in Bangladesh?'. Available at www.wionews.com/opinions-blogs/is-islamic-radicalism-on-the-rise-in-bangladesh-346627 [last accessed 21 April 2022].

Naqvi, Saba (2021) 'Opposition Bets on Hindutva to Counter BJP'. Available at www.tribuneindia.com/news/comment/opposition-bets-on-hindutva-to-counter-bjp-313446 [last accessed 2 December 2021].

Opindia (2020) 'Killer TikTok: How Teens Used the App to Post Suicide Videos, Film Killer Stunts and Glorify Anti-social Behaviour'. Available at www.opindia.com/2020/06/tiktok-banned-suicides-murders-inciter-hatred-glorification-of-antisocial-behaviour/ [last accessed 19 April 2022].

Pacepa, I. M., Rychlak, R. J (2013) *Disinformation: Former Spy Chief Reveals Secret Strategies for Undermining Freedom, Attacking Religion, and Promoting Terrorism* (New York: WND Books).

Pal, J., Chandra, P., Vydiswaran V. (2016) 'Twitter and the Rebranding of Narendra Modi', *Economic and Political Weekly*, 51 (8). Available at www.epw.in/journal/2016/8/twitter-and-rebranding-narendra-modi.html [last accessed 8 June 2021].

Papacharissi, Z. (2016) 'Affective Publics and Structures of Storytelling: Sentiment, Events and Mediality', *Information, Communication & Society*, 19 (3). Available at https://doi.org/10.1080/1369118X.2015.1109697 [last accessed 4 June 2021].

Parthasarathy, Suhrith (2018) 'Understanding Secularism in the Indian Context', *The Hindu*. Available at www.thehindu.com/opinion/lead/the-secular-condition/article22347527.ece [last accessed 10 June 2021].

Perry, Valery (ed.) (2019) *Extremism and Violent Extremism in Serbia* (Germany: Ibidem Press).

Print (2019) 'No Debate, No Discussion, No Dissent, and the Constitution is Changed'. Available at https://theprint.in/opinion/no-debate-no-discussion-no-dissent-and-the-constitution-is-changed/272436/ [last accessed 21 April 2022].

Prothom Alo (2020) 'Dhormiyo o jati goto shonkhya loghu ra bhalo nei' ['Religious & Ethnic Minorities are Not Fine']. Available at www.prothomalo.com/amp/story/opinion/column/ধর্মীয়-ও-জাতিগত-সংখ্যালঘুরা-ভালো-নেই [last accessed 27 March 2021].

Reinemann, C., Aalberg, T., Esser, F., Strömbäck, J., de Vreese, C (2017) 'Populist Political Communication, Toward a Model of its Causes, Forms and Effects', in T. Aalberg, F. Esser, C. Reinemann, J. Strömback, C. de Vreese (eds), *Populist Political Communication in Europe* (London: Routledge).

Resolve Network (2018) 'Bangladesh and Violent Extremism: Resolve Network Research 2016–2017'. Available at https://resolvenet.org/system/files/2018-10/RSVE_16-17BGD_ResearchCompendium_FINAL.pdf [last accessed 21 April 2022].

Sen, Amartya (2006) *The Argumentative Indian* (New York: Penguin Books).

Shankaran, Sanjiv (2015) 'Ambedkar Did Turn Down Proposals to Include "Socialist" and "Secular" in Constitution's Preamble'. Available at https://timesofindia.indiatimes.com/blogs/cash-flow/ambedkar-did-turn-down-proposals-to-include-socialist-and-secular-in-constitutions-preamble/ [last accessed 24 April 2022].

Shirky, Clay (2011) 'The Political Power of Social Media', *Foreign Affairs* 90 (1). Available at www.cc.gatech.edu/~beki/cs4001/Shirky.pdf [last accessed 24 May 2021].

Sinha Palit, Parama (2020a) 'Online Hate Speech Is a Challenge for India's Foreign Policy'. Available at https://thediplomat.com/2020/10/online-hate-speech-is-a-challenge-for-indias-foreign-policy/ [last accessed 29 May 2021].

Sinha Palit, Parama (2020b) 'Fake News and Covid-19: India's Diplomatic Challenges', in Isha Dubey (ed.), *Articulations of a Pandemic: Researching and Navigating South Asia in the times of Covid-19* (Chakra).

Subramanian, Samanth (2020) 'How Hindu Supremacists Are Tearing India Apart'. Available at www.theguardian.com/world/2020/feb/20/hindu-supremacists-nationalism-tearing-india-apart-modi-bjp-rss-jnu-attacks [last accessed 1 June 2020].

Swain, Ashok (2020) 'India Must Stop Spreading Hindu Nationalism to its Global Diaspora'. Available at https://asia.nikkei.com/Opinion/India-must-stop-spreading-Hindu-nationalism-to-its-global-diaspora [last cited 15 June 2021].

Tharoor, Shashi (2012) *Pax Indica: India and the World of the 21st Century* (New Delhi: Penguin).

Udupa, Sahana (2018) 'Enterprise Hindutva and Social Media in Urban India'. Available at www.tandfonline.com/doi/full/10.1080/09584935.2018.1545007 [last accessed 7 April 2021].

Venkatesh, Archana (2019) 'Right-Wing Politics in India', *Origins* 13 (1). Available at https://origins.osu.edu/article/right-wing-politics-india-Modi-Kashmir-election [last accessed 30 March 2021].

Wade, Stuart (2019) 'Islamophobia in the UK: A UK Response to Islam and the Influence of Social Media in Shaping Attitudes towards Muslim Communities', dissertation, Lancaster University.

Waikar, Prashant (2018) 'Reading Islamophobia in Hindutva: An Analysis of Narendra Modi's Political Discourse', *Islamophobia Studies Journal*, 4 (2). Available at www.scienceopen.com/hosted-document?doi=10.13169/islastudj.4.2.0161 [last accessed 18 April 2022].

Wire (2021) 'Right Wingers Tweet Morphed Video of AIUDF Chief Saying "India Will Become Islamic Nation"'. Available at https://thewire.in/politics/right-wingers-tweet-morphed-video-of-aiudf-chief-saying-india-will-become-islamic-nation [last accessed 7 April 2021].

Wolfe, L., Copeland, L. (1994) *Violence against Women as Bias-Motivated Hate Crime: Defining the Issue in the USA* (Washington, DC: Center for Women Policy Studies).

Yardi, S., Boyd, D. (2010) 'Dynamic Debates: An Analysis of Group Polarization Over Time on Twitter' *Bulletin of Science, Technology & Society*, 30 (5). Available at https://doi.org/10.1177/0270467610380011 [last accessed 14 May 2021].

Zaharna, R. S., Uysal, Nur (2016) 'Going for the Jugular in Public Diplomacy: How Adversarial Publics Using Social Media Are Challenging State Legitimacy', *Public Relations Review*, 42.

Zaharna, R. S. (2003) 'Asymmetry of Cultural Styles & the Unintended Consequences of Crisis Public Diplomacy'. Available at http://fs2.american.edu/zaharna/www/crisisPD-ab.html [last accessed 18 April 2021].

4 The Offshore Hindu Nation

The Indian Ocean in the Hindu Nationalist Imagination, 1990–2019

Sara Perlangeli

In a much-publicized address at the Shangri-La dialogue in Singapore, an annual gathering of foreign policy officials from the Asia-Pacific region, Indian Prime Minister Narendra Modi declared, somewhat blandly, that 'the Indian Ocean has shaped much of India's history. It now holds the key to our future' (Modi, 2018). The speech was hailed as a major commitment to the region from a country that had, until then, been somewhat reluctant to embrace such a role (Roy-Chaudhury, 2018). What a heightened Indian profile in the Indian Ocean entails is a moot point, both in the Indian foreign policy establishment and strategic circles surrounding it (see Schöttli, 2019). Yet that an adherent of Hindu nationalism is in power as India's Prime Minister may have some bearing on the actual contours of India's role that issue from these debates. In this context, ideas about India's role in the Indian Ocean region articulated in Hindu nationalist circles have acquired renewed relevance.

This chapter shines a light on some of these ideas, primarily ones articulated outside officialdom and developed in an ambiguous relationship with it, and possibly representing the ideological backdrop of more visible government actions. In particular, it explore the ways in which individuals associated with the Hindu nationalist project have written about the Indian Ocean and its littoral over a period of thirty years, starting in the early 1990s, when Indian foreign policy was gradually reoriented seaward, and continuing to this day, as the deepening and expansion of India's engagement in the Indian Ocean has become a key foreign policy priority for the Modi government. In so doing, it considers the role that such narratives may play in advancing the ideological commitments of the Hindu nationalist movement, as well as in galvanizing constituencies willing to embrace its causes, by attributing specific identities to India and other countries along the Indian Ocean. The chapter focuses on a middlebrow inflection of Hindu nationalist ideology, as articulated in the pages of the English-language weekly magazine *Organiser*, and show how generally consistent ideological positions may issue not from an unchanging ideological charter, but rather from extemporaneous forms of engagement with the world beyond India's borders.

In line with the analytical approach of this volume, this chapter is primarily interested in the identity and global vision that the sources under

DOI: 10.4324/9781003305132-6

analysis put forward for India. In so doing, its starting point is an acknowl-edgment of the intersubjective nature of identity construction (see Wendt 1992: 401). In particular, in paying attention to the centrality of interaction with both domestic and foreign 'others', this chapter attends to the pains-taking ideological labour that domestic actors perform in attempting to produce and reproduce identities by engaging with the world beyond India's borders. Crucially, this serves not only to advance foreign policy objectives, but also to realize the broader goals – domestic and international – of the Hindu nationalist movement. Identity and interaction are therefore the con-ceptual keystones of this endeavour, for it is by ascribing certain cultural traits to the societies they encounter over the course of their reporting that *Organiser* contributors come to articulate their own visions of India's own identity and appropriate international conduct.

In attending to these analytical concerns, the chapter moves away from an overwhelming focus on state-centric or elite understandings of Indian foreign policy and the state's seaward turn (see Chacko, 2014; Hall, 2019; Mohan, 2012). It is my contention that perspectives articulated in non-specialist cir-cles, though perhaps sparser and lacking in analytical rigour, form a reper-toire of ideas against which foreign policy initiatives may be understood, besides representing a valuable and understudied archive of ways of engaging with the international beyond the state. In moving both beyond the state and elite epistemic communities, the chapter focuses on the ways in which *Orga-niser* renders the Indian Ocean into a meaningful space for the Hindu nationalist constituencies by retelling developments along the Indian Ocean littoral, in a manner that cultivates certain ideological dispositions, or alle-giances, among these constituencies. From an analytical standpoint, this entails attending to the role played by interpellation in the narratives that it considers. In Althusser's (1971: 174) framing, interpellation is the process by which individuals recognize themselves within a specific ideology, thus turn-ing into 'subjects' of that ideology. How, then, the chapter asks, do these narratives enable individuals to recognize themselves in Hindu nationalist representations of the international that may seem, geographically at least, quite distant from their lived experience?

For this to occur, the chapter argues that it is necessary that the narratives articulated in *Organiser* have an interpellative potential, or the ability to cultivate allegiance to Hindu nationalist objectives among their con-stituencies. This depends on the projection, onto these distant places, of modes of belonging and political action drawn from the Indian mainland – the context with which *Organiser*'s constituencies are presumably most familiar. In this manner, the domestic is refracted through the international, and the littoral of the Indian Ocean is constructed as an offshore replica of the Hindu India that *Organiser*, and Hindu nationalists more generally, advocate. At the same time, the cultivation of ideological dispositions among domestic constituencies depends on the articulation of a distinct ideological programme that charts onto foreign places some of the objectives of the

Hindu nationalist movement. Throughout, the identities that *Organiser* contributors construct for themselves and the foreign and domestic 'others' they
encounter, as well as for India, act as the main rhetorical hinge of this
endeavour.

This chapter proceeds as follows. First, it situates my contribution in relation to the literature on Hindu nationalism and Indian foreign policy, and
defines the specific inflection of Hindu nationalist ideology that the chapter's
sources represent. It then moves on to a more substantive analytical part, in
which the analysis considers how *Organiser*'s ideological commitments are
articulated in relation to topical developments along the Indian Ocean littoral. The chapter does so by dissecting, first, the magazine's treatment of
cultural commonalities along the eastern wing of the Indian Ocean, and
second, the identification, in the same region, of much the same competitive
dynamics between majorities and minorities that characterize the Hindu
nationalist rendering of India's domestic space, so that social cleavages at
home neatly transpose onto ones abroad, and vice versa. Emphasis on such
commonalities – in both cultural practices and social cleavages – helps
Organiser articulate an ideological programme in relation to the Indian
Ocean, onto which some of the goals and priorities of the Hindu nationalist
movement are mapped, as the chapter shows in the final section.

The Hindu Nationalist Foreign Policy Paradox and *Organiser*

The electoral ascendance of the Hindu nationalist Bharatiya Janata Party
(BJP) from the late 1980s has generated renewed interest in the relationship
between ideological commitments and foreign policy, and often puzzlement
at the apparent lack of any immediate connection between the two, despite
the textual richness of Hindu nationalism and the BJP's own rootedness in
such a milieu. On the one hand, interventions seeking to unveil the relationship between Hindu nationalist ideology and foreign policy outcomes have
largely interpreted the former as a set of domestically generated notions
about appropriate international conduct, sometimes subject to constraints
emanating either from the world outside or from within a well-entrenched
foreign policy tradition (Chacko, 2012; Chatterjee Miller & Sullivan de
Estrada, 2017: 29; Ogden, 2014). In so doing, these studies have attempted to
move beyond government or elite epistemic communities, and have taken
into account the influence of worldviews and individual agency on policy
outcomes (Hall, 2017; Hall, 2019). Yet ideas seem to matter in these accounts
only as variables in a process that has policy outcomes as its most important
part. Rarely are they examined as modes of engaging with the international
that are worthy of analysis in their own right.

On the other hand, there have been attempts at tracing the contours of
Hindu nationalist ideology as a foreign policy orientation, largely based on
close readings of paradigmatic texts. Such an orientation, or 'grand strategy''is, in Bajpai's (2003: 252–253) view, deeply revisionist and has as its

objective the achievement of Hindu supremacy, whereas for Sagar (2009: 809; 2014: 254) it simply amounts to an ersatz realism wherein the maximization of national power on the international stage is hindered by ethno-nationalist priorities (see also Basrur, 2017: 10–13). Hall (2019) attempts a similar exercise: on his reading, Hindu nationalist ideas are 'intellectually malnourished' (Hall, 2019: 149), offering little guidance with respect to policymaking and therefore incapable of shaping policy outcomes.

This chapter seeks to broaden the field of enquiry to show that there exists in fact a non-technocratic, middlebrow public that engages with loosely defined foreign policy issues. It does not argue that ideas emerging in such public spheres are wholly non-statist, or inherently non-elite because of their relative distance from state power or elite epistemic communities. Indeed, as the literature on Hindu nationalism has shown, organizations in this ecosystem are enmeshed in relationships of mutual dependence, to the extent that the BJP has been repeatedly unable to emancipate itself from its mother organization, the Rashtriya Swayamsevak Sangh (RSS), which presides over a sprawling network of domestic subsidiaries and foreign franchises of a Hindu nationalist ideological bent, together forming the so-called the Sangh Parivar (Jaffrelot, 2013: 890). As a result, a productive engagement with the Hindu nationalist thought-world, and indeed, with the ideological landscape of Indian foreign policy, requires acknowledging agency far beyond its traditional sites.

Organiser is a useful starting point for such an endeavour. The magazine represents an English-language, middlebrow variant of Hindu nationalism, often voicing its more activist constituencies (see Andersen & Damle, 1987: 115). It belongs to a specific milieu that is perhaps closest to what Basu terms 'metropolitan *Hindutva*' (Basu, 2017: 15), an Anglophone intellectual sphere grounded in Hindu nationalism and developed as an alternative to a postcolonial liberal intelligentsia framed as obsolescent and deracinated (Basu, 2017: 16). By contrast, metropolitan *Hindutva* considers itself 'more alive to the national spirit, its language more accessible to the People and its creed more expressive of what this People ostensibly aspires to' (Basu, 2017: 17).

Similarly, claiming to speak from a more legitimate position of (Hindu) nationalist common sense, *Organiser* seeks to embody an 'Indian school of learning … [that is] worthy of the size and past achievement that the country represents' (Rajaram, 1998: 2; see also Hansen, 1996: 610). While it may employ a peculiar register, in its worldview, the metropolitan *Hindutva* embodied by *Organiser* fits within the broad contours of Hindu nationalist ideology. Indeed, even while acknowledging that there is no unchanging '*Hindutva* orthodoxy' (Anderson & Longkumer, 2018: 372), there nonetheless remains a core set of common ideological commitments advanced across the vast Hindu nationalist universe, and which *Organiser*, too, espouses. These are a concern with the continued dominance and assertion of a national majority defined on ethno-religious grounds as Hindu, and a corresponding twin effort to identify seemingly existential threats to which such a majority is said to be exposed, and to mobilize against these perceived threats. By weaving these ideological commitments in its reports on current developments along the Indian Ocean, *Organiser* articulates its vision of India's identity both at home and on the world stage, as is shown in the rest of this chapter.

Civilizational Diasporas Along the Eastern Indian Ocean

A crucial step in setting the stage for the ideologically laden representations of the Indian Ocean produced by *Organiser* is the characterization of the region – particularly its eastern flank – as inherently 'Hindu', if not religiously, then culturally so. In casting one's eye over distant shores, similarities help establish translatability for domestic audiences. The terms of *Organiser*'s engagement with the region are thus primarily drawn from the Indian mainland. The extemporaneous articulation of ideology, then, requires establishing translatability, which in turn entails emphasizing likeness over difference, as *Organiser* makes clear.

In particular, central to such Hindu nationalist narratives is a totalizing view of Hinduism that characterizes all outward cultural flows originating from the Subcontinent as the transmission of Hindu customs, irrespective of the actual nature of these cultural exports. Hinduism is thus produced as a 'synthetic concept' that fixes diverse practices around an 'ideal core' (see Hansen, 1999: 66–67). Anything that approximates this core is taken as Hindu, and, as such, as evidence of the inherently Hindu character of those who embrace such practices. In the thought-world of *Organiser* writers, pictorial references to Hindu myths in the halls of power of Southeast Asian countries – in Jakarta, 'a majestic six-horse marble chariot adjacent to the Presidential bungalow depicting the *Gitopadesha* by Lord Krishna to Arjuna' (Agarwal, 1992: 14) – or the official celebration of Hindu festivals serve as evidence of such claims. Equally relevant is the emphasis *Organiser* writers place on the ordinariness of displays of Hindu practices, for it signals their penetration of the domain of the everyday, and ultimately, their deep entrenchment in the region. Reports from Southeast Asia are replete with the images of pupils re-enacting the Ramayana, streets with unmistakably 'Hindu/Sanskrit names' (Pandit, 2009: 11), Hindu deities adorning postal stamps (Sethi, 2007: 38), banknotes and state insignia, and references to Hindu symbols in the names of banks and airlines (Hussain, 1998: 19).

So persuasive are these public shows of 'Hinduness' that they are taken as the expression of a national culture that transcends locally rooted allegiances and reflects the acceptance of Hinduism as the hegemonic cultural form, if not at the religious level, then at least at a deeper 'cultural' one. Indonesians, for instance, are said to be truly 'secular' in their outlook, for 'ask them what their religion is and pat would come the reply: Islam. But again ask them about their culture. And they would have no compunction in asserting that it is no different from that of Hindus in Bharat' (Agarwal, 1992: 14), an

Organiser writer suggests. Islam, then, is unmistakably alien, its 'five-hundred year' [*sic*] presence 'sitting like a dome over the millennia-old Hindu civilizational foundations and pillars', the remains of a 'thriving civilisation that was of Indian origin' (Pandit, 2009: 11). Indonesians, as descendants of such a civilization, are said to be 'attitudinally still very Hindu – gentle and inclusive' (Pandit, 2009: 11). On this reading, Hinduism represents the true cultural essence of the land and holds primacy over all other forms of identification by reason of its antiquity. Representing this vast region as inherently Hindu, then, produces a space that is strikingly similar to India, onto which analogous modes of belonging are projected, largely through an overriding emphasis on a common Hindu cultural substratum as the main determinant of popular allegiances.

Southeast Asia thus emerges as home to what may be called a 'civilizational diaspora' of the Hindu nation. In this expansive understanding, such a diaspora does not have any direct connection with the Indian mainland: it does not merely comprise the descendants of Indian migrants that moved across the Bay of Bengal, in very large numbers, throughout the nineteenth and early twentieth centuries (Amrith, 2013: 104), nor does it rely on collective, conscious self-identification with an ethnic homeland (Vertovec, 1997: 281). Rather, diaspora here is a label that originates from outside the community, and one that *Organiser* attaches indiscriminately to Southeast Asia as a whole rather than to specific groups that migrated from India. In so doing, Hindu nationalists create a common genealogy that constructs diasporas out of non-migrant people, who thus become the embodiment of the inherently Indian – and specifically Hindu – character of the littoral regions they inhabit. For one *Organiser* columnist, for instance, India's diaspora was formed over three waves of migration that span a significant period of human history and include not just the colonial-era forced migrations of indentured labourers or the postcolonial ones of workers and professionals, but also Ashoka's 'civilisational mission' to spread Buddhism across Asia, whose legacy includes the nineteenth century Buddhist revivalist Anagarika Dharmapala in colonial Ceylon (Menon, 2006: 16). Crucially, Buddhism here does not merely stand as a religious signifier; rather, it is a synecdoche for 'Hindu culture', of which, in a long-established Hindu nationalist trope, 'it [is] a constituent', its 'essential spirit' making it a part of the 'commonwealth of Hindu Dharma' (Madhok, 1969: 183).

The projection of diasporic tropes onto Southeast Asia has to be seen in the broader context of the *Sangh Parivar*'s domestic concerns, and the cultivation, towards that end, of ideological dispositions among its domestic constituencies. Seen from this perspective, the category of diaspora serves to frame this region in terms that are intelligible to domestic audiences (in so far as the eastern Indian Ocean is represented in a way that emphasizes a shared Hindu identity), as well as to mobilize loyalties and legitimize Hindu nationalist claims, rather than to identify groups of people. In this sense, the emphasis on the essentially Hindu character of Southeast Asia has a dual character: it is *interpellative*, in its representation of the eastern wing of the Indian Ocean through tropes that bring out a high degree of similarity with India and thus enable *Organiser*'s constituencies to identify with the ideological content of these narratives; but it is also *instrumental*, in helping to advance the broader agenda of the Hindu nationalist movement. This was especially stark in the context of the Ram Setu agitation in the mid-2000s in India, which saw the RSS mobilize against the dredging of the Sethusamu-dram shipping canal between the Gulf of Mannar and the Palk Bay. A key reason for Hindu nationalist opposition to the project was the fact that construction work would destroy a chain of shoals that supposedly formed the Ram Setu, a bridge that, in Valmiki's *Ramayana*, Hanuman built for Ram to cross over the ocean to Sri Lanka and rescue his wife Sita (Jaffrelot, 2011: 320).

In this context, *Organiser* contributors often turned to Southeast Asia to bolster their arguments for the preservation of the site, constructing, in the process, the Ram Setu as a universal object of worship and Ram an unob-jectionably historical figure. That Ram really existed could not be doubted, *Organiser*'s writers held, for 'crores of Hindus and non-Hindu countries like Indonesia, Thailand and Communist regime of Laos firmly believe in the historicity of Sri Ram and events related to that period' (Sethi, 2007: 38). The philatelic record, too, seemed to prove that Ram did exist, for 'if this had not been the case, the rulers of these countries would never have issued postal stamps of Ram, Sita, Jamwant and Raja Janak of Mithila' (Sethi, 2007: 38). Moreover, that foreign governments readily embraced Hindu symbols and practices – even in states where Hindus are not a majority – served as a counterpoint to their neglect by India's Congress-led government. In the words of the *Hindutva* firebrand Sadhvi Rithambara, the project highlighted the government's inability to rise to its role as a guardian of the Hindu faith worldwide:

> Sri Ram's importance is not confined to India alone. The Ramayan is an integral part of traditional culture in Buddhist Burma, Thailand, Cam-bodia and many other parts of the world. In Malaysia and Indonesia, the Ramayan was popular long before the conversion of the local com-munities to Islam. Millions of Hindus living outside India believe India to be a sacrosanct land where their Gods once walked. They consider the people of India to be the custodians of their ancient pilgrimage sites and expect that these sacred heritage places will be protected from the scourges of hostile and irresponsible forces.
>
> (Rithambara, 2007: 62)

This is a rather typical formulation of *Organiser*'s favoured ethnocentric reading of Southeast Asia as a Hindu space, in a subordinate relationship with India, which, as the embodiment of a Hindu nation, is expected to lead the way. The inescapable Hinduness of Southeast Asia is, moreover, a staging ground for the formulation of expectations (of Indian governments as defenders of the Hindu faith) and loyalties (that cultural kinship will enable these countries to coalesce around India). In so far as the characterization of the eastern wing of the Indian Ocean as essentially Hindu carries this corollary, the construction of a civilizational diaspora here constitutes an attempt not to describe the social world that Hindu nationalists inhabit, but to reshape it in the image of *Hindutva*: it is, in other words, an exercise in worldmaking.

Littoral Majoritarianism

Precisely because of the cultural similarities mentioned above, which allow for easy comparisons, Southeast Asia is an important point of reference for the articulation of Hindu nationalist ideology. The construction of the eastern wing of the Indian Ocean as an offshore replica of the Indian mainland hinges not only on the emphasis on cultural similarities explored above, but also on the reproduction, in this region, of some of the domestic strategies of the Hindu nationalist movement. This is made possible by the projection of domestic grievances onto the foreign space that Southeast Asia represents, as was the case in the Ram Setu agitation, and the concomitant reframing of local issues affecting these countries in terms that are intelligible to domestic audiences in India, which are explored below.

In this context, the tropes of Hindu nationalist mobilization in India are the main lens through which *Organiser* understands social unrest in the region, in a process that, as Tambiah notes with reference to ethnic riots in South Asia, 'denudes local incidents and disputes of their contextual particulars' and builds such incidents into 'larger collective issues of national or ethnic interest' (Tambiah, 1996: 81). Thus, in the world of *Organiser* writers, ethnic tensions in Southeast Asia are a flashpoint for international conspiracies. If, for *Organiser*, the identification of Hindu cultural artefacts along the ocean's eastern littoral points to the essential Hinduness of this area, the magazine's understanding of ethnic tensions complicates the picture, for, as the analysis shows below, it reinscribes the region within a discursive tension between majorities and minorities that is constitutive of *Hindutva* ideology.

The main object of interest for Hindu nationalists seems to be the condition of Hindus in Malaysia, which *Organiser* claims should be 'a cause of concern for the Hindus all over the world, especially for the Hindus of India' (Anon, 1998: 17). Their predicament is, in the weekly's pages, not merely borne out of local circumstances as a result of the nativist policies of successive governments, but it ultimately is a mirror of the condition of Hindus in places where they are not an overwhelming majority. Conversions, hate crimes, and the demolition of Hindu temples in Malaysia in the mid-2000s become, in this context, a commentary on the nefarious intentions of Muslims worldwide. In the words of a high-ranking Hindu nationalist leader,

'Islam', personified, is responsible for 'ethnic cleansing' in Malaysia, Indonesia and Thailand, reducing Hindus to a minority, in much the same way as in 'Assam, Eastern UP, [and] some parts of West Bengal' (Togadia, 2007: 2). The Islamist threat that some *Organiser* writers see lurking over the fate of Hindus in Malaysia, then, is a global issue, but also one that is easily translatable in an Indian context. A local dispute in Malaysia over the construction of a Hindu temple on a site adjacent to a madrasa is described, ominously, as having engendered an 'Ayodhya-like situation' (Anon, 1998: 17), referring to the controversy around the Babri Masjid in Ayodhya, a mosque that according to Hindu nationalists lay atop a Hindu temple and therefore had to be torn down, as it indeed was. A columnist pondering over the possibility that Malaysia may become a 'Jihadistan' dominated by 'Wahhabis' begins his plea for India to take action against 'religious extremism' abroad by inviting the reader to take note of the omnipresence of 'Wahhabis' at home, 'at the seat behind you on the Delhi-Hyderabad flight or the Kolkata-Patna train' (Nalapat, 2007: 2). India, Malaysia and the rest of the world, then, constantly fold into one another.

There is, in these discourses, a constant back-and-forth between domestic space and the international – to such an extent that this slippage is in fact central to their narrative about an international conspiracy against Hindus. This conspiratorial language has long been part of the Hindu nationalist repertoire, central as it is to the construction of Hindus as a threatened majority that the *Sangh Parivar* proposes to consolidate and protect (Hansen, 1999: 108). As *Organiser* rails against the high-handedness of a 'Wahabi Islamist racist regime' (Anon, 2010: 4) in Malaysia that discriminates against Hindus, 'Muslim intransigence' in the Philippines and 'extra-territorial sentiments' inherent in 'the nature of Islam' (Anon, 1999: 15), it also entrenches a sense of existential threat to the very survival of Hindus in India as well, for today's minorities may well become tomorrow's majorities, if India's Muslims join hands with their religious brethren abroad, thus confirming their status as 'external majorities in disguise' (see Appadurai 2006: 112). In this manner, the utopia of a homogenously Hindu nation, towards which the *Sangh Parivar* tends, appears to be imperilled; yet it is precisely in this that *Hindutva* finds the rationale for its own existence: in its promise to offer protection from uncontrollable global flows by mobilizing a threatened majority.

The discursive slippage between India and Southeast Asia that this chapter has so far outlined, substantiates demands for greater assertiveness on behalf of a transnational Hindu nation. *Organiser*'s construction of 'Islamist' regimes in Southeast Asia as a global, existential threat is seen as calling for an equally global response. In the words of an *Organiser* contributor, because Hinduism is practiced by 'many non-Hindustanis', 'it is time not only for Malaysians Hindus but Hindus all over the world to identify themselves as Hindus' so as to 'retain their faith and culture and assert their rights' (Malarmannan, 2008: 8). This appeal for a geographically dispersed community to come together surely reflects a long-running commitment to diaspora outreach in the *Sangh Parivar* (see Jaffrelot & Therwath, 2012: 345). Yet, perhaps unsurprisingly for a magazine whose readership is primarily Indian, *Organiser*'s writing about a Muslim threat to Hindus abroad and at home, or in fact its emphasis on the omnipresence of Hindu cultural artefacts in Southeast Asia, is less shaped by the concerns of local actors in the region than by the magazine's own attempts to advance its domestic agenda by casting *Hindutva* tropes over a region characterized as remarkably similar to India. In so doing, *Organiser* constructs a representation of the eastern wing of the Indian Ocean that welds the local with the global but projects the resulting image back onto India. For, as Grant (2005: 328) puts it, in order to translate for a vast Hindu nationalist constituency, the 'stories of the global' formulated in this context have to be 'visible on the streets'. The global, then, also has to make sense on a more minute, local scale: the interpellative potential of these representations, or their ability to have readers recognize themselves in Hindu nationalist ideology, lies precisely in their seamless switching between different geographical scales.

This consideration can square the blanket characterization of Southeast Asia as a Hindu space with the potentially contradictory identification, in the same region, of an existential threat to Hindus worldwide. Both narratives lead to the same conclusion, at least according to the internal logic of *Organiser*'s own arguments: the Indian state has a duty of care to Hindus across the globe, and failure to do so is an indictment of the shaky secular foundations of the state. If geographical scale-switching enables Hindu nationalists to cultivate domestic constituencies through the work of interpellation, this constant moving, at a discursive level, from domestic to foreign spaces also serves to articulate the preferred identities and policy stances that India should embrace, as the analysis will show in the next section. The cultivation of Hindu nationalist ideological dispositions among *Organiser*'s constituencies ultimately depends on two rhetorical moves. On the one hand, there is a constant switching between geographical scales that translates, for a domestic audience, the relevance of these foreign spaces by projecting onto them tropes and dynamics drawn from more geographically proximate places. On the other hand, the interpellative potential of this genre of writing depends on the articulation of a tangible, yet so far unaccomplished, ideological agenda in relation to such places – an issue to which the chapter now turns.

From National to Ethno-National Interest

Underpinning *Organiser*'s representations of the eastern littoral of the Indian Ocean explored so far is the assumption that Indian foreign policy should be dictated not by the advancement of a merely 'national' interest, but rather by addressing possibly narrower, ethno-national concerns, with a view to the *Sangh*'s domestic priorities and its overall objective to unite and consolidate a Hindu nation. On this view, then, the national interest – presupposing state action on behalf of an internally unspecified citizenry – requires reframing: what Hindu nationalists propose is the promotion of ethno-national interests that coincide with the priorities and concerns of the Hindu nation. The Indian Ocean littoral is thus turned into a region holding vast potential for India, and in relation to which an alternative vision of Indian nationhood, and indeed of the state's international relations, may be not only articulated, but also realized.

Insisting on the inherent Hinduness of swathes of the Indian Ocean – particularly Southeast Asia, as already shown – is central to this endeavour, generating an expectation for India to stand as a guardian of transnational Hindu interests. Any inability to do so – as was the case with the Ram Setu controversy – is interpreted as a broader failure of Indian leadership, as has been seen. *Organiser* contributors counter this by articulating an alternative vision of appropriate international conduct that would align with the core ideological tenets of Hindu nationalism. Central to such a vision is the notion of India's cultural centrality, which frames the state as a beacon for its Indian Ocean neighbours, which are, in turn, framed as eagerly awaiting Indian guidance. This forms a hierarchy along the Indian Ocean, one that suggests at once relatedness, in so far as it brings the region together on the basis of cultural commonalities, and rank, for the emphasis rests invariably on the Indian origin of such commonalities. In this Indo-centric hierarchy, the bonds forged along the Indian Ocean, then, appear fundamentally unequal. Yet this hierarchy is articulated not as a ranked relationship with foreign aliens, but as bonds of kinship between a mother state and its cultural offspring: it is what may be called a kinship-based hierarchy.

A number of articles appeared in the pages of *Organiser* bear this out, often bringing together the eastern and western flanks of the Indian Ocean. For instance, during a 1994 interaction with the mayor of Nairobi and the vice-mayor of Mombasa, an RSS general secretary, H.V. Seshadri, is said to have realized that Kenyans 'are eager and open minded ... to emulate the good and benevolent aspects of Hindu culture' (quoted in Anon, 1994: 9). More recently, looking to the other side of the Ocean, RSS chief Mohan Bhagwat, also quoted in the pages of *Organiser*, suggested, 'there is an expectation' in Southeast Asian countries that 'Bharat should lead them and stand by them through thick and thin' owing to both 'common economic interests' and a 'deep cultural relationship' that continues to be remembered to this day 'with gratitude, joy, and happiness' (Bhagwat, 2011: 2).

As has already been shown, the cultural relationship Bhagwat alludes to is consistently framed, in the pages of *Organiser*, as entailing shared adherence to Hindu customs. Consequently, building on such ties, too, effectively amounts to the realization of India's potential as a Hindu country, and that of Indians as 'protectors, preachers and defenders of Hindudom' (Boal, 1958: 8) – a position *Organiser* contributors have long embraced. It is in this sense that such contributions reframe the idea of national interest in ethno-national terms and, in the process, turn the Indian Ocean into an arena in which India may externalize its identity as a Hindu state. Such a move, then, both targets and redefines India's domestic identity and the kind of behaviour that should flow from it. Here too is the now-familiar switching between different geographical scales, and indeed a simultaneous addressing of the categories of domestic and international, which remains central to the functioning of interpellation.

Srinivasan Kalyanaraman's work, frequently serialized in the pages of *Organiser* and circulated online in self-published format, instantiates this dynamic. In claiming for themselves a kind of locally grounded expertise made legitimate by this very indigeneity, Kalyanaraman's publications channel the middlebrow inflection of Hindu nationalism that *Organiser* also encapsulates. This concern with indigeneity is not merely a rhetorical move but lies at the heart of the reframing of India's role in the Indian Ocean region that he proposes. Driving his work is the advocacy of what he calls a 'Hindu Mahasagar Parivar', or an Indian Ocean Community, that, modelled after the now-superseded European Community, would 'link up the nations that have followed common traditions' (Kalyanaraman, 2012a: 54) and be governed by '*dharma*', on this reading, the true cultural essence of the Indian Ocean (Kalyanaraman, 2012b). For him, the establishment of an Indian Ocean community would represent the outward, yet peaceful, expansion of a domestic Hindu *rashtra*, or a polity that would come about 'when all citizens of Bharat call themselves Hindu, affirming their national identity, a shared identification, a shared cultural heritage received from ancestors' (Kalyanaraman, 2008: 46). It is in this context, I would suggest, that *Organiser*'s emphasis on the inherently Hindu character of much of the Indian Ocean should be read, alongside the domestic goals of the Hindu nationalist movement (of which the establishment of a Hindu polity is a central one). In sum, in switching between different geographical scales, and advancing ideologically laden representations of parts of the Indian Ocean, *Organiser* contributors make a relatively distant arena intelligible to their constituencies in ways that align with the mobilizing imperatives of Hindu nationalism.

Conclusion: Foreign Policy and Identity Beyond the State

Against the backdrop of the deepening of India's foreign policy engagement in the Indian Ocean, and the proliferation of debates regarding the exact nature of these new commitments, this chapter has sought to explore how a middlebrow inflection of Hindu nationalism, finding its voice in the pages of the weekly magazine *Organiser*, has framed India's role in the region. Throughout, it has shown that consistent ideological positions can be articulated through generally haphazard forms of engagement with the world beyond India's borders – ones that the literature on Hindu nationalism and foreign policy has so far shunned, preferring instead to focus on paradigmatic texts and policy outcomes.

The analysis has argued that an interpellative potential, or ability to cultivate allegiance to Hindu nationalist objectives among certain constituencies, is not inherent in the narratives analysed but rather depends on the presence of two key elements. First, a switch between different geographical scales renders distant places more proximate to domestic constituencies and thus easier to identify with. Second, the presence of a clearly articulated ideological content suffuses such representations with the tropes and objectives of the Hindu nationalist movement and envisions, in these places, the realization of some of the programmatic goals of the movement. The identification of civilizational diasporas of the Hindu nation along the eastern shores of the Indian Ocean serves this purpose, as does the singling out of a littoral majoritarianism in the region and the reconceptualization of India's conduct in the region that *Organiser* contributors put forward. More generally, narratives advanced in relation to a clearly identifiable 'culturalist' slant that emphasizes the commonality of cultural and religious practices, and, indeed, of threats to Hindu communities, tend to be successful in producing interpellative potential.

Like the other contributions in this volume, this chapter has put identity centre stage. By attributing certain identities to societies along the Indian Ocean, it has shown how *Organiser* contributors also articulate their own visions of India's own identity and appropriate international conduct, besides advancing their own ideological programme. India emerges, from such an exercise, as a 'natural' leader in the region, whose position of pre-eminence derives from its role as a cultural and religious fountainhead. Its position in relation to the region is thus premised on cultural kinship and hierarchy, the former justifying the latter. India's identity as a cultural hegemon – a staunchly Hindu one – therefore structures the region along a hierarchical axis, according to the narratives explored here.

It remains to be seen, however, what this means for government-sanctioned foreign policy endeavours. On the one hand, this study has sought not to establish a causal link between the narratives put forward in *Organiser* and specific policy outcomes. Rather, it has explained how a form of extemporaneous engagement with the international, beyond the established centres of foreign policymaking and outside the fixity of an ideological charter, can serve to reinforce ideological commitments. Yet on the other hand, the permeable boundaries between the BJP as a political party and the RSS as a social movement – whose positions *Organiser* often voices – raise important questions. The character of the BJP as a 'movement party' with 'independent ideological, activist commitments that are further fortified by its ties to the RSS' (Basu, 2015: 26) can open foreign policy debates to multidirectional influences that may reasonably be expected to emanate from the intellectual sphere embodied by *Organiser*. The recent ascendancy of a number of RSS-adjacent organizations as fora for policy discussion and advice (Hall, 2019: 98), and specifically, their ability to weld traditional foreign policy issues with the culturalist slant typical of Hindu nationalist milieux seems to point in that direction. In Tremblay and Kapur's (2017) analysis, the involvement of such epistemic communities in the policy process is symptomatic of the 'Hinduization of foreign policy' under Modi. Defining engagement with foreign policy too narrowly, then, is unhelpful for analytical purposes. As an insurgent force seeking to reshape not only the political field but also public discourse, the Hindu nationalist movement has relied on several channels for the dissemination of its ideas. Examining both the contents of these ideas and the ever-expanding avenues through which they are disseminated is more pressing than ever.

Bibliography

Agarwal, B. (1992) 'Indonesian Vice-President Inaugurated Hindu Conference in Bali invoking "Om Swasti Astu", "Om Shanti, Shanti"', *Organiser*, 27 September, p. 14.

Althusser, Louis (1971) *Lenin and Philosophy and Other Essays*, tr. Ben Brewster (New York: Monthly Review Press).

Amrith, Sunil (2013) *Crossing the Bay of Bengal: The Furies of Nature and the Fortunes of Migrants* (Cambridge, MA: Harvard University Press).

Andersen, Walter K. and Damle, Shridhar D. (1987) *The Brotherhood in Saffron: The Rashtriya Swayamsevak Sangh and Hindu Revivalism* (Boulder, CO: Westview Press).

Anderson, Edward and Longkumer, Arkotong (2018) 'Neo-Hindutva: Evolving Forms, Spaces, and Expressions of Hindu Nationalism', *Contemporary South Asia*, 26 (4): 371–377.

Anon (1994) 'There is Ekatmata between Hindus Here and Abroad: Interview with Shri H.V. Seshadri, RSS General Secretary after His Recent Sojourn beyond the Shores of Bharat', *Organiser*, 20 February, p. 9.

Anon (1998) 'Hindu Temples Evoke Muslim Fury', *Organiser*, 7 June, p. 17.

Anon (1999) 'Islam Targets Philippines', *Organiser*, 23 May, p. 15.

Anon (2010) 'India Should Be Concerned about Human Rights Issues of Pravasi Bharatiyas', *Organiser*, 17 January, p. 3.

Appadurai, Arjun (2006) *Fear of Small Numbers: An Essay on the Geography of Anger* (Durham, NC: Duke University Press).

Bajpai, Kanti (2003) 'Indian Conceptions of Order and Justice: Nehruvian, Gandhian, Hindutva, and Neo-Liberal', in Rosemary Foot, John Lewis Gaddis and Andrew Hurrell (eds), *Order and Justice in International Relations* (Oxford: Oxford University Press).

Basrur, Rajesh (2017) 'Modi's Foreign Policy Fundamentals: A Trajectory Unchanged', *International Affairs*, 93 (1): 7–26.

Basu, Amrita (2015) *Violent Conjunctures in Democratic India* (Cambridge: Cambridge University Press).

Basu, Manisha (2017) *The Rhetoric of Hindu India: Language and Urban Nationalism* (Cambridge: Cambridge University Press).

Bhagwat, Mohan (2011) 'Sarsanghachalak's Vijayadashmi Message: Work for a Strong, Prosperous Bharat', *Organiser*, 16 October, pp. 2–4.

Boal, V. R. (1958) 'Thanks to "Secularism" Hindus in East Africa Are a Lost People', *Organiser*, 19 May, p. 8.

Chacko, Priya (2012) *Indian Foreign Policy: The Politics of Postcolonial Identity from 1947 to 2004* (New York: Routledge).

Chacko, Priya (2014) 'The Rise of the Indo-Pacific: Understanding Ideational Change and Continuity in India's Foreign Policy', *Australian Journal of International Affairs*, 68 (4): 433–452.

Chatterjee Miller, Manjari and Sullivan de Estrada, Kate (2017) 'Pragmatism in Indian Foreign Policy: How Ideas Constrain Modi', *International Affairs*, 93 (1): 27–49.

Grant, Will J. (2005) 'The Space of The Nation: An Examination of the Spatial Productions of Hindu Nationalism', *Nationalism and Ethnic Politics*, 11 (3): 321–347.

Hall, Ian (2017) 'Narendra Modi and India's Normative Power', *International Affairs*, 93 (1): 113–131.

Hall, Ian (2019) *Modi and the Reinvention of Indian Foreign Policy* (Bristol: Bristol University Press).

Hansen, Thomas Blom (1996) 'Globalisation and Nationalist Imaginations: Hindutva's Promise of Equality through Difference', *Economic and Political Weekly*, 31 (10): 603–616.

Hansen, Thomas Blom (1999) *The Saffron Wave: Democracy and Hindu Nationalism in Modern India* (Princeton, NJ: Princeton University Press).

Hussain, M. (1998) 'Lord Ganesha Blesses Indonesian Currency', *Organiser*, 20 September, p. 19.

Jaffrelot, Christophe (2011) *Religion, Caste and Politics in India* (London: C. Hurst & Co).

Jaffrelot, Christophe (2013) 'Refining the Moderation Thesis. Two Religious Parties and Indian Democracy: The Jana Sangh and the BJP between Hindutva Radicalism and Coalition Politics', *Democratization*, 20 (5): 876–894.

Jaffrelot, Christophe and Therwath, Ingrid (2012) 'The Global Sangh Parivar: A Study of Contemporary International Hinduism', in Abigail Green and Vincent Viaene (eds.), *Religious Internationals in the Modern World*, (London: Palgrave Macmillan), pp. 343–364.

Kalyanaraman, S. (2008) 'Oppose Communal Budgeting', *Organiser*, 27 January, pp. 42–46.

Kalyanaraman, S. (2012a) 'Bahubhasha Bharati Saraswati: Imperative of Rastram in Indian Ocean Community', *Organiser*, 29 January, pp. 54–56.

Kalyanaraman, S. (2012b) *Indian Ocean Community: Uniting Nations on Path of Progress* (Herndon, VA: Sarasvati Research Center).

Madhok, Balraj (1969) *Portrait of a Martyr: Biography of Dr. Shyam Prasad Mookerji* (Bombay: Jaico).

Malarmannan (2008) 'Hindu Identity Makes the Difference', *Organiser*, 13 January, p. 8.

Menon, M. S. N. (2006) 'India as Catalyst of Civilisation', *Organiser*, 8 January, p. 16.

Modi, Narendra (2018) 'Keynote Address at Shangri La Dialogue', 1 June. Available at www.mea.gov.in/Speeches-Statements.htm?dtl/29943/Prime+Ministers+Keynote+Address+at+Shangri+La+Dialogue+June+01+2018 [last accessed 1 January 2022].

Mohan, C. Raja (2012) *Samudra Manthan: Sino-Indian Rivalry in the Indo-Pacific* (Washington, DC: Carnegie Endowment for International Peace).

Nalapat, M. D. (2007) 'Will Malaysia Become a Jihadistan?', *Organiser*, 23 December, p. 2.

Ogden, Chris (2014) *Hindu Nationalism and the Evolution of Contemporary Indian Security: Portents of Power* (Oxford: Oxford University Press).

Pandit, S. (2009) 'Elections in Indonesia: A Test for Inclusive Indonesian Islam', *Organiser*, 5 July, p. 11.

Rajaram, N. S. (1998) 'Towards Creating an Indian School of Thought', *Organiser*, 24 May, p. 2, 19.

Rithambara, S. (2007) 'An Assault on the Soul of India', *Organiser*, 11 November, pp. 61–63.

Roy-Chaudhury, Rahul (2018) 'Modi's Vision for the Indo-Pacific Region', 2 June. Available at www.iiss.org/blogs/analysis/2018/06/modi-vision-indo-pacific [last accessed 1 January 2022].

Sagar, Rahul (2009) 'State of Mind: What Kind of Power Will India Become?', *International Affairs*, 85 (4): 801–816.

Sagar, Rahul (2014) '"Jiski Lathi, Uski Bhains": The Hindu Nationalist View of International Politics', in Kanti Bajpai, Saira Basit and V. Krishnappa (eds), *India's Grand Strategy: History, Theory, Cases* (New Delhi: Routledge), pp. 234–257.

Schöttli, Jivanta (2019) '"Security and Growth for All in the Indian Ocean" – Maritime Governance and India's Foreign Policy', *India Review*, 18 (5): 568–581.

Sethi, L. (2007) 'A Philatelic Record of Sri Ram', *Organiser*, 11 November, p. 38.

Tambiah, Stanley J. (1996) *Leveling Crowds: Ethnonationalist Conflict and Collective Violence in South Asia* (Berkeley, CA: University of California Press).

Togadia, P. (2007) 'This Is State-Sponsord Jehad', 9 December, *Organiser*, p. 2.

Tremblay, Reeta Chowdhari and Kapur, Ashok (2017) *Modi's Foreign Policy* (New Delhi: Sage Publications).

Vertovec, Steven (1997) 'Three Meanings of "Diaspora", Exemplified among South Asian Religions', *Diaspora: A Journal of Transnational Studies*, 6 (3): 277–299.

Wendt, Alexander (1992) 'Anarchy is what States Make of it: The Social Construction of Power Politics', *International Organization*, 46 (2): 391–425.

Part II

Deepening Great Power Relations

5 The Elusive Settlement

India–China Negotiations Over 'The Boundary Question'

Stephen P. Westcott

2020 saw a marked deterioration in China–India relations, arguably to their lowest nadir since the 1960s. The year had started promisingly following the 'informal summit' between President Xi Jinping and Prime Minister Modi at Mamallapuram in October 2019 and a reportedly constructive Special Representatives Meeting in December 2019. However, in early May 2020, Chinese and Indian border forces began to confront each other at several places along the Line of Actual Control (LAC), the poorly defined and disputed *de facto* border between the two states. These clashes eventually culminated in the lethal skirmish in the Galwan Valley on the evening of 15 June 2020 which saw the first combat fatalities in nearly 45 years. This violence shocked both sides, as previous confrontations between patrols mostly just resulted in posturing as they sought to enforce their territorial claims. To prevent further escalations, a flurry of diplomatic activity was undertaken in an effort to end the crisis, with negotiations promptly raised from *ad hoc* meetings between officers on the ground to formal talks between the regional commanders and top diplomats from both sides.

Through both formal discussions and back-channel negotiations, India and China were able to defuse the immediate flashpoints and eventually secure a mutual withdrawal in several, though not all, areas. India and China also came to a 'five-point consensus', formally agreed to on the sidelines of the 2020 Shanghai Cooperation Organisation meeting in Moscow. In essence, the consensus recognized the need for a mutual withdrawal and for negotiations to devise new confidence building measures to return 'peace and tranquillity' to the border. Naturally, this has proven easier said than done, with both sides digging into their positions either side of the LAC and ramping up infrastructure construction where they can. Nevertheless, although the standoff along the LAC entered its second year in 2022, the negotiations have succeeded in curtailing brinkmanship and defusing the worst of tensions.

The 'boundary question' as it is officially referred to by Chinese and Indian diplomats has been the major source of distrust and tension between the two sides since relations first broke down over the issue in 1959. Thus, as long as the international border remains actively disputed, geopolitical crises

DOI: 10.4324/9781003305132-8

akin to that caused by the Galwan Valley skirmish remain a possibility and the most likely source of conflict between the two Asian powers. China and India evidently remain cognisant of this fact and have actively sought ways to mitigate any potential confrontations between their border forces. Indeed, there have been over 70 rounds of formal discussions and six major treaties signed between the two states concerning their disputed border. This is in addition to the countless informal talks and backchannel negotiations that have focused on the border dispute. Yet, despite these efforts, progress towards an actual resolution of the border dispute is scarcely more advanced today than the early 1980s when negotiations started in earnest.

This situation is curious for several reasons. Firstly, most of the disputed territory is uninhabited, consisting of rugged and heavily forested terrain in the east and a barren desolate plateau in the west. Secondly, despite the nationalist rhetoric and posturing, neither side has a strong historical claim to the disputed territory which previously existed as something of a no-mans-land buffer zone between the two. Thus, common sense would suggest that this territory would not be too difficult for the two sides to divide and settle. Yet, each side insists on maintaining their incompatible border claims and demonstrate no public indication that they are willing to consider a compromise. This then leads to the third and final oddity with the disputed Sino-Indian border; that the negotiations over its resolution have continued unabated for forty years without either side significantly altering their positions. Most border negotiations either demonstrate some tangible progress leading to an eventual resolution or become shelved once it becomes apparent that both sides are unable to come to a consensus (Guo, 2012: 151–158). However, the Sino-Indian border negotiations have become something of a diplomatic ritual between the two states. For at least the past 15 years, Indian and Chinese representatives have met annually to reiterate their state's position on the border's location and agree that an early settlement is in both states' interests before adjourning without any ostensible progress being made.

In this chapter, I explore why border negotiations between India and China have become stalemated and why both sides continue holding ostensibly fruitless negotiations. Specifically, I argue that the Sino-Indian border's location has become an issue of national prestige for both states, prompting both states to obstinately maintain their incompatible positions on the border dispute. Thus, the border negotiations have remained deadlocked and made little tangible progress towards resolution. Yet, while the negotiations have failed in their primary mandate of resolving the boundary question, they have nonetheless evolved into a near indispensable channel of communication between the emerging great powers. Hence, both states have maintained the negotiations, with formal meetings taking place at least annually since 1981.

This argument is unpacked in this chapter in three main sections. First, it provides a basic overview of the Sino-Indian border dispute, outlining both sides positions as to where the border should lie. Then it discusses how national prestige impacts border dispute negotiations. This second section defines this underexplored concept and explains that states typically cherish their status within the international hierarchy, both as a key part of their self-identity and for functional political reasons. When a border dispute becomes tied to their prestige, states become concerned about damage to their reputation and attempt to save face, usually by obstinately maintaining their position and refusing meaningful concessions. Finally, it explores how these concerns about national prestige have impacted the Sino-Indian border negotiations, following the developments from the initial talks to the efforts to pacify the border and finally the current deadlocked discussions. Here it is explored how both India's and China's identity imbues them with a sense of entitlement to great powers status. However, they have often been frustrated by what they perceive as a lack of respect and recognition, ultimately compelling both to maintain their incompatible positions rather than risk appearing weak and damaging their valued prestige. Yet the negotiations have proven to become a mechanism for managing rather than resolving the dispute ensuring that they have continued despite the deadlock.

The Contours of the Sino-Indian Border Dispute

As illustrated in Figure 5.1, the Sino-Indian border dispute can be divided into two main areas, an eastern sector and a western sector. In the east, the dispute revolves around what is now the Indian state of Arunachal Pradesh, which the Chinese claim is part of southern Tibet. The crux of the dispute in the east is a dispute over the validity and exact location of the 'McMahon Line' which India claims as its border. The McMahon Line was border drawn up between British India and Tibet as part of the proceedings of the 1913–1914 Simla Convention which was held to determine the status of Tibet following the collapse of the Qing Empire. However, China maintains that Tibet was one of its autonomous provinces, not an independent country, and thus did not hold the authority to independently negotiate with other states. Thus, the Chinese maintain that the McMahon Line is an illegitimate imperial creation and that the border should follow foothills of the Assam Himalayas instead (Deepak, 2005: 62–70; Miller, 2013: 60–61).

Further complicating matters is that India reinterpreted the McMahon Line's location in the early 1960s and has maintained its position through to the current day. Specifically, India argues that the clear intention of the agreement was to have the border follow the crest of the Assam Himalayas, which would fix the border north of the cartographic line in several places. While China has tacitly accepted the McMahon Line should be used as the basis for a border in the east, it has refused to allow India to unilaterally redefine where the Line should be drawn. Additionally, China has reportedly indicated that it considers the incorporation of the monastic town of Tawang into Tibet to be the key concession it wants before any resolution can be

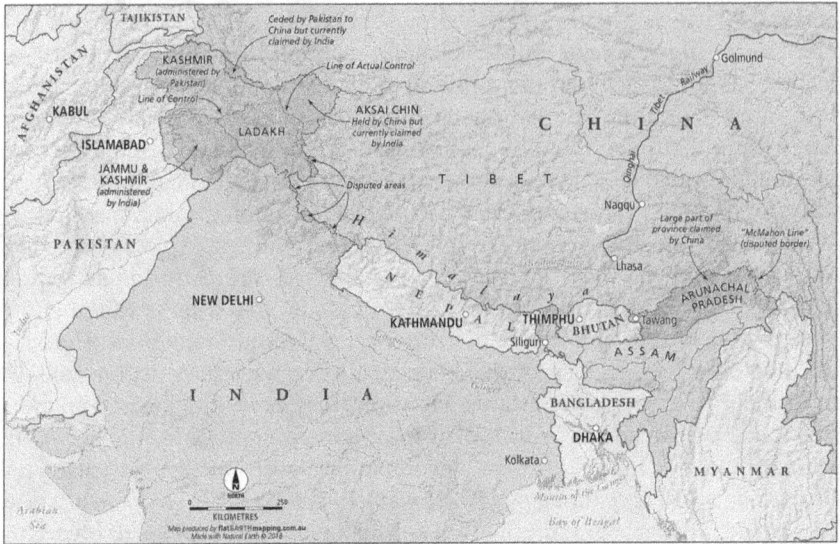

Figure 5.1 The Sino-Indian border dispute.
Source: Stephen P. Westcott

agreed to. In essence, China's argument is that although Tawang is south of the McMahon Line, it was in practice governed by Tibetan authorities until 1950 when India dispatched an military expedition to establish control over the town (Garver, 2011: 109–111; Smith, 2014: 76–77). India rejects this position as it considers Tawang to have been ceded by Tibet in Simla Convention and that it has since become an integral part of Arunachal Pradesh.

In the western sector, the dispute focuses around the ownership of several pockets of territory, the largest and most salient of which is the uninhabited and desolate Aksai Chin plateau. Historically, the Aksai Chin was effectively a no-mans-land between India, Tibet and Central Asia, crossed only by the occasional shepherd, trade caravan or explorer. Although British India did make a few sporadic attempts to establish a clear border with Imperial China, none of these efforts progressed far. Thus, the north-western frontier was still labelled 'undefined' in official maps upon India's independence. Despite this ambiguous frontier, India adopted the position that the Aksai Chin was traditionally administered as part of the Ladakh region of Jammu and Kashmir. Thus India amended their maps in 1954 to remove the undefined label and draw their border to encompass the Aksai Chin (Garver, 2001: 88–89; Kalha, 2014: 72–73). In contrast, China considers the Aksai Chin to be part of Xinjiang, citing its use by local pastoralists and its role a key trade route from centres such as Kashgar and Yarkand into Tibet. Furthermore, the Aksai Chin was one of the key routes into Tibet that the People's Liberation Army used in 1950, with China building an important supply road that ran through the plateau in 1956 (Garver, 2001: 82–84; Shankar, 2018: 33–34).

Adding to the territorial dispute in the western sector is the ambiguity as to the exact location of the LAC separating the two side's forces in the region. This ambiguity in the LAC is in part the result of the inhospitable terrain which makes efforts are clear delimitation difficult but also in part due to the fluctuation in both sides' actual control on the ground since the 1962 Border War. The inability for China and India to agree over where their respective control extended to and what time period should count has led to several areas where the two sides' claimed LAC are known to overlap. This dispute within a dispute has been a major source of contention within the negotiations and generated most of the recent confrontations on the border as both sides have dispatched patrols into these grey areas to uphold their territorial claims (Shankar, 2018: 42; Deepak, 2020: 30–32).

National Prestige and Border Disputes

When considering the causes of the Sino-Indian border dispute's continuing intractability, it is apparent from both side's obstinance that there are deeper issues at stake beyond disputed historical ownership and the simple coveting the disputed territory. While these factors clearly have played a role, both India and China have also associated their handling of the boundary question with their sense of national prestige from an early stage. As national prestige is a recognized but largely unexplored motivating factor behind state behaviour in international relations, there is merit in first defining what it is and how exactly it impacts upon interstate border disputes.

National prestige is defined here as *the recognition of, and respect for, a state's importance within international affairs, as determined by other states assessments its achievements, qualities and/or capacities.* While prestige is inherently intersubjective, formed from the consensus of the broader international community's opinion of one of its members, it is important to note that a state still has the agency to shape international opinion of itself. Specifically prestige is gained by 'doing deeds or possessing things' (O'Neill, 1999: 194). The actual 'deeds' and 'things' that bestow prestige are highly varied and depend on the situation, but typically comprise a mixture of state's recent accomplishments and current military strength and diplomatic acumen. Hence, states attempting to enhance or maintain their prestige seek to acquire assets or deliberately act in a manner they believe will enhance their esteem in the eyes of others (Larson et al., 2014: 20–23; Wood, 2014: 100).

Although national prestige is intangible and more difficult to reliably acquire and maintain than conventional metrics such as military power, states still view it as important for two key reasons. The first reason is psychological, as the government and general population of a state typically care about their country's performance relative to others and desire to secure as high a standing as feasible for it. Furthermore, for many states national prestige plays an important role in their national identity, with the polity often placing a significant value on having their state recognized as an important player in international affairs (Wood, 2014: 102–103). Hence, people often feel pride and gain self-esteem from global recognition of their state's importance while experiencing shame, anxiety or resentment should it have a poor international standing (Onea, 2014: 130–131; Wohlforth, 2009: 35–36).

The second reason is more functional, with a state's standing in the international hierarchy informing them of the privileges and treatment they can expect when engaging with other states. As Robert Gilpin argued:

> prestige, rather than power, is the everyday currency of international relations ... in the conduct of diplomacy and the resolution of conflict amongst states there is actually relatively little use of overt force or, for that matter, explicit threats. Rather, the bargaining among states and the outcome of negotiations are determined principally by the relative prestige of the parties involved.
>
> (Gilpin, 1981: 31)

In other words, a state with high prestige can often influence events and ensure that it can obtain its preferred outcomes without needing to resort to coercion or bribery. In contrast, a state with lower prestige can expect to see its concerns ignored should they inconvenience or simply not interest more prestigious powers (Larson, Paul and Wohlforth, 2014: 18–19). Thus, for both national identity and practical political concerns, states normally conduct their foreign policies in a manner they believe will enhance their national prestige, or at least avoid having it diminished.

Arguably, national prestige's most visible impact and utility for a state is within the diplomatic arena, where it provides some structure to the anarchical system by establishing an informal hierarchy among states that goes beyond raw power (Khong, 2019: 130). This hierarchy allows governments to identify their 'peer group' of states that they are considered equal to. States loosely measure their position within the international hierarchy in relations to others in terms of 'face', or the public treatment or deference a state can expect based upon its position within the international system. A state's face is generally considered to be 'lost' when a state is publicly forced to accede to another's will or is otherwise humiliated, especially by a state that is considered inferior in rank. Face is 'saved' or 'gained' when a state is able to, at least ostensibly, negotiate a good deal for itself or successfully demonstrated resolve when confronted with a threat or challenge (O'Neill, 1999: 139–140).

While ranking prestige is far from a precise science and is not necessarily a zero-sum game given several states can occupy the same peer group, prestige is still considered a scarce resource in international relations. After all, not everyone can be considered a great power, or even a middle power, and places at the top are often limited to no more than a handful. This naturally leads to social competition between states for greater recognition and influence within the broader international community while guarding against any erosion of their position (Xie, 2019: 173–175). This situation is often exacerbated when a state considers there to be an imbalance between their self-perceived international position and the respect shown to them by other states. Naturally it is not uncommon for a state to feel as though there is a degree of disparity in this regard. Nonetheless, some appear to be overly sensitive or perennially dissatisfied with the level of respect that they receive (Khong, 2019: 130–132; Onea, 2014: 134–136). Such states, especially if they are rising or declining powers, typically have a strong sense of entitlement and can be a destabilizing influence in international affairs as they seek to address this perceived imbalance. In particular, these prestige conscious states become highly sensitive to any potential manoeuvres that could undermine their position or enhance a rival's prestige at their expense (Pu, 2018: 57–60; Wohlforth, 2009: 38–39).

When national prestige concerns become attached to an interstate border dispute, the issue shifts from being purely a consideration of the geopolitical value of the contested territory or the merits of a state's historical/legal claims. Instead, it becomes a question of how a resolution could impact the states' position in the international hierarchy. While a state could gain prestige through its negotiation skills and magnanimous offers at resolution, prestige sensitive states are often more concerned about being viewed as being compelled to accept poor deals or being outmanoeuvred by their rival claimant. Thus, such countries feel incentivized to adopt an intransigent stance in border negotiations as a means to save face rather than yielding to the demands and risking appearing weak before an international audience (Hensel and Mitchell, 2005: 276; O'Neill, 1999: 165–170).

This situation is often exacerbated when one of the states considers itself equal or superior to its higher ranked rival, and therefore more worthy of deference from them, or views their rival as in competition for the same prestigious international position (Xie, 2019: 179). Such a prestige sensitive state will likely view genuine resolution proposals as insults, take umbrage at otherwise innocuous behaviour and confuse minor incidents with active challenges to its international position (Larson, Paul and Wohlforth, 2014: 22–23). For the rival claimant, such a position will be unacceptable, if not offensive, and encourages it to establish firmer non-negotiable positions of its own in order to avoid losing face itself. Hence, when at least one state in a border dispute senses that its national prestige is at risk, its behaviour compels both sides entrench their positions ensuring that even minor disputes become intractable.

National Prestige and the Sino-Indian Border Negotiations

When considering how national prestige has impacted the Sino-Indian border dispute, it is first necessary to understand what factors India and

China believed made them prestigious. For both states, the foundation of their sense of national prestige lies with their identity as 'civilizational states' and the natural heirs of great pre-colonial empires that preceded them (Acharya, 2020; Deepak, 2020). In viewing themselves as effectively the successors to their respective civilizations, both India and China believe that they are not only owed of respect for their contributions to humanity but that they should naturally hold an esteemed position in the international hierarchy. Yet, until recently, Western powers have overshadowed both states, leading them to feel that their rightful place was being denied and their positions are not taken seriously by the international community. Hence, they have been notably sensitive to fluctuations of prestige, actively seeking ways in which they can enhance it while remaining alert for potential slights and keen to preserve face whenever possible (Freedman, 2016: 808–809; Miller, 2013).

These concerns have inevitably bled into the India–China bilateral relationship, with both perceiving the other as a potential obstacle to their path to become a great power. India in particular has concerns that its national prestige is at risk of being diminished by China. Since independence India has also considered itself to be a great power in its own right due to its regional dominance, democratic/anti-colonialist credentials and pacifistic and pluralist values (Engelmeier, 2009; Wojczewski, 2018). On the basis of these virtues India appointed itself to a position of leadership among the Asian states and Non-Aligned Movement, even initially attempting to position itself as China's 'big brother' in the 1950s. However, as China's ideology, and more recently its economy, began to eclipse India's and gain greater respect throughout the international community, India became palpably concerned that China was actively undermining its efforts to emerge as a great power (Deepak, 2020: 13–14; Pu, 2018: 61–62). China for its part has been generally dismissive of India's pretences of being a great power, an attitude that only further exacerbated India's concerns (Pardesi, 2021).

These concerns have ensured that the Sino-Indian border dispute became a focal point for India relatively early as it became particularly sensitive to showing any potential sign of weakness in the face of perceived Chinese encroachment. Hence, the Sino-Indian border dispute became the perfect stage for India to demonstrate resolve by standing firm against 'autocratic coercion' while remaining true to its identity as a non-aggressive state. Furthermore, especially following its defeat in the 1962 Border War, India has been keen to regain or preserve face by obstinately maintaining their position towards the border, lest they be viewed as being forced to concede territory. This obstinate position has only compelled China to insist upon its own stance on the border dispute in order to preserve face and maintain its authority in what it perceives as unreasonable demands imposed by a 'lesser' state. It is this mutual prestige dynamic that has seen both sides make little progress in harmonizing their incompatible positions even after several rounds of border negotiations.

Initial Efforts at Negotiations (1958–1962 and 1981–1991)

After India achieved independence in 1947 and the People's Republic of China was proclaimed in 1942, both states sought to effectively ignore the ambiguous border they inherited. This was done in part so that China and India focus on their respective internal and regional issues that needed more urgent consideration. Yet this policy of avoiding discussing the border's location was also adopted by both sides in an attempt to consolidate their position as close to their border claims and thereby achieve a *fait accompli* before negotiations started (Fravel, 2008: 70–71; Shankar, 2018: 32–34). This position became increasingly untenable by the late 1950s after India discovered that China had constructed a major highway through the Aksai Chin region and border patrols began to confront each other. After some low-level discussions between Chinese and Indian officials failed to break any ground, the Indian Prime Minister Jawaharlal Nehru wrote to his counterpart Premier Zhou Enlai in December 1958, effectively marking the start of negotiations over the dispute.

In his letter, Nehru attempted to obliquely raised the subject by declaring that China was publishing 'incorrect' maps and requesting they be revised to reflect the 'well known boundaries' (Ambekar and Divekar, 1964: 112–116). Zhou Enlai's response in January 1959 that China and India clearly had different understandings of where their border lay and proposed that the two sides maintain the status quo while negotiations continued. The correspondence became increasingly acrimonious as the two state leaders sought to elaborate on their 'fair' and 'equitable' positions while denouncing their counterpart's stance as 'shocking' and 'unreasonable' (Ambekar and Divekar, 1964: 120–166). Furthermore, the increasingly evident gulf between the two sides' position on the border only served to highlight and trigger other resentments between the two sides. Indeed, by the time Nehru agreed to meet Zhou in April 1960 for direct talks on the border, it was apparent that the discussion had evolved from a simple disagreement over the historical and legal basis of their shared border to become an issue of their treatment by the other.

Thus, national prestige concerns became a central issue for both sides relatively early on in the border negotiations, although India was clearly more affected by a sense that its international standing was on the line. For India, its belief that its prestige was at stake during at this initial phase was derived from several concerns. The first and foremost was India's concern that any compromise would ultimately diminish their international standing while enhancing China's, especially among the Afro-Asian states among whom India was increasingly being ignored in favour of China's more radical anti-imperialism credentials (Garver, 2001: 113–124; Maxwell, 2013: 166). Another key prestige concern of India's was that China simply did not take India seriously as a peer. Indian officials believed their state to be the successor state of the various great empires that dominated South Asia which were at least equal to China (Pardesi, 2015: 2–4). Thus, India felt that it could not be seen as offering any significant concessions towards China, lest it lose its international standing and potentially invite further challenges from China or other states.

In contrast, China's prestige concerns at this stage largely emanated from its concern of being taken advantage of and desire to restore China's position as a great power after a century and a half of predation by imperialist countries (Chung, 2004: 4–5; Freedman, 2016: 809–812). One of the primary means by which China sought to accomplish this was by reversing the unequal treaties and regaining 'lost' territory. For China, its border with India was just one such a humiliating legacy, especially the McMahon Line which had been drawn and enforced without China's consent. Hence, Premier Zhou often stressed during his communications with Nehru that China considered the McMahon Line delimiting the eastern sector as an illegitimate imperial creation and a stain upon its national prestige (Miller, 2013: 73–76).

China's concern over its prestige was further inflamed by the unfortunate timing of India's territorial claims. The Sino-Indian dispute emerged in earnest during the great famines caused by the Great Leap Forward and significant unrest caused by Beijing's policies, including the 1959 Tibetan uprising. This led China to suspect that India saw it as a stepping stone to imperial grandeur and was thus trying to capitalize on China's weakness to seize territory and turn Tibet into a buffer zone (Garver, 2006: 89–91; Pardesi, 2021: 10–13). Such concerns regarding its national prestige were exacerbated by the fact that India clearly thought of itself as the senior partner in the relationship. Indeed, Chinese officials often grated under India's condescending adoption a 'mentor' role over China throughout the 1950s and frequent efforts to claim credit for positively influencing China's policies (Garver, 2001: 117–120; Miller, 2013: 66–71).

Nonetheless, China during this period sought to propose what they considered to be a mutually face-saving deal in the 'package deal'. In essence, this proposal sought to formalize the *status quo*, with China formally accepting India's control below the McMahon Line in exchange for India accepting China's control of the Aksai Chin (Haksar Papers, 1960). However, while China clearly considered this to be a fair and sensible exchange of territorial claims, India saw it as a request to cede vast swaths of its territory that no great power could contemplate. Thus, to preserve face internationally and assuage public pressure domestically, Indian officials refused to contemplate anything other than minor altercations to its claimed borders, obstinately insisted that the Chinese withdraw from all Indian claimed territory. This tactic did maintain India's prestige in the short term as it was able to demonstrate, to the admiration of several international states, that it was determined to resist what it claimed internationally illegal actions (Garver, 2001: 89–91). However, the often 'arrogant' and 'perfunctory' treatment from Indian officials not just irritated Zhou, it exacerbated concerns that India considered itself superior and did not respect China's position (Maxwell, 2013: 173; Miller, 2013: 74).

Despite these issues, negotiations were actively pursued by both sides as it was recognized that they were essential to defuse the crisis and come to a final settlement. This was formally conducted through the Officials Talks on the China–India Border in which diplomates and experts from both sides presented and examined the evidence in support of each side's claims. Yet, these deliberations did little to help the situation as, after three rounds of discussions in 1960, neither side was able agree over the evidence (Chung, 2004: 104; Deepak, 2005: 233–235). Indeed, the Officials Talks only resulted in each side becoming convinced of the validity of their own claims and the weakness of their rivals. Several unofficial discussions between the midlevel officials from both sides throughout 1961 and 1962 also failed to break any ground in the dispute. With the negotiations deadlocked in late 1961, the Indian government fatefully decided to implement the Forward Policy. Essentially, this policy was effort to change the facts on the ground by establishing military border posts as close to India's claimed border as possible in order to strengthen India's claim to the territory (Maxwell, 2013).

Although India attempted to conduct the Forward Policy in a non-violent manner, China saw this move as a provocative and insulting challenge by its neighbour who was attempting to bully it out of its own territory. This ultimately led Chinese officials to believe that only a 'self-defensive counter-attack' would disabuse India's arrogance and force it to take China and its position seriously (Garver, 2006: 109–110; Shankar, 2018: 36). Thus, after the Chinese assault was launched on 20 October 1962, Zhou justified China's attack by declaring that 'the Indian government has put to the Chinese Government humiliating conditions such as forced on a vanquished party ... both our countries are sovereign states and neither can force its unilateral demands on the other. India has its self-respect, so has China' (MEA, 1963: 10).

Although China launched the war in part with the aim to 'knock Nehru to the negotiating table' (Garver, 2006: 115–119; Fravel, 2008: 194–196), the quick and decisive defeat of the Indian Army reverberated throughout the Indian national psyche. The Indian public believed that their state had been betrayed by China and India's parliament promptly rejected any border negotiations while China still occupied the 'sacred soil of India' (Chung, 2004: 106–107). Despite its resistance, India's aura of leadership among the developing and non-aligned states was shattered. Only Malaysia and Cyprus voiced support for India while most non-Western states sought to remain neutral, attempted to mediate or supported China's perspective (Garver, 2001: 124–125). This humiliation effectively relegated India to a middle tier regional power for the remainder of the twentieth century. Furthermore, the loss has a significant impact on Indian identity, shaking its faith in non-violence and ensuring post-war India embraced more martial and pragmatic values it has held since (Pardesi, 2015: 4). Thus, the compromises necessary to settle the border dispute remained unpalatable for India, especially in the decade after the 1962 Border War lest it lose further face by seemingly capitulating to an aggressor.

Border negotiations only resumed in 1981 after time and a generational change in leadership had allowed bilateral relations to sufficiently thaw. Yet, although both sides were evidently committed to continuing the Border Talks, as they were simply known, prestige concerns quickly ensured that the negotiations became deadlocked again. For India, although the high emotions generated by the 1962 Border War had gradually dissipated, it still felt the need to regain face to rectify the damages done by its humiliating loss. This primarily manifested in India vehemently rejecting the *status quo* package deal when China reproposed it, arguing that accepting would effectively 'legitimize theft' and insisting that the border be negotiated in a 'sector-by-sector' manner (Garver, 2001: 102–103). Notably, India also sought to tie Chinese recognition for its claims to Kashmir and Sikkim into a resolution to the border dispute in an effort to compel some international legitimacy for its contentiously acquired territory. However, China refused to expand negotiations beyond the traditional contours of the dispute and the matter was eventually dropped (Chung, 2004: 111–112; Singh, 2011: 86).

While the Chinese approached the negotiations more pragmatically, it was unwilling to let India dictate the direction of the discussions and generally treat them discourteously. In particular, China was incensed by Indian presumptions that Beijing did not have a strong claim to the eastern section and thus it would be the easiest to solve. Hence, when in 1985 the Chinese agreed to India's instance that the sections be negotiated separately, it also took the opportunity to reassert its claims in the eastern sector and particularly Tawang (Deepak, 2020: 32). While this represented a hardening of its position, China apparently felt it necessary to avoid making unreciprocated concessions to India and remind the Indian side that China had a legitimate claim to the territory (Garver, 2001: 104–106; Singh, 2011: 87–88). With both sides unwilling to contemplate a mutually face-saving resolution, negotiations quickly became deadlocked with neither side yielding or able to wedge their rival into concessions. Nonetheless, both sides clearly recognized the importance of continuing engagement with their rival, especially as a formal channel of communication and means to manage border friction, such as the 1986–1988 Sumdorong Chu standoff (Chung, 2004: 113–114; Deepak, 2005: 324). A breakthrough in the negotiations was made when Prime Minister Rajiv Gandhi visited Beijing in 1988. While this visit saw a general reset in China–India relations, arguably the most significant development was the agreement to elevate the border negotiations by forming the Joint Working Group (JWG) (Kalha, 2014: 204–207).

From Pacification to Deadlock and Asymmetric Rivalry (1991–2021)

Shortly after Rajiv Gandhi's visit, the international situation changed dramatically for both China and India when the Cold War ended. China had effectively become a pariah for its brutal suppression of the Tiananmen Square protests in 1989 and maintaining its Marxist-Leninist regime. India for its part had just lost its major economic partner when the Soviet Union collapsed and found its identity as a non-aligned state redundant in a unipolar world. Hence, as the former Indian Foreign Secretary, J. N. Dixit, who initially represented New Delhi during at JWG talks noted, 'parallelism, if not a convergence of interests, existed between China and India on the forgoing matters [the changing international system post-Cold War] because both countries had similar objectives and concerns. The ground was thus fertile to initiate positive interaction' (Dixit, 1996: 232).

Yet it was clear that significant territorial concessions were off the table as neither side wished to agree to anything that could be construed as weakness abroad or domestically. Hence, after some preliminary discussions in 1991, the JWG managed to break some ground and come to a consensus over a broad code of conduct to pacify the border and generally reduce tensions. This was formulized in 1993 when China and India signed the 'Agreement on the Maintenance of Peace and Tranquillity along the Line of Actual Control in the India–China Border Areas', the first treaty between the two sides over their borders. This was followed shortly after by a second treaty in 1996, the 'Agreement on Confidence Building Measures in the Military Field along the Line of Actual Control in the India–China Border Areas'. Both of these treaties effectively amounted to a non-aggression treaty, renouncing the use of force on the border, committing to a negotiated settlement, formally recognizing the LAC and laying out a code of conduct for how the border forces should interact (Deepak, 2020: 63–64; Menon, 2016: 17–19).

The negotiations briefly again stalled over the issue of trying to determine where the LAC actually lay. As they had previously agreed to do, China and India exchanged maps of the middle sector and the western sector of the dispute during the twelfth and fourteenth JWG meetings. However, the number and scope of the discrepancies between the two side's view on where the LAC lay opened up another arena for debate and the discussions became stuck again (Kalha, 2014: 215–216). In an effort to get negotiations moving again, the two sides agreed in 2003 to establish the Special Representative Mechanism (SRM). The SRM consisted of China's and India's most senior diplomatic officials with their advisors and quickly superseded the JWG to become the main diplomatic mechanism for conducting the border negotiations. Initially the SRMs showed promise, with the Chinese and Indians agreed in 2004 to a three-stage process for addressing the 'boundary question': (1) establishing the political parameters for and guiding principles for coming to a resolution, (2) establish the framework for the final resolution and (3) to delimitate and demarcate the agreed border (Deepak, 2020: 65–66). The first stage of this process was completed relatively quickly, with the 'Agreement on the Political Parameters and Guiding Principles for the Settlement of the India–China Boundary Question' signed during Premier Wen Jiabao's visit to New Delhi in 2005.

However, following the 2005 Agreement the Sino-Indian border negotiations stalled as prestige concerns began to emerge for both sides again. By the mid-2000s China's remarkable economic and military rise had shifted its prestige calculus, imbuing it with the belief that it has become the penultimate power in the international system, second only to the US. This created an 'asymmetry of status and perception' in China's favour, ensuring that China typically does not take India's sensitivities or interests seriously (Pardesi, 2021; Pu, 2017). For India, which evidently aspires to be recognized as a great power, such an attitude from a state it considers to be its peer is viewed as contemptuous at best or a systematic policy to diminish Indian prestige at worst. As India's accomplishments and capabilities have gradually begun to match its great power aspirations over the past decade and other states have begun to acknowledge New Delhi's rise, India's irritation with China's refusal to treat it as a peer has only grown. Thus, India has been increasingly seeking ways that it can assert itself towards China and force the Chinese to take its concerns seriously. The border dispute has provided the perfect medium for India to apply such pressure on China and make a display of standing firm (Xie, 2019: 178–180).

For China, the situation is a little more complicated in that its prestige concerns in the negotiations have less directly about India but rather what other states will glean from their interactions. While China clearly does not consider India to be a peer competitor and remains generally disdainful of their 'great power dreams', it does recognize that India is an ambitious state (Pardesi, 2021: 13–14). Therefore, China recognizes India could complicate things as it seeks to expand its global influence and contend with the US, and potentially other powers such as Japan, for its place at the top of the international hierarchy. China has become particularly sensitive towards the 'China threat' theories that have been occasionally promoted by India, considering them effectively slander intended to smear its international image as a peacefully rising state (Deng, 2008: 97–108). Furthermore, China clearly feels isolated within its peer group and remains alert to any efforts by the US and others to marginalize it. Thus, China has been particularly sensitive to India's growing alignment with the United States and Japan, concerned that they will not just geopolitically encircle it but will act to limit its influence in international affairs (Pardesi, 2021: 15–16; Pu, 2018: 63).

These growing concerns that their prestige was being eroded by the other's actions ultimately induced both sides to obstinately maintain their maximalist stance, aware that their positions are incompatible but believing that any compromise would result in an avoidable loss of face. In practice, this has seen China insist that India at a minimum agrees to its 'reasonable requests' for territorial adjustments in the eastern section of the dispute, especially around the monastery town of Tawang (Deng, 2008: 153–154; Garver, 2011: 109–111). India, for its part, rejected such demands as 'outrageous' claiming that Tawang as a populated centre is 'non-negotiable', all while consistently and publicly pressing its own claims to the Aksai Chin (Kalha, 2014: 210–228; Smith, 2014: 59–62). Despite a flurry of SRM dialogues in 2006 and 2007 in an attempt to break the impasse, the SRMs became an annual event after 2007 as the two sides seeming recognized the futility of continuing to negotiate at such intensity. Shortly after the negotiations became deadlocked, both sides began actively patrolling up to their interpretation of the LAC to strengthen their claim to legitimately occupy the disputed territory.

Notwithstanding these provocations, both sides were evidently interested in finding a way to keep the channel of negotiation open and occasionally manage crises on the border as and when they emerged. The importance of maintaining this dialogue became increasingly apparent throughout the 2010s as confrontations became increasingly common and the levels of force employed by both sides gradually escalated. Following each clash, the SRM has proven pivotal for finding face-saving means for resetting bilateral relations and re-establishing 'tranquillity' on the border (Shankar, 2018: 41–43; Xie, 2019: 182–184). Increasingly, the SRMs have also been used as a high-level mechanism discussing bilateral issues unrelated to the dispute, such as China's opposition to imposing sanctions of Pakistan-based terrorists or India's restrictions on Chinese firms (Deepak, 2020: 67–68). Hence, with the bilateral tensions caused by their simultaneous pursuit of further international power and prestige, both states have seen the benefit in keeping active an official dialogue with which they can defuse tensions and maintain a degree of coexistence.

Interestingly, in recent years the SRMs has increasingly become just part of a broader patchwork of formal and back-channel talks on the Sino-Indian boundary question. While some of these engagements appear to have been genuine attempts move the dialogue forward, most have been reactive efforts to either manage or smooth over a crisis. Of note has been the 'Working Mechanism for Consultation and Cooperation on Indo-China Border Affairs', which was formed in 2012 and became the primary forum for coordinating the mutual drawdown during 2020–2021 border standoff (Deepak, 2020: 73). Yet, although these discussions have allowed China and India to maintain the mutually beneficial atmospherics that they are addressing their disagreement civilly, they have proven no substitute for an actual resolution.

Conclusion: Stalemated Negotiations and the Elusive Settlement

In reviewing how China and India have approached talks over the Sino-Indian border dispute, it becomes apparent that concerns over their national prestige have prompted both sides to adopt incompatible and intractable positions. Interestingly, both states share the same basic concern that the prestige attributed to them by the international community has been inferior to what they considered their rightful place as great powers (Deng, 2008: 155; Garver, 2001: 345–349). Despite the lack of any clear historical or legal ownership over the territory they dispute, the disparity between their self-perceived national prestige and their treatment in international affairs ensured that both sides came to see the other's border claims as a challenge.

Although there was a brief productive period in the post-Cold War era when China and India held an equivalent international status, the gulf between China's and India's understanding of where the LAC lay, let alone where the border should be fixed, continued to create problems in the negotiation. By the mid-2000s, both sides came to see the other as an obstacle to their rise as an international power, prompting them to harden their position and remain unwilling consider any resolution that could be construed as a concession. Nonetheless, both sides have seen the continuing utility of a formal mechanism to help manage border crises as and when they occur and attempt to smooth over differences before they become a problem.

Yet, managing crises is not a serious substitute for resolution. The increasingly violent border clashes over the past decade have no doubt brought home to both sides the potential consequences of leaving an actively contested border remain. Nonetheless, India's and China's national prestige remain a prominent stumbling block. India in particular has been unable to reconcile its identity an emerging great power and deserving international leader with position in the current hierarchy. Viewing China as a rival great power contender that has been undermining its rise, India quickly adopted a publicly unyielding stance on the border as a means to show resolve and enhance its prestige. Its history of being humbled in the 1962 Border War and being unable to extract any meaningful concessions from China has only added to India's desire to save face by insisting upon its territorial claims. China for its part, although it has been far more successful than India in achieving what it believes is its rightful great power status, it has never felt secure or respected in its position. Thus, it has considered India's border demands to be insulting and has responded with maximalist positions of its own in an effort to compel India to take its position seriously.

With both states viewing concessions as potentially damaging to their cherished national prestige and their perceived rightful place, Sino-Indian border negotiations are likely to remain stalemated for the foreseeable future. Thus, while both sides recognize the precariousness of the status quo on the border, simply returning to a state of 'tranquillity' along the border rather than pushing for a resolution will likely remain too tempting. As long as India and China continue to value their national prestige, fear appearing irresolute and perceive their rightful place in the international hierarchy as being in the great powers club, a negotiated settlement to the border dispute will remain elusive.

References

Acharya, A. (2020) 'The Myth of the "Civilization State": Rising Powers and the Cultural Challenge to World Order', *Ethics and International Affairs*, 34 (2): 139–156.

Ambekar, G. V. and Divekar, V. D. (1964) *Documents on China's Relations with South and South-East Asia*. Bombay: Allied Publishers.

Chung, C. (2004) *Domestic Politics, International Bargining and China's Territorial Disputes*. Abingdon: Routledge.

Deepak, B. R. (2005) *India and China 1904–2004: A Century of Peace and Conflict*. New Delhi: Manak Publications.

Deepak, B. R. (2020) *India and China: Beyond the Binary of Friendship and Enmity*. Singapore, Singapore: Springer.

Deng, Y. (2008) *China's Struggle for Status: The Realignment of International Relations*. New York: Cambridge University Press.

Dixit, J. N. (1996) *My South Bloc Years: Memoirs of a Foreign Secretary*. New Delhi: UBS Publishers.

Engelmeier, T. F. (2009) *Nation-Building and Foreign Policy in India: An Identity-Strategy Conflict*. New Delhi: Cambridge University Press India.

Fravel, M. T. (2008) *Strong Borders, Secure Nation: Cooperation and Conflict in China's Territorial Disputes*. Princeton, NJ: Princeton University Press.

Freedman, J. (2016) 'Status Insecurity and Temporality in World Politics', *European Journal of International Relations*, 22 (4): 797–822.

Garver, J. (2001) *Protracted Contest: Sino-Indian Rivalry in the Twentieth Century*. Seattle, WA: University of Washington Press.

Garver, J. (2006) 'China's Decision for War with India in 1962', in A. I. Johnston and R. S. Ross (eds) *New Directions in the Study of China's Foreign Policy*. Stanford, CA: Stanford University Press, pp. 86–130.

Garver, J. (2011) 'The Unresolved Sino-Indian Border Dispute: An Interpretation', *China Report*, 47 (2): 99–113.

Gilpin, R. (1981) *War and Change in World Politics*. New York: Cambridge University Press.

Guo, R. (2012) *Territorial Disputes and Conflict Management: The Art of Avoiding War*. London: Routledge.

Haksar Papers (1960) 'Record of Talks between P.M. and Premier Chou En Lai Held between 20 April 1960 and 24 April 1960'. P. N. Haksar Papers (I–II Installments), Wilson Center Digital Archive. Available at http://digitalarchive.wilsoncenter.org/collection/71/sino-indian-border-war-1962 (Accessed: 20 July 2017).

Hensel, P. R. and Mitchell, S. M. (2005) 'Issue Indivisibility and Territorial Claims', *GeoJournal*, 64 (4): 275–285. doi:10.1007/s10708-005-5803-3.

Kalha, R. S. (2014) *India–China Boundary Issues: Quest for Settlement*. New Delhi: Pentagon Press.

Khong, Y. F. (2019) 'Power as Prestige in World Politics', *International Affairs*, 95 (1): 119–142.

Larson, D. W., Paul, T. V. and Wohlforth, W. C. (2014) 'Status and World Order', in T. V. Paul, D. W. Larson and W. C. Wohlforth (eds), *Status in World Politics*. New York: Cambridge University Press, pp. 3–29.

Maxwell, N. (2013) *India's China War*. Revised and updated edition. Dehra Dun: Natraj Publishers.

MEA (1963) *Notes, Memoranda and Letters Exchanged Between the Governments of India and China October 1962–January 1963*. Whitepaper 8. New Delhi: Ministry of External Affairs, p. 126.

Menon, S. (2016) *Choices: Inside the Making of India's Foreign Policy*. Washington, DC: The Brookings Institution.

Miller, M. C. (2013) *Wronged by Empire: Post-Imperial Ideology and Foreign Policy in India and China*. Stanford, CA: Stanford University Press.

Onea, T. (2014) 'Between Dominance and Decline: Status Anxiety and Great Power Rivalry', *Review of International Studies*, 40 (1): 125–152.

O'Neill, B. (1999) *Honor, Symbols and War*. Ann Arbor, MI: University of Michigan Press.

Pardesi, M. S. (2015) 'Is India a Great Power? Understanding Great Power Status in Contemporary International Relations', *Asian Security*, 11 (1): 1–30.

Pardesi, M. S. (2021) 'Explaining the Asymmetry in the Sino-Indian Strategic Rivalry', *Australian Journal of International Affairs*, 75 (3): 341–365.

Pu, X. (2017) 'Ambivalent Accommodation: Status Signalling of a Rising India and China's Response', *International Affairs*, 93 (1): 147–163. doi:10.1093/ia/iiw002.

Pu, X. (2018) 'Asymmetrical Competitors: Status Concerns and the China–India Rivalry', in T. V. Paul (ed.), *The China–India Rivalry in the Globalisation Era*. Washington, DC: Georgetown University Press, pp. 55–73.

Shankar, M. (2018) 'Territory and the China–India Competition', in T. V. Paul (ed.), *The China–India Rivalry in the Globalisation Era*. Washington, DC: Georgetown University Press, pp. 27–53.

Singh, Z. D. (2011) 'After the Hiatus: India–China Border Diplomacy Since the 1970s', *China Report*, 47 (2): 83–98.

Smith, J. M. (2014) *Cold Peace: China–India Rivalry in the Twenty-First Century*. Lanham, MD: Lexington Books.

Wohlforth, W. C. (2009) 'Unipolarity, Status Competition and Great Power War', *World Politics*, 61 (1): 28–57.

Wojczewski, T. (2018) *India's Foreign Policy Discourse and its Conceptions of World Order: The Quest for Power and Identity*. Abingdon: Routledge.

Wood, S. (2014) 'Nations, National Identity and Prestige', *National Identities*, 16 (2): 99–115.

Xie, C. (2019) 'How Status-seeking States can Cooperate: Explaining India–China Rapprochement After the Doklam Standoff', *India Quarterly*, 75 (2): 172–189.

6 India–Japan Alignment in the Indo-Pacific

Astha Chadha and Yoichiro Sato

Upon independence, the newly independent and partitioned India refrained from the Cold War bloc politics and bandwagoning with either the US or USSR, under its non-alignment approach which remained a crucial part of Indian foreign policy much after the end of the Cold War (Chacko, 2014; Harshe, 1990). An erstwhile colonizer, Japan, restrained by US alliance structures, was forced into adopting a pacifist identity for coming decades (Sato & Hirata, 2008). Thus, as both India and Japan were emerging from the devastation of the second world war, their newly adopted identities rather supported a mutually amicable relationship during the Cold War. Independent India became among the first states to recognize Japanese sovereignty post Second World War and signed a peace treaty with it in 1952. Japan in 1961 recognized the need to firmly place Japan in Asian security architecture by declaring India and Japan as the 'natural pegs' (Ghosh, 2008; Jain, 2017: 14) of this system. While India supplied iron ore towards Japanese post-war reconstruction, Japanese loans and development aid to India became the base of their economic relations for the next few decades until the global geopolitics took another turn in Cold War period. But the relationship between New Delhi and Tokyo was far from stable.

The US–Japan alliance (as elaborated in the US–Japan Security Treaty) had put a constraint on Japan's relations with India, which was engaged in border wars with neighbouring China and Pakistan and began spearheading the Non-Alignment Movement. Japan normalized its relations with China in 1970s, and India had been pushed out of Japan's engagement in Southeast Asia, of which India was no longer considered a part (Horimoto 2015: 100, Jain 2017: 16). As India remained ideationally constrained by strategic neutrality while following a socialist model of economic growth, Japan's alliance with the US and its free market-driven capitalist model pulled New Delhi and Tokyo in opposite directions politically as well as economically. Despite an improvement in ties in the post-Cold War 1990s, their relations further deteriorated with India's nuclear tests in 1998, pushing Japan to suspend its Official Development Assistance (ODA) to India, only resuming it in 2000 after the US–India rapprochement (Lalwani & Byrne, 2019). When India opened its economy post-Cold War to foreign investment and globalization,

DOI: 10.4324/9781003305132-9

India–Japan relations then improved with growing trade and signing of several agreements to boost investment and development projects in India (Brewster, 2010).

However, bilateral ties picked an upward trajectory after 2014 when India's Prime Minister Narendra Modi and his Japanese counterpart Shinzo Abe elevated Indo-Japanese relations to a 'Special Strategic Global Partnership', typified by cooperation in technology, defence, space and nuclear energy (Basrur, 2017; Chhibber, 2018). After several decades, the states were aligning their respective strategic visions underpinned by development goals to assist the rise of India as an Asian power of substantial standing. Japan became the only state besides Russia to have regular bilateral summits with India. With an eye on regional geopolitics amid China's economic growth and strategic connectivity projects like Belt and Road Initiative (BRI) that challenged US hegemony, India and Japan signed a 'Vision 2025' statement in 2017, outlining spheres of cooperation in the Indo-Pacific, expanding India's role beyond the Indian Ocean and positioning Japan as a leader in response to regional security challenges (Rai, 2018).

Unlike the US that defined the Indo-Pacific as stretching from west coast of America to east coast of India in line with the reach of its newly named Indo-Pacific Command in 2018, India and Japan recognized the geostrategic region inclusive of the whole Indian Ocean encompassing the east coast of Africa. The New Delhi and Tokyo partnership gained ground beyond their respective territories as they launched joint development programmes in other Indian Ocean states, complementing their Indo-Pacific vision of it being a free, open and inclusive region with a rule-based order. However, the elevated bilateral relationship has suffered several bottlenecks in the context of their respective strategic relationships with China and the US. This chapter raises the following questions: How has India–Japan relation transformed over time into a resilient partnership? What are the strategic arrangements in the Indo-Japanese bilateral relationship that continue to thrive? and how have China and the US impacted the India–Japan relationship at the bilateral and multilateral levels?

The authors will use the realist-constructivist framework, which incorporates a realist emphasis on material factors and power together with incorporation of ideas for a complete understanding of global politics (Barkin 2003: 338). In other words, realist-constructivism does not compromise the realists' core focus on material interests and accepts the role of identities and norms to serve the material interests of states, in either scenarios of competition or conflict (such as inter-state) or cooperation (such as within an alliance) (Sato and Hirata 2008: 5–6). Employing a realist-constructivist perspective allows for a detailed analysis of the material as well as non-material aspects that impact the India–Japan relationship. Through the realist lens, the chapter examines the degree to which balance of power strategies are employed by the two states, in the backdrop of their relations with the US as well as China. The constructivist approach helps examine the key normative characteristics of New Delhi and Tokyo's foreign policies towards each other and the impact of their foreign policy norms on their respective Indo-Pacific visions.

Collaboration in India's Strategic Locations

India's view of Japan as a reliable development partner was largely due to the complementary nature of Japanese capital when invested in India's resource-rich and labour-abundant economy. The India–Japan rapprochement and India's transformation to catch up on lost decades of progress came at an opportune time when Japan's relations with China on the security front were witnessing deterioration (Jain, 2010). This provided Japan with a way of diversifying its economic partnership in the medium term, which had been entwined mainly with China. Politically, it also coincided with India's move beyond the constraints of non-alignment to strategic autonomy and eventual multi-alignment as New Delhi embraced globalization, having balanced international relationships, and playing a greater role regionally and beyond.

India–Japan relations have received a great push through complementing objectives of New Delhi's Look East Policy and Japan's greater engagement policy towards South Asia towards the end of 1990s. However, the new millennium set the stage for improved bilateral relations between the two Asian democracies with the visit of Japanese Prime Minister Yoshiro Mori who signed the Global Partnership between Japan and India with his Indian counterpart Prime Minister Vajpayee (Chadha, 2020c; Yoshimatsu, 2019). As a result, bilateral trade picked up and Japanese foreign direct investment (FDI) into India increased during the early 2000s and New Delhi surpassed Beijing as Tokyo's largest ODA beneficiary in 2003.

Realizing the need to establish a security partnership with India that had been establishing itself as a regional economic power, Prime Minister Abe's 2007 speech in the Indian Parliament laid the foundations for strategic

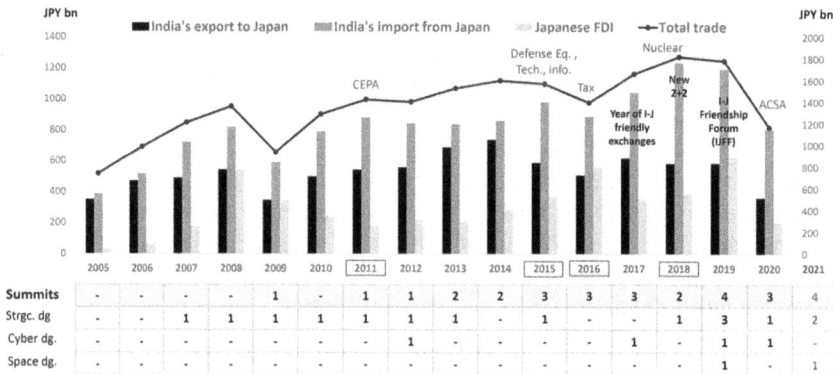

Figure 6.1 India–Japan relations (pre-pandemic): trade, FDI and strategic ties.
Source: adapted from Chadha (2020c)

cooperation among democratic states in Asia and the Pacific, leading to the 2007 edition of the US–India Malabar naval exercises off Okinawa that included Japan for the first time (Paul, 2012; Yoshimatsu, 2019). New Delhi and Tokyo also signed the 'Joint Declaration on Security Cooperation' in 2008, followed by 'Comprehensive Economic Partnership Agreement (CEPA)' in 2011 (Chadha, 2020a; MOFA Japan, 2011) under the leadership of Prime Minister Manmohan Singh. The impact of these agreements, among others, can be seen in Figure 6.1.

Japan was among one of the first states visited by the new Indian Prime Minister Narendra Modi in 2014, setting up the 'Japan Plus' division within the Ministry of Commerce to resolve grievances by Japanese firms operating in India, which had risen from 267 in 2006 to 1,156 in 2014 (JETRO, 2021; SAM & Co. and FICCI, 2020: 18). By November 2014, Japanese FDI worth $17.6 billion in pharmaceutical, automobile and services accounted for 7.4% of the total FDI into India (Economic Times, 2014). The Modi administration changed the Look East Policy into the Act East Policy (AEP), which gave a boost to New Delhi and Tokyo's infrastructure and connectivity projects in India's vulnerable northeast, which is threatened by insurgency from neighbouring China, Bangladesh and Myanmar. These projects aim at linking the northeast to the rest of India as well as Association of South East Asian States (ASEAN) countries like Myanmar and Thailand.

Prime Minister Modi and Prime Minister Abe signed an agreement to launch the 'India–Japan Act East Forum' in 2017, wherein several infrastructure projects including roads, highways, hydropower stations and bridge construction, were launched in India's northeastern states of Meghalaya and Mizoram, along with forest managements and hydropower undertakings in Sikkim, Nagaland, Tripura, and Meghalaya (JICA, 2018). India's engagement of Japan in its geo-strategically critical northeast had crucial implications for Indo-Chinese border disputes in the region and China's launch of its Belt and Road Initiative (BRI). For Tokyo, these initiatives marked the first time it had set foot in the area since the Japanese imperial presence in Battle of Kohima and Imphal against British India in 1944. Connectivity projects were also aimed at facilitating the movement of troops into India's northeast amid increased Chinese presence close to the contested Line of Actual Control (LAC) and improving surveillance of insurgency activities across Bangladesh and Myanmar (Barua, 2020; Chadha, 2020b). Furthermore, Japan's ODA loans that had been instrumental in railway and urban projects in Delhi were extended to other metropoles like Bengaluru, Mumbai, and Chennai in 2017 including the Mumbai-Ahmedabad High Speed Rail (Shinkansen) project and multi-modal transport network. India also made an exception by partnering with Japan towards laying optic fibre cables as well as installing a 15-megawatt diesel power plant on its strategically located Andaman and Nicobar Islands, vital to offset Chinese presence in Indian Ocean through its own network of ports in India's strategic backyard (Bose, 2022; JICA, 2022).

India–Japan strategic alignment has also permeated defence agreements in past two decades. While the 2007 Quadrilateral summit among India, Japan, the US, and Australia was short-lived after Australia pulled out of the same later, the 2007 edition of bilateral US–India Malabar naval exercise included Japan. Tokyo and New Delhi also signed the Security Cooperation agreement in 2008, followed by the establishment of several diplomatic dialogue mechanisms at the level of security advisors, defence ministers and coast guards. Japan was permanently added to the US–India Malabar exercise in the Bay of Bengal in 2015. Alongside existing exercises JIMEX (biennial naval) and Sahyog-Kaijin (Coast Guards), more exercises were launched in all corners of India, including Dharma Guardian (in Mizoram in 2018), SHINYUU Maitri (joint air force exercise since 2019 in West Bengal), air anti-submarine naval exercise (2017 in Goa), and MINEX (mine countermeasure exercise in 2019 in Kerala). Further, a 'Defense Equipment and Technology Transfer' agreement was signed in 2015 between the two states alongside mutually agreed measure for protection of classified military information.

The establishment of the 'India–Japan Defense Industry Forum' in 2017 was aimed at pushing investments in the defence sectors of both states but which faced some domestic challenges in terms of achieving closer defence cooperation. For New Delhi, its defence industry is in a relatively nascent stage and military equipment is largely procured from partners like Russia, France, and the US (Wezeman et al. 2022: 7). For Tokyo, despite the signing of the 2018 'Civil Nuclear Arrangement' with India, engagement with India (which is a non-signatory nation to the Nuclear Non-Proliferation Treaty) has been challenged domestically. In terms of military action, issue like expanding the role of Japanese self-defence forces through an amendment of Article 9 of Japan's constitution (which restricts it from waging war), or concerns over the degree of sensitive information-sharing with other nations also persist in Tokyo (Hatakeyama, 2021). On the investments front, despite being a preferred destination for overseas subsidiary of Japanese businesses, India's lack of adequate infrastructure and bureaucratic delays in process have adversely affected India's attractiveness for Japanese FDI in addition to the Covid-19 pandemic's negative economic impacts.

Cooperation in the Indo-Pacific Region

When the US unveiled its 2017 Indo-Pacific strategy as a counter to the China-led vision of world trade and sea routes under its BRI, Japan had pitched its Indo-Pacific vision of a free, open and rule-based order in the region. India announced the complementary vision of SAGAR (Security and Growth for All in the Region) for the Indo-Pacific to practically engage in multi-alignment. But the region has been a rough terrain for the India–Japan partnership where despite partial successes of their collaboration, neither holds absolute diplomatic influence when compared with a stronger Chinese presence. Though India shares close cultural and socio-political proximity in its neighbourhood dating for centuries and Japan has been a key ODA donor to several states in the Indian Ocean, the recent contestation in the region has uncovered several new realities. These include fault lines in India's relations with its neighbours and Japan's lack of political influence in the Indian Ocean states compared to the indispensability of China in the political and economic landscape of the wider Indo-Pacific.

The Asia Africa Growth Corridor (AAGC) was among the first India–Japan partnership projects announced in 2016 in line with their Indo-Pacific vision of bringing equitable growth, development and connectivity to the region, besides security interests. Against the backdrop of increasing Chinese investments in Africa, such as in Djibouti where Beijing established a military base in the debt-ridden state, India and Japan offered 'quality' infrastructure projects and skill development in Africa that kept people at the heart of their initiatives (Chadha, 2022). In this way, India announced $10 billion in lines of credit and $600 million in grants under the AAGC, while Japan was among the highest ODA contributors to Africa offered $30 billion in investments in the region (Beri 2017: 3; MOFA Japan 2017: 117; Vivekananda International Foundation 2018: 9). The two states also offered development funds and infrastructure projects in key Indian Ocean island states like Mauritius, Seychelles and Comoros, each of which had undertaken Chinese development loans (Bhaumik, 2020; Chadha, 2020a). Since the Indo-Pacific included the east coast of Africa, the Indian Ocean and the Pacific Ocean for New Delhi and Tokyo, they also launched several projects in key maritime areas showing a deeper strategic convergence (Chadha, 2021b).

India–Japan ties can also be illuminated through their respective bilateral relations with a number of states in South Asia. In this regard, both India and Japan view Bangladesh as key to their Indo-Pacific visions of linking South and South-East Asia. New Delhi had extended LoCs (line of credit) to Dhaka worth $ 862 million, followed by another in 2017 of $ 2 billion and a subsequent pledged $4.5 billion for infrastructure projects including railways, roads, airports, power, shipping etc. (Ministry of External Affairs, 2017). Japan, on the other hand, agreed to build Matabari port after cancellation of China-backed Sonadia port few kilometres away (Pearson 2015; JICA 2021: 5). In turn, the Maldives, an archipelago of over 1,200 islands in the Indian Ocean lies along the major sea lines of communication (SLOCs) in the region. After Maldivian President Yameen joined the BRI, the Maldives cancelled the Milan 2018 naval exercise with India, which initiated the return of New Delhi's helicopters and other military assets (Verma 2020: 160–161). But after the opposition leader Ibrahim Solih was elected President in 2018, India then offered $400 million loans and $100 million grant towards the 'Greater Male Connectivity Project', the largest infrastructure undertaking in the Maldives, alongside $1 billion loan to payoff Chinese debt amounting to 25% of its GDP, and 80% of total foreign debt in 2018 (Kuronuma, 2018). Japan also opened an embassy in Maldives in 2016, began offering financial assistance in 2020 such as a $7.6 million grant towards strengthening Maldives National Defense Force Coast Guard and $5.6 million towards assistance for fighting COVID-19 pandemic (Embassy of Japan in Maldives, 2020a, 2020b).

Sri Lanka has also emerged as the diplomatic battleground for India and Japan against China's increasing naval presence, undisclosed submarines in the Indian Ocean and huge infrastructure investments under the BRI such as the Hambantota port. Because of Sri Lanka's proximity to the Indian mainland and the importance of SLOCs for Japan, India and Japan partnered in Sri Lanka towards a $250 million LNG import terminal in West Sri Lanka's Kerawalapitiya (Press Trust of India, 2017). In 2019, India and Japan also signed a trilateral agreement with Sri Lanka to develop and operate Colombo port's East Container Terminal, retaining a 49% stake. The Sri Lankan government unilaterally cancelled the agreements in early 2021 over domestic concerns of foreign ownership and offered development of the West Container Terminal at the same port to India and Japan in compensation (Press Trust of India, 2021). Elsewhere, for India, Myanmar is key to the India–Myanmar–Thailand Trilateral Highway, the Kaladan multi-modal transport project and the Mekong–India economic corridor. Japan, on the other hand, had invested over $1 billion in Myanmar in 2010s, with several Japanese companies operating in the Thilawa Special Economic Zone (JICA, 2020a; Japan Times, 2018). Both New Delhi and Japan also extended grants and medical assistance to battle Covid-19 pandemic in the country (JICA, 2020b). But after the 2021 military coup, the ongoing and proposed projects by India and Japan suffered an additional setback, with both states prioritizing their national interests and bilateral ties with Myanmar amid their diplomatic inability to exert influence in the state whose military maintains close ties with Beijing (Banerjee & Basu, 2021).

Elsewhere, India and Japan have been increasingly engaging with ASEAN states since 2010, offering development assistance (such as with Thailand and Cambodia), while also engaging in joint exercises and offering military equipment such as submarines, boats, and military training to the region (in Indonesia and Vietnam) (Chakraborti & Chakraborty, 2020; Liao & Dang, 2019). New Delhi and Japan share the view that their development assistance and security enhancement in the Indo-Pacific can augment equitable growth in the region and maintain peaceful rule-based order. Thus, while for India, Indo-Pacific is a partnership mechanism, which enables it to engage with other regional powers in issue-based alignments to play a larger security role, Japan sees the Indo-Pacific as an opportunity to forge security arrangements with other states beyond its waters to overcome its relative absence from regional security affairs since the end of Second World War.

Both India and Japan have respectively embraced the free and open Indo-Pacific vision as their own core strategy in the region. While Japan has been increasing its military roles despite maintaining certain degree of its post-World War Two pacifism, it has adopted a unique role of playing the facilitator of regional cooperative mechanisms. India has moved beyond its Cold War non-alignment into a proactive space where it practices multi-alignment as it cultivates its partnerships with all states through multi-lateralism or bilateralism. India's principled foreign policy approach is thus, complementary to Japanese multilateral initiatives, in a way that they abso-lutely converge at best, and remain non-conflicting and different at worst. This dynamic between Japan and India can support and straighten their relationship in the long run with the commitment from both sides to deepen this partnership through mutual acceptance and encouragement of each other's strategic roles in the Indo Pacific.

The Beijing Challenge and the India–Japan Response

Japan re-established diplomatic relations with China in 1972, after its occu-pation of parts of China under Imperial Japan. Thus, Japanese relations with China have been overshadowed by Japanese 'guilt' and China gradually rising from economic backwardness to surpass Japan as an economic power. India's relations with China, on the other hand, have been oscillating between rivalry and friendship ever since the establishment of bilateral dip-lomatic relations between them in 1950. As shown in Chapter 5 of this volume, these have involved longstanding territorial disputes concerning Tibet, Aksai Chin and Arunachal Pradesh. The first decade of the 2000s saw increased engagement between India and China towards resolution of the border disputes. Sikkim was recognized as part of India in 2003, followed by establishment of strategic partnership between India and China in 2005 as well as reopening of border trade after four decades of economic isolation. But the dispute over Arunachal Pradesh continued.

In 2000, after opening its economy to globalization and liberalization, India established strategic relations with the US and Japan, with the latter diverting its ODA loans from China into India. In 2004 China overtook the US as Japan's largest trading partner. After the 2005 anti-Japan protests in China over Tokyo's efforts to rewrite part of imperial history, FDI from Japan that was concentrated in China began flowing into other growing economies like India (Horimoto, 2015). By 2007 Japan had also become cautious about China's assertions over the Senkaku Islands in East China Sea, territorial claims over the whole of South China Sea which holds some key SLOCs, and growing presence in the Indian Ocean (Midford, 2015; Sato, 2017: 247–250). Despite Chinese protests over the 2007 Quad summit and Malabar Exercise involving India, Japan, the US and Australia, Tokyo con-tinued to push for greater engagement with India that emerged as a regional economic hub and was embracing a new mode of strategic autonomy. China also expressed concerns over the 2008 'India–Japan Defense Cooperation Agreement', but Japan and the US supported India on its territorial sover-eignty over Arunachal Pradesh with an Asia Development Bank (ADB) loan for the region's development in 2009 despite Chinese protests.

China launched the BRI (including the Silk Road Economic Belt and the Maritime Silk Road) in 2013 and established its Asian Infrastructure Investment Bank (AIIB) to finance infrastructure projects connecting China with Europe and the Pacific through the South China Sea. Japan under Prime Minister Abe did not join the initiative as it threatened Japan's regional leadership by placing China at the centre of regional connectivity and installed the AIIB against existing institutions like the ADB (Iida, 2018: 2–3). In 2015, Japan expressed the need for cooperation with China through engagement between the ADB and the AIIB, as well as between Japanese infrastructure projects and the Chinese BRI, however, Beijing maintained that Japan should cooperate with China through the BRI framework (Iida, 2018). Japan did not join the BRI due to its opaque terms such as concerns of governance of projects as well as debt sustainability concerns in the recipient countries of Chinese loans.

Meanwhile, India refused to join the BRI due to sovereignty issue and territorial disputes with China after the Depsang standoff in Aksai Chin (in Jammu and Kashmir) in 2013. Despite several summit meetings with Beijing, New Delhi also began raising concerns over Beijing's assertion in the South China Sea and protested over the presence of Chinese troops in Chumar across the LAC and also that the China-Pakistan Economic Corridor (CPEC) passed through India-claimed and Pakistan-administered Kashmir. Refusal to join the BRI marked yet another policy convergence between India and Japan. India and Japan launching of the AAGC in 2016, in line with India's SAGAR vision, was further designed to counter China's encirclement of India's maritime boundary and to enable Japan's Free and Open Indo-Pacific strategy. In 2016, Japan also took steps to introduce security laws that allowed it the right to collective self-defence without violating its Constitutional provisions (Sato 2017; Kumar 2018: 31).

Overall, New Delhi and Tokyo have pursued soft balancing approach in their cautious stance towards the BRI and aggressive Chinese foreign policy in the region, while also trying to cooperate with China in their separate ways. China's emergence as a large security player in the region is a threat to Indo-Pacific norms and security visions of Japan and India. To that measure, the Indo-Pacific collaboration for India and Japan is a measure to ensure their strategic presence in the region. China's bilateral partnerships with New Delhi and Tokyo, despite territorial disputes between India–China and island disputes between Japan-China, imply that India and Japan understand each other's issues but face limitations in disengaging from China completely. But more important implication of this triangular relationship is that neither Japan, nor India seek each other's commitment towards disengagement from Beijing but engage in complementary strategies towards the economic giant. Despite mutual threat perceptions of Chinese aggression and military visibility, Japan seeks to engage with China through various multilateral institutions and cooperative mechanisms. On the other hand, India's multi-engagement is underpinned by its acceptance of multipolarity in the inclusive

Indo-Pacific which can accommodate the peaceful rise of both India and China.

India's Strategic Autonomy and Japan's Alliance with the US

The US has played a critical role in security of the Asia-Pacific, a region that has some key SLOCs that account for over half of the global energy trade. While at the end of Second World War, Japan agreed to an arrangement to be a US ally in Asia and a base for American interests and policies in the region, post-independence India struggled to resist becoming subservient under another power after its colonial experience (Atanassova-Cornelis & Sato, 2019). India's launch of the Non-Aligned Movement further distanced it from the Western powers, while drawing it closer to the Soviet Union during the Cold War.

Several events in the last three decades of the twentieth century set the ground for tumultuous Indo-American relations, where relations with China were prioritized, and hence the US established its alliance with Pakistan which served as an intermediary between Sino-American talks and engagement (Sisson & Rose, 1990). Subsequently, the US assisted Pakistan in the 1971 Bangladesh War of Independence, while India placed an emphasis on non-alignment and strategic autonomy from either the US or Russia. However, India–Russia defence relations, and India's socialist economic model, and the 1998 nuclear tests by New Delhi that made it a nuclear power in the region, further deteriorated India's relations with the US and Japan which imposed economic sanctions (Limaye, 2006: 225–248). Pakistan's geostrategic location also served the US interests in the Middle East, as well as US interests in Afghanistan in later years.

While Japan was the only nation to assist India in its foreign exchange crisis in the early 1990s, overall contemporary India–Japan relations shadowed the trajectory of India–US relations (Limaye, 2006: 225–248). US President Bill Clinton eventually lifted economic sanctions against India (introduced as a result of the 1998 nuclear tests) and visited India in 2000 after two decades of diplomatic vacuum, followed by the Japanese Prime Minister who signing the 'India–Japan Global Partnership' agreements months later (Verma, 2020: 187–188). In turn, the India–US Strategic Partnership agreement in 2004 made way for the 2006 'India–Japan Global and Strategic Partnership'. The next year Japanese Prime Minister Abe delivered his 'Confluence of Two Seas' speech before Indian Parliament and launched his proposal for a Quad forum.

The US foresaw the need to launch connectivity projects in Asia, linking Central Asia to East Asia. Obama's refocusing on Afghanistan after withdrawing US troops from Iraq aimed at multi-lateralizing the post-conflict reconstruction efforts in Afghanistan to shift the cost onto other stake holders (Mann, 2013). However, since the US proposal of building a 'Silk Road' in 2011 was accompanied by necessary economic-political reforms, several Central Asian states preferred unconditional Chinese loans and thus their support for the Beijing backed One Belt One Road or BRI initiative (Clinton, 2011a, 2011b). The US pivot to Asia also led to the launch of tri-lateral US–Japan–India dialogue at ministerial level. Thereafter, the Indo-Pacific as a geostrategic concept of free, open and rule-based vision gained international political weight against the China-led BRI which aimed to link Chinese markets with the rest of the world through China-financed infra-structure development. After the signing of the 'US–India Joint Strategic Vision for the Indo-Pacific' in 2015, Japan and India signed the 'India–Japan Vision 2025' agreement, instating Japan as a regular member of the Malabar exercise in 2015 followed by 2016 'India–Japan Civil Nuclear Agreement' (Department of Foreign Affairs and Trade, 2017; Jung et al., 2020).

The US's proactiveness laid the groundwork for Indo-Japanese relations to flourish post 2000 but especially since 2011. However, India has been wary of US-led alignment arrangements since Cold War. Despite improved strategic and military ties with Washington, New Delhi has shown reluctance in being a US balance against China in the Indo-Pacific or even accepting increased the US presence in its maritime neighbourhood due to apprehensions over US dominance as well as its relations with Pakistan. Hence, India's strategy has been to form issue-based alignments for national interests while prior-itizing strategic autonomy. Though this has not had a major and direct impact on the growing Indo-Japanese relations, US policies towards Asia in general has impacted India's relations with US rivals like Russia and Iran, both of which are India's strategic partners for trade in military equipment and energy respectively. For example, US sanctions on Iran have restricted India from engaging in oil imports from Tehran while also jeopardizing India's Chabahar port investments in Iran, which is crucial for India's trade with Afghanistan and Central Asia (Chadha, 2021a; Teja, 2015; Zahid Shahab & Bhatnagar, 2018).

The US initiative towards the resurgence of Quad in 2017 did not culmi-nate into anything more than a consultation mechanism till 2020, since all four states continued to issue separate statements, wherein India was careful not to mention China but only cooperation and joint initiatives. It was only at the 2021 Quad meeting that a joint statement was launched declaring a rule-based maritime order in the East and South China Seas, alongside joint initiatives to combat the Covid-19 pandemic with vaccine manufacturing by India, with support from other states (Rej, 2021; White House, 2021). The Indo-Pacific, including the Quad mechanism within it, has a huge strategic and symbolic value. In the present geopolitical order, it allows like-minded states to collaborate towards deterring China from belligerence while also offering the other smaller states an alternative route to development part-nerships. Its significance has increased during the pandemic since dealing with the health crisis and manufacturing massive vaccination supplies would be a daunting task unless states collaborate in the Indo-Pacific and beyond. However, India has been very cautious in its engagement in trilateral and quadrilateral arrangements in the Indo-Pacific to balance its relations with China, thus refraining from joining several initiatives like the Blue Dot Network or achieving depth in trilateral frameworks, such as the US–Japan–Australia triad (Goodman et al., 2020; Sarkar, 2020; United States Department of State, 2020).

While India has responded to China's presence in the Indian Ocean by signing the 'Basic Exchange and Cooperation Agreement' with the US for strategic information sharing, and 'Acquisition and Cross Servicing' agreements with all members of the Quad, India–Japan do not hold the same official position over US Freedom of Navigation Operations (FONOPs) in the Indo-Pacific (Hindu, 2020). The US presence in Japan is crucial to Japanese security amid threats from China or North Korea, and hence Japan has not protested the most rigorous openness of the seas advocated through US FONOPs (freedom of navigation operation) in the South China Sea and elsewhere despite the US not being a signatory of the United Nation Convention on Law of the Seas. India on the other hand holds important strategic autonomy and territorial sovereignty to signify itself as a net security provider in the Indian Ocean region, which it considers to be its strategic backyard. Therefore, India strongly protested the 2021 US FONOPs close to Lakshadweep archipelago, an undisputed Indian territory (Peri, 2021).

The Indo-Pacific, is thus, a geopolitical rationale for the US to wield its supremacy and influence in the region, not only against China but also against any other state that aims to be a regional power. Japan sees itself as a US ally and the fulcrum of US policy towards Asia, and thus an indispensable part of the Indo-Pacific geopolitical order (Sato, 2019, 2020, 2021). But India's view of the Indo-Pacific has been a work-in-progress: it has progressed from being New Delhi's last resort amid geopolitical frictions and deteriorating security situation in its neighbourhood, to a soft balance against Chinese aggression, and now an opportunity for India to assert its strategic autonomy and carve a space for its ambitions in the region which it sees as being inclusive and multipolar. However, India maintains reservations over accepting the nature of Indo-Pacific as a containment measure against China.

Conclusions: Emerging Geopolitical Challenges and Evolving Collaboration

India's gradual move from non-alignment to multi-alignment has created a welcome space for strategic partners like Japan to assist India's rise as a regional power. India–Japan alignment is exemplary for its depth and scope of cooperation among two states not bound by formal alliance or treaty. The two states, over the years have recognized areas of mutual action and coordination, with an emphasis on infrastructure development, investments and economic growth. A re-emerging Japan's technological and financial capabilities have complemented multi-aligned India's large growing market and young population. The two states have also effectively cooperated in defence and strategic geographies of India. However, a recent economic slowdown in India, exacerbated by bureaucratic delays and then the pandemic, has decelerated Indo-Japanese trade and investments.

In a broader perspective, while India–Japan relations have been welcomed by the US, the defence engagements and security cooperation have alerted China. New Delhi and Tokyo have partnered in port development and infrastructure projects in Indian Ocean states, as well as in several Africa and Southeast Asian countries, offering a 'quality' alternative to the Beijing-led BRI that has left several states debt-ridden. Despite challenges in economically disengaging from China, the complementarity between India's multi-alignment, and India–Japan FOIP (Free and Open Indo-Pacific) cooperation allows enough space to accommodate any divergence in their respective policy preferences in the Indian Ocean and Western Pacific.

The US has been a great influence in the formation and trajectory of India–Japan relations, owing to the US–Japan security alliance, which puts Japan as America's pivot to Asia. But for India, strategic autonomy is crucial for its policy of issue-based alignments. This also reflects in India and Japan's objectives and vision for the Indo-Pacific, where they share the Quad platform and agree on the nature of the threat from China but view the geopolitical frictions differently. India views the Indo-Pacific as a partnership mechanism, which enables it to engage with other regional powers in issue-based alignments to play a larger security role. On the other hand, Japan sees the Indo-Pacific as an opportunity to forge security arrangements with other states beyond its waters to overcome its self-imposed restrictions on the right to collective defence. The US and its partners such as India and Japan aim to balance against China's rise, but the role of Quad has been limited as a joint policy platform. However, the pandemic has offered a new window of opportunity for India and Japan to cooperate not only mutually but also with the US and Australia towards regional prosperity, while also signalling collective symbolic deterrence to China.

New Delhi and Tokyo have largely refrained from their distinct positions on geopolitical challenges to hinder the upwards trajectory of their collaboration. At present, their special strategic partnership thrives, not only on absence of vastly opposing ideologies or territorial disputes, but also on mutual recognition of their valuable roles as economic powers and security providers in the Indo-Pacific region. Emerging challenges in and beyond their immediate neighbourhoods, such as the global pandemic, eroding democratic rule in Myanmar or Russia's attack on Ukraine in 2022, call for clear positions of the two states on these issues and their ability to reckon long-term impacts of these events on regional and global security architecture. At the same time, for as long as India and Japan can continue to prioritise national interests in line with their distinct identities, norms and principles such that they remain non-conflicting with their mutually shared values and visions, the partnership would remain potent to steer the course of Indo-Pacific peace, prosperity and security.

Acknowledgement

This work was supported by JSPS KAKENHI Grant Number JP18K01494.

References

Atanassova-Cornelis, E. & Sato, Y. (2019). The US–Japan Alliance Dilemma in the Asia-Pacific: Changing Rationales and Scope. *International Spectator*, 54(4), 78–93.

Banerjee, S. & Basu, P. (2021). India–Japan Partnership in Third Countries: A Study of Bangladesh and Myanmar. *ORF Issue Brief*, 460, 1–18.

Barkin, J. S. (2003). Realist Constructivism. *International Studies Review*, 5(3), 325–342.

Barua, T. (2020). The Look East Policy/Act East Policy-driven Development Model in Northeast India. *Jadavpur Journal of International Relations*, 24(1), 101–120.

Basrur, R. (2017). Modi's Foreign Policy Fundamentals: A Trajectory Unchanged. *International Affairs*, 93(1), 7–26.

Beri, R. (2017). *AAGC: Towards India–Japan Development Cooperation in Africa*. RIS/AAGC.

Bhaumik, A. (2020). S Jaishankar in Seychelles, Doval in Colombo: India Ups Outreach to Indian Ocean Region to Counter China. Retrieved from www.deccanhera ld.com/national/s-jaishankar-in-seychelles-doval-in-colombo-india-ups-outreach-to -indian-ocean-region-to-counter-china-920645.html.

Bose, S. (2022). India–Japan Collaborations: Andaman and Nicobar Islands in Focus. Retrieved from www.orfonline.org/expert-speak/India–Japan-collaborations/.

Brewster, D. (2010). The India–Japan Security Relationship: An Enduring Security Partnership? *Asian Security*, 6(2), 95–120.

Chacko, P. (2014). The Rise of the Indo-Pacific: Understanding Ideational Change and Continuity in India's Foreign Policy. *Australian Journal of International Affairs*, 68(4), 433–452.

Chadha, A. (2020a). India and the Seychelles: Economics First, Defense Later. Retrieved from https://thediplomat.com/2020/12/india-and-the-seychelles-econom ics-first-defense-later/.

Chadha, A. (2020b). India's Foreign Policy towards Japan: Special Partnership amid Regional Transformation. *Ritsumeikan Journal of Asia-Pacific Studies*, 38(1), 2020.

Chadha, A. (2020c). India's Strategy towards Japan & FOIP amid Regional Transformations: Analysis from the Realist and Constructivist Perspectives. Unpublished master's thesis, Ritsumeikan Asia Pacific University.

Chadha, A. (2021a). India's COVID-19 Strategy and Implications for its Relations in the Indian Ocean. *Ritsumeikan Journal of Asia Pacific Studies*, 39(1), 81–104.

Chadha, A. (2021b). The Heavenly Land and the Land of the Rising Sun: Historical Linkages, Security Cooperation and Strategic Partnership. *Contemporary Japan*, 1–2.

Chadha, A. (2022). India's Relations with Africa: Evaluating Changes in India's Africa Policy during COVID-19. In N. M. Raman (ed.), *Reimagining South Asia: Multilateralism in the Contemporary Times* (pp. 10–29). Pentagon Press.

Chakraborti, T. & Chakraborty, M. (2020). *India's Strategy in the South China Sea* (1st ed.). Routledge.

Chhibber, B. (2018). India–Japan Relations: Breaking New Ground in the Strategic Partnership. *World Affairs: The Journal of International Issues*, 22(3), 94–103.

Clinton, H. (2011a). Remarks on India and the United States: A Vision for the 21st Century. 20 July.

Clinton, H. (2011b). America's Pacific Century. *Foreign Policy*, 11 October.

Department of Foreign Affairs and Trade. (2017). Foreign Policy White Paper. Retrieved from dfat.gov.au/sites/default/files/minisite/static/4ca0813c-585e-4fe1-86e b-de665e65001a/fpwhitepaper/foreign-policy-white-paper/chapter-three-stable-and-prosperous-indo-pacific/geo-economic-competition.html#figure-3-1.

Economic Times. (2014). India Sets up Japan Plus Investment Team to Speed Up Proposals. *The Economic Times*, October 10. Retrieved from https://economictimes.india times.com/news/economy/policy/india-sets-up-japan-plus-investment-team-to-speed-up -proposals/articleshow/44765782.cms?from=mdr [last accessed 31 May 2021].

Embassy of Japan in Maldives. (2020a). The Government of Japan Provides Medical Equipment Worth USD 5.6million to Strengthen Health Sector of the Maldives. 7 June.

Embassy of Japan in Maldives. (2020b). The Government of Japan Pledges Equipment Worth USD 7.6 Million to Strengthen the Operational Capability of the Maldives National Defence Force Coast Guard. 22 November.

Garge, R. (2016). The India–Japan Strategic Partnership: Evolving Synergy in the Indo-Pacific. *Australian Journal of Maritime & Ocean Affairs*, 8(3), 257–266.

Ghosh, M. (2008). India and Japan's Growing Synergy: From a Political to a Strategic Focus. *Asian Survey*, 48(2), 282–302.

Goodman, M. P., Runde, D. F. & Hillman, J. E. (2020). *Connecting the Blue Dots*. Center for Strategic and International Studies.

Harshe, R. (1990). India's Non-Alignment: An Attempt at Conceptual Reconstruction. *Economic and Political Weekly*, 25(7–8), 399–405.

Hatakeyama, K. (2021). *Japan's Evolving Security Policy: Militarisation within a Pacifist Tradition*. Routledge.

Hindu. (2020). India and US Sign BECA. *The Hindu*, 28 October. Retrieved from www.thehindu.com/news/international/india-and-us-have-signed-beca/article329623 24.ece [last accessed 31 June 2021].

Horimoto, T. (2015). Japan-India Rapprochement and Its Future Issues. In *Toward the World's Third Great Power: India's Pursuit of Strategic Autonomy* (pp. 99–126). Iwanami Shoten. Retrieved from www2.jiia.or.jp/en/digital_library/japan_s_diplomacy.php.

Iida, M. (2018). *Japan's Reluctant Embrace of BRI*. Stiftung Wissenschaft und Politik, Berlino (Session 3). In German Institute for International and Security Affairs.

Jain, P. (2010). Japan–India Relations: Peaks and Troughs. *The Round Table*, 99(409), 403–412.

Jain, P. (2017). Twin Peaks: Japan's Economic Aid to India in the 1950s and 2010s. *JICA Research Institute*, February(139), 1–46.

Japan Times. (2018). Japanese Investment in Myanmar Soars to All-Time High. *The Japan Times*, 29 May.

JETRO. (2021). *Japanese Business Establishments in India*. JETRO.

JICA. (2018). JICA Continues to Invest in Improving Transitability by Extending ODA Loan of Approximately INR 2,500 Crore for the North East Road Connectivity Project.

JICA. (2020a). Signing of Japanese ODA Loan Agreements with Myanmar: Comprehensive Support for Economic and Social Development. 21 January.

JICA. (2020b). JICA Provides Myanmar 43 billion Japanese Yen Concessional Financing to Support Development of Logistics Infrastructure and Recovery of SMEs from COVID-19 Epidemic Loss. 4 November.

JICA. (2021). *Ex-Ante Evaluation (for Japanese ODA Loan)*. Japan International Cooperation Agency.

JICA. (2022). Signing of Grant Agreement with India: Support for the Improvement of Power Supply in Andaman and Nicobar Islands. 14 April.

Jung, S. C., Lee, J. & Lee, J. Y. (2020). The Indo-Pacific Strategy and US Alliance Network Expandability: Asian Middle Powers' Positions on Sino-US Geostrategic Competition in Indo-Pacific Region. *Journal of Contemporary China.*

Kumar, S. (2018). *India's National Security: Annual Review 2016–17.* Routledge.

Kuronuma, Y. (2018). India Offers Maldives $1bn in Loans to Help Repay China debt. *Nikkei Asia,* 28 November.

Lalwani, S. & Byrne, H. (2019). Great Expectations: Asking Too Much of the US-India Strategic Partnership. *Washington Quarterly,* 42(3), 41–64.

Liao, J. C. & Dang, N. T. (2019). The Nexus of Security and Economic Hedging: Vietnam's Strategic Response to Japan–China Infrastructure Financing Competition. *The Pacific Review,* 33(3–4), 669–696.

Limaye, S. (2006). Japan and India after the Cold War. In Y. Sato & S. Limaye (eds), *Japan in a Dynamic Asia: Coping with the New Security Challenges.* (pp. 225–248). Lexington Books.

Lintner, B. (2019). *The Costliest Pearl: China's Struggle for India's Ocean.* Hurst & Company.

Mann, J. (2013). *The Obamians: The Struggle Inside the White House to Redefine American Power.* Penguin Books.

Midford, P. (2015). Japan's Approach to Maritime Security in the South China Sea. *Asian Survey,* 55(3), 525–547.

Ministry of External Affairs. (2017). India–Bangladesh Joint Statement during the State Visit of Prime Minister of Bangladesh to India. 8 April.

MOFA Japan. (2011). Japan-India Economic Partnership Agreement. Ministry of Foreign Affairs of Japan. Retrieved from www.mofa.go.jp/policy/economy/fta/india.html.

MOFA Japan. (2017). *White Paper on Development Cooperation 2017: Japan's International Cooperation.* MOFA Japan.

Paul, J. M. (2012). India–Japan Security Cooperation: A New Era of Partnership in Asia. *Maritime Affairs: Journal of the National Maritime Foundation of India,* 8(1), 31–50.

Pearson, N. O. (2015). Japan beating China to the Port in Bangladesh. *Japan Times,* 5 July. Retrieved from www.japantimes.co.jp/news/2015/07/05/national/politics-diplomacy/japan-beating-china-to-the-port-in-bangladesh/l [last accessed 31 May 2021].

Peri, D. (2021). India Protests against US Naval Exercise Sans Consent. *The Hindu,* 9 April. Retrieved from www.thehindu.com/news/national/india-protests-us-naval-exercise/article34279034.ece [last accessed 31 May 2021].

Press Trust of India. (2017). India, Japan JV to Set up LNG Import Terminal in Sri Lanka. *Hindustan Times,* 24 May. Retrieved from www.hindustantimes.com/business-news/India–Japan-jv-to-set-up-lng-import-terminal-in-sri-lanka/story-lwUzqdG98TVEZMgmYOQgFN.html [last accessed 31 May 2021].

Press Trust of India. (2021). Sri Lanka Says it Scrapped Port Deal as Indian Firm Rejected Terms. *The Hindu,* 13 February. Retrieved from www.thehindu.com/news/international/sri-lanka-says-it-scrapped-port-deal-as-indian-firm-rejected-terms/article33829461.ece [last accessed 31 May 2021].

Rai, A. (2018). Quadrilateral Security Dialogue 2 (Quad 2.0)–A Credible Strategic Construct or mere 'foam in the ocean'? *Maritime Affairs,* 14(2), 138–148.

Rej, A. (2021). In 'Historic' Summit Quad Commits to Meeting Key Indo-Pacific Challenges. *The Diplomat,* 13 March.

SAM & Co. and FICCI. (2020). *India–Japan: Time to Seize New Opportunities.*

Sarkar, M. G. (2020). China and Quad 2.0: Between Response and Regional Construct. *Maritime Affairs*, 16(1), 110–130.

Sato, Y. (2017). Conclusion: Abe's Japan- Manifestation of a Quiet Transformation in Power and Values. In S. Hidekazu & Y. Sato (eds), *Re-rising Japan: Its Strategic Power in International Relations* (p. 264). Peter Lang.

Sato, Y. (2019). Japan's Indo-Pacific Strategy: The Old Geography and the New Strategic Reality. *Journal of Indo-Pacific Affairs*, 2(4), 107–119.

Sato, Y. (2020). Free and Open Indo-Pacific: The Region in Japan's Perspective. *Issues and Insights*, 20, 12–15.

Sato, Y. (2021). Japan's Strategic Indo-Pacific Vision. In C. Moldicz & G. Kovács (eds), *The Rise of Global Strategies: Edited by Csaba Moldicz and Gabriella Kovács* (pp. 167–186). Budapest Business School, University of Applied Sciences, Oriental Business and Innovation Center.

Sato, Y. & Hirata, K. (2008). Introduction: Constructivism, Rationalism, and the Study of Norms in Japanese Foreign Policy. In Y. Sato & K. Hirata (eds), *Norms, Interests, and Power in Japanese Foreign Policy* (p. 279). Palgrave Macmillan.

Sisson, R. & Rose, L. E. (1990). Pakistani Politics: Image and Legacy. In *War and Secession: Pakistan, India, and the Creation of Bangladesh* (pp. 8–10). University of California Press.

Teja, J. (2015). India–Iran Relations in a New Context. *American Foreign Policy Interests*, 37(2), 87–94.

United States Department of State. (2020). Blue Dot Network. Retrieved from www. state.gov/blue-dot-network/ [last accessed 31 May 2021].

Verma, A. (2020). *The Heavenly Land and the Land of the Rising Sun: Historical Linkages, Security Cooperation and Strategic Partnership.* KW Publishers.

Vivekananda International Foundation. (2018). *India Africa: A Partnership for Growth.* Vivekananda International Foundation.

Wezeman, P. D., Kuimova, A. & Wezeman, S. T. (2022). *Trends in International Arms Transfer, 2021.*

White House. (2021). Quad Leaders' Joint Statement: 'The Spirit of the Quad'. Retrieved from.whitehouse.gov/briefing-room/statements-releases/2021/03/12/qua d-leaders-joint-statement-the-spirit-of-the-quad/ [last accessed 10 December 2021].

Xianghui, Z. (2019). China's Mega-Projects in Myanmar: What Next? *ISEAS – Yusof Ishak Institute*, 84, 1–11.

Yoshimatsu, H. (2019). The Indo-Pacific in Japan's Strategy towards India. *Contemporary Politics*, 25(4), 438–456.

Zahid Shahab, A. & Bhatnagar, S. (2018). The India-Iran-Pakistan Triad: Comprehending the Correlation of Geo-economics and Geopolitics. *Asian Studies Review*, 42(3), 517–536.

7 A Comparative Analysis of Russian and French Strategies towards India and South Asia

Aleksei Zakharov

Since 2018 Indian and international scholars have pointed out how Paris replaced Moscow as a sole consistent supporter of Indian interests in the international arena (Rajagopalan, 2019). Three broad reasons are cited to explain why France has emerged for India as a 'new Russia'. For one, Paris is perceived to be such a comfortable partner for New Delhi that Indian leaders can utilize the term 'alliance' without any harm to its traditional stance on 'strategic autonomy' and cautious approach towards alliance making. Narendra Modi's reference to 'InFra' as an 'alliance of India and France' (MEA, 2019), that he made during his speech in Paris in August 2019 is a case in point. Moreover, New Delhi and Paris, albeit both being United States (US) partners, 'share a healthy scepticism of American policies' (Pande, 2019) and strive for independence in foreign policy decision-making. Secondly, in the changing realities of the twenty first century India and France are drawing closer together and are cooperating 'on military nuclear propulsion and other sensitive areas' (Mohan, 2018) previously reserved only for Soviet Union / Russia. Finally, France has proven to be a more reliable partner since Russia's support on Kashmir turned 'lukewarm' as Moscow is now following an ambiguous policy on sensitive issues for India 'feeling squeezed' (Rajagopalan, 2019) between China and India and has also established a closer cooperation with Pakistan.

As observed by Rakesh Sood, 'the test for a strategic partnership is not that there must be convergence on all issues; the test is that where there are differences, these are expressed in private and not publicly' (Sood, 2020). This notion used to be a salient feature of India–USSR relations, but most lately finds rising evidence in India–France partnership. New Delhi, however, would scarcely acknowledge officially any difference in the treatment of its strategic partners, apparently appreciating each and promoting relationships with them in accordance with India's national interests. Although some Indian markets remain quite competitive for great powers, there is no sign that Paris has been seeking to edge Russia out of its positions. As the French Ambassador to India Emmanuel Lenain delicately noted, when asked if France has acquired Moscow's role, 'being Russia in India is quite a compliment' (quoted in Sibal, 2020).

DOI: 10.4324/9781003305132-10

Beyond the discourse of France as 'a new Russia', there is much complementarity between the two as both these partnerships respond to India's
desire to explain its national identity to the world and being relied upon by
New Delhi on its way to global prominence. Firstly, Paris and Moscow are
staunch advocates of multi-polarity which India has viewed as a core element
of its global and, more narrowly, Asian affairs. With some differences concerning how to approach Asia and its subregions, which will be addressed
further in this chapter, France and Russia are among those states who have
endorsed neither a superpower dominance in the region, nor a return to
bipolarity. India's 'multi-alignment policy' appears to fit well into President
Macron-promoted 'strategic autonomy' concept for France and the European Union (EU) and allows New Delhi to find new convergences across
the Indo-Pacific with Paris and Brussels. The activation of India's foreign
policy under the Narendra Modi government and the shift from 'non-alignment' to 'multi-alignment' were initially misinterpreted by many in Russia as
a tilt towards the West, particularly the US. However, against the backdrop
of US-China rivalry, there has been a growing understanding of India's role
as an independent centre of the multipolar world. Russian experts believe
that Moscow should seek to preserve 'strategic autonomy' and avoid slipping
down to the position of China's junior partner. A report with ideas for a new
Russian foreign policy suggested that Russia should spearhead a 'new non-
alignment movement' and cooperate with India in order for this movement
to become united (Karaganov et al., 2020: 65).

Secondly, in the last twenty years Moscow and Paris have supported
India's inclusion to the global high table. However, although both capitals
favour New Delhi's quest for a permanent United National Security Council
(UNSC) membership, the odds are against the reform of this organization.
Moreover, as a French journalist, who has been working on India for a long
time, pointed out, the support of India's UNSC place by France and other
major powers is 'a lip service allowing [it] to secure positions in other
spheres' (author's interview, Paris, 2019). Thirdly, France and Russia share
India's concerns about the terrorism threat and have portrayed themselves as
primary partners on this track. By acceding to denounce 'cross-border terrorism' and the activity of Pakistan-based terrorist groups, Paris and
Moscow have been playing to India's critical diplomatic goal of juxtaposing
its own identity against the *'other'*, its traditional enemy Pakistan.

Fourthly, India has utilized its relations with France and Russia for projecting a certain image. In its dialogue with France Indian officials feel comfortable making references to 'shared values of democracy and freedom'
while with Russia they tend to emphasize 'non-interference in internal
affairs'. What matters for New Delhi is that neither of partners – though for
different reasons – passes judgments on India's human rights record. Lastly,
unlike the US, which had a period of 'estrangement' with India throughout
the Cold War, both Russia and France can avail of positive reflection of their
India policies' legacy associated in Indian collective memory with their

backup on sensitive political issues and investments in India's technological capabilities.

This chapter explores the trajectories of India's strategic partnerships with Russia and France and identifies factors that have shaped these relationships. How have India's longstanding principles and values influenced these partnerships? How have alignments with Moscow and Paris allowed Indian governments to further their goal of economic and technological development, promote diplomatic narratives of 'cross-border terrorism' and maintain equidistance between great powers avoiding military alliances? As both Russia and France seem to play integral roles in India's multi-alignment policy, which has gained momentum under Bharatiya Janata Party (BJP) government, what is their contribution to New Delhi's pursuit of power and status?

Historical Background

The Dubious Trajectory of France's and Russia's India Policies in 1990s

The dissolution of the Soviet Union significantly affected India's foreign policy, making New Delhi more vulnerable to external and internal challenges. The first half of 1990s was an unstable and complicated period for India's ties with both France and Russia. A major reason for such state of relationships was caused by Paris and Moscow's close interactions with Islamabad at the politico-military level and their policies on nuclear non-proliferation. Since the Cold War, Pakistan had remained a large importer of French defence equipment – especially aircraft, warships, submarines and rockets – and surpassed India on total volumes of military orders by the end of 1990s, though the general trend turned in favour of India after 1996 (Racine, 2002: 169). The contract between France and Pakistan for three Agosta-90B submarines, signed in 1994, which included provisions of technology transfer, was also an issue of acrimony for New Delhi. Another point of divergence was Paris's refusal to carry on enriched uranium supplies to the Tarapur plant following the end of bilateral agreement in 1993 and France joining the Nuclear Suppliers Group. Nevertheless, France was keeping up close diplomatic contacts with India. The 1994 visit to India by French Minister of External Affairs Alain Juppé reconfirmed French interest to preserve the political dialogue and boosted their economic relationship (Racine, 2002: 161, 187).

Russia cosied up to Pakistan at the beginning of 1990s and it was mainly a strong pro-Western lobby, represented by then Foreign Minister Andrey Kozyrev and other government officials, who argued for improving ties with Pakistan. This intention was driven by the following motives:

• to indicate the new Russia's approach to the region and, thus, appease the West;

- to get a better place to tackle the Taliban in Afghanistan;
- to increase control over the situation in Central Asian Republics; and
- to get access to the warm-water ports of Arabian Sea.

(Mohanty, 2001: 33)

There were however different, sometimes opposing, approaches in Moscow to relations with India. Even in Russia's Foreign Ministry there was no unity as different factions could not agree on either preserving cooperation with India or promoting relations with Pakistan. The first school of thought, prevalent in the academic community and parliament, favoured retaining a special relationship with India and developing working relations with other South Asian states, including Pakistan. The second group, mostly associated with Kozyrev, suggested Russia should stop looking at regional develop-ments 'through Indian spectacles' as it could have been harmful for relations with Pakistan and other actors (Shukla, 1999: 252). Only in 1996 when Yev-geny Primakov took up the post of Foreign Minister, did the gradual restoration of Russia's ties with India begin. Just two months after his appointment, Primakov visited India, which became his first foreign destination as the head of Russian foreign policy.

The Commencement of Strategic Partnerships

Jacques Chirac had been invited as a Chief Guest for India's Republic Day in January 1998 and confirmed his visit regardless of a change of government in New Delhi. His tour of India was rich in symbolism and paved the way for the Indo-French strategic partnership. The visit was 'a watershed' at the political level of cooperation and reflected 'the enhanced consideration given to India by the French decision makers' (Racine, 2002: 160–161). The eco-nomic side of the trip gained symbolical importance with President Chirac's arrival to Mumbai being accompanied by the large group of French entre-preneurs and his meeting with representatives of Indian business community. He called for boosting industrial cooperation in the aerial domain, in com-munications, space, urban development and financial services, and expressed France's readiness to share its technologies and know-how (Élysée, 1998a). In New Delhi, President Chirac emphasized an 'insufficient level of ties' and committed to restore the foundations for 'a more solid and dynamic part-nership' (Élysée, 1998b). He also underlined that the objective of his visit was to 'propose to build a strong relationship between [the] two countries, a global partnership developed on complementarities and shared interests' (Élysée, 1998b).

By contrast, Russian President Boris Yeltsin had decided to postpone his trip to India in early 1998. The confusion concerning this decision was fuel-led by media reports providing contradictory explanations. The Kremlin press-service tried to downplay the situation by stating that the visit had been postponed by 'mutual consent' and the initial preparation had been only 'preliminary' while a diplomatic source told the Interfax agency that the reason for rescheduling trip was 'important domestic political events in India' (quoted in RFERL, 1998b). The latter contradicted earlier remarks by presidential spokesperson Sergey Yastrezhembskiy who had claimed that the domestic situation could not affect Russia–India relations. In any case, the postponement came as a surprise for Indian officials. An even more damaging event for the relationship could have been another postponement by Yeltsin in November 1998, which provoked rumours about the state of his health. However, it was then Prime Minister Primakov who went to India to keep up momentum of bilateral ties and discuss pending agreements.

In 2000, New Delhi and Moscow signed an agreement on strategic partnership which indicated an attempt to revitalize bilateral ties. The status of 'strategic partnership' infused new energy in a bilateral relationship that had evidently soured during the turbulent 1990s, though Vladimir Putin later claimed that the agreement 'merely committed to paper what was already a reality' (Kremlin, 2001). The declaration on strategic partnership allowed for the institutionalization of high-level exchanges and led to regular bilateral summits held annually until the pandemic year of 2020.

The Intersection of Interests in Key Areas of Competition

Defence

It is hard to overestimate India's significance as a defence market for Russia and France. According to SIPRI data, India was the main recipient of arms for both countries with its share of 23% and 21% of all Russian and French defence exports respectively in the period of 2016–2020 (Wezeman et al., 2021: 2). Notably, over the last five years as Paris and New Delhi completed several contracts, France's share of India's defence market has been rising and France even emerged as the second largest supplier of weaponry. Imports from Russia, on the contrary, have been gradually decreasing as a clear sign of New Delhi's attempt to diversify its sources of arms. That said, notwithstanding the threat of US sanctions, India made a firm decision to go ahead with a S-400 SAM deal with Russia and did not renege on the orders for frigates, fighter jets and helicopters. As some researchers assume, these and some other previous deals may 'lock India into several decades of dependence for supplies and parts' (Lalwani et al., 2021: 28–29) from Russia. In conjunction with Moscow's readiness to share sensitive technologies, such dependence might allow Russia to retain its position of major arms supplier to India in the coming years.

Significantly, even during the India–China crisis in Eastern Ladakh in June 2020 Moscow kept open the lines of military equipment export to India's armed forces and 'responded positively to every defence requirement that India has had' (Embassy, 2021). From its part, Paris also agreed to expedite the delivery and enlarge the batch of Rafale jets weeks after the Galwan clash between Indian and Chinese troops. Hence, both Moscow and Paris are keen to demonstrate their reliability as India's traditional suppliers of defence equipment.

Obviously, Moscow and Paris have been competitors in the Indian defence market with France coming on the heels of Russian positions in several domains of military-technical cooperation with India. For instance, MiG and Dassault were bidding for tender on the Medium Multi-Role Combat Aircraft that New Delhi announced in 2007. Following a lengthy procurement procedure, the Rafale fighter jet emerged as the winner while the MiG-35 did not even qualify for the final cut. At one point, during a pricing uncertainty and lack of progress over the Rafale contract, Russia, particularly amid its tensions with France over the Ukraine crisis and Paris's subsequent delay of Mistral-class warships delivery, was seeking to influence India's position, which included offering to sell more Su-30MKI instead of Rafale jets (Bodner, 2015). Another example of competition is India's tender on the conventional submarines' procurement under the long-delayed P75I project. France's Naval Group and Russia's Rubin Design Bureau are among five foreign original equipment manufacturers that have been bidding for the project reportedly valued at US$5.6 billion. Even though the requests for proposals are yet to be issued by Indian Ministry of Defence, there are some indications that the submarines 'would come from the French shipbuilder' (Chanda, 2020).

In general, India seems to have chosen France as a favourable source for the diversification of its defence imports. Indian procurements from French manufacturers are out of the scope of sanctions and are unlikely to provoke any dissent from the US. Even Moscow is seemingly less uneasy when New Delhi opts for French offers rather than American ones. The Indo-Russian defence partnership may still be rather enduring as it remains 'the one and only' track of cooperation that neither side would be eager to lose. It appears that India would like to keep Russia by its side and might continue to rely heavily on Russian-origin equipment, particularly the most sophisticated ones that cannot be replaced by other exporters. The case in point here is Russia's provision of India with access to nuclear submarine technology which its major competitors – France and the US – have not proposed so far (Unnithan, 2021).

Being two of the largest arms exporters in the world, Russia and France seek to expand their market shares across the wider Asian region. Even though both promise India not to supply its adversaries with the weaponry already shared with Indian military, obviously they cannot entirely bypass them. From the Russian side, there has been an advanced stage of military cooperation with China. Some of Russia's state-of-the-art equipment (S-400 SAM, Su-35 fighter jets) were sold to China before India, and Russia has been assisting China with developing a missile attack early warning system, which was seen in India as an indication of a growing strategic partnership (Rajagopalan, 2019), if not of a looming alliance. France has also maintained defence ties with Beijing, though at a considerably lower level. An important difference is the trajectory of France's and Russia's respective cooperation with Pakistan, including in defence. Given the deterioration of France–Pakistan relations, it is hard to expect any significant deals in the near-term while the Islamabad–Moscow connection continues to gain momentum with Russia being ready to provide 'assistance to the strengthening of Pakistan's counterterrorism capability, which includes the supply of relevant equipment' (MOFA, 2019). Clearly, such 'assistance', once materialized, would raise hackles in New Delhi which has serious doubts about how and where Pakistan could utilize Russian-made weaponry.

Space

Foreign assistance has been an integral part of India's achievements in space. In a way, the history of India's space programme is a history of foreign collaboration. During the Cold War era the programme had relied heavily on help from the Soviet Union, France, West Germany, the United States and, to a lesser extent, Japan (Bhatia, 1985: 1021). For France, India is its oldest partner in space. Back in the 1960s India became the second international partner of the French space agency – Centre National d'Etudes Spatiales (CNES) – after the US. Both the USSR and France, along with the US, aided India in setting up the Thumba Equatorial Rocket Launching Station (TERLS) and provided assistance to India's Rohini rockets programme (Lele, 2015: 13). The first rockets launched from the TERLS were two-stage rockets imported from the Soviet Union ('M-100') and France ('Centaure'). In the 1970s, following the agreement between the Indian Space Research Organisation (ISRO) and the Soviet Academy of Sciences, the USSR helped fabricate an Indian designed and manufactured satellite called 'Aryabhatta', which was launched from Kapustin Yar range using a Soviet rocket in 1975 (Bhatia, 1985: 1017). The close cooperation with Moscow enabled India's first and the only cosmonaut Rakesh Sharma to visit space on board the Soyuz T-10 in 1984.

Just in line with the general decline of their bilateral relationship at that time, Russia–India space cooperation in the 1990s had seen a considerable downfall. The most memorable and humiliating moment for the ties was Moscow's reneging on the cryogenic engines deal, having refused to transfer cryogenic technology under the pressure from the US Washington expressed concerns that India could have used the cryogenic technology to develop missiles and equated the potential transfer from Russia with the violation of Missile Technology Control Regime (MTCR). Ultimately, Russia sold the engines, which allowed India to develop its Geosynchronous Satellite Launch Vehicle programme, albeit after a long delay. However, the controversy would remain in the Indian memory for years to come as a reminder that even a reliable Russia may go back on its commitment. Interestingly, before imposing sanctions on ISRO and Russia's former space agency Glavkosmos, the

US proposed the same technology to India. Apart from Glavkosmos, the American company 'General Aerodynamics' and the French 'Arianespace' were keen to sell the cryogenic technology, but at a higher price. Before India made its choice to partner with Glavkosmos, the US was not invoking the issue of violation of MTCR regulations (Mohanty, 2001: 42).

Since the 1990s Russia's own space programme has faced various difficulties, preventing the development of collaboration with India in this domain. Despite signing several agreements like the agreement on space cooperation and MoU on joint activities in human spaceflight programme (MEA, 2008), there had been scarce progress on this track between the two sides. Moreover, the 2007 agreement on joint lunar research and exploration was terminated after ISRO- in the wake of Roscosmos-led moon mission failure in 2013 – had decided to realize a land rover component for the Chandrayaan-2 on its own (Jayaraman, 2013). On a positive note, Russia has helped India with its human space mission Gaganyaan. Even despite the pandemic, four Indian cosmonauts underwent training at Gagarin Cosmonaut Training Centre in 2020–2021. ISRO would like to increase technical interaction with Roscosmos and has announced establishing a liaison unit in Moscow. The two sides have also been discussing setting up of ground stations for their navigation satellite systems – Indian NavIC and Russian GLONASS – in their respective territories, which should enhance the accuracy of satellite navigation signals (MEA, 2020). Another topic for further talks is Russia's offer of its semi-cryogenic rocket engine technology along with critical components for India's human space capsule (Mint, 2019).

The Indo-French space cooperation in the same period has been focused on such areas as satellites development and launching services. The successful projects implemented by the countries include the Megha-Tropiques earth observation satellite, utilized for atmospheric studies in tropics, and satellite SARAL, applied for studying the circulation of ocean currents and measuring ocean surface topography (Lele, 2015: 17–19). It appears that, unlike cooperation with Russia, which has turned into being more technical in nature over the last decade, India's interaction with France is more dynamic and comprehensive. The intention by Indian and French agencies to continue collaboration in satellites development and build 'a constellation of satellites [for the Indian Ocean] carrying telecommunications and radar and optical remote-sensing instruments' (Economic Times, 2020) points to shared geopolitical visions for the region. Once developed, it will be the first space-based system in the world capable of tracking ships continuously.

Nuclear Energy

The 1974 Indian nuclear explosion drew public criticism from the international media and concerns from many governments on proliferation grounds. The congratulatory telegram from André Giraud, administrator general of the French atomic energy commission, to India's Department of Atomic

Energy, was unique as it contrasted with negative public statements from across the world, reticence from the USSR and a low-key response from the US. This was, however, followed with the reassessment of nuclear cooperation with India by the government of Valéry Giscard d'Estaing (Sarkar, 2021: 302). 1998 saw nuclear tests conducted by India and Pakistan which seriously affected the security situation in South Asia and led to the UNSC's resolution condemning India's and Pakistan's actions. Although Russia and France were part of the P5's joint communiqué, both did not support the economic sanctions imposed on India and Pakistan by the US and Japan (Balz and Drozdiak, 1998). France emerged as the only P5 member who was not openly criticizing India for the tests.

Moscow's reaction to the tests was ambivalent. Russia officially joined the chorus of international criticism of the nuclear tests, as President Yeltsin stated that 'India has let us down with this decision, [but] I believe we can still achieve a change in their position' (UPI, 1998a). Moscow's stance was explained by the convergence of Russian and US approaches to non-proliferation, including in South Asia, and attempts to dissuade India and Pakistan from nuclear testing (Topychkanov, 2018: 253–254). At the same time, Russia continued to maintain cooperation with the Indian nuclear sector. Just a month after the nuclear tests, Moscow and New Delhi, to the significant displeasure of the US State Department, signed a supplementary document to the 1988 agreement on the construction of two nuclear reactors in India. Hence, despite the opposition from the US and other Nuclear Suppliers Group members, Moscow proceeded with construction activities at the Kudankulam site (Balachandran, 2012). As of 2022, Russia is the only country to build nuclear reactors on Indian soil with the Kudankulam power plant extension to two operating reactors and four other units being under construction.

Even though civilian nuclear energy has been one of the most talked about areas of Indo-French cooperation, the two sides have struggled to make progress in the implementation of their agreements. France has actively appealed to the international community to allow civilian nuclear cooperation with India. Following the US–India nuclear deal of 2008, France was among the first to sign a US$9.3 billion framework agreement for the construction of two reactors in Jaitapur, Maharashtra (Saint-Mézard, 2015: 3, 7). Since then, new contracts between Indian and French leaders were signed implying the construction of more reactors. Jaitapur plant has seen the completion of all required land acquisitions and received all the necessary approvals from Indian Ministry of Environment and Forrest. The process of project realization, however, stumbled upon changes in the French partner company since EDF took over nuclear reactor business from Areva which had initially began negotiations.

Geopolitical Considerations across Multiple Geographies

Since the beginning of the twenty first century, Russia's and France's policies towards South Asia have seen various twists and turns, including their changing visions vis-à-vis Pakistan, the Afghan crisis and other regional issues which, to a great extent, have been defined by their larger geopolitical considerations as well as domestic policies.

The Indo-Pacific and Greater Eurasia

Before outlining its vision for the Indo-Pacific, France has always stressed its interests as a legitimate regional actor belonging to the Indian Ocean Rim, basing its claim on possession of overseas territories of La Réunion and Mayotte in the Southwest Indian Ocean and a substantial military presence in the Northwest Indian Ocean, with two inter-services bases located in Djibouti and UAE (Saint-Mézard, 2015: 4). About 93% of the French exclusive economic zone is located in the Pacific and Indian Oceans, more than 1.5 million French people live in the Indo-Pacific region and more than 8,000 soldiers are stationed there. Apart from a purely geographical attachment to the region, Paris pursues a range of geopolitical and geoeconomic objectives, including ensuring maritime security, developing maritime surveillance capabilities, ensuring the safety of international waters and vital sea lines of communications, promoting the blue economy and connectivity, and strengthening strategic partnerships (Pajon, 2020: 168–170). The French Indo-Pacific strategy set out by Emmanuel Macron in 2018 contains an outlook for France as 'a mediating, inclusive and stabilizing power' (Ministry of Europe, 2021). The emphasis on multipolarity, multilateralism and inclusivity is significant as it makes the French approach similar to the Indian vision articulated by Prime-Minister Modi at Shangri-La Dialogue in June 2018.

Unlike France, Russia does not position itself as an Indo-Pacific state. Russian officialdom has been wary of this geopolitical concept equating it with the US's Indo-Pacific strategy. Being a Northern Pacific power, Russia has a limited presence in the Indian Ocean in the recent years, beyond regular naval exercises with India (called 'Indra') and sporadic port calls by Russian warships. Moreover, Moscow is opposed to the Quad grouping comprising Australia, India, Japan and the US regarding this format as 'a closed bloc', openly 'anti-Chinese' (Lavrov, 2020) and as a 'structure similar to NATO' (Lavrov, 2021).

Since 2014 Russia's external policies have been driven by two theoretical concepts: 'a pivot to the East' and 'a Greater Eurasia partnership'. The second concept is a genuine continuation of the first that Russia was compelled to announce in 2014 in the wake of the Ukraine crisis, which acted as a trigger for the breakdown in the country's relations with the US and the EU. The idea of 'Greater Eurasia', formally unveiled by Vladimir Putin in June 2016, conceives of a new Eurasian partnership including not only Russia's partners from the Eurasian Economic Union (EAEU), but also the friendly countries from the extended neighbourhood – China, India, Pakistan and Iran – and even the EU's members. As part of this, Moscow hopes that the Eurasian project may be promising in 'harmonising various integrational groups' (MFA 2020), including the Shanghai Cooperation Organisation (SCO), the EAEU, the Association of Southeast Asian Nations and the South Asian Association for Regional Cooperation, which reflects intention to extend the 'Greater Eurasia' concept to all states of South and Southeast Asia.

Afghanistan and Pakistan

The tense situation in Afghanistan, which broke out after the Taliban took control in 1996, has been the prime focus of both India and Russia's attention. In the late 1990s and early 2000s, New Delhi and Moscow supported the anti-Taliban Northern Alliance and provided logistical and material assistance and limited military support (Menon, 2019; Trenin et al., 2014: 2–3). Moscow's main concern over the Afghan situation has always been to prevent the spill-over effect of insecurity and instability on its territory. United in their stance against terrorist groupings, Moscow and New Delhi acted against the Taliban and, as a result, shared common ground regarding Islamabad's role in the region. However, the situation began to change in the 2010s with the decline of US power in the region, in Afghanistan in particular, and the shift in Russian foreign policy approaches towards South Asia. Since then, Russia's rapprochement with Pakistan has revolved around the Afghan issue, overall regional security and some particular economic projects.

Although Moscow's engagement with Islamabad has considerably increased since 2014, it is erroneous to overstate Pakistan's role for Russian regional interests. Pakistan can neither be sufficiently a lucrative market for Russia's products, nor a close geopolitical partner. Islamabad may preserve some value in Russia's geopolitical constructs being regarded as a 'key player' in Eurasia which ought to be considered not only for security reasons, but also as a potential transit hub for transport corridors. Moreover, Russia's diplomatic initiatives for the Afghan crisis settlement, be the 'Moscow format' or the SCO-Afghanistan Contact Group, have consistently implied Pakistan's importance in regional affairs.

France was involved in military operation in Afghanistan from 2002 to 2014 as part of US-led operation 'Enduring Freedom' and NATO's International Security Assistance Force. The whole French participation in the campaign was aimed at securing and stabilizing the Kabul region (mainly the Kapisa and Surobi districts) and training the Afghan national army. For Paris involvement in the Afghan theatre was important not only as a counter-terrorism measure, but as an indication of a great power status (Monsoni, 2009). Even though French troops' presence in the country was not popular domestically, the Nicolas Sarkozy government responded to NATO demands of additional troops' contribution and even made the decision to reintegrate with NATO military command (Kreps, 2010: 205). Some incidents with casualties among French soldiers (such as the Uzbin Valley Ambush in

August 2008) led to an emotional response in the public space and made the troops' presence in Afghanistan a matter of domestic discussion. Following a series of losses of the French contingent in late 2011 – early 2012, President Sarkozy announced suspension of training and combat aid operations by the French Army in Afghanistan. The process of troops' withdrawal was accelerated shortly after the election of François Hollande in May 2012 and was fully completed by the end of 2014 (Lafaye, 2021).

Kashmir

During the Cold War the USSR shielded India from criticism at the United Nations and in several cases was the only state to veto resolutions on the issue of Kashmir. In the 1990s however, following outreach from Pakistan Moscow's stance, especially in contrast to previous decades, became more ambiguous. New Delhi's confidence in Moscow's support was shattered after the visit of a Russian delegation to Islamabad in December 1991. The joint communiqué succeeding the talks mentioned 'the deteriorating human rights conditions in Kashmir' and also stated that 'the Russian side acknowledged Pakistan's position [on the dispute] and expressed hope that the issue would be resolved peacefully through negotiations between Pakistan and India on the basis of international agreements' (quoted in Bakshi, 1999: 1376). Indian observers and officials could not ignore the fact that for the first time Moscow referred to 'international agreements' – failing to mention the 1972 Simla Agreement – and acknowledged the existence of a human rights problem (Bakshi, 1999: 1376). President Yeltsin during his trip to India in January 1993 attempted to dispel Indian doubts by saying that Russia 'supports India's position on Kashmir firmly and unwaveringly' (Mohanty, 2001: 56). But his assurance had a short-term effect, because two months later the 'K' question was raised by Foreign Minister Kozyrev during his official visit to Pakistan.

By the end of 1990s Moscow began to support India's stance more consistently but did not rule out a mediatory role between India and Pakistan, if both would demand it. In June 2002, amidst high tensions between New Delhi and Islamabad, President Putin launched a mediation effort by inviting Atal Bihari Vajpayee and General Pervez Musharraf to Moscow for talks after holding separate meetings with each of them in Almaty, Kazakhstan. New Delhi, however, rejected this idea. A similar episode took place in 2019 after the Pulwama terror attack and airstrike exchanges between India and Pakistan. In response to the tense situation Russian Foreign Minister Sergey Lavrov did not exclude Moscow helping to mediate between the two countries and providing the venue for their talks. This 'offer' was accepted by Pakistan's Foreign Minister Shah Mahmood Qureshi, who expressed readiness to discuss the settlement, with Moscow's assistance (MOFA, 2019). India, in contrast, stated that the mediation issue was a 'fiction' and that the two sides would manage without any intermediaries (Embassy, 2019).

France's position on the issue has been clearly neutral with a perceptible pro-India course since late 2000s. In general, Paris has expressed the view that the issue should not be internationalized, but to be resolved at the bilateral level – repeating principles on the issue for Indian diplomacy. New Delhi had however expected a tougher approach from French diplomacy against Pakistan and the problem of cross-border terrorism. Throughout the 1990s and 2000s Paris preferred not raising it explicitly, but rather considered it wise to keep Islamabad engaged (Racine, 2002: 171). Unlike Russia, France has never offered to mediate between the two, even at the peaks of crisis.

Overall, both Russia and France, though generally supporting India's view of the issue, have had similar concerns regarding the potential escalation of the regional situation. In August 2019, neither Moscow nor Paris blocked Beijing's push to hold closed-door consultations on Kashmir issue, which were brought onto the UNSC agenda for the first time since 1965 (United Nations, 2019). However, in terms of perception Paris has been regarded as a defender of India's case, while Moscow's remarks on Kashmir in recent years have been less consistent in recent years creating space for interpretations and doubts (Mitra, 2019).

Conclusions and Prospects for India's Engagement with Russia and France

Taking stock of the evolution of French and Russian regional approaches, several parallels may be drawn. First, South Asia does not hold immense significance in Russia and France's respective foreign policy priorities, but the rise of Asia and India's increasing role in global affairs have made both Moscow and Paris ramp up their regional policies. Russia and France approach the region through different geopolitical visions: Moscow views South Asia through the continental prism as part of its Eurasian policy, whereas France has stepped up its regional presence by strengthening naval engagements in the Indo-Pacific. India is prone to remain an indispensable part of both strategies, particularly given New Delhi's attempts to maintain a neat balance between its maritime and continental policies.

Secondly, geopolitically France and Russia have little to vie for in the region. Neither Paris nor Moscow perceive South Asia as its sphere of influence, hence their competition in India's defence market will unlikely affect their relationship. For that matter, their divergences on Ukraine/Eastern Europe or Central Africa are more likely to act as irritants for their bilateral dialogue. Both have limited engagement in the regions of primary significance to the other. While Moscow has a nascent presence and influence in the Indian Ocean Region, France is not sufficiently involved in Eurasian affairs. Hence, each side will continue to provide India with a separate geostrategic and diplomatic agenda. Thirdly, Paris and Moscow have been instrumental for India's pursuit of global status and regional influence. Both capitals have been vocal supporters of India's inclusion in major international organizations, including the UNSC. India has also benefitted from regional cooperation with France in the Indian Ocean Region – in terms of access to French naval bases and joint naval exercises and patrols. Russia in its turn is providing Indian diplomacy with some leeway in Eurasia through interactions at the SCO and a closer engagement on the Afghan track in the wake of Kabul takeover by the Taliban.

Fourthly, since both states' interaction with New Delhi will develop along similar sectors, there may well be some natural competition for India's defence tenders between the two, though it is quite improbable that France and Russia will find themselves in a rivalry mode. Moreover, India is better off having both partners offer its state-of-the-art equipment, technologies and solutions in key areas, so that it can choose what best fits its demands and budget. From an Indian angle, there is a complementarity between France and Russia as know-how suppliers, be it in defence or space, though Indo-French cooperation in these spheres in the last decade seems to have been more dynamic than the Indo-Russian one. Fifthly, regardless of Pakistan's geopolitical role, both Moscow's and Paris's engagement with Islamabad is likely to be of limited nature. The trends in their relations with Pakistan, however, will have implications for cooperation with India. Russia's dalliance with Islamabad, even if issue-based, security- and Afghan-centred, will unavoidably unnerve India. Although Moscow continuously reassures New Delhi of not crossing India's 'red lines' in its partnership with Islamabad, this mutual understanding seems to be working until another Russia-Pakistan high-level dialogue occurs or when there is a discussion of Russia's military supplies to Pakistani armed forces. In France's case, the deterioration of its relationship with Pakistan eliminated the source of potential friction with India allowing Paris to express even more solid support to Indian positions on terrorism threats and other regional issues.

Overall, Russia retains its special position in a row of India's partners with critical importance as a traditional defence and energy supplier. The divergent perceptions of China and the US however created tensions limiting the potential for deepening partnership. Even as Moscow stands out from the rest of Indian partners with its readiness to share sensitive technologies, Russia's engagement with China and Pakistan have eroded India's trust and may constrain the scope of Indo-Russian cooperation in South Asia and the Indo-Pacific. Russia's invasion of Ukraine in February 2022 has brought additional pressure on Indian diplomacy and decision-making, though it has not led to the breakdown of ties with Moscow. New Delhi's reaction to the war in Ukraine highlighted its continuous strive to maintain a delicate equilibrium between Russia and the West while striking a balance between its diplomatic position and long-held principles. Even though New Delhi issued an explanation of vote at the UN General Assembly underlying importance of 'commitment to international law and respect for sovereignty and territorial integrity of all states' (Tirumurti, 2022), it has stopped short of openly criticizing Russia's actions.

Such approach may be explained by three factors. Firstly, even as the geopolitical situation in Europe rapidly shifted from a build-up of tension to an armed conflict, New Delhi has retained its fidelity to traditional principles of the conduct of international affairs. Presumably, India's government believes that maintaining neutrality in the times of surging antagonism between Russia and the West would allow it to achieve the core goal – that of seizing maximum opportunities from engagements with all sides. Secondly, in Indian collective memory Moscow is still remembered as a supporter of India's case in the global arena during the Cold War era – be it on Western resolutions against Kashmir, the annexation of Goa or the 1971 India–Pakistan war. There is still much continuity in how Indians have viewed USSR/ Russia's role in critical junctures for India's rise. Thirdly, New Delhi's stance is evidently driven by pragmatic considerations, such as an obvious dependency on Russia's arms supplies and the prevention of a Russia-China alliance which appears to be looming large against the backdrop of disruption in Moscow's political, economic, technological and even cultural ties with the Western powers.

France is positioning itself as a broader strategic partner for India, particularly in maritime security in the Indian Ocean. Indo-French relations are devoid of geopolitical bottlenecks with their visions for the Indo-Pacific regions being in sync. Paris also remains consistently cognisant of India's strategic concerns and diplomatic principles, adhering to which often results in New Delhi's nuanced view of regional crises. Even on the issue of conflict in Ukraine, Paris has chosen an arguably more accommodative approach to India's position than many other Indian partners. Such French adjustment to India's interests and practices coupled with a broader geopolitical concord holds promise for future cooperation and opens up avenues for a closer partnership in various domains.

References

Bakshi, Jyotsna (1999) 'Russian Policy Towards South Asia', *Strategic Analysis*, 23 (8): 1367–1397.

Balachandran, G. (2012) 'Kudankulam Nuclear Power Plant and Civil Nuclear Liability', *IDSA Issue Brief*, 9 November. Available at https://idsa.in/issuebrief/Kudankulam NuclearPowerPlantandCivilNuclearLiability_BalachandranPatil_091112 [last accessed 15 April 2021].

Balz, Dan and Drozdiak, William (1998) 'US Responds with Penalties, Persuasion', *The Washington Post*, 14 May. Available at www.washingtonpost.com/wp-srv/inatl/long term/southasia/stories/penalties051498.htm?noredirect=on [last accessed 25 May 2020].

Bhatia, Anita (1985) 'India's Space Program: Cause for Concern?', *Asian Survey*, 25 (10): 1013–1030.

Bodner, Matthew (2015) 'Russia Angles to Snatch $20Bln Indian Fighter Jet Deal From France', *The Moscow Times*, 16 February. Available at www.themoscowtim es.com/2015/02/16/russia-angles-to-snatch-20bln-indian-fighter-jet-deal-from-france -a43948 [last accessed 11 April 2021].

Chanda, Amit (2020) 'France and India Talk Submarines as Rafale Fighters Are Delivered', *Nikkei Asia*, 5 November. Available at https://asia.nikkei.com/Politics/International-relations/France-and-India-talk-submarines-as-Rafale-fighters-are-de livered [last accessed 27 April 2021].

Economic Times (2020) 'Indo-French Satellites to Trace Illegal Spillage of Oil by Ships: French Space Agency', *The Economic Times*, 4 October. Available at https://econom ictimes.indiatimes.com/news/science/indo-french-satellites-to-trace-illegal-spillage-of-oil -by-ships-french-space-agency/articleshow/78476853.cms?from=mdr [last accessed 15 June 2021].

Élysée (1998a) 'Discours de M. Jacques Chirac, Président de la République, devant les communautés d'affaires indiennes et françaises', *Élysée*, 24 January.

Élysée (1998b) 'Discours de M. Jacques Chirac, Président de la République, sur le développement des relations politiques, économiques et culturelles entre la France et l'Inde et la création d'un forum d'initiatives indo-français', *Élysée*, 26 January.

Embassy (2019) 'Interview of Ambassador of India to Russia D.B. Venkatesh Varma to Kommersant'. Available at https://indianembassy-moscow.gov.in/Interview-of-Amba ssador-kommersant-05-04-2019.php

Embassy (2021) 'Interview of Ambassador with Lenta.ru on 8th February'. Available at https://indianembassy-moscow.gov.in/ambassador-interviews-08-02-2021-1.php [last accessed 29 April 2021].

Jayaraman, K. S. (2013) 'India Drops Russia from Chandrayaan-2 Lunar Mission', *Space News*, August 15. Available at https://spacenews.com/36795india-drop s-russia-from-chandrayaan-2-lunar-mission/ [last accessed 29 May 2021].

Karaganov, Sergey *et al.* (2020) *Protecting Peace, Earth, and Freedom of choice for All Countries. New Ideas for Russia's Foreign Policy* (Moscow: Higher School of Economics Publ. House), p. 65.

Kremlin (2001) 'Statement for the Press and Answers to Questions Following Negotiations with Indian Prime Minister Atal Bihari Vajpayee', *Kremlin*, November 6. Available at http://en.kremlin.ru/events/president/transcripts/21390 [last accessed 5 May 2021].

Kreps, Sarah (2010) 'Elite Consensus as a Determinant of Alliance Cohesion: Why Public Opinion Hardly Matters for NATO-led Operations in Afghanistan', *Foreign Policy Analysis*, 6 (3): 205.

Lafaye, Christophe (2021) 'L'engagement de l'armée française en Afghanistan: 90 morts pour rien?', *The Conversation*, 14 September. Available at https://the conversation.com/lengagement-de-larmee-francaise-en-afghanistan-90-morts-pour-rien-167555 [last accessed 29 April 2022].

Lalwani, Sameer, O'Donnell, Frank, Sagerstorm, Tyler and Vasudeva, Akriti (2021) 'The Influence of Arms: Explaining the Durability of India-Russia Alignment', *The Journal of Indo-Pacific Affairs*, 4 (1): 2–41.

Lavrov, Sergey (2020) 'Foreign Minister Sergey Lavrov's Remarks at the General Meeting of the Russian International Affairs Council, *The Ministry of Foreign Affairs of the Russian Federation*, 8 December. Available at https://archive.mid.ru/ en/foreign_policy/news/-/asset_publisher/cKNonkJE02Bw/content/id/4470074 [last accessed 24 April 2022].

Lavrov, Sergey (2021) 'Foreign Minister Sergey Lavrov's Interview Given to Channel One's Bolshaya Igra (Great Game) Talk Show', 1 April. Available at https://mid.ru/ ru/foreign_policy/news/1418821/?lang=en [last accessed 24 April 2022].

Lele, Ajey (2015) 'Space Collaboration between India and France: Towards a New Era', *Asie Visions*, 78: 13–19.

MEA (2008) 'Memorandum of Understanding between the Indian Space Research Organisation and the Federal Space Agency on Joint Activities in the Field of Human Spaceflight Programme', 5 December. Available at www.mea.gov.in/Portal/LegalTreatiesDoc/RU08B0377.pdf [last accessed 1 June 2021].

MEA (2019) 'Translation of Prime Minister's Address at Community Reception in Paris', 24 August. Available at https://mea.gov.in/Speeches-Statements.htm?dtl/31760/Translation_of_Prime_Ministers_Address_at_Community_Reception_in_Paris [last accessed 11 May 2021].

MEA (2020) 'Gaganyaan Gives a Boost to India-Russia Space Partnership', 25 January. Available at https://indbiz.gov.in/gaganyaan-gives-a-boost-to-india-russia-space-partnership/ [last accessed 26 April 2022].

Menon, Rhea and Rajiv, Sharanya (2019) 'Realizing India's Strategic Interests in Central Asia', December. Available at www.india-seminar.com/2019/724/724_rhea_and_sharanya.htm [last accessed 24 April 2022].

MFA (2020) 'Foreign Minister Sergey Lavrov's Remarks and Answers to Questions at a Plenary Session of the Raisina Dialogue International Conference, New Delhi, 15 January 2020'. Available at www.mid.ru/ru/foreign_policy/news/-/asset_publisher/cKNonkJE02Bw/content/id/3994885?p_p_id=101_INSTANCE_cKNonkJE02Bw&_101_INSTANCE_cKNonkJE02Bw_languageId=en_GB [last accessed 16 April 2021].

MFA (2021) 'Foreign Minister Sergey Lavrov's Remarks and Answers to Media Questions at a Joint News Conference with Foreign Minister of the Islamic Republic of Pakistan Makhdoom Shah Mahmood Qureshi, Islamabad', 7 April. Available at www.mid.ru/foreign_policy/news/-/asset_publisher/cKNonkJE02Bw/content/id/4666612?p_p_id=101_INSTANCE_cKNonkJE02Bw&_101_INSTANCE_cKNonkJE02Bw_languageId=en_GB [last accessed 10 June 2021].

Ministry of Europe (2021) 'French Strategy in the Indo-Pacific', July. Available at www.diplomatie.gouv.fr/en/country-files/asia-and-oceania/the-indo-pacific-region-a-priority-for-france/[last accessed 5 December 2021].

Mint (2019) 'Gaganyaan: Russia Offers India Semi-cryogenic Engine Technology', 25 August. Available at www.livemint.com/science/news/gaganyaan-russia-offers-india-semi-cryogenic-engine-technology-1566735729879.html [last accessed 26 April 2022].

Mitra, Devirupa (2019) 'In a First, Russia Talks of UN Resolutions on Kashmir', *The Wire*, 18 August. Available at https://thewire.in/diplomacy/kashmir-article-370-russia-un-security-council [last accessed 14 June 2021].

MOFA (2019) 'Telephone Call between Foreign Minister and the Foreign Minister of the Russian Federation', 1 March.

Mohan, C. Raja (2018) 'France: India's New Russia', *The Indian Express*, 9 March. Available at https://indianexpress.com/article/opinion/columns/france-indias-new-russia-emmanuel-macron-narendra-modi-5091279/ [last accessed 08 June 2020].

Mohanty, Arun (2001) *Indo-Russian Relations: From Yeltsin to Putin* (1991–2001) (Moscow: IKAR), pp. 33–56.

Monsoni, Guillem (2009) 'Redefining France's Role in Afghanistan: Need for better Strategy', 22 January. Available at https://idsa.in/idsastrategiccomments/redefiningFranceRoleinAfghanistan_gmonsonis_220109 [last accessed 28 April 2022].

Pajon, Céline (2020) 'France's Indo-Pacific Strategy and the Quad Plus', *Journal of Indo-Pacific Affairs*, 3 (5): 165–178.

Pande, Aparna (2019) 'In Modi Era, France Has Replaced Russia as India's New Best Friend', *The Print*, 22 August. Available at https://theprint.in/opinion/in-m

odi-era-france-has-replaced-russia-as-indias-new-best-friend/280431/ [last accessed 08 June 2020].

Racine, Jean-Luc (2002) 'The Indo-French Strategic Dialogue: Bilateralism and World Perceptions', in Sumit Ganguly (ed.), *India as an Emerging Power* (London: Frank Cass), pp. 161–187.

Rajagopalan, Rajeswari Pillai (2019) 'A New India-France Alliance?' *The Diplomat*, 3 September. Available at https://thediplomat.com/2019/09/a-new-india-france-allia nce/ [last accessed 08 June 2020].

Rajagopalan, Rajeswari Pillai (2019) 'Russia-China Strategic Alliance Gets a New Boost with Missile Early Warning System', 28 October. Available at www.orfon line.org/research/russia-china-strategic-alliance-gets-a-new-boost-with-missile-early -warning-system-57094/ [last accessed 11 June 2021].

RFERL (1998b) 'Yeltsin Trip to India Postponed', 6 January. Available at www.rferl. org/a/1141566.html [last accessed 5 June 2021].

Saint-Mézard, Isabelle (2015) *The French Strategy in the Indian Ocean and the Potential for Indo-French Cooperation* (RSIS), pp. 3–7.

Sarkar, Jayita (2021) 'From the Dependable to the Demanding Partner: The Rene-gotiation of French Nuclear Cooperation with India, 1974–80', *Cold War History*, 21 (3): 301–318.

Shukla, Vinay (1999) 'Russia in South Asia: A View from India', in Gennady Chufrin (ed.), *Russia and Asia: The Emerging Security Agenda* (Stockholm: SIPRI), p. 252.

Sibal, Sidhant (2020) 'France Replaces Russia as India's Best Friend? New Delhi Says Both Are Important', 6 June. Available at www.dnaindia.com/india/report-fra nce-replaces-russia-as-india-s-best-friend-new-delhi-says-both-are-important-28270 89 [last accessed 07 June 2020].

Sood, Rakesh (2020) 'Why France Is a Reliable Strategic Partner for India', 20 Jan-uary. Available at www.orfonline.org/research/why-france-is-a-reliable-strategic-pa rtner-for-india-60480/ [last accessed 05 June 2020].

Tirumurti, T.S. (2022) 'Statement by Ambassador T.S. Tirumurti Permanent Repre-sentative of India to the United Nations. Explanation of Vote,'2 March. Available at www.pminewyork.gov.in/IndiaatUNGA?id=NDUyNA, [last accessed 27 April 2022].

Topychkanov, Petr V. (2018) 'US–Soviet/Russian Dialogue on the Nuclear Weapons Programme of India', *Strategic Analysis*, 42 (3): 251–259.

Trenin, Dmitri, Kulakov, Oleg, Malashenko, Alexey and Topychkanov, Petr (2014) 'A Russian Strategy for Afghanistan After the Coalition Troop Withdrawal'. Available at https://carnegieendowment.org/files/CMC_Article_Afganistan_Eng14.pdf [last accessed 24 April 2022].

United Nations (2019) 'UN Security Council Discusses Kashmir, China Urges India and Pakistan to Ease Tensions', *UN News*. Available at https://news.un.org/en/ story/2019/08/1044401 [last accessed 27 May 2021].

Unnithan, Sandeep (2021) 'Why India Could Be Leasing a Second Nuclear Powered Attack Submarine from Russia', *India Today*, 4 September. Available at www.india today.in/india-today-insight/story/why-india-is-leasing-a-second-nuclear-powered-a ttack-submarine-from-russia-1849277-2021-09-04 [last accessed 27 April 2022].

UPI (1998a) 'Yeltsin Regrets Indian Nuclear Test', 12 May. Available at www.upi. com/Archives/1998/05/12/UPI-Focus-Yeltsin-regrets-Indian-nuclear-test/437889494 5600/ [last accessed 22 April 2022].

Wezeman, Pieter D., Kuimova Alexandra and Wezeman Siemon T. (2021) *Trends in International Arms Transfers, 2020: SIPRI Fact Sheet* (Stockholm: SIPRI), p. 2.

8 India and the United States

Friends Elsewhere, Foes at the United Nations

Chirayu Thakkar

In 2009, Teresita Schaffer, former Deputy Assistant Secretary of State for South Asia, wrote in an essay that it is 'conventional wisdom that the United States and India can work together bilaterally, but not multilaterally' (Schaffer, 2009: 79). Schaffer made this observation a year after both India and the US ratified the Civilian Nuclear Agreement and a year before President Barack Obama loudly and clearly endorsed India's bid for a permanent seat at the UN Security Council (UNSC) in 2010. For those who have seen the nadir of 1998 – the point at which New Delhi became an almost pariah for Washington for crossing the nuclear red line – this was nothing short of a bilateral high point. Yet, when Schaffer wrote her essay, India's support was zero on those UN General Assembly (UNGA) votes marked as 'important' by the US State Department (excluding consensus votes).

The contemporary story of India–US relations is one of a profound paradox. On the one hand, trade, strategic, commercial, defence, and people-to-people ties have risen meteorically between 2000–2019. Contrasting this bilateral warmth, their lack of alignment in the global governance arena is more characteristic of their Cold War-era discord. During the Cold War, its non-aligned identity and developmental interests put India naturally in a diametrically opposed position to the US. However, the end of the Cold War, the liberalization of the economy, and the eventual embrace of Washington in the early 2000s should have reoriented India's global governance posturing. However, as I demonstrate through voting numbers, neither altering identity nor changing interests modified India's voting behaviour. The key question is why the improved bilateral warmth has not permeated multilateral decision-making? Or, in the words of Schaffer, why India and the US can work together bilaterally, but not multilaterally?

In this chapter, I answer this question in two parts. First, while the early 1990s marked the end of the Cold War, though taking away the essential backdrop for the non-alignment project, it also marked the beginning of India's formal campaign for a UNSC permanent seat. The 'status seeker' identity of an emerging power that wants a higher status in global governance overpowered its other identities and interests, including the new-fangled warmth with Washington. Tactically, the logic of numbers game, the policy

DOI: 10.4324/9781003305132-11

of non-alienation towards larger voting blocs, and preserving the rights of the UNGA against the Council, among others, became some of the decisive factors driving New Delhi's multilateral calculus. Second, some thematic and state-specific choices that India has made over the years further constrained it from cooperating with Washington and its emerging partners in the West. The chapter deliberately excludes multilateral financial and trade organizations such as the World Bank, International Monetary Fund, or the World Trade Organization, which have a different dynamic even if New Delhi might share certain attitudes within those organizations (Narlikar, 2006). Apart from statistics and India's stated positions recorded through statements and voting explanations, the analysis is also informed by interviews with a dozen Indian and US diplomats, including former ambassadors, permanent representatives, and diplomats from respective bureaus.

The chapter is organized into four sections. The first section identifies the central puzzle examining India's voting records for all UNGA votes as well as 'important' votes as marked by the US State Department. This is not merely a vacuous academic exercise, as I demonstrate, but also an ongoing policy debate in Washington. The second section outlines the first part of the argument by establishing the provenance of India's formal campaign and its impact on India's multilateral calculus. The third section examines India's thematic and state-specific choices through a qualitative analysis of its voting behaviour. The concluding section captures some emerging trends where New Delhi has deliberately accommodated Washington. It also raises a crucial point that both states' behaviour within the UN is dictated by their respective positions and not by the strength of their bilateral ties. It indicates a relative impermeability of international organizations where the changing external context and emerging warmth between major powers is reflected quite gradually. If India's behaviour continues to be dictated by the imperatives of higher status and power, the US remains an unflinching, status-quoist permanent member. Hence, both these states are locked into an adversarial position within multilateral institutions, which will continue to remain in place until India's status inconsistency (i.e. its desire for a permanent UN Security Council seat) is resolved.

Understanding and Quantifying the Puzzle

Changing identity and interests have profoundly impacted India's foreign policy outlook in the past few decades. Two events played a seismic role in this paradigm shift. The first was the end of the Cold War, which until then provided the essential backdrop for India to remain non-aligned between two blocs. The second was its embrace of the West, or the US in particular, after the nadir of May 1998 nuclear tests, when New Delhi briefly became a near pariah for Washington. No other work has captured this shift better than C. Raja Mohan's *Crossing the Rubicon*. As Raja Mohan pithily notes, 'India's engagement with the world since the early 1990s posits a fundamental change of course and a reconstitution of its core premises. Whether it was the de-emphasis of non-alignment or the new embrace of the US ... a radically different foreign policy orientation emerged *by the turn of the millennium*' (Raja Mohan, 2003: 262–263, emphasis added). What Raja Mohan documented in the early 2000s was a mere inflection point. Today, India is a vital pillar of the Quad, widely considered a US-led alliance against China; it has in place four military logistics and intelligence sharing pacts with Washington; its trade ties with the US are swelling and only second to China; and the political warmth between the two sides is unprecedented.

One would naturally expect the reconstitution of core foreign policy premises to be reflected in all foreign policy domains, including multilateralism. For instance, as the former Soviet states adopted democracy and capitalism, their UN voting started aligning with that of the US (Kim & Russett, 1996), even before they were formally inducted into the North Atlantic Treaty Organization (NATO) security architecture. On global governance issues, it is generally observed that plural democracies with a free-market economy, the rule of law, and strategic proximity with the US tend to make choices similar to the US. It is an indicator of their assimilation into the US-led liberal international order. However, when one puts India's support to the US on 'important votes' as marked by the US State Department since the turn of the millennium, the picture is baffling. Of all the US's strategic partners, India's support is only slightly better than Pakistan and Egypt (see Figure 8.1), neither of which can boast any trade, defence, or strategic ties with the US compared to India. To put the numbers in context, both Japan and Australia – the two other Quad members along with the United States and India – have aligned 80 percent of the time with the US while India's alignment stands dismally at about 20 percent.

Two caveats are necessary here. First, US positions are not always static. They can vary dramatically between and within administrations (for policy fluctuations across administrations, see Thakkar, 2021a: 3). An extreme example is the Trump administration's decision to declare Jerusalem as Israel's capital, something which when put to vote (ES-10/L.22), some of the US and Israel's closest allies could not endorse. Second, sometimes, the US's stance is at stark variance with normatively desirable choices. For example, the Trump administration did not join a near-unanimous UNGA resolution declaring the Covid-19 vaccine as a global good (Lederer, 2020). However, most 'important votes' pertain to policy issues that are consistent across administrations, and on which, Washington expects support from allies and partners.

Comparing India's overall percentage agreement with the US, Russia, and China (see Figure 8.2), one notes a secular trend continuing prior to and after the Cold War save for some quirks vis-à-vis the Soviet Union around its disintegration. The larger question is why India's UNGA voting has registered such consistency despite major foreign policy reorientations over the years.

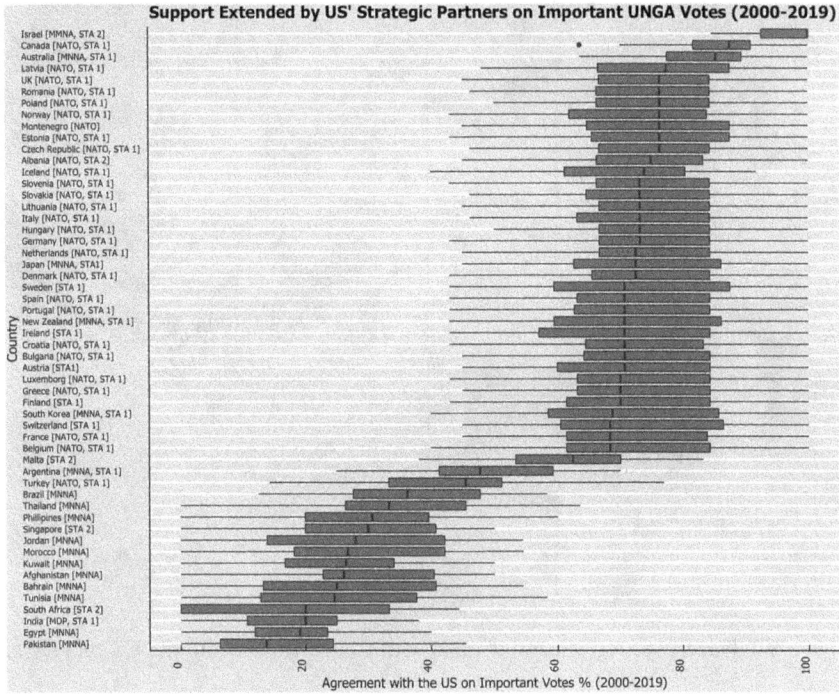

Figure 8.1 Support extended by US strategic partners on important UNGA votes (2000–2019).
Source: Chirayu Thakkar

The editors of a noted contribution on Indian multilateralism observed that 'post-Cold War India has started to reflect a more pragmatic, *realpolitik* approach to multilateralism and multipolarity – which is evident in its multiple alignment policy' (Sidhu, et al., 2013: 5). To an extent, this observation is appropriate as India neither demonstrates the dogmatism of the past nor resorts to the shrill anti-Western rhetoric that used to upset Western diplomats. Nor is there a non-aligned caucus in the UNSC anymore. Despite these indicators, voting numbers present a different story. And that story offers a much cautious version compared to what scholars have been projecting. For example, elsewhere Raja Mohan notes that given the significant rise in India's capabilities, its global governance outlook is reorienting from 'universalism of the weak' towards 'internationalism of the strong' (Raja Mohan, 2010). Later, in an essay on the evolution of Indian multilateralism, Raja Mohan defines the post-2000 Indian multilateralism as 'responsible multilateralism' marked by the 'erosion of traditional third worldism' (Raja Mohan, 2013: 35ff). However, scholars and practitioners examining India's behaviour closely differ in their assessment. Amrita Narlikar's work on India's negotiation strategies finds New Delhi's sustained emphasis on

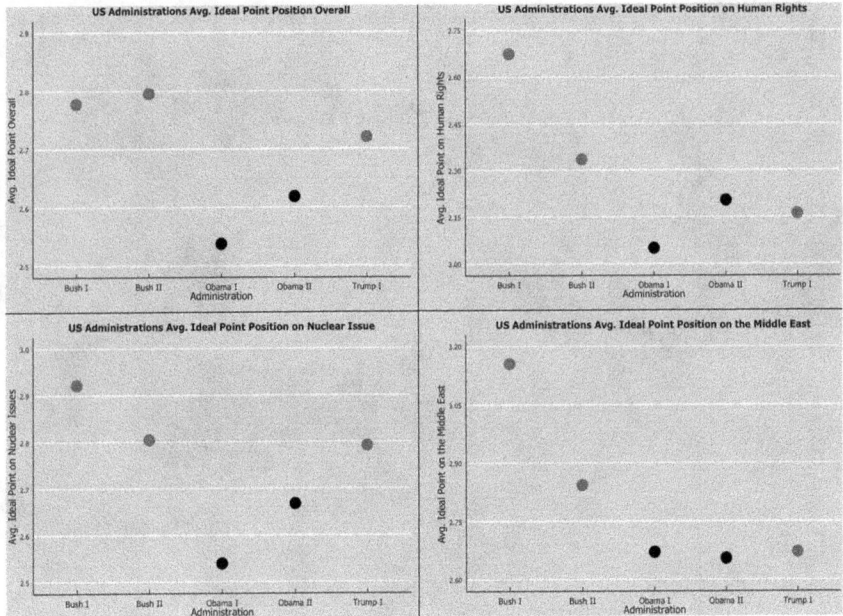

Figure 8.2 Percentage Agreement of India with China, Russia, and the US on Overall
UNGA Voting
Source: Bailey, Strezhnev & Voeten (2017)

distributive strategies regardless of its continuously augmenting economic
and political stature (Narlikar, 2006). Similarly, India's former Foreign
Secretary Shyam Saran notes, 'this tradition of activism [at the UN] continues today, although it is manifest in a posture different from that of the
cold war era, responding to a vastly transformed international geopolitical
terrain and a greatly transformed India itself' (Saran, 2013: 44). As noted,
indeed there are some changes in the form of this activism. Nevertheless, the
central puzzle remains. Why did India's altering identity and interests, strategic proximity to the West, and changing international environment not
impact its multilateral positions?

The lack of US–India convergence on global governance issues is not
merely an Indian foreign policy puzzle, it is an ongoing policy debate in
Washington too. From time to time, US diplomats and analysts have asked:
can India be a meaningful partner of the US in global governance? (Dormandy, 2007; McDonald & Patrick, 2010; Schaffer, 2009). From the US
viewpoint, it is both an insignificant and a significant question depending on
one's approach towards the relationship and expected payoffs. The first is a
lenient and pragmatic view that overlooks the US's divergences with India in
multilateral forums as the relationship pays economic, strategic, and political
dividends bilaterally, whereas the costs of divergences at the multilateral level

are negligible. This view also believes that 'India's interests will be parallel to those of the US more often than not, but they will not be identical. Regardless, *this should not be the test of a responsible international stakeholder*' (Dormandy, 2007: 128; emphasis added).

In contrast, the second view stringently gauges Washington's multilateral interests against its investments. The US's stakes in India have been steadily increasing – it has invested in India as a counterbalance to China, installed it into the nuclear order, and is prepared to support New Delhi's bid to join the global high table in the UNSC when the time comes. These investments in India's future are underwritten by India's assessment as being a state that has the necessary traits of an international ally – being a pluralist democracy and free-market economy, embracing the rule of law, and a host of other shared values. Such hopes from India augmented as it shed the shibboleths of non-alignment and Third Worldism. As an undeclared ally or a major partner, Washington 'looks ... for endorsement – or at least not overt rejection – of American policy positions. This expectation has resulted in disappointment in Washington when Indian officials appear to embrace positions that Americans see as impossible to understand' (Kaye, et al., 2015: 28). Hence, in private exchanges, US diplomats remind their Indian counterparts that India's 'obstinate role [at the UN] is increasingly at odds with our emerging strategic proximity' (Wikileaks Cable: 06NEWDELHI4827_a).

In policymaking so far, the lenient view has trumped the stringent one as India's dissonance with the US has not imposed a major cost – some of New Delhi's positions may be status quo-ist, moralist, Third World-ist, or frozen in the time warp of the Cold War, but they do not include a disruptive agenda that threatens the foundations of the liberal international order. Such accommodation from Washington has allowed New Delhi to continue its *à la cartism* – creating issue-based alignment with various global powers in international forums – without preventing it from negotiating its rise with the US (Kaye, et al., 2015). With a changing global order facing an unprecedented strain on rules by a common adversary like China, the costs of their inability to work together in the global governance arena can be much higher today.

Continuity over Change

Despite the radical reconstitution of foreign policy foundations since the end of the Cold War, voting records at the UN indicate significant continuity and subtle changes. I explain this puzzle of multilateralism in two parts. In the first part, I argue that the end of the Cold War was coeval with the inception of India's formal campaign for UNSC permanent membership, which accentuated the element of a 'number games' in India's multilateral calculus. Instead of unshackling New Delhi from its non-aligned club, the imperative of the numbers game further deepened its engagement to preserve the group's cohesion, which India can marshal to its advantage when the time of UN reform comes. In the second part, I look at other areas in two sub-sections – thematic choices and region-specific issues – to indicate that not all continuity can be explained by the logic of numbers game. Here, I investigate other compulsions forcing India to continue its Cold War-era postures in numerous domains, limiting its cooperation with its emerging partners (i.e. Washington and the West).

India's UNSC Campaign and the Numbers Game

During the Cold War, the Non-Aligned Movement (NAM) within the UNGA allowed India to exhibit leadership as an active third bloc, even though the underlying rationale of the movement was independence from blocs. As Shyam Saran testifies, historically, non-alignment activism at the UN has 'provided a useful platform on which India could mobilize the numerically growing constituency of newly emerging independent states in support of its own policy objectives' (Saran, 2013: 44). In the 1980s and even in the early 1990s, the animating goals were more equitable and distributive outcomes in global governance that would favour many, including India, and not a chosen few from the First World. It was a convenient union of a non-aligned identity with developmental interests. The disintegration of the Soviet Union in 1991 eliminated the *raison d'être* for non-alignment whereas the liberalization of Indian economy, forced by the International Monetary Fund in the wake of the balance of payment crisis, in the same year started chipping away developmental imperatives.

Although poverty alleviation still remains a challenge, in roughly a decade by 2003, India had formally joined the donors club with its own development assistance program (Chaturvedi & Mendiratta, 2015). Moreover, New Delhi embraced Washington at the turn of the millennium as non-proliferation wonks in the US made peace with India's nuclear status, and eventually, by 2005, they were working overtime to install India in the global nuclear order (Raja Mohan, 2006). Neither of the three transformations – the end of the Cold War, increased economic heft, and the proximity to Washington – was able to reorient India's multilateral outlook entirely. By the early-1990s, it was because another potent variable was impacting India's multilateral calculus – its formal campaign to acquire a UNSC seat.

Although India made its UNSC permanent seat ambitions abundantly clear since independence, it did not culminate into a formal campaign until 1994. Indian diplomats usually credit Brajesh Mishra, India's permanent representative between 1979 and 1981, who later served as India's first National Security Advisor under the Vajpayee administration, for initiating the push for equitable representation in the Security Council (Mukerji, 2018; Sreenivasan, 2008). Brajesh Mishra, as India's Permanent Representative to the UN, galvanized ten non-aligned countries to move a joint resolution in the General Assembly (A/34/246) on 14 November 1979 that demanded equitable representation and increase in the membership of the Council. Despite ground-breaking efforts, the text of Mishra's resolution demanded enlargement of the Council on the grounds of increased UN membership. The text did not press for the expansion of permanent members.

However, the banal text's dormant existence continued on the Assembly's agenda until it resurfaced in 1992 in a newer form on the eve of the UN's golden jubilee (Permanent Mission of Saint Vincent and the Grenadines, 2018, p. 15). In 1992, India introduced a new resolution (A/RES/47/62) that sought proposals from member states on the expansion of the Council, based on which an Open-ended Working Group under the President of the General Assembly was formed in the subsequent year (A/RES/48/26). On the Indian side, who re-initiated this process remains a mystery. In his memoirs, Sreenivasan (2008), then Deputy Permanent Representative, claims to have suggested to his boss Chinmaya Gharekhan, then India's Permanent Representative to the UN, that he seek member states' opinions (which Amb. Gharekhan refused to corroborate in personal correspondence with the author). Both Gharekhan (2006) and J. N. Dixit (1996), then Foreign Secretary, are also silent about who initiated the proposals in their own recollections. Even if the 1992/1993 resolutions elicited opinions and formed working groups, the resolution texts do not mention expansion in the permanent category. Only from 1995 onwards, in the proceedings of the working group, was the possibility of adding permanent members entertained officially for the first time (cf. A/49/965).

Some scholars attribute the inception of India's quest to Prime Minister Rao's speech at a Security Council summit organized by British Prime Minister John Major in January 1992 (Malone & Mukherjee, 2013: 170). However, if one closely examines the speech, Rao's emphasis is still tied to expanding membership, similar to the 1979 Brajesh Mishra resolution, without making a clear call for India's permanent representation. Rao stated, 'as the composition of the General Assembly has trebled since its inception, the size of the Security Council cannot remain constant any longer' (Ministry of External Affairs, 1993). The MEA's *Foreign Affairs Records* for 1993 then shows that Indian ministers and diplomats had started canvassing for an expanded permanent membership and pitching New Delhi's case in their bilateral interactions. In the same year, at the 48th General Assembly, India's junior foreign minister, Dinesh Singh, indirectly claimed for India's inclusion by emphasizing criteria for permanent members. It was only in 1994 that India's then Commerce Minister and head of UNGA delegation, Pranab Mukherjee, made an explicit case for India's permanent membership. Speaking at the 49th General Assembly on 3 October 1994, Mukherjee stated that 'on the basis of any criteria – population, size of economy, contribution to the maintenance of international peace and security and to peace-keeping or future potential – India deserves to be a permanent member of the Security Council' (Mukherjee, 1994).

Subsequently, when asked in the *Lok Sabha*, whether India has formally staked a claim for permanent membership, another junior minister, R. L. Bhatia, referred to Pranab Mukherjee's statement (Lok Sabha, 1994a: 27), making apparent that the UNGA speech was the formal proposition from the Indian government's perspective. In the same session of the parliament, a resolution affirming the need for UN Security Council reform was passed

(Lok Sabha, 1994b: 2–3). Although Mukherjee got this historic opportunity of formally inaugurating India's UNSC quest, being the Commerce minister, he gave the credit to Prime Minister Rao (Mukherjee, 2016).

The formal campaign vastly impacted India's multilateral calculus, providing New Delhi with fresh grounds to continue investing in the cohesiveness of the non-aligned group. First, Indian decision-makers understood that on the judgement day of UNSC reform, it needed the goodwill of as many blocs and constituencies as possible. Any reform process would need concurrence, with a two-thirds majority, of the UNGA, where the principle of 'one state, one vote' applies. By the end of the Cold War, UNGA voting had become a numbers game with most states voting cohesively on group lines (Iida, 1998). Given that the numbers game between two constituencies of varying size – the developing world as represented by the G77/NAM and the much smaller developed world – it was natural that India would be swayed by size. This realization grew stronger after India, along with Brazil, Germany, and Japan (the G4), failed to secure necessary support in 2005 for their UNSC reform proposal (A/59/L.64), despite the significant concession of forgoing veto powers for newly minted permanent members. Moreover, India's developmental challenges were not dissipating anytime soon despite the growing aggregate economic might, making common cause with the G77/NAM constituency expedient in certain cases.

Second, given the desire to be in the good books of as many constituencies as possible, India acquired a key voting trait of offending as few groups as possible. Hence, India's once practiced policy of non-alignment transformed into a policy of non-alienation, which requires it to not alienate any major bloc, group, or constituency in international forums. A corollary of this thought was, as one former diplomat identified to me, if India's vote is not going to change the outcome, it is better to abstain than alienate by voting with the minority (Indian diplomat quoted in Thakkar, 2021a: 5). Thus, India became notoriously known for abstentions, a policy criticized domestically as too risk-averse (Malik, 2012).

Third, until India does secure a position at the global high table, it wants as many issues as possible to be dealt with at the UNGA level, where it can assert its leadership and secure its interests. Therefore, New Delhi actively resists any attempt at expansion of the council's remit. For instance, when the UNSC called an informal meeting (known as Arria-formula meeting) on 'The Security Dimension of Climate Change,' India reacted adversely as it was understood to be the P5's way of encroaching on a global issue. Speaking at the meeting, India's then Deputy Permanent Representative, Manjeev Singh Puri registered protest by pointing out that 'merely adding the words security dimension, [the issue of climate change] does not become a matter fit for discussing in the Security Council' (Puri, 2013). Some scholars also maintain that India actively tries to expand the UNGA clout against the UNSC, leading the P5 to agree to expand the council to defuse the threat of a strong assembly (Mukherjee & Malone, 2013). Some Indian diplomats, such as former Deputy Permanent Representative Ajai Malhotra, have candidly confessed that India's 'real interest' in exploiting the UNGA-UNSC divide 'is to promote its candidacy to join the UN Security Council' (Wikileaks Cable: 06USUNNEWYORK1033_a).

These three traits define India's approach towards numbers. The final factor that impinges on India's decision-making is the attitude of India's decision makers, both the political/strategic elite and diplomats. Indian political leaders and strategic thinkers hanker for a multipolar world, meaning India would not lean towards any one state on all issues, trying to balance between major powers. On the other hand, some Indian diplomats have been known for a dogmatic commitment towards non-alignment (later recast as 'strategic autonomy'), even after the end of the Cold War (Schaffer & Schaffer, 2016). Their personal outlook continued to manifest as a certain frigid approach towards the West incommensurate with the increasing political warmth. India's former Permanent Representative Nirupem Sen, who some foreign diplomats identified as an 'unreformed Communist' (Wikileaks Cable: 06USUNNEWYORK1254_a) and a 'dyed-in-the-wool NAM advocate' (Wikileaks Cable: 09NEWDELHI877_a), is a case in point. Given his acerbic rhetoric and uncooperative attitude towards the US at the time when India was negotiating the Nuclear Deal, Foreign Secretary Shyam Saran had to deputize another diplomat, Ajai Malhotra, to look after Washington's complaints (Wikileaks Cable: 06USUNNEWYORK1033_a). With a generational shift, such legacy dogmatism no more seems to be the case these days.

India's 'status inconsistency' (Basrur & Sullivan de Estrada, 2017: 7) – defined here as the discrepancy between New Delhi's permanent seat aspiration and its current status – has shaped distinct behavioural dynamics. It is underpinned by a unique logic of numbers game that has not allowed the newer foreign policy orientation to decisively permeate its multilateral behaviour. India's newfangled multialigned identity and its proximate interests to Washington have not overpowered the blend of identity and interests of a perpetual 'status seeker' at the UN. Hence, a perplexing foreign policy duality emerged for New Delhi. Outside the UN, India hewed closely to its emerging partners in bilateral and plurilateral arrangements; inside the UN, the bonds of non-alignment with its past partners remain unfazed. This frustrated and flummoxed many in the West, most recently during the 2022 Ukraine–Russia crisis. However, it seems that until New Delhi's status inconsistency remains unresolved, this foreign policy duality will continue. Some of the continuities in New Delhi's behaviour is enforced by substantive constraints, which I examine in the subsequent section.

Thematic and State-Specific Choices

As the well-known maxim goes, where one stands depends on where one sits. India's divergence with the US also remains a function of particular choices it has made in international affairs, both for major governance themes and state- or region-specific foreign policy tilts. In this section, I first examine some key thematic areas where India and the US are at variance followed by country- and region-specific divergences.

On the key issue of non-proliferation, India mostly votes against resolutions pressing for treaties such as the Non-Proliferation Treaty or Comprehensive Nuclear Test Ban Treaty, to which it remains a non-signatory. India has always believed that these treaties are discriminatory in nature and perpetuate 'nuclear apartheid,' with the world divided into nuclear haves and have-nots (Singh, 2007). Instead, India presses for total and non-discriminatory elimination of nuclear weapons through two annual resolutions – 'Reducing Nuclear Danger' (draft text: A/C.1/73/L.43) and the 'Convention on the Prohibition of the Use of Nuclear Weapons' (draft text: A/C.1/73/L.44) – which is met with stiff opposition from the P5, including the US and its treaty allies. The case of India–US disagreement on nuclear weapons is a classic case of what Bailey et al. (2017: 7) term as the difference between 'revealed preferences' versus 'true preferences'. While both states revealed preferences – the US's maintaining the privileges of the five nuclear weapons states (NWS) and India's insistence on total nuclear disarmament – are at odds with each other, they are not their true preferences. In reality, Washington has made peace with India's nuclear status. Regardless, the discrepancy in their revealed preferences remains due to both states structural differences as a recognized NWS and as an unrecognized one. The difference on conventional weapons is less stark (Schaffer, 2009: 73).

On economic issues, usually dealt within the Second Committee of the General Assembly, India mostly sides with the Global South on trade liberalization, debt relief, development assistance, global economic and financial governance, and sustainable development, among others. Interestingly, Indian diplomats identify themselves in the 'grey zone' between the developing and the developed worlds (Wikileaks Cable: 06NEWDELHI4827_a). Even if India has entered into the G20 club and frequently flirts with the G7 by virtue of its aggregate economic might, its developmental imperatives neatly resonate with G77. Therefore, within the Second Committee and outside – be it financial and trade institutions such as WTO or international climate negotiations – India is often found under the Global South's tent clamouring for distributive justice (Narlikar, 2006). Such rhetoric also provides New Delhi with a convenient shield to ward off international pressures, when the world expects it to do more based on its aggregate size. For instance, when India was getting isolated in the world opinion for not yet committing to 'net-zero' carbon emissions, India's Commerce Minister Piyush Goyal parried such salvos by conveniently placing itself with the developing world, which is yet to enjoy fully the fruits of low-cost energy to pursue their development agenda (Laskar, 2021). Analysts in Washington have usually flagged in red this Indian trait of assuming the 'developing country' mantle and hewing closely with the NAM bloc (McDonald & Patrick, 2010), to which Indian analysts advise of utilizing this goodwill to bridge the gap between both worlds (Pant & Thakkar, 2021).

Another important sticking point between both states is the human rights records of third countries. Indian diplomats privately admit the US approach as 'finger pointing' and 'name and shame' to which India does not readily agree to (Wikileaks Cable: 06NEWDELHI759_a). India's reservations are threefold. First, in the past, India has been at the receiving end in multi-lateral organizations for the management of secessionist movements within its territory, particularly in Kashmir. On the debate between 'external-intervention', even a non-military one, and 'sovereignty', New Delhi has been consistently and squarely on the sovereignty side due to its own desire to prevent external interventions in the Kashmir dispute. Such a stance hardened after militancy erupted in Kashmir, a reversal from its interven-tionist stance during the 1971 Bangladesh war (Chacko, 2018). For such an unflinching posture, Indian strategic thinkers are sometimes called 'sovereignty hawks' (Ganguly & Sridharan, 2013). Second, India sees human rights resolutions as a precursor to regime change operations, which then become a theatre for great power politics, for instance in Syria or Libya (Puri, 2016). In UN parlance, the issue falls under the rubric of Responsi-bility to Protect, a doctrine India finds difficult to embrace (Hall, 2019). Finally, as one Indian diplomat pointed it to me, there is a fundamental dif-ference in approach between both states: the American side believes naming someone brings them to the negotiation table, while the Indian side thinks that name-calling should be the last resort (Indian diplomat quoted in Thakkar, 2021a: 6). Given New Delhi's beliefs in political solutions, it does not readily agree to naming and shaming, which it believes forecloses the path of diplomacy.

While the US feels that India fails to adequately support it on human rights issues, India has a reciprocal feeling for Washington due to its luke-warm support on India's pet project of 'Comprehensive Convention on International Terrorism'. Given the continuous assault India faces from terror groups emanating from Pakistan, it has been at the forefront of sup-porting international instruments to curb and combat terrorism. Currently, India is a party to all 13 multilateral anti-terror instruments (Ministry of External Affairs, 2014). India first plunged into action in 1996/97 to negoti-ate a global convention on terrorism through a General Assembly resolution (A/RES/51/210) that formed an Ad Hoc Committee. After six years, the Committee produced its first draft in 2002 (A/57/37), which has since been in limbo due to the politics surrounding it. As India's former Permanent Representative Syed Akbaruddin indicated, the Arab world remains the key holdout as an overarching definition of terrorism can adversely affect the Palestinian movement (Lakshman, 2020). Nevertheless, the US is also known to pull the plug on this issue behind the scenes, which New Delhi resents. There are also other legacy issues, such as decolonization, UN administra-tion, a larger say in peacekeeping operations by troop contributing countries, and the powers of the Secretary General, among others, where India and the US have differed historically and continue to do so.

Apart from thematic choices, India, like any other state, has to take sides between feuding countries at the UN. On the enduring issue of Israel-Palestine, where the US unwaveringly supports Israel, India has leaned towards the Palestinian cause because of its energy dependency on the Arab world and having significant Muslim population at home. More recently, India has occasionally taken Israel's side (Basu, 2019) to indicate flexibility, signal some sort of equanimity to Tel Aviv, and most importantly, hint to the Arab world that India's support to Palestine is dependent on their reciprocal neutrality on the Kashmir issue between India and Pakistan. Another set of state-specific issues are those where the US and Russia are in direct contestation. Russia has been the top supplier of critical arms and ammunition to India, as well as a consistent veto provider in the UNSC when the United States was still balancing between India and Pakistan. Moreover, with an increasingly belligerent China, New Delhi wants Moscow to remain neutral in an India–China crisis scenario. India's dilemma of choosing between a historical relationship (Russia) and an emerging relationship (US) becomes more acute when it is an elected member on the Council, as happened during 2011–12 (including cases like Syria) as well as most recently during a 2021–22 stint concerning the Russia–Ukraine conflict.

Significantly, India has altered its stance from supporting the Soviet Union during the Hungarian Crisis in 1956 and the Soviet invasion of Afghanistan in 1979 to a neutral position as seen concerning the Russian annexation of Crimea in 2014. However, during the 2014 Crimean annexation, India extended vocal support to Moscow by stating that Moscow has 'legitimate Russian interests' (PTI, 2014), despite abstaining from the UNGA resolution (68/24). However, abstentions in cases where Washington and Moscow are in direct conflict are ironically not construed as abstentions in the Western media. India was widely censured for not condemning Russian war on Ukraine in 2022. Although India continues its balancing act for obvious reasons – multipolarity, arms dependence, Russian neutrality with China, and historical partnership, the West fails to appreciate that India draws a red line concerning Russia's methods of achieving its political goals. When New Delhi realized that poisoning ex-spy Sergei Skripal was unacceptable, it abstained from an Organization for the Prohibition of Chemical Weapons vote, which Moscow lost in part due to 17 abstentions (Roy Choudhary, 2018). Similarly, India, which had thoroughly eschewed from condemning Russian aggression in Ukraine, censured the dastardly killing of civilians in Bucha. Despite such red lines, given its overall tendency of not pointing fingers which forecloses the path of diplomacy, something I have discussed earlier, it is unlikely India will get openly confrontational with Moscow.

India's voting patterns have also been more consistent with China's than the US. It is primarily because China and India both want to court the developing world (Sullivan de Estrada & Foot, 2019). Sometimes, India accommodates China in the hope of calmer north-eastern borders, which has proven futile with increasing instances of Chinese aggression. However, China has not been a major friction point so far between India and the US. On the contrary, given Beijing's continued belligerence, it has been a uniting factor for India and the US. There are still other states that India cannot condemn unequivocally for one reason or the other. For example, what India has called the 'three problem children' (Wikileaks Cable: 04NEWDELHI7674_a) in the bilateral relationship – Myanmar, Sudan, and Iran – are the ones that remain unfavourable to the US for human rights or nuclear issues. India has to consider gaining energy supplies with Iran and Sudan. With Myanmar, New Delhi remains mindful of its historical ties, considerable bilateral cooperation on border management, and warding off Chinese influence in its backyard. On Iran, the US wants India's support at the International Atomic Energy Agency, which it receives occasionally but not always. Within its neighbourhood, India must take sides as a reliable friend if a state is ever at odds with the US, such as with Mauritius in the Diego Garcia case. Mauritius is at loggerheads with the United Kingdom over the sovereignty of Diego Garcia, an island in the Indian Ocean that hosts one of the most critical US military bases (Thakkar, 2021c). In the General Assembly, and later at the International Court of Justice, India had to weigh in on the Mauritian side, even if half-heartedly to the displeasure of both US and the UK.

Conclusions: An Ally in the Making?

The previous section examined in detail why the strategic proximity between India and the US in the last two decades has not reflected multilaterally, but it would be remiss to portray the ties as entirely adversarial. Moreover, as Harsh Pant and I (Pant & Thakkar, 2021) have noted elsewhere in detail, most of these divergences do not harm core US interests, save for its balancing act with Russia. India's current positions on a number of issues are far from opposed, if not enthusiastically aligned, including containing China, preventing nuclear proliferation in Iran and North Korea, enhancing maritime security, emphasizing a rules-based world order, combating climate change and promoting free-market democracies.

Both sides have actively cooperated on many issues due to India's changing identity and interests, emerging geopolitical necessities, or simply to meet the US's expectations. An example of India's evolving interest and identity that has spurred cooperation is climate diplomacy. During this period, New Delhi has understood that it can neither continue to blame the industrialized north as it used to do at the summits in Rio de Janeiro (1992) and Kyoto (1995) nor afford the disasters that would knock on its door due to climate inaction. As the third largest carbon emitter currently, India has realized that it must be a part of any global solution, which also accords it the opportunity to shape the conversation. Hence, New Delhi shed its activism and adopted a cooperative stance during the Paris negotiations (Jayaram, 2021). Since then, India has not only been at the forefront of meeting its annual targets but has also demonstrated climate leadership by instituting the International Solar Alliance for sunshine countries (Thakkar, 2021b).

The second factor compelling India to work with the US and the West is the emerging threat from a common adversary like China. Both sides have seemed to realize that it is not enough to form alliances like the Quad-rilateral Security Dialogue (the Quad) to uphold and enforce norms, it is also vital to come together to set norms for a rules-based order. Hence, any attempt by Beijing to game multilateral institutions brings India and the US ever closer, as was seen in the combined efforts of Indian, American, and European diplomats to prevent 'Xi Jinping thought' from infiltrating UN resolutions (Sirohi, 2018). Finally, at times, India understands that for the sake of the bilateral relationship, it has to show flexibility in some areas to make up for some of the positions where it cannot give in to the US demands. On a resolution moved against Guantanamo Bay at the UNHRC by Cuba, India voted in support of the US, something that mattered to Washington. After the vote, S. Jaishankar, then Joint Secretary (Americas) and now India's foreign minister, invited the Political Counsellor from the US Embassy in New Delhi to ensure that Washington has registered India's positive vote, when India was the only one to stand with the US, besides its NATO allies (Wikileaks Cable: 05NEWDELHI3080_a).

These occasions of cooperation are incidental and not strategic. Both states have desired cooperation as was evident from the 'Global Issues Dialogue' instituted jointly in the early 2000s, which has intermittently remained in action, most recently in its new format called the 'Dialogue on UN and Multilateral Issues'. However, these recommendations are palliatives offered to address the symptoms and not the cause. The cause is the structural adversity in which both states are locked, a situation created by their respective identities and interests. New Delhi is a 'status seeker' that wants a permanent UNSC seat, which Washington demurs. An unwieldy and expanded Council is not in US interests. If India's aspirational status has influenced its behaviour, so does the US's status as a P5 member. In this regard, Ambassador Akbaruddin documents a UN election where India bested the UK for a judgeship at the International Court of Justice (Akbaruddin, 2021). The most crucial upshot of the memoir was the P5's way of preserving their collective rights, including Washington's efforts to help the UK that year and China the subsequent year. As I have noted in the book's review, 'at the height of Trump's acrimony towards China in 2020, Chinese judge Xue Hanquin received not only Washington's vote but also its non-national nomination, something denied to a 'friend' of America such as India' (Thakkar, 2022: 38). Unless New Delhi's status inconsistency is resolved, adversarial relations will continue to prevail in their multilateral interactions. If anything, it is the relative impermeability of the multilateral arena where the external strength of ties between two states may not be adequately reflected due to internal dynamics. Group cohesion, status inconsistency, or commitments to principles can prevent states from standing with their 'friends' within multilateral institutions. Hence, India and the US are friends elsewhere, but foes at the UN.

Acknowledgements

This chapter builds off an earlier policy memo published with the Henry L. Stimson Center in Washington, DC as part of the 2020 South Asian Voices Visiting Fellowship (cf. Thakkar 2021a). I would like to thank Christopher Clary, Samir Lalwani, Akriti Vasudeva, Brigitta Schuchert, Elizabeth Threlkeld, and Frank O'Donnell for their feedback while at Stimson.

References

All UN documents are referred to in this chapter through their numbers. They can be accessed from www.undocs.org. All Wikileaks cables are referenced through their canonical ids. They can be accessed from https://wikileaks.org/plusd/. The *Voting Practices in the United Nations* reports marking 'important votes' issued by the US Department of State can be accessed at www.state.gov/voting-practices-in-the-uni ted-nations/.Akbaruddin, Syed (2021) *India vs UK: The Story of an Unprecedented Diplomatic Win* (New Delhi: HarperCollins).

Bailey, M. A., Strezhnev, A. & Voeten, E. (2017) 'Estimating Dynamic State Preferences from United Nations Voting Data', *Journal of Conflict Resolution*, 61 (2): 430–456.

Basrur, Rajesh & Sullivan de Estrada, Kate (2017) *Rising India: Status and Power* (London: Routledge).

Basu, Nayanima (2019) 'In a First, India Votes in Favour of Israel at UN Against Palestine Human Rights Body'. *The Print*, 11 June. Available at https://theprint.in/ diplomacy/in-a-first-india-votes-in-favour-of-israel-at-un-against-palestine-human-r ights-body/248543/ [last accessed 1 December 2021].

Chacko, Priya (2018) 'Foreign Policy, Ideas and State-Building: India and the Politics of International Intervention', *Journal of International Relations and Development*, 21: 346–371.

Chaturvedi, Sachin & Mendiratta, Shashank. (2015) 'Principles of South–South Cooperation and Emerging Evidence from Indian Engagements', in Manmohan Agarwal & John Walley (eds), *World Scientific Reference on Asia and the World Economy, Vol 1* (Singapore: World Scientific), pp. 109–133.

Dixit, Jyotindra Nath (1996) *My South Block Years: Memoirs of a Foreign Secretary* (New Delhi: UBS Publishers).

Dormandy, Xenia (2007) 'Is India, or Will it Be, a Responsible International Stakeholder?', *The Washington Quarterly*, 30 (3), 117–130.

Ganguly, Sumit & Sridharan, Eswaran (2013) 'The End of India's Sovereignty Hawks?' *Foreign Policy*, 13 November.

Gharekhan, Chinmaya (2006) *Horseshoe Table: An Inside View of the UN Security Council* (New Delhi: Pearson).

Hall, Ian (2019) 'India and the Responsibility to Protect', in Harsh V. Pant (ed.) *New Directions in India's Foreign Policy: Theory and Praxis* (New York: Cambridge University Press), pp. 149–171.

Iida, Keisuke (1998) 'Third World Solidarity: The Group of 77 in the UN General Assembly', *International Organization*, 42 (2): 375–395.

Jayaram, Dhanasree (2021) *Climate Diplomacy and Emerging Economies: India as a Case Study* (New Delhi: Routledge).

Kaye, Charles R., Nye, Joseph S. & Ayres, Alyssa (2015) *Working with a Rising India: A Joint Venture for the New Century* (New York: Council on Foreign Relations).

Kim, Soo Yeon & Russett, Bruce (1996) 'The New Politics of Voting Alignments in the United Nations General Assembly', *International Organization*, 50 (4): 629–652.

Laskar, Rezaul H. (2021) 'India: Rich Nations Must Do More On Green Goals'. *Hindustan Times*, 1 November. Available at www.hindustantimes.com/india-news/develop ed-nations-must-make-more-efforts-to-help-achieve-net-zero-carbon-emissions-piyush-goyal-101635703707462.html [last accessed 1 December 2021].

Lakshman, Sriram (2020) 'By any Calculus, India Qualifies for UNSC Permanent Seat: Syed Akbaruddin'. *The Hindu*, 29 April. Available at www.thehindu.com/op inion/interview/by-any-calculus-india-qualifies-for-unsc-permanent-seat-syed-akbar uddin/article31465932.ece [last accessed 1 December 2021].

Lederer, Edith M. (2020). 'UN Assembly Approves Pandemic Resolution: US, Israel Object'. *Washington Post*, 11 September. Available at www.washingtonpost.com/ world/middle_east/un-assembly-approves-resolution-on-dealing-with-the-pandemic/ 2020/09/11/f0e98360-f4ab-11ea-8025-5d3489768ac8_story.html [last accessed 1 December 2021].

Lok Sabha (1994a) *Lok Sabha Debates (English Version), Tenth Lok Sabha, Twelfth Session, Vol. XXXVI(4), 12 December* (New Delhi: Lok Sabha Secretariat).

Lok Sabha (1994b) *Lok Sabha Bulletin – Part I, Tenth Lok Sabha, XII Session, No. 334* (New Delhi: Lok Sabha Secretariat).

Malik, Ashok (2012) 'A Case in Absentia', *Pragati*, 3 November.

Malone, David M. & Mukherjee, Rohan (2013) 'Dilemmas of Sovereignty and Order: India and the UN Security Council', in Waheguru Pal Singh Sidhu, Pratap Bhanu Mehta & Bruce Jones (eds), *Shaping the Emerging World: India and the Multilateral Order* (Washington, DC: Brookings Institution Press), pp. 157–176.

McDonald, K. C. & Patrick, S. M. (2010) *UN Security Council Enlargement and US Interests* (New York: Council on Foreign Relations).

Ministry of External Affairs (1993) *Foreign Affairs Record 1992* (New Delhi: Ministry of External Affairs, Government of India).

Ministry of External Affairs (2014) 'Nuclear Security in India'. Available at www. mea.gov.in/Images/pdf/Brochure.pdf [last accessed 1 December 2021].

Mosler, Martin & Potrafke, Niklas (2020) 'International Political Alignment During the Trump Presidency: Voting at the UN General Assembly', *International Interactions*, 46 (3): 481–497.

Mukerji, Asoke Kumar (2018) 'The Impact of Multilateralism on India', *Indian Foreign Affairs Journal*, 13 (4), 335–344.

Mukherjee, Pranab (1994) 'Speech by Mr. Pranab Mukherjee'. Available at www.pm inewyork.gov.in/pdf/uploadpdf/77859lms44.pdf [last accessed 1 December 2021].

Mukherjee, Pranab (2016) *The Turbulent Years 1980–1996* (New Delhi: Rupa).

Mukherjee, Rohan & Malone, David Malone (2013) 'India and the UN Security Council: An Ambiguous Tale', *Economic and Political Weekly*, 48 (29): 110–117.

Narlikar, Amrita (2006) 'Peculiar Chauvinism or Strategic Calculation? Explaining the Negotiating Strategy of a Rising India', *International Affairs*, 82 (1), 59–76.

Pant, Harsh V. & Thakkar, Chirayu (2021) 'The United States and India: Multi-laterally Abridged Allies', 23 August. Available at www.cfr.org/blog/united-states-a nd-india-multilaterally-abridged-allies [last accessed 1 December 2021].

Permanent Mission of Saint Vincent and the Grenadines (2018) *Handbook on Security Council Reform* (New York: Permanent Mission of Saint Vincent and the Grenadines to the United Nations).

PTI (2014) 'Russia Has Legitimate Interests in Ukraine: Shivshankar Menon', Business Standard, 6 March. Available at www.business-standard.com/article/international/russia-has-legitimate-interests-in-ukraine-shivshankar-menon-114030600962_1.html [last accessed 1 December 2021].

Puri, Hardeep Singh (2016) *Perilous Interventions: The Security Council and the Politics of Chaos* (New Delhi: HarperCollins Publishers).

Puri, Manjeev Singh (2013) 'Extempore Remarks by Ambassador Manjeev Singh Puri', New York. Available at www.pminewyork.gov.in/pdf/uploadpdf/94572pmi12.pdf [last accessed 1 December 2021].

Raja Mohan, C. (2003) *Crossing the Rubicon: The Shaping of India's New Foreign Policy* (New Delhi: Viking).

Raja Mohan, C. (2006) *Impossible Allies: Nuclear India, United States, and the Global Order* (New Delhi: India Research Press).

Raja Mohan, C. (2010) 'Rising India: Partner in Shaping the Global Commons?', *The Washington Quarterly*, 33 (3): 133–148.

Raja Mohan, C. (2013) 'The Changing Dynamics of India's Multilateralism', in Waheguru Pal Singh Sidhu, Pratap Bhanu Mehta & Bruce Jones (eds), *Shaping the Emerging World: India and the Multilateral Order* (Washington, DC: Brookings Institution Press), pp. 25–42.

Roy Choudhary, Dipanjan (2018) 'India Abstains on Voting on Proposal on UK Spy Case at The Hague', *Economic Times*, 5 April. Available at https://economictimes.indiatimes.com/news/defence/india-abstains-on-voting-on-proposal-on-uk-spy-case-at-the-hague/articleshow/63633890.cms [last accessed 1 December 2021].

Saran, Shyam (2013) 'India and Multilateralism: A Practitioner's Perspective', in Waheguru Pal Singh Sidhu, Pratap Bhanu Mehta & Bruce Jones (eds), *Shaping the Emerging World: India and the Multilateral Order* (Washington, DC: Brookings Institution Press), pp. 43–56.

Schaffer, Teresita C. (2009) 'The United States, India, and Global Governance: Can They Work Together?', *The Washington Quarterly*, 32 (3): 71–87.

Schaffer, Teresita C. & Schaffer, Howard B. (2016) *India at the Global High Table: The Quest for Regional Primacy and Strategic Autonomy* (Washington, DC: Brookings Institution Press).

Sidhu, Waheguru Pal Singh, Mehta, Pratap Bhabu & Jones, Bruce (2013) 'A Hesitant Rule Shaper?', in Waheguru Pal Singh Sidhu, Pratap Bhanu Mehta & Bruce Jones (eds), *Shaping the Emerging World: India and the Multilateral Order* (Washington, DC: Brookings Institution Press), pp. 3–24.

Singh, Jaswant (2007) *In Service of Emergent India: A Call to Honor* (Bloomington, IN: Indiana University Press).

Sirohi, Seema (2018) 'India-US-EU Combine Halts China's Belt and Road Initiative at the UN'. *The Wire*, 12 December. Available at https://thewire.in/diplomacy/india-china-belt-and-road-united-nations [last accessed 1 December 2021].

Sreenivasan, T. P. (2008) *Words, Words, Words: Adventures in Diplomacy* (New Delhi: Pearson Longman).

Sullivan de Estrada, Kate & Foot, Rosemary (2019) 'China's and India's Search for International Status Through the UN System: Competition and Complementarity', *Contemporary Politics*, 25 (5): 567–585.

Thakkar, Chirayu (2021a) *India and the United States: Friends Elsewhere, Foes at the UN* (Washington, DC: Henry L. Stimson Center). Available at www.stimson.org/2021/india-and-the-united-states-friends-elsewhere-foes-at-the-un/ [last accessed 1 December 2021].

Thakkar, Chirayu (2021b) 'India-US Nuclear Trade and Cooperation: Potential for the Biden Administration', *South Asian Voices*, 5 February. Available at https://southasianvoices.org/india-u-s-nuclear-trade-and-cooperation-potential-for-the-biden-administration/ [last accessed 1 December 2021].

Thakkar, Chirayu (2021c) 'Overcoming the Diego Garcia Stalemate', *War on the Rocks*, 12 July. Available at https://warontherocks.com/2021/07/overcoming-the-diego-garcia-stalemate/ [last accessed 1 December 2021].

Thakkar, Chirayu (2022) 'Review: India vs UK: The Story of an Unprecedented Diplomatic Win', *International Affairs*, 98 (1): 349–350.

Part III
Articulating a Diplomatic Vision

9 Institutionalization of Paradiplomacy in India

Aayushi Liana Shah, Nomita Prithviraj,
Vedant Mehra and Vishwesh Sundar

In August 2019, the government of the southern Indian state of Andhra Pradesh organized a diplomatic outreach event in coordination with the Indian Ministry of External Affairs (MEA) in Vijayawada. During this event, the Chief Minister of Andhra Pradesh, Y. S. Jagan Mohan Reddy, held direct interactions with Ambassadors of different Indian states and announced the state's plans of opening investment promotion offices in the foreign capitals of Tokyo and Seoul (Hindu, 2019). A few months later, in February 2020, a similar diplomatic outreach event was organized in Chennai by the Government of Tamil Nadu (ANI, 2020). Here too, the then Chief Minister Edappadi Palaniswami held personal interactions with the high-level attendees urging them to facilitate stronger ties between their respective Indian states and the state of Tamil Nadu through economic cooperation (Sekar, 2020). Both of these diplomatic outreach events were arranged as part of the MEA's increasing effort to involve state governments in India's economic diplomacy, and point towards the growing federalization of Indian foreign policy (ANI, 2020).

This phenomenon of subnational actors actively participating in foreign policy and diplomatic initiatives in parallel to their central government is termed 'paradiplomacy' (Duchacek, 1990). In the Indian context, this is a relatively new development. Historically, the central government has retained absolute authority on foreign policy matters (Asthana & Jacob, 2017). The economic liberalization of the country during the 1990s, in tandem with the emergence of coalition politics, propelled a shift that allowed Indian state governments to negotiate with the central government for increased engagement in foreign policy. State governments became increasingly involved in international activities, with their respective Chief Ministers taking up the role of 'Chief Diplomats' (Wyatt, 2017). A prominent example of this is the current Indian Prime Minister, Narendra Modi, who, during his tenure as the Chief Minister of Gujarat, became a pioneer for Indian paradiplomacy. From organizing investor summits to market Gujarat's good governance and investor-friendly brand to attending World Economic Forum meetings and engaging with Gujarati diaspora abroad, Modi built an international profile for his state. This was notable as it was done within a constitutional

DOI: 10.4324/9781003305132-13

framework in which foreign policy is the exclusive domain of the central government (Wyatt, 2017).

The initial efforts aimed at the institutionalization of paradiplomacy have been achieved through the development of new norms, rules and institutions, which were earlier sporadic, ad-hoc and reactionary (Jacob, 2016). Simultaneously, the central government is taking a cautious approach to avoid the interests of subnational units clashing with or superseding the national strategic interests. To this extent, the central government still holds a veto over paradiplomatic projects and engagements, with Indian states having no constitutional or judicial remedy to challenge it (Jacob, 2016). In this chapter, the authors examine *the role of domestic political actors in shaping Indian foreign policy in the twenty first century.* To begin with, a short overview of the theoretical underpinnings of paradiplomacy, its development in the West and the Indian context are provided. This is followed by a discussion on the three factors that guide the cautious process of the institutionalization of paradiplomacy within the unique federal context of India.

Crucially, the foreign policy of India is underpinned by its values and identities as well as the interactions with external actors (Manikam & Puspitasari, 2021). The identity of India is an amalgamation of regional identities, cultures and values that coalesce to form a larger national identity. There has been a long history of regions in India leveraging their relations with their neighbours for trade and economic ties. In this chapter, the authors elaborate on how regional identities have been instrumental in the evolution of paradiplomacy, and how this has been facilitated by the national government in the pursuit of India's great power ambitions.

Paradiplomacy: Academic and Theoretical Discussions

Paradiplomacy refers to the foreign policy activities and diplomatic engagements adopted by subnational entities of a sovereign state in parallel to the foreign policy activities of the national governments (Duchacek, 1990). Paradiplomacy is a relatively new term in the lexicon of international relations and gained academic popularity only in the 1970s and 1980s. The preoccupation of major International Relations theories with the nation-state as the unit of analysis meant that paradiplomacy remained at the margins of academic debates in international relations (Duran, 2015). According to the realist school, international politics is determined by the structural realities of the anarchic world order, which in turn is influenced by the power-seeking behaviour of the nation-states that form it (Heywood, 2011). On the contrary, classical liberalism postulates the possibility of cooperation and peaceful norm development in world politics, in which nation-states still remain the principal actor (Burchill, 2005).

Growing paradiplomatic developments in the 1970s prompted International Relations theorists to acknowledge and accommodate non-central governments as actors in world politics. Constructivist theories that emerged in the following decades could explain paradiplomacy as it focuses on identities and cultures in influencing the interactions of nation-states (Reus-Smit, 2005; Wendt, 1992), whereby 'paradiplomacy in this respect is seen as an effort by subnational actors to build their own identities' (Utomo, 2019: 38). Despite the growing relevance and prominence of paradiplomacy in International Relations, the initial discourses on the topic was almost exclusively focused on its practice in the federal democracies of the West. This could be because paradiplomacy has been most visible in these states (Lecours, 2008), with some even leading the efforts at institutionalizing this process. Institutionalization can be understood as the process of establishing institutions and/or rules and norms that serve as distinct channels for decision making. Kuznetsov (2015: 31) lists the six principal ways in which paradiplomacy is institutionalized, which are: (i) the establishment of a regional ministry responsible for international affairs of the constituent unit; (ii) opening of permanent subnational offices in foreign states, which is also termed as 'paraconsulates'; (iii) facilitating official visits of regional authorities to foreign states; (iv) the participation of local authorities in international events organized by foreign actors; (v) the participation of local governments in transborder multilateral networks to resolve issues of regional importance; and (vi) the participation in international events organized by foreign actors within the official delegation of the central government. The pace and scope of institutionalizing paradiplomacy are influenced by several factors such as the area of paradiplomatic activity, the ethnic composition of the population and the federal set-up of the country. It can be observed that the paradiplomatic aspirations of subnational units are generally successful in areas that are traditionally considered 'low politics' and when the interests of the subnational unit are complementary to – rather than in contradiction to – national interests. Furthermore, states that have a significant minority population with a distinct regional identity have especially been at the forefront in formalizing paradiplomacy (McHugh, 2015).

At times, extreme forms of regional nationalism and a fear of secessionism have been detrimental to the spread of paradiplomacy. These apprehensions are stronger in the newly formed and multi-ethnic democracies of Asia, Africa and the Middle East, which have thus favoured unitary governments. Such states fear that the decentralization of foreign policy could be a slippery slope towards independence or autonomy. This severe form of paradiplomacy is called 'protodiplomacy' (Aguirre, 1999). In these states, subnational governments practice paradiplomacy 'simply on practice and experience, guided by common sense and normative boundaries' (Tavares, 2016: 63). The incidental and ad-hoc nature of paradiplomacy practiced in the developing world and the inadequacy of institutions to formalize this process can also explain the lack of literature on paradiplomacy in the developing world. This is true in the Indian context too and a few sources, such as Tewari (2017) and Jain & Maini (2017), provide a brief discussion on the institutional aspects of paradiplomacy in India.

Centre can leverage the benefits of cooperative

and competitive federalism

Institutionalisation

of paradiplomacy

Enhances bureaucratic efficiency   Channel for states to portray

their economic and soft power

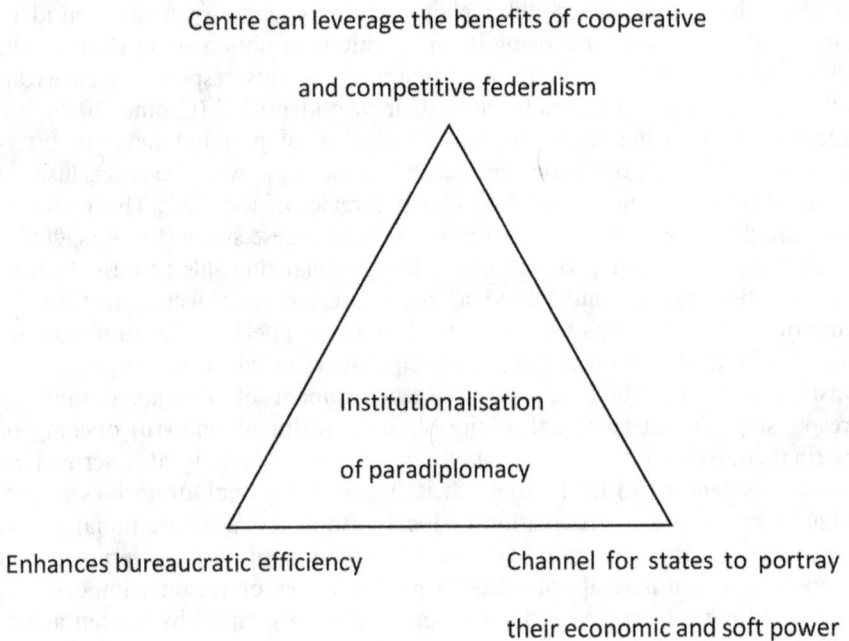

Figure 9.1 Motivations for the institutionalization of paradiplomacy in India.
Source: chapter authors

However, the purpose that the institutionalization of paradiplomacy serves in India has not yet been discussed in academic literature. Therefore, the primary question that this chapter seeks to answer is *'why have initial steps to institutionalize paradiplomacy been undertaken in India?'* We argue that paradiplomacy serves three purposes (see Figure 9.1): (i) it aids the central government to leverage the benefits of cooperative and competitive federalism; (ii) it serves as a channel for state governments to portray their economic and soft power; and (iii) it enhances bureaucratic efficiency. Although we highlight three distinct reasons for institutionalizing paradiplomacy in India, in reality, it is fluid, and can serve multiple or all purposes too.

Cooperative and Competitive Federalism

The Seventh Schedule of the Indian Constitution lists 'diplomatic, consular and trade representation' and 'participation in international conferences and associations' under the exclusive competence of the central government (Bywalec, 2018: 58). Consequently, the Indian Constitution has traditionally had a unitary bias. However, starting in the 1990s, factors such as the rise of coalition politics and the initiation of the New Economic Policy reforms led the central government to relinquish its absolute autonomy over foreign policy, especially in the economic and social realm. Nowadays, the central government in India is actively encouraging states to compete with each other in attracting foreign investments and enhancing foreign trade as long as they are congruent with national policies (Jain and Maini, 2017). As will be discussed in the next section, the same holds true for the projection and utilization of regional identities by states in their overtures to foreign actors.

Narendra Modi's success in conducting paradiplomacy also prompted him to bring the idea to the national forefront through his 2014 national election campaign, where he repeatedly underlined the need for greater involvement of states in India's foreign policy (Bywalec, 2018). After becoming Prime Minister, Modi announced his government's strong desire to cooperate with state governments to achieve India's diplomatic objectives and work towards a more inclusive centre-state relationship. In achieving this goal, in October 2014, the Ministry of External Affairs took the significant step of creating a 'States Division' to facilitate direct coordination between the ministry and subnational units on matters relating to external relations and diplomacy (Tewari, 2017). The objective of this institution is to facilitate states to 'promote exports, tourism and attract more overseas investment and expertise' (PTI, 2014a). The States Division also assists Indian states in identifying target external states and regions for engaging in commercial and cultural diplomacy (PNS, 2016). Moreover, the States Division gives Chief Ministers of India's states 'direct briefings on investment opportunities and international collaboration, and also sometimes organizes meetings with the target state's ambassador' (Jacob, 2016: 16). Additionally, the Division provides training and capacity building assistance to states and Union Territories in areas relating to external linkages such as trade and investments (PTI, 2014a).

The inception of the States Division has made Chief Ministers the chief entrepreneurs of their respective states. State governments are becoming more forthcoming and proactive in sending and hosting international delegations from foreign states and inter-governmental organizations. Presently, the five-year report cards of the Chief Ministers are evaluated by the electorate based on the value of foreign investments brought into the state and the number of jobs created as a result, in addition to other factors (Vadlamannati, 2012). This phenomenon has led Chief Ministers and their cabinet ministers to vie aggressively with their counterparts in other Indian states to make foreign trips and attract foreign investments. For instance, the incumbent Chief Minister of Kerala, Pinarayi Vijayan, made four visits to the United Arab Emirates since assuming office in 2016 to propose investment opportunities with the Abu Dhabi National Oil Company and Abu Dhabi Investment Authority, and other Kerala expatriate organizations (Mathrubhumi, 2020; Saseendran, 2019). The States Division has been pivotal in arranging these trips and coordinating between the states and Indian missions abroad. The division assists the states 'in building bridges with the [foreign] states in which they have a special interest on account of proximity or the presence of diaspora from that state' (Sreenivasan, 2017). This practice could, however, also have the disadvantage of political leaders utilizing these trips for furthering personal gains, such as securing funding for their respective political parties through diaspora engagement (Jenkins, 2003).

Promotion of Regional Economic and Soft Power

According to Pietrasiak et al. (2018), economic and cultural interests are key motivators for paradiplomacy within a globalized world. In this process, subnational governments foster direct connections with foreign governments and other inter-governmental organizations with the aim of promoting the region's commercial and cultural diplomacy. Bywalec (2018) argues that the regional identities of subnational units (i.e. here the states of India are also instrumental in influencing their international orientation). As Tewari (2017) points out, in federal democracies with periodic elections, state government leadership is often keen to utilize the globalized market economy for their state's development and to strengthen their own political prospects. Several Indian state governments draw on incentives such as the furthering of international trade, foreign investments and economic development, in order to conduct and institutionalize paradiplomacy, often with the encouragement of the central government. In this regard, the Government of India has arguably been generous, albeit cautious, in relinquishing its absolute autonomy in areas of foreign economic relations (Asthana and Jacob, 2017).

It is increasingly becoming common to see Chief Ministers leading Indian delegations to bilateral talks and international conferences. The former Chief Minister of Andhra Pradesh Chandrababu Naidu led an Indian business delegation to China in 2015 for boosting bilateral cooperation. Similarly, the former Chief Minister of Maharashtra, Prithviraj Chavan, led the Indian delegation to participate in the World Economic Forum in 2014 (Bywalec, 2018). Likewise, foreign government officials have also started appreciating the federal nature of the country's politics (Stancati, 2012). Moreover, as the geo-economics centre of India has shifted away from Delhi, heads of foreign states have started making additional stops in cities such as Mumbai, Chennai, Hyderabad and Kolkata. Foreign governments have also begun setting up foreign trade offices across India to directly negotiate with states over trade and investment issues before seeking approval from the Centre (Jha, 2014).

The gradual decentralization of foreign economic policy has also resulted from India's World Trade Organization (WTO) commitments, since its accession to the organization in 1995. Some of the rules contained in the WTO agreements relate to agriculture and its allied sectors, which fall within the exclusive executive competence of the states in India (Jha, 2014). The central government at the time received criticism for not consulting the states before accepting the treaty commitments. Some states, such as West Bengal, Punjab and Tamil Nadu, even took the central government to court for having made international commitments on issues where it lacks authority (Jenkins, 2003). To assuage the situation, the central government, under the leadership of the then Prime Minister Vajpayee, convened the 'Chief Ministers' Conference on the WTO' in 2001 to address the grievances and reservations of Indian states regarding their commitments under the WTO agreement (Natarajan, 2019). The states were also advised to set-up WTO cells to enhance centre-state cooperation and coordination on WTO-related issues (Tewari, 2017).

Another recent trend that can be noticed is the inception of 'investment summits' that has become an opportunity for states to showcase their economic achievements and highlight their areas of comparative advantage to attract foreign and domestic investments for economic development. For example, the Indian state of Gujarat has the distinction of being the first in India to institutionalize state investment summits such as the bi-annual 'Vibrant Gujarat' Summits in 2003 (Maini, 2015). Following Gujarat's success, almost all states across India now organize such investment summits. In the span of just two months in 2018, at least five states (Andhra Pradesh, Assam, Maharashtra, Uttar Pradesh, West Bengal) held summits attended by foreign delegations, resulting in billions of dollars' worth of financial commitments to regional projects (Ministry of External Affairs, 2018). Furthermore, for the first time, the Economic Survey of India for 2017–2018 published the data on India's international trade split across different Indian states. Taken together, these facts indicate the willingness of the central government towards institutionalizing paradiplomacy to promote economic interests. Prime Minister Modi himself stressed that these state-level investment summits are intended to ease doing business, with an added objective of bolstering cooperative and competitive federalism among the state and central governments (Maini, 2015).

Alongside the economic interests, state governments in India are actively pursuing various strategies to promote their regional identities and culture. The Indian Council for Cultural Relations (ICCR), with centres in twenty countries around the world, is also an important facilitator for such efforts (Indian Council for Cultural Relations, n.d.). State governments often join hands with the ICCR in their conduct of cultural paradiplomacy. Furthermore, in recognition of the immense regional diversity in India, it can also be argued that increasing involvement of state governments bodes well for the vibrancy of Indian cultural diplomacy. To institutionalize this process, state governments have begun to set-up cultural and language centres in various states. For example, West Bengal promotes its indigenous culture and heritage on an international scale under the aegis of 'Biswa Bangla'. In 2015, a Memorandum of Understanding (MoU) was signed between West Bengal and the Chinese province of Yunnan to pave the way for the first overseas Biswa Bangla showroom in the city of Kunming, with talks currently underway to open stores in London and Singapore as well (PTI, 2014b, 2015a). A similar initiative was taken by the government of Kerala in 2017 during the visit of the ruler of Sharjah (an Emirate of the United Arab Emirates), H.H. Sheikh Dr. Sultan Muhammad Al Qasimi, to the state when it proposed the establishment of a Kerala Culture Centre in Sharjah (New Indian Express, 2017). This proposed centre is intended to foster closer cultural ties between Kerala and the Emirate, which has a large diaspora from the state (Government of Kerala, 2017).

Additionally, states turn to paradiplomacy for promoting regional languages. The states in India have been divided along linguistic lines, highlighting the centrality and sensitivity of languages within India's cultural diversity. On an institutional level, many departments and chairs for Indian languages have been established in foreign states, with notable contributions of the respective Indian state governments and often in collaboration with the ICCR. For instance, during Chief Minister Mamata Banerjee's visit to the United Kingdom (UK) in 2015, there was an exchange of MoUs between the University of Cambridge and the Presidency University in West Bengal for the study of the Bengali language (PTI, 2015b). The state government has also sponsored scholarships for students studying Bengali at the School of Oriental and African Studies in London (Sinha, 2015). Similarly, after the successful creation of a Tamil Chair at Harvard University in the United States (US), the state government of Tamil Nadu has proposed setting up Tamil Chairs in renowned universities across the globe, including in the UK, Malaysia and Sri Lanka. These efforts aim to protect and project the Tamil language and culture, while also helping the diaspora to retain ties with their home country and state (New Indian Express, 2018a).

When it comes to paradiplomacy, the diverse cultural and linguistic identities of the different subnational regions in India can thus be perceived as enhancing the scope of India's national identity in the international sphere, rather than taking away from it. This is also encouraged by the national government, as evidenced by the active involvement of its bodies, such as the ICCR and the States Division of the MEA in the cultural paradiplomacy of the states.

Enhancing Bureaucratic Efficiency

The cautious devolution of foreign policy to Indian states has also been a logical and necessary consequence of the shortage of human resources faced by the MEA. The Indian diplomatic system extends from the MEA Headquarters in New Delhi to 123 Embassies and 53 Honorary Consulates worldwide (Ministry of External Affairs, n.d.). Yet, this vast system is staffed by only 1,200 diplomatic staff, which includes 820 Indian Foreign Service (IFS) 'A' officers, 230 Grade IFS 'B' officers and approximately 150 officers on deputation from other central government ministries (Rana, 2020). In comparison, the diplomatic corps of other large states such as China and the US is estimated to be 7,500 and 13,790, respectively (Ahluwalia, 2021). An overstretched diplomatic corps has long impacted the MEA's ability to efficiently process information received from India's different missions and manage multiple diplomatic negotiations simultaneously (Shukla, 2019). In these circumstances, paradiplomacy offers a tool for New Delhi to supplement its human resource shortage by involving and delegating certain tasks to state level officials and achieve bureaucratic efficiency.

This is especially evident in the spheres of consular affairs and diaspora engagement, as Indian state governments have started engaging with Non-Resident Indians (NRIs) from their respective states through NRI cells and departments. The initiative taken by the Kerala Government in its outreach towards the 3.5 million strong Keralite diaspora population residing in Gulf States is a prominent example (Bywalec, 2018). To address the concerns and welfare of the large diaspora population, the state government has set up a department called the Non-Resident Keralites' Affairs Department, or NORKA-Roots (Wyatt, 2017). The department serves as a kiosk for the Keralite diaspora to interact with the Indian state government, access important information about legal protections and facilitate their rehabilitation on return to the state (NORKA-Roots, n.d.). The states of Haryana and Andhra Pradesh have also set up NRI cells aimed at providing grievance redressal mechanisms for their diasporas and safeguarding their investments (Kumar, 2017; New Indian Express, 2018b). Some of these institutions also aim at tapping the resources of their diaspora. For instance, in Punjab, the state government has established a NRI Affairs Department, which oversees the program 'Mera Pind Mera Shehar' ('My Village My City') to encourage Punjabi migrants to contribute to healthcare and other development initiatives of their native areas (Government of Punjab, n.d.). With direct communication between Indian diaspora communities and state governments on key issues facilitated through these institutions, the MEA has been able to delegate some of its tasks and duties to the states.

Using paradiplomacy as a tool to involve and delegate tasks to states is also visible in the nature of assignments undertaken by different Indian State WTO cells. These institutes were set-up following the Chief Minister's Conference of 2001 to enhance centre-state coordination on WTO-related issues. The cells facilitate information sharing between the federal actors on agricultural commodity prices and aid cooperation in the drafting of protection strategies (Tewari, 2017). Specific WTO cells, such as in Karnataka have also been successful in ensuring congruence of interests for different stakeholders involved by linking local needs with national interests and international regulations (Jayaram, 2006). As consequence, the burden for New Delhi to engage with domestic and international actors to enable similar outcomes and consensus has been reduced. Another initiative that indicates New Delhi's will to involve its states in the conduct of India's foreign policy is the setting up of MEA Branch Secretariats in the cities of Chennai, Kolkata, Guwahati, Hyderabad and Mumbai (Jacob, 2016). Overseen by the States Division, the Secretariats engage in functions of liaising between the state governments and the MEA to promote international investments, facilitate clearances of state delegations for foreign visits and organize meetings of local officials with Indian diplomats and staff in the foreign consulates present in their respective states (One India, 2007).

As stated earlier, paradiplomacy can also be institutionalized through the establishment of norms or rules in decision making relating to foreign policy. A few norms established by the MEA aim at enhancing the communication between state governments and the Indian Embassies abroad. One of the norms established in 2016 calls for Indian ambassadors to go to Indian state capitals, interact with local bureaucrats and help facilitate interaction between respective state governments and the ambassador's country of posting (Indian Express, 2016). The goal of this norm is to empower Indian state government officials to liaise with Indian ambassadors directly and position their respective states for investment opportunities and deepen ties with foreign governments. Several ambassadors have already done so, such as Nandini Singla, the ambassador to Mauritius in 2022, who has adopted her home state of Karnataka to boost ties (Deccan Herald, 2016). In another example, previous Indian ambassadors to the counties of Israel, Croatia, Macedonia and Iceland adopted the state of Goa to expand relations and cooperation during their tenures (NavHind Times, 2018).

To further consolidate the growing collaboration of state and central governments in conduct India's foreign policy, it has been decided that recruits to the IFS would be sent on secondments to Indian state governments (Schaffer & Schaffer, 2016). This informal rule is now institutionalized during the training of IFS officers at the Foreign Services Institute, Shimla. For instance, 33 officer trainees of the 2014 batch of IFS spent a month in different state capitals and districts to familiarize themselves with state officials and the respective state's development plans. Mid-career IFS officers are also being increasingly encouraged to acquaint themselves with the economic prospects of two Indian states of their choice (Roche, 2015). Familiarity with the local conditions helps Indian diplomats in promoting investment opportunities in the respective states while simultaneously furthering India's larger economic and political interests. For Indian state governments and local bureaucrats, these changed norms provide capabilities of prompt access and engagements with foreign governments and investors through specific channels, saving the effort of routing similar requests through the MEA Headquarters in New Delhi. The interactions between IFS officers and state government officials through these informal processes are of great significance in India's federal context. This is because, even though economic and development initiatives such as 'Make in India', 'Digital India' and 'Skill India' are launched by the central government, they ultimately have to be realized in cooperation from both the bureaucracy and political leadership at the Indian state level (Roche, 2015).

Conclusions: Institutionalizing Paradiplomacy in India: Nascent Yet Ambitious

In this chapter, the authors examined the role of domestic political actors in shaping Indian foreign policy in the twenty first century. The three factors steering the institutionalization of paradiplomacy in India were highlighted and argued to be; (i) the promotion of cooperative and competitive federalism; (ii) the pursuit of commercial and cultural diplomacy by states; and (iii) the enhancement of bureaucratic efficiency. In reality, there is a considerable overlap in the purposes served by the paradiplomatic institutions. This is a fluid process with institutions serving multiple or all the three grounds for institutionalization. For instance, the States Division of the MEA is driven by all three factors and serves as a bridge between Indian state governments and foreign governments. The active involvement of state governments in Indian foreign policy making is indicative of the central government's intent to utilize the country's diverse subnational actors and identities as instruments to achieve its diplomatic and foreign policy objectives. The cautious institutionalization of paradiplomacy is realized through the development of new norms, rules and institutions, and has facilitated the strengthening of India's position and identity as an economic and diplomatic power in international affairs.

As elaborated previously, almost all elements of institutionalization of paradiplomacy as explained by Kuznetsov (2015) – barring the establishment of paraconsulates or foreign ministries at the regional level – can be seen in India and thus, one must not undervalue these developments. In 2016, there were even newspaper reports that the southern Indian state of Telangana went to the extent of establishing a foreign ministry, though this was later rejected by the MEA (Asthana & Jacob, 2017). Moreover, the examples discussed in this chapter are by no means exhaustive. Initiatives such as the establishment of the Special Economic Zones or Border Haats (markets) in border states to enhance trade with neighbouring states can also be considered institutional arrangements to further paradiplomacy. Yet, the institutionalization of paradiplomacy in India is still in its nascency in comparison to that of several federal democracies of the West, such as Belgium or Canada. For example, the Government of Flanders in Belgium has established a Flanders Department of Foreign Affairs and also has foreign representation (or paraconsulates) in many capitals around the world (Embassy of Belgium, n.d.).

At the same time, one must also not be tempted to inflate these developments because most of the paradiplomatic engagements in India still continue to be ad hoc, sporadic in nature and provisional upon the outcomes of the political bargains between the Centre and the states. Furthermore, in a few cases the institutions to further paradiplomacy have been created on paper but suffer from many structural problems due to a shortage of resources or the lack of a clear mandate. For instance, some of the WTO cells have largely been ineffective in their functioning due to a lack of interest from the states and the Centre in setting up these cells and a lack of sufficient follow-up on its recommendations. The WTO cells also suffer from severe staffing and financial constraints. Consequently, these cells have either remained dormant or have become defunct (Jayaram, 2006).

Additionally, there are no uniform guidelines from the Centre on the powers and responsibilities of these institutions. For instance, the establishment and the effectiveness of the NRI Cells or the state WTO Cells relies largely on state governments being proactive. There are also no mechanisms in place to check the effectiveness of these institutions and while there is an 'alliteration soup' of state-level investment summits in India, most remain about optics rather than investments. Many of the proposed MoUs are also not translated into actual investments (Kishore, 2018). For instance, a study by the Centre for Monitoring Indian Economy concluded that only a fourth of the investment announcements between 2003 and 2016 have been completed (Varma, 2018). Furthermore, at present, there seems to be little effort taken by the Centre and the states towards a systematic and long-term approach towards establishing institutions to decentralize foreign policy decision-making.

Paradiplomatic activities are generally successful in the areas of low politics, as is the case in India too. The central government has guarded authority over areas of high politics, such as on issues relating to political, strategic or security issues of foreign policy. The MEA also seeks to strike a delicate balance between state governments' interests and its own jurisdiction, as illustrated earlier in the case of Telangana's proposed foreign ministry. While there are indeed instances of state governments being involved in political or security issues of foreign policy, especially with regard to relations with the neighbouring states, these have generally been for pragmatic reasons or political compulsions. The case of a regional political party such as the Dravida Munnetra Kazhagam affecting India's United Nations High Commissioner for Refugees stance on the Sri Lankan civil war is a typical example (Blarel, 2019). However, this can be seen as a one-off event with little chance of being institutionalized in the future. Overall, while this chapter focuses on the role of state governments in institutionalizing paradiplomacy, as demonstrated above, other subnational actors can also influence India's foreign policy. Subsequently, the role of regional political parties or cities in furthering paradiplomacy could be an interesting consideration for future research.

References

Aguirre, Iñaki (1999) 'Making Sense of Paradiplomacy? An Intertextual Enquiry about a Concept in Search of a Definition', *Regional & Federal Studies*, 9 (1): 185–209.

Ahluwalia, Pranay (2021) 'Rebooting India's Foreign Ministry', *The Diplomat*, 2 October. Available at https://thediplomat.com/2021/10/rebooting-indias-foreign-m inistry/ [last accessed 15 November 2021].

ANI (2020) 'TN CM Chairs Inaugural Session of Diplomatic Outreach Summit on Investment Opportunities', *ANI*, 21 February. Available at www.aninews.in/news/na tional/general-news/tn-cm-chairs-inaugural-session-of-diplomatic-outreach-summit-on- investment-opportunities20200221234910/ [last accessed 26 December 2021].

Asthana, Anamika & Jacob, Happymon (2017) 'The Growing Power of States in India's Foreign Policy', *International Negotiation*, 22: 317–343.

Blarel, Nicolas (2019) 'Coalition Politics and the Making of Indian Foreign Policy: A New Research Program'. *India Review*, 18 (5): 582–595.

Burchill, Scott (2005) 'Liberalism', in S. Burchill & L. Andrew (eds), *Theories of International Relations*, 3rd edition (Basingstoke: Palgrave Macmillan), pp. 55–83.

Bywalec, Grzegorz (2018) 'Paradiplomacy in India As Exemplified by the State of Gujarat', in Malgorzata Pietrasiak, Grzegorz Bywalec, Tomasz Kamiński, Dominik Mierzejewski & Michal Słowikowski (eds), *Paradiplomacy in Asia: Case studies of China, India and Russia* (Łódź: Łódź University Press), pp. 39–90.

Deccan Herald (2016) 'New Ambassador to Portugal from Hubballi', *Deccan Herald*, 9 June. Available at www.deccanherald.com/content/551300/ambassador-portugal-hubballi.html [last accessed 18 October 2021].

Duchacek, Ivo (1990) 'Perforated Sovereignties: Toward a Typology of New Actors in International Relations', in Hans J. Michelmann & Panayotis Soldatos (eds), *Federalism and International Relations: The Role of Subnational Units* (Oxford: Clarendon Press), pp. 1–33.

Duran, Manuel (2015) *Mediterranean Paradiplomacies: The Dynamics of Diplomatic Reterritorialization* (Leiden: Brill).

Embassy of Belgium (n.d.) 'Policy'. Available at www.flanders.org.za/Flanders/Foreign-Affairs [last accessed 29 December 2021].

Government of Kerala (2017) 'Sharjah Ruler Sheikh Sultan's Historic Visit', *Kerala Calling*, 38 (1): 6–10.

Government of Punjab (n.d.) 'Mera Pind Mera Shehar – Nurture Your Roots – Make a Difference'. Available at http://nripunjab.gov.in/mera-pind.htm [last accessed 14 October 2021].

Heywood, A. (2011) *Global Politics* (Basingstoke: Palgrave Macmillan).

Hindu (2019) 'Diplomatic Outreach Programme Today', *The Hindu*, 9 August. Available at www.thehindu.com/news/cities/Vijayawada/diplomatic-outreach-programme-today/article28918484.ece [last accessed 26 December 2021].

Indian Council for Cultural Relations (n.d.) 'Indian Cultural Centers Abroad List View'. Available at https://iccr.gov.in/indian-cultural-center-map-list-view [last accessed 14 December 2021].

Indian Express (2016) 'South Block Initiative: Indian Envoys to Facilitate Trade Link between States & Countries of Posting', *Indian Express*, May 28. Available at https://indianexpress.com/article/india/india-news-india/south-block-initiative-indian-envoys-to-facilitate-trade-link-between-states-countries-of-posting-2822694/ [last accessed 25 October 2021].

Jacob, Happymon (2016) *Putting the Periphery at the Center: Indian States' Role in Foreign Policy* (Washington, DC: Carnegie Endowment for International Peace).

Jain, Purnendra & Maini, Tridivesh Singh (2017) 'India's Subnational Governments Foray into the International Arena', *Japanese Journal of Political Science*, 18 (2): 286–312.

Jayaram, Suprita (2006) 'Functioning of WTO Cells in India: A Critique'. Available at https://cuts-citee.org/pdf/fwto.pdf [last accessed 21 October 2021].

Jenkins, Rob (2003) 'India's States and the Making of Foreign Economic Policy: The Limits of the Constituent Diplomacy Paradigm', *Publius*, 33 (4): 63–81.

Jha, Prakash Chandra (2014) 'Federalism, Regionalism and States' Paradiplomacy in India', in Lancy Lobo, Mrutuyanjaya Sahu & Jayesh Shah (eds), *Federalism in India: Towards a Fresh Balance of Power* (Delhi: Rawat Publications), pp. 234–260.

Kishore, Roshan (2018) 'Can Investor Summits Tackle Uttar Pradesh's Development Challenge?', *Hindustan Times*, 26 February. Available at www.hindustantimes.com/india-news/can-investor-summits-tackle-uttar-pradesh-s-development-challenge/story-T8eMAAVn057AWQYIk6YnzO.html [last accessed 25 December 2021].

Kumar, Anil (2017) 'Haryana to Set Up Two NRI Cells', *The Hindu*, 12 July. Available at www.thehindu.com/news/national/other-states/Haryana-to-set-up-two-NRI-cells/article17026782.ece [last accessed 15 November 2021].

Kuznetsov, Alexander (2015) *Theory and Practice of Paradiplomacy* (New York: Routledge).

Lecours, André (2008) *Political Issues of Paradiplomacy: Lessons from the Developed World* (The Hague: Clingendael Institute).

Maini, Tridivesh Singh (2015) 'Making India's Investor Summits More Effective', *The Diplomat*, 16 January. Available at https://thediplomat.com/2015/01/making-investor-summits-more-effective/ [last accessed 15 November 2021].

Manikam, Alam Syamsidar Mutu & Puspitasari, Irfa (2021) 'The Significance of India's National Identity in Foreign Policy to One Belt One Road (OBOR)', in *Proceedings of Airlangga Conference on International Relations (ACIR 2018) – Politics, Economy, and Security in Changing Indo-Pacific Region* (Surabaya: Science and Technology Publications), pp. 428–433.

Mathrubhumi (2020) 'Kerala Ministers Make Most Number of Visits to UAE for Personal Purpose', *Mathrubhumi English*, 1 December. Available at https://english.mathrubhumi.com/news/kerala/kerala-ministers-make-most-number-of-visits-to-uae-for-personal-purpose-1.5247289 [last accessed 28 December 2021].

McHugh, James T. (2015) 'Paradiplomacy, Protodiplomacy and the Foreign Policy Aspirations of Quebec and Other Canadian Provinces', *Canadian Foreign Policy Journal*, 21 (3): 238–256.

Ministry of External Affairs (n.d.) 'Indian Missions Abroad'. Available at www.mea.gov.in/indian-missions-abroad-new.htm [last accessed 18 December 2021].

Ministry of External Affairs (2018) 'State Summits across India Draw Big Investments', *IndBiz*, 28 February. Available at https://indbiz.gov.in/state-summits-across-india-draw-big-investments/ [last accessed 18 December 2021].

Natarajan, Aishwarya (2019) 'Democratization of Foreign Policy: India's Experience with Paradiplomacy', *Law and Development Review*, 12 (3): 797–818.

NavHind Times (2018) 'Four Indian Ambassadors "Adopt" Goa for Promotion', *The NavHind Times*, 6 July. Available at www.navhindtimes.in/four-indian-ambassadors-adopt-goa-for-promotion/ [last accessed 17 October 2021].

New Indian Express (2017) 'Kerala Seeks Housing Project in Gulf City', *The New Indian Express*, 26 September. Available at www.newindianexpress.com/states/kerala/2017/sep/26/kerala-seeks-housing-project-in-gulf-city-1662653.html [last accessed December 28, 2020].

New Indian Express (2018a) 'Tamil Nadu Government to Create Tamil Chairs in Top Global Universities', *The New Indian Express*, 29 June. Available at www.newindianexpress.com/states/tamil-nadu/2018/jun/29/tamil-nadu-government-to-create-tamil-chairs-in-top-global-universities-1835341.html [last accessed December 20, 2020].

New Indian Express (2018b) 'Two Cells Set Up to Assist Investors, NRIs in Andhra Pradesh', *The New Indian Express*, 13 September. Available at www.newindianexpress.com/states/andhra-pradesh/2018/sep/13/2-cells-set-up-to-assist-investors-nris-in-andhra-pradesh-1871306.html [last accessed 1 November 2021].

NORKA-Roots (n.d.) 'Services'. Available at https://norkaroots.org/ [last accessed 15 October 2021].

One India (2007) 'MEA to Open its Branch Secretariat in Chennai on Aug 25', *One India*, 23 August. Available at www.oneindia.com/2007/08/23/mea-to-open-its-bra nch-secretariat-in-chennai-on-aug-25-1187872683.html [last Accessed 15 October 2020].

Pietrasiak, Malgorzata (2018) 'The International Activity of Federal Subjects of the Russian Federation on the Case of the Far East', in Malgorzata Pietrasiak, Grze-gorz Bywalec, Tomasz Kamiński, Dominik Mierzejewski & Michal Słowikowski (eds.), *Paradiplomacy in Asia: Case studies of China, India and Russia* (Łódź: Łódź University Press), pp. 39–90.

PNS (2016) 'States Division Helping MEA Identify Target States', *The Pioneer*, 15 March. Available at www.dailypioneer.com/2016/india/states-division-helping-mea -identify-target-states.html [last accessed 26 December 2021].

PTI (2014a) 'Section in MEA to Boost States' Efforts to Woo FDI, Push Exports', *The Economic Times*, 26 November. Available at https://economictimes.indiatimes. com/news/economy/policy/section-in-mea-to-boost-states-efforts-to-woo-fdi-push-e xports/articleshow/45286160.cms?from=mdr [last accessed 10 December 2020].

PTI (2014b) 'Several Pacts Signed during Mamata's Singapore Visit', *India Today*, 20 August. Available at www.indiatoday.in/india/east/story/mamta-banerjee-singapore-vi sit-pacts-signed-west-bengal-cm-204908-2014-08-20 [last accessed November 20, 2021].

PTI (2015a) '"Biswa Bangla" Brand to be Taken Overseas: West Bengal CM, Mamata Banerjee', *DNA India*, 19 June. Available at www.dnaindia.com/india/rep ort-biswa-bangla-brand-to-be-taken-overseas-west-bengal-cm-mamata-banerjee-20 97116 [last accessed 26 December 2021].

PTI (2015b) 'West Bengal and Britain Sign 21 MoUs', *Business Standard*, 28 July. Available at www.business-standard.com/article/pti-stories/west-bengal-and-brita in-sign-21-mous-115072800025_1.html [last accessed 20 December 2020].

Rana, Kishan (2020) 'The MEA's Structural Reforms Are Promising, but Not Suffi-cient', *The Wire*, 18 November. Available at https://thewire.in/government/minis try-external-affairs-reform-foreign-policy [last accessed 18 November 2021].

Reus-Smit, C. (2005) 'Constructivism', in S. Burchill & L. Andrew (eds), *Theories of International Relations*, 3rd edition (Basingstoke: Palgrave Macmillan), pp. 188–212.

Roche, Elizabeth (2015) 'Diplomats Work on an Added Role: Showcase States Abroad', *Livemint*, 27 July. Available at www.livemint.com/Politics/HY9v wUl6wc782xNPyZCmMN/Diplomats-work-on-an-added-role-showcase-states-abr oad.html [last accessed 10 December 2020].

Saseendran, Sajila (2019) 'Kerala CM Pinarayi Vijayan Lands in UAE for 4-Day Visit', *Gulf News*, 13 February. Available at https://gulfnews.com/uae/kerala-cm-pinarayi-vija yan-lands-in-uae-for-4-day-visit-1.62046795 [last accessed 10 December 2020].

Schaffer, Teresita Currie & Schaffer, Howard Bruner (2016) *India at the Global High Table: The Quest for Regional Primacy and Strategic Autonomy* (Washington, DC: Brookings Institution Press).

Sekar, D. (2020) 'Facilitate More Investments in Tamil Nadu, Edappadi K Pala-niswami Urges Envoys', *Deccan Herald*, 22 February. Available at www.decca nchronicle.com/nation/politics/220220/facilitate-more-investments-in-tamil-nadu-ed appadi-k-palaniswami-urge.html [last accessed 26 December 2021].

Shukla, Srijan (2019) 'With Just 1,400 Diplomats, India's Foreign Influence Is Severely Limited', *The Print*, 10 April. Available at https://theprint.in/diplomacy/ with-just-1400-diplomats-indias-foreign-influence-is-severely-limited/219288/ [last accessed 20 October 2021].

Sinha, Kounteya (2015) 'Mamata Help for Bengali Course in UK', *The Times of India*, 22 July. Available at https://timesofindia.indiatimes.com/india/Mamata-help-for-Bengali-course-in-UK/articleshow/48166158.cms [last accessed 20 December 2021].

Sreenivasan, T. P. (2017) 'States in Indian Diplomacy: When Sharjah Ruler Visited Kerala', *The Hindu*, 6 October. Available at www.thehindu.com/opinion/lead/states-in-indian-diplomacy/article19803262.ece [last accessed 20 October 2021].

Stancati, Margherita (2012) 'Why Hillary Clinton Went to Kolkata to See "Didi"', *The Wall Street Journal*, 7 May. Available at www.wsj.com/articles/BL-IRTB-15399 [last accessed 20 October 2021].

Tavares, Rodrigo (2016) *Paradiplomacy: Cities and States as Global Players* (Oxford: Oxford University Press).

Tewari, Falguni (2017) *Paradiplomacy in India: Evolution and Operationalisation* (Mumbai: Observer Research Foundation).

Utomo, Ario Bimo (2019) 'Reimagining City Identities in Globalisation: A Constructivist Study on City Paradiplomacy', *Global South Review* 1 (2): 33–48.

Vadlamannati, Krishna Chaitanya (2012) 'A Race to Compete for Investment among Indian States? – An Empirical Investigation'. Available at www.uni-heidelberg.de/md/awi/professuren/intwipol/regional.pdf.

Varma, Subodh (2018) 'Investment Summits: All Dressed Up and Nowhere to Go', *News Click*, 23 February. Available at www.newsclick.in/investment-summits-all-dressed-and-nowhere-go [last accessed 25 December 2021].

Wendt, A. (1992) 'Anarchy Is What States Make of it: The Social Construction of Power Politics', *International organization*, 46 (2): 391–425.

Wyatt, Andrew (2017) 'Paradiplomacy of India's Chief Ministers', *India Review* 16 (1): 106–124.

10 Futures in the Making

An Analysis of Indian Climate Policy Articulations

Miriam Prys-Hansen

It will be known to most observers that India has a complicated relationship with the global climate regime, as manifested in the United Nations Framework Convention on Climate Change (UNFCCC). Recently, this found expression at the UNFCCC Conference of the Parties in November 2021 (COP26). Here, the Indian government on the one hand surprised the world, including some Indian climate policy experts, by announcing a 2070 net-zero goal. On the other hand, the conference also saw India's well-covered and widely criticized last minute intervention, in which it, at least at first glance, forced the international community to retreat from a consensus on the phase-out of coal to a phase-down of coal. Once the mood had cooled down, analyses painted a more favourable picture of India, in which its focus on the need to develop and the obstacles towards a fast phase-out of coal, as well as the failure of the developed world to quickly phase-out fossil fuels themselves, were framed in a more balanced perspective. This instance has nevertheless painted an illuminating picture of India's difficult dual identity as both a developing country that first and foremost has the obligation to lift its population out of poverty, to develop its economy and infrastructure, to provide energy security, and, contrastingly, as a proactive global leader that is willing to take on international responsibilities and contribute to burden-sharing for instance through South-South cooperation within the International Solar Alliance (ISA).

India's multiple 'climate identities' discourses have been discussed in the literature. The timelines of shifts and continuities are well known and much written about (e.g. Dubash 2019), which is why they will not need to be repeated at length here. While what has been described as 'Third Worldism' (Isaksen & Stokke, 2014) or 'growth-first realism' (Dubash, 2013: 197) has emerged and persisted as a very powerful identity for India in the past 30 years of global climate summitry, the realities of India's intense vulnerability, rising international pressures and the actual domestic realization that dangerous climatic change is unstoppable without an engaged India have involved the development of new discourses, described as 'win-win' (Isaksen & Stokke, 2014: 114) or 'sustainable development realists' (Dubash, 2013: 197) as well as bursts of proactive engagement and, aspirational leadership. It

DOI: 10.4324/9781003305132-14

is unclear whether there will be a 'winner' among these competing identities and discourses, which makes it difficult to develop reliable scenarios of how India's climate governance, both nationally and internationally, will progress.

This chapter takes a novel look at Indian climate policies and investigates the future, or more specifically how political elites imagine the future to be. The analysis of these 'climate imaginaries' is a missing piece in the research of Indian global climate governance. Building on scholarship on socio-technic futures (Milkoreit, 2017; Muiderman et al., 2020), I argue that climate imaginaries or 'visions of climate futures' are a necessary ideational foundation for legitimate and adequate climate policies today and thus have a great impact on present political decision-making. This kind of research is important for a volume on India's (global) identities, as the uncertainties and fluidity of climate futures allow for an important impact of identity, memories, experiences and practices to shape the kinds of futures actors can and want to imagine. Looking into the implicit and explicit climate imaginaries in Indian climate policy articulations will also contribute to a better understanding of their respective definition of the problems, challenges and opportunities associated with climate change and plausible solutions, as well as ascriptions of responsibilities for taking action in bringing about a desirable future.

After briefly introducing some theoretical foundations for researching images and visions of future, as well as a brief overview of India's position in the global regime, I present the empirical findings of how the future – and India's role in it – is imagined in Indian domestic and international climate policy statements, as well as their relevance to studying 'Global India'.

Future Visions and Climate Imaginaries

There is not much literature on national or global environmental politics that systematically discusses the role of visions of the future, the conditions under which they come into being and the impact they have on climate policy-making; but there are a few useful starting points (see Milkoreit, 2017; Oomen et al., 2021). However, four kinds of future visions are discussed, which I detail here. First, the literature proposes that the creation and contestation of imaginaries is political. Any societal and political transformation requires debates about the future, as the future is uncertain and can be negotiated. This also requires thinking about the ideational and structural power of those involved in societal deliberation processes in order to understand whose visions prevail and become intersubjectively shared (Milkoreit, 2017: 1). Inversely, if shared visions of those futures are missing in society, it reveals a lack of possible solutions and pathways to counter undesirable effects of climate change.

Second, future visions do not exist in a vacuum but always involve 'beliefs about values, norms and ways of life' (Milkoreit, 2017: 2) that shape what kinds of goals (and, thus, futures) society *should* pursue. Moreover, memories, narratives and explanations of what happened in the past, i.e. particular weather-events and their explanations, shape what can be thought and done in the present. For climate imaginaries scientific knowledge and the inclusion of nature are also essential because both are necessary for understanding environmental conditions and limitations for future societies. What counts as legitimate information is largely determined by the scientific community, as presented, for instance, in the reports of the Intergovernmental Panel on Climate Change (IPCC). To what extent decision-makers follow scientific advice is a different matter, but it seems hard to contest that the science constrains the scope of future visions.

Third, future visions can be not only desirable but also undesirable, and still bear motivational potential for action: either in order to reach a desired future, or to prevent an undesired future through action in the present or near-term future (Milkoreit, 2017: 14; Oomen et al., 2021: 5). Often, the literature distinguishes between emancipatory and apocalyptic catastrophism. While the latter is 'guided by (a) dystopian imagination of the future and humans' hubris to control the climate' (Asayama, 2015: 90), the former views climate through a more optimistic lens by considering 'global climate risk as an opportunity' (Asayama, 2015: 91) for change. Both future visions demand action in the present, but the understanding of how effective behaviour must look like differs. Fourth, as we move into the realm of politics and strategic decision-making, we need to consider that 'the act of futuring' may be driven by various, including politico-strategic, motivations. Oomen et al. define futuring as 'the identification, creation and dissemination of images of the future shaping the possibility space for action' (Oomen et al., 2021: 2–3). I am interested in precisely the relationship between images of the future and the possibility space of governments when negotiating solutions for climate change. If different future visions trigger different solution pathways and we assume that decision-makers are aware of this, we can expect a strategic use of the future visions they produce and share with others. When applied to governmental climate policies, both internal and external, the multiple influences, identities and interests that shape future visions, are likely to lead to variable and often fluid visions of the future across venues, actors, scales and audiences.

India's Climate Present and Climate Future

The following describes a central aspect of India's climate future; 'if India follows a high-carbon path in its economic development, international society as a whole will be unable to keep to the 2°C goal established in the Paris Agreement' (Chatzky, 2019). As it stands, India's rekindled economic growth of 2021 led to a growth in CO_2 emissions of 1.4% when compared to 2019, leaving India roughly at the same level of emissions as the EU, at 2.35Gt (its per capita emissions remain a 60% below the global average) (International Energy Agency, 2021a: 12). This is more than three times as much as in 2005, despite considerable improvements in the CO_2-intensity of its industrial production, for example. Yet, population growth and rapid urbanization will further increase energy demand in the next decades and energy-related CO_2 emissions are projected to increase by 45% until 2040 (International Energy Agency, 2021a: 12). Thus, while the need for new energy infrastructures will, even on a low-carbon development path, lead to a doubling of energy consumption up to the year 2030, this also offers plentiful opportunities: Should the needed investments flow into low-carbon solutions that might lower the prices for solar installations and high-efficient LED technologies (Carrington & Safi, 2017), this may have an exemplary effect on the whole world.

India has already expanded its investment in solar photovoltaics, and this investment has been greater than in all fossil fuel sources of electricity generation taken together. Still, the annual average share of solar and wind energy for the entire country was only 8.2% in 2021 and a rebound in coal demand above 2019 levels drove a significant increase in emissions in India. Overall, 80% of India's total energy demand since 1990 are made up of coal, oil and biomass and, more importantly, 'coal has strengthened its role as the dominant energy source, maintaining its strong position [44% of demand up from 33% in 2000] in power generation as well as being the fuel of choice for many industries' (International Energy Agency, 2021b).

All of this requires the Indian government to take regulative decisions *now* to provide for sufficient improvements in energy efficiency, for example, and it had the chance to chart its plans at the COP in November 2021. It has committed to five pledges: to increase non-fossil energy capacity to 500GW by 2030, to meet 50% of its energy requirements from renewable energy by 2030, to reduce the total projected carbon emissions by 1 billion tonnes by 2030, to reduce the carbon intensity of the economy by more than 45% by 2030, and, as mentioned above, to achieve net-zero carbon emissions by 2070 (Tomar et al., 2021). Yet, it is unclear whether and how some of the at least partially very ambitious goals can be achieved.

India's energy production, consumption and respective CO_2 emissions are, however, not the only important factors to consider when charting India's climate futures. In addition, India's overwhelming vulnerability to weather-related disasters that may be triggered and intensified by climate change, has become once more visible in 2021. This was evidenced for instance in the Uttarakhand floods in February in the surroundings of the Nanda Devi National Park with over 200 people being killed or missing; the series of landslides in Mumbai with 32 people killed, floods and landslides in Maharashtra with over 200 people dead or missing in July; severe flooding in the Saurashtra region in Gujarat with at least six people found dead in September; and the South India floods in November, but also millions of people suffering from extreme heat in June and July as the monsoon rains were delayed in New Delhi and surroundings. It is projected that even under a moderate mitigation scenario (rather than a business-as-usual projection of greenhouse gas emissions), some urban areas of India might become unliveable by 2100 and that more than 80% of India's population lives in areas that are 'highly vulnerable to extreme hydro-met disasters' (Mohanty & Wadhawan, 2021).

The multiple pressures of climate vulnerability, the continued need for poverty alleviation, the population growth but also the opportunities offered by investments in renewable energies give no clear indication of the future directions of Indian domestic and global climate governance ambitions. While its own climate vulnerabilities turn successful regional and global climate initiatives into a necessity for India (Prys-Hansen, 2022), India also continues to make its own climate action conditional on the actions of developed countries and exposing its traditional 'Third-Worldism' identity. Additionally, the Indian government positions itself as global leader in tackling vulnerabilities and helping other states of the Global South to do so, for instance through the ISA, which stands at least in partial contradiction to the previous two points. If we look to the national level of climate policymaking, the ambiguities in India's climate policies become once more visible: while its leadership in climate matters is 'real' in one sense, it is also adequate to describe India's nationally determined contributions as being 'in reality fairly modest' (Mohan & Wehnert, 2019: 276). Strong reductions in emission intensity took already place between 2005 and 2011, so that, arguably, India 'has very much played it safe about international commitments' (Mohan & Wehnert, 2019: 276). Hence, it is reasonable to suspect that at least some of India's global climate leadership posturing has been a means of increasing its diplomatic clout rather than providing effective solutions to the problem, when domestically, the government has yet to develop a roadmap for the phase-out of fossil fuels, for example.

Considering the review of literature on both the politics of the future and Indian climate policymaking, I come to the following research questions for this chapter: When looking at two different arenas (international / domestic) of climate policy articulation, how is the future constructed and talked about? Are there differences and similarities? What kinds of different norms, values or principles are appealed to? And what responsibilities are assigned and to whom? I attempt to answer these questions by means of a qualitative text analysis, using Atlas.ti with a team of three coders. First, we collected a total of 151 speeches, reports and statements by the Indian political elite, including the President, the Prime Minster, the Minister of Environment, the Minister for Energy, and other representatives of the Indian government both at national and international venues between 2006 and 2021, focusing on periods around the COPs. We include two different governments, under Prime Minster Singh (2004–2014) and Prime Minster Modi (since 2014), and hence cover potential variation across party lines and venues. I thus investigate only the elite, official discourse on climate change. This seems justified, as most of the (little) literature on India's climate change policy at the national-international nexus argues that the climate change topic has largely been dominated by the central government. Mostly, at the national level, it is linked to development policies and used as a strategic aspect of foreign policy. This is somewhat in contrast with India's often ambitious reporting on domestic mitigation activities.

One of the key arguments in the 'domestic' literature is that there is a lack of institutionalization of climate policymaking in India, but that instead 'climate institutions have been … layered upon existing bodies' (Pillai & Dubash, 2021). This has integrated climate policy making into other strategic objectives. Another important factor to consider is, as said above, the change of government from the Congress-led United Progressive Alliance (UPA) under Manmohan Singh, who served as Prime Minister from 2004 to 2014, to the Bharatiya Janata Party (BJP)-led National Democratic Alliance under Narendra Modi, who has held the office since 2014. Most of the foreign-policy literature in general and climate diplomacy in specific finds a considerable amount of continuity between the two governments. This may point towards a solidified material and/or ideational basis of policies, for example, in the relationship of people to nature or the legacy of Gandhi, and that the changes in climate policy and its articulation mainly arise out of growing knowledge, but also growing pressures from the global level as well as from internal, and mostly societal, forces (Dubash, 2019; Pant, 2019; Saran & Jones, 2017).

We coded the material for visions of climate futures regarding 'agency' (who influences the future and to what degree), time ('when' is this envisioned future happening), scope (is the future of local, national, or global extent), the particular reference to climate change (water, biodiversity, human survival and so on), and the normative evaluation of this future. Moreover, the ascription of responsibilities for actions associated with the vision have been tracked. Throughout the coding process, I reiteratively refined the specific sub-categories for these codes and added codes for reoccurring other themes.

Indian Domestic and International Climate Imaginaries

I first looked for *general* images of the future that may guide Indian climate action at home or abroad. Yet, there is little concrete or even abstract talk about what future is expected and, accordingly, which actions need to be taken by whom in relation to this future. Prime Minister Singh at times voiced concern at a *national* stage about the basic shape of the development path India should take, as in the following example:

> humanity's approach to climate change and other global challenges has to be need based, not greed based, as Gandhi taught us. So, I sometimes reflect on whether we should follow the same unsustainable path the industrialized countries took to develop and modernize their societies. Ecological devastation of whatever cause or origin will have far greater

consequences in India than in the West. We need to recognize our own reality and have an informed and rational debate on what is in our enlightened self-interest.

(Singh, 2009b)

Statements by Prime Minister Modi (since 2014) regarding Indian environmental futures, generally are much more optimistic, as in this statement:

India will prosper both economically and environmentally. India will build more roads and India will have cleaner rivers. India will have better train connectivity and also greater tree coverage. India will build more homes for our citizens and at the same time create quality habitats for animals ... This balance is what will contribute to a strong and inclusive India.

(Modi, 2019b)

The kind of, this points towards strong, identity-based commitments that require present and future engagement on climate change in order to follow prescribed paths of actions, especially at the national level where India's main responsibility will continue to lie:

in line with our tradition of living in harmony with nature and culture of deep respect for the planet, we are taking ambitious action on expanding clean & renewable energy, energy efficiency, afforestation and bio-diversity. Today, India is creating new records in collective effort for climate adaptation, mitigation and resilience and forging multilateral alliances. India is among the top countries in the world in terms of installed renewable energy, wind and solar energy capacity.

(Modi, 2021c)

These statements point at a necessity of Indian present and future climate action mostly domestically, but also a certain optimism about this future. We also find only few references to India's vulnerability and its ramifications for the future; and if so, any descriptions of vulnerabilities are often accompanied by presentations of policy initiatives that will be taken or have already been taken by the government to solve the problem. Interestingly, official statements addressing actual natural disasters like the severe flooding, did, for the most, not make any direct links to climate change.

At the international level, considering both India's vulnerability as well as its vocal history of demanding adequate climate action from developed countries, I expected India to actively engage in a politics of the future, that uses doom and gloom scenarios to push for action by others. Yet, one of the most apparent patterns in the collected documents is, again, the general absence of gloomy future visions about the adverse impacts of climate change in India, particularly in international venues. This is remarkable in comparison to the statements of other nations severely endangered by climate change, including the speech by Tuvalu's foreign minister at COP26 held standing knee deep in seawater to highlight his nations endangerment by rising sea levels. Thus, at least in official statements, India's intense climate vulnerabilities are not projected into the future and thus play only a little role in its public climate imaginaries.

A second emergent pattern in both national and international venues and across time is the need for, but also the certainty of, future economic development in India. Addressing the international community at COP17 in Durban in 2011, Jayanthi Natarajan, Minister of Environment and Forests, argued that:

> We must also not forget that, for a very large number of poor in the developing world, the world has not changed. ... [T]hey cannot be expected to be legally bound to reduce their emissions when they have practically no emissions ... [Therefore, the] [e]radication of their poverty and social and economic development is the primary goal.
>
> (Natarajan, 2011)

This pattern also continues after 2014. In a speech at COP20 in Lima, Prakash Javadekar, Minister of Environment, Forests and Climate Change stated that:

> The new Government in India ... represents the hopes and aspirations of more than a billion Indian people for growth and inclusive development' and further claims that ... [w]e are determined to ensure development to all these people and provide them with basic services of energy, water, sanitation, healthcare, education and employment.
>
> (Javadekar, 2014)

According to the statements, this intended economic development will be in line with environmental protection or is even a prerequisite for it. In 2018, Sushma Swaraj, External Affairs Minister, stated that:

> The schemes and projects of the government to address the development needs of our people balance the three pillars of sustainable development – economic growth, social development, and environmental preservation.
>
> (Swaraj, 2018)

In contrast to the record of developed countries, India describes it thus as its 'destiny' to achieve a sustainable transformation of its economy. This pertains to the widespread idea that India will be 'amongst the most responsible (countries) in ensuring a high rate of growth of the real GDP-Green Domestic Product' (Ramesh, 2010). Presenting India's global role at a national venue, Prime Minister Modi emphasized also to a national audience the nexus of poverty reduction and sustainable development, and the way that India can exercise leadership:

> today India is recognized as one of the countries of the world that fulfil all the resolutions taken in their interest and the interest of the world. I am confident that India will be leading the world in achieving Poverty Elimination and Sustainable Development Goals.
>
> (Modi, 2019a)

Third, the Indian government across time also consistently assigns responsibilities for future burden-taking to others, above all developed countries: India insists on developed countries to provide the necessary financial support for its own but also other developing countries' sustainable transformation. In two different submission documents from 2018, the Government of India states that '[i]t is observed that financial support is required to be transferred from developed countries to developing countries to carry out many of the suggested activities' (Government of India, 2018a). Other forms of responsibility ascription pertain to individual, developed-country 'lifestyles' that need to be changed, a future prescription that, in both governments, is largely limited to statements at international venues, for example by Prime Minster Modi in the framework of the G20; 'when we speak of targets, we must not only reduce the use of fossil fuel, but also moderate our lifestyle' (Modi, 2015a). Similar statements are made at other occasions, yet this is a new development with the premiership of Narendra Modi.

Fourth, I assessed principles and values that are considered to determine a 'good' and desirable future. Above all, moral considerations of equity are an important factor in the 'politics of the future' by the Indian governments. They serve as basic principles according to which present *and* future responsibilities should be distributed, again, both nationally and internationally, as well as across governments. Since developed countries' economic growth was based on greenhouse gas intensive industries, India has long considered itself and other developing countries entitled to the same right. In 2014, Prakash Javadekar, State Minister for Environment, Forests & Climate Change: noted that: '[i]t should be able to address the genuine requirements of the developing countries by providing them equitable carbon space to achieve sustainable development and eradicate poverty' (Javadekar, 2014).

This seems to be in contrast with India's multiple assertions that sustainable growth is possible and how well India is dealing with this transformation. Instead, it points to a more realistic imaginary of the short- and mid-term future which will be characterized by high emissions from India and other developing countries. Calling for equitable carbon space aims at justifying the current – and probably ongoing – increase in emissions while the sustainable development vision is supposed to serve as an outlook for what is intended beyond that in the more long-term future. In addition, India insists on the future relevance of the 'principles and provisions of the Convention'

(Government of India, 2018b), above all, common but differentiated responsibility. Despite its more limited importance in the Paris Agreement, India
projects this norm into the future because it benefits substantially from it and
'anything else would be morally wrong' (Modi, 2015b).

With regard to other values used by the Indian government, it is noticeable
that equity plays a relatively large role in the international context, while it is
not discussed in the national context, i.e. within Indian society, despite considerable gaps between the carbon footprints in different sections of society
and, for instance, the capacities of different Indian regions or states to mitigate emissions. The debate on this instead seems replaced by a call to order
and harmony among Indians when it comes to climate futures, as expressed
by the Ministry of Environment, Forests & Climate Change:

> the Indian conception of life is embodied in a coherent world-view in
> which all its aspects exist in a state of inter-related harmony, ... the
> human being is part of a well-ordered system in which all aspects of life
> and nature have their place, and are not in opposition, but in harmony
> with each other. This harmony between humans and nature is integral to
> the Indian tradition and ethos.
>
>   (Ministry of Environment, Forest and Climate Change, 2015)

Even though Prime Minister Singh's government uses fewer spiritual references, it still often refers to Indian culture, which is inherently in unison with
nature and can thus carry green economic growth. The Singh government
also expressed this internationally, for example at COP16:

> ecological preservation and celebration of biodiversity is embedded in
> Indian culture in myriad ways. India will ... be amongst the most
> responsible in ensuring a high rate of growth of the real GDP – Green
> Domestic Product. That is my solemn assurance to the world community
> today on behalf of the Government of India. Environmental stewardship
> demands responsive leadership. That is India's calling.
>
>   (Ramesh, 2010)

Repeatedly, the Indian government thus emphasizes the natural connection
and inseparableness between the Indian people and nature, describing it, as
said above, as the foundation of all climate action, both at home and abroad.
A comparison between the Modi and the Singh governments shows some
variance. Prime Minister Singh includes democracy, the rule of law and religious freedom among India's national values, in addition to the connection
to nature and the resulting environmental responsibility. This domestic
statement is exemplary:

> friends, I know you will agree with me that the real strength of our
> country will come from an overriding sense of national purpose. We need

to return our economy to the high growth path. Above all, we need to strengthen the values that define us – democracy, rule of law, individual liberties, social and religious harmony and commitment to global peace.

(Singh, 2013)

Singh's government also cites the closeness to nature of Indians and its leaders at the international level, placing it in a context that legitimizes India's climate policy and leaves little room for critical debate:

these [Indian] leaders' beliefs ... were deeply rooted in our civilizational legacy, which emphasized the need for harmony between Man and Nature, rather than Man triumphing over Nature. ... the concept of sacred groves, sacred trees and sacred animals created a spiritual framework of conservation, which is still observed in many parts of our country.

(Mukherjee, 2008)

Modi takes up the link between environmental awareness and development in front of national audiences. However, in addition to general value statements, strong references to Hinduism also emerge, as was expected, 'our scriptures have always taught us the balance of the relationship of animals and nature; hostility and totality; and creature and Shiva' (Modi, 2021b). By highlighting the closeness between the environment and India's history as well as beliefs, the impression is created, that the Indian government cannot act differently but in continuous harmony with nature:

balance between development and environment is an important part of our ancient tradition, which we are also making the strength of self-reliant India. ... everything we do for ourselves directly affects our environment. Therefore, India's efforts are also increasing regarding the efficiency of its resources.

(Modi, 2021b)

These spiritual references appeal to the level of beliefs, identity and memories, also transcending the need for scientific verification.

Another aspect I looked for in the collected statements is the role of technology and science. Particularly in the Modi government, technology plays a crucial role in optimistic climate imaginaries. What is called 'the 'Make in India' vision' (Mukherjee, 2015), for example, refers to state-of-the-art technologies in railway systems and the contribution to it by research in order to 'create a wholesome eco-system to transform India into a manufacturing hub' (Mukherjee, 2015). The values and spiritual expressions described above can also be seen as a rhetorical initiator for technological change and India's role in it, as in this statement already from 2013; 'with the vision of Jawaharlal Nehru and Indira Gandhi, India has built a strong indigenous base of science and technology ... we shall concentrate effort in frontier areas of science and technology to put ourselves abreast of advanced nations. I am confident our scientists will rise to this challenge' (Gandhi, 2013). The role of science and technology thus becomes a national task, particularly as it pertains competing or at least catching up with the global North. The Indian government thus also increasingly emphasizes its role as a technology leader, especially in the context of the ISA, as illustrated by R.K. Singh, responsible for the Ministry of New and Renewable Energy, at an ISA assembly: 'It is time for all of us to get together to make energy access using solar and renewable energy available. We have successfully done this in India, and it can be replicated globally' (Ministry of New and Renewable Energy, 2021). While this plays to the tune of India's identity as a global power of the Global South, present across this volume, with regard to climate change, this, however, clearly also involves a strategic interest in creating more self-sufficiency.

A pattern that rhetorically ties both the spiritual references as well as India's global reach is the presentation of India as a model of success in the fight against climate change. This narrative is especially present with a view to the future and is used by both the Singh and Modi governments, not least to circumvent criticism of their own climate goals. This vision of the future also includes poverty alleviation, for example nationally addressed by President Patil during the Singh government:

> we are presenting a new template of a society where livelihoods can be secured for millions of underprivileged and the aspirations of our youth for a better life can be met; a society where massive developmental projects do not impinge on the security of the ecology and environment; a society that is open, democratic and transparent.
>
> (Patil, 2012)

The Modi government continues this narrative at the national level, especially pertaining to renewable energies, and also often links it to social justice; 'India has taken a lead in addressing these issues of energy access. In our success, I see hope for the world that problems of energy availability can be suitably addressed' (Modi, 2019a).

At the same time, government officials often point to the constraints India faces with its huge population and comparatively low financial resources. Despite these adversities, they express that India is a global player in the fight against climate change:

> the world once used to see India as a challenge to climate change because of its huge population. Today the situation has changed. Today our country is emerging as the leader of climate justice and is a big force against a formidable crisis.
>
> (Modi, 2021b)

This self-dramatization, however, is largely absent at the international level, which is not particularly surprising in view of the only minor concessions made in terms of total emissions targets.

Lastly, I assessed views on the scope and venue at which climate governance should ideally take place. First, overall, Indian governments generally express optimism about the prospects of future international cooperation, despite their often-critical interventions at the COPs over the years. In 2011, the Minister of Environment and Forests declared that '[w]e are fully behind you to ensure that Durban CoP becomes a successful CoP for climate change' (Natarajan, 2011) and Prime Minister Modi affirmed in 2015 that '[w]e will succeed if we have the wisdom and courage to craft a genuinely collective partnership that balances responsibilities and capabilities with aspirations and needs. I am confident that we will' (Modi, 2015b).

As said above, however, there is also a considerable shift of blame or responsibility from the national to the international level, particularly taking place in domestic settings, as expressed by Prime Minister Singh:

> I would like to emphasise that Climate Change is a challenge of global dimensions. It deserves a global and a collaborative response. It is unfortunate that the global discourse on Climate Change has become enmeshed with arguments about maintaining economic competitiveness or level playing fields. Climate Change is becoming the pretext for pursuing protectionist policies under a green label.
>
> (Singh, 2009a)

The UPA government thus presented a clear image in that domestic level responsibilities are not to be meddled with by international agreements and binding commitments for the future, whereby 'it is to our advantage to build a low-carbon Indian economy and to be even ambitious in this regard. But this is a national effort dictated by our own growth choices. When it comes to multilateral negotiations on dealing with climate change, the dynamics are different' (Saran, 2008). This emphasis on the sovereignty of economic decision making by the Special Envoy for Climate Change is pointing to, at least in previous governments, strong sense of the separation of the domestic and global level climate discourse: 'whatever action we take domestically ..., let it be clearly understood that there is no legal obligation on the part of India, under existing international instruments, to take on binding emissions reduction obligations, now or in the post 2012 period' (Saran, 2008).

While I could not identify similar statements by officials from the Modi government, which marks an important change from the first to the second decade of the 2000s, there are remnants of this in India's refusal to agree to a coal phase-out at COP26.

Conclusions: Identity *and* Strategy Shape Climate Futures

This chapter traced the expressed climate future imaginaries of Indian government officials during the current Modi and the past Singh administration. I reviewed literature on the role of future visions for policymaking and subsequently illustrated important patterns in India's climate visions in speeches directed at international and national audiences. This literature led to expectations of differences in visions across national and international venues emanating from different levels of access, power differentials, varying discourses and norms, for example. Visions are centrally related to identity, memories, past experiences, and religious or spiritual perspectives on nature, in the case of climate change, however, also are constrained by necessities of science, technology and strategic interests of all kinds. The role of Indian identity, particularly the role of Hinduism, is often used to point to the inevitability of Indian future climate action; yet, there is politicization of the future to consider, which lets us expect a considerable strategic interest in voicing or avoiding particular imaginaries of the future.

For instance, both on international and national levels, there are not too many direct references to how the future will look like. It is not entirely surprising that a political elite would avoid descriptions of apocalypse; however, the prevalence of optimism and confidence in positive outcomes, particularly in the case of India, are somewhat surprising. Backed by the severe, negative effects of climate change the country and the entire region are facing already, one would expect a greater emphasis on this specific future scenario, which could be imagined to be employed in a strategic manner as well. Despite its economic rise, India still depends financial and technological support, yet the negative impacts of climate change, however, are more explicitly communicated nationally than internationally. This might have to do with the issue that, internationally, it is easier to shift responsibility to other actors (i.e. developed countries) while on the domestic level, the speakers (i.e. government representatives) can be held accountable more immediately.

If futures are described, directly or indirectly, national and international future visions are much alike, albeit a few critical differences. Most domestic rhetoric, across time and governments, emphasis India as an outstanding example that will lead to a better future of sustainable development and renewable energy technologies, both with worthwhile impacts on India itself, but also both developing and developed countries. The patterns of principles to shape the future are also using similar anchors that are also well known from the general debate of Indian climate policy – i.e. the principle of 'common but differentiated responsibilities', the role of equity and justice and demands for international financial support. All of these points remain stable across time and venue. When looking at the potential strategic deployment of this imaginary, intention of envisioning this future perspective is to demonstrate that sustainable and climate-friendly economic growth is not only the goal, but India is on the right path of making it possible. Yet, by emphasizing the voluntary and ambitious nature of their targets, India at the same time puts itself in a favourable light, which is not surprising given the context of international negotiations, but also – already in advance – leaves a loophole open for the possibility of failing. If it was the latter case, India would not be to blame since its targets were still 'only' voluntary.

As said above, both governments describe climate futures as an inherent part of Indian philosophy of life. However, while the Singh government considered this as part of a general social transformation in which community values such as democracy and religious freedom must be preserved, the Modi government focuses on the economic efficiency of the measures as well as Hindu references, appealing to an underlying but essential ideational driver of climate policies and imaginations. Responsibility for a positive climate future is attributed by both governments to the international community, especially in the area of financing and concrete emission targets. The policy field in which India presents itself as a pioneer is that of the energy transition and related technologies. This role is articulated much more strongly in domestic politics and the presence of this vision increases over time, which, also, clearly has to do with the availability and affordability of solar power technologies. At the same time, the international community is used to externalize frustration in the national context to justify the failure of international climate agreements, which should primarily affect the global North, as well as measures that could potentially curtail the economy.

What we failed to observe are clear links to particular governance solutions that are proposed; responsibilities are assigned but not in any way different in which this has happened for past and present over the past 30 years of climate negotiations. There are no clear visions painted in the actual negotiation statements and discussions, instead stronger connections to the past, to traditions and underlying values are made in order to present the own position in a favourable light. This links to Milkoreit's argument about the need for future visions in order to develop effective counterstrategies, if those future visions are not desirable. Without clear visions of how India will be impacted by climate change, no strong countermeasures can be designed to limit negative impacts. This is potentially concerning as, particularly in a field that requires anticipatory governance, the absence of formulations that allow for a debate of how the future will and should be are concerning. This is not only an issue for India, but for the world.

Acknowledgements

I would like to thank Lena Funke, Simon Kaack and Clara Scheuber for their research assistance for this chapter. I would further like to acknowledge that the coding frame used is based on a framework on social constructions of climate futures, which was developed together with colleagues at University of Hamburg, namely Lars Guenter, Michael Brüggemann, Simone Rödder, Michael Schnegg, Katharina Kleinen-von Königslöw, Youssef

Ibrahim, Christopher Pavenstädt, Coral O'Brian, Inga Janina Sievert and Jana Lüdemann.

This work was (partly) funded by the German Research Foundation under Germany's Excellence Initiative – EXC 177 CliSAP – 'Integrated Climate System Analysis and Prediction' (2017-2018) – and subsequent Excellence Strategy – EXC 2037 'CLICCS – Climate, Climatic Change, and Society' – (2019–2022) Project Number 390683824, contribution to the Center for Earth System Research and Sustainability of Universität Hamburg.

References

Asayama, Shinichiro (2015) 'Catastrophism toward "Opening Up" or "Closing Down"? Going beyond the Apocalyptic Future and Geoengineering', *Current Sociology*, 63: 89–93.

Carrington, Damian & Safi, Michael (2017) 'How India's Battle with Climate Change Could Determine all of our Fates', *The Guardian*, 6 November. Available at www.theguardian.com/environment/2017/nov/06/how-indias-battle-with-climate-change-could-determine-all-of-our-fates (last accessed 24 June 2021).

Chatzky, Andrew (2019) *Envisioning a Green New Deal: A Global Comparison* (New York: Council on Foreign Relations).

Dubash, Navroz K. (2013) 'The Politics of Climate Change in India: Narratives of Equity and Cobenefits', *WIREs Climate Change*, 4 (3): 191–201.

Dubash, Navroz K. (2019) *India in a Warming World: Integrating Climate Change and Development* (Oxford: Oxford University Press).

Gandhi, Sonia (2013) Seventh Plan – An Expression of People's Aspirations. New Delhi. Available at www.inc.in/media/speeches/seventh-plan-an-expression-of-people-s-aspirations.

Government of India (2015) 'First Biennial Update Report to the United Nations Framework Convention on Climate Change', December. Available at https://unfccc.int/resource/docs/natc/indbur1.pdf [last accessed 7 March 2022].

Government of India (2018a) Submission by India (2018) On SBI Agenda Item 18: Ways of Enhancing the Implementation of Education, Training, Public Awareness, Public Participation and Public Access to Information so as to Enhance Actions under the Paris Agreement. New Delhi.

Government of India (2018b) India's 2018 Submission to the Fiji Momentum for Implementation. New Delhi. Available at www.unfccc.int/sites/SubmissionsStaging/Documents/201805010125—India%20on%20Pre-2020%20-%20Submission.pdf.

International Energy Agency (2021a) 'Global Energy Review 2021'. Available at www.iea.org/reports/global-energy-review-2021 [last accessed 4 January 2021].

International Energy Agency (2021b) 'India Energy Outlook'. Available at www.iea.org/reports/india-energy-outlook-2021 [last accessed 20 December 2021].

Isaksen, Kari-Anne & Stokke, Kristian (2014) 'Changing Climate Discourse and Politics in India. Climate Change as Challenge and Opportunity for Diplomacy and Development', *Geoforum*, 57: 110–119.

Javadekar, Prakash (2014) Minister of State with Independent Charge for Environment, Forests & Climate Change at High Level Segment; 20th Conference of the Parties (COP-20). 9 December, Lima. Available at https://unfccc.int/files/meetings/lima_dec_2014/statements/application/pdf/cop_20_hls_india.pdf.

Milkoreit, Manjana (2017) 'Imaginary Politics: Climate Change and Making the Future', *Elementa: Science of the Anthropocene*, 5 (62).

Ministry of Environment, Forest and Climate Change (2015) Climate Friendly Lifestyle Practices in India. New Delhi. Available at https://moef.gov.in/wp-content/up loads/2017/08/Lifestyle-Brochure_web_reordered.pdf.

Ministry of New and Renewable Energy (2021) Fourth Assembly of the International Solar Alliance closes with a promise to achieve $1 trillion global in solar investments by 2030. New Delhi. Available at https://pib.gov.in/Pressreleaseshare.aspx? PRID=1765671.

Modi, Narendra (2015a) Lead Intervention by Prime Minister at G20 Working Lunch on Development and Climate Change. Antalya, 15 November. Available at www.mea.gov.in/Speeches-Statements.htm?dtl/26027/Lead_Intervention_by_Prime_ Minister_at_G20_Working_Lunch_on_Development_and_Climate_Change_ November_15_2015.

Modi, Narendra (2015b) Statement by Prime Minister at COP 21 Plenary Paris, 30 November 2015. Paris. Available at www.mea.gov.in/Speeches-Statements.htm?dtl/26071/

Modi, Narendra (2019a) PM at PETROTECH 2019 in Noida. Greater Noida. Available at www.pmindia.gov.in/en/news_updates/energy-is-the-key-driver-of-socio -economic-growth-pm-at-petrotech-2019/?comment=disable.

Modi, Narendra (2019b) PM Modi: Speech at the Release of the 'Tiger Census Report' in New Delhi 29/07/2019. New Delhi. Available at www.pmindia.gov.in/en/ news_updates/pms-speech-at-the-release-of-tiger-census-report-2018-in-new-delhi-o n-29-july-2019/?comment=disable.

Modi, Narendra (2021a) PM's Address at the Virtual Vesak Day Celebrations on Buddha Purnima, 26 May 2021. New Delhi. Available at www.pmindia.gov.in/en/ news_updates/pms-address-at-the-virtual-vesak-day-celebrations-on-buddha-purni ma/?comment=disable.

Modi, Narendra (2021b) PM's Speech on World Environmental Day Event on June 5th. New Delhi. Available at www.pmindia.gov.in/en/news_updates/pms-sp eech-on-the-world-environment-day/?comment=disable.

Modi, Narendra (2021c) PM's Departure Statement Ahead of His Visit to Rome and Glasgow. New Delhi. Available at www.pmindia.gov.in/en/news_updates/pms-depa rture-statement-ahead-of-his-visit-to-rome-and-glasgow/?comment=disable

Mohan, Aniruddh & Wehnert, Timon (2019) 'Is India Pulling its Weight? India's Nationally Determined Contribution and Future Energy Plans in Global Climate Policy', *Climate Policy*, 19 (3): 275–282.

Mohanty, Abinash & Wadhawan, Shreya (2021) *Mapping India's Climate Vulnerability – A District Level Assessment* (New Delhi: Council on Energy, Environment and Water). Available at www.ceew.in/sites/default/files/ceew-study-on-climate-cha nge-vulnerability-index-and-district-level-risk-assessment.pdf [last accessed 20 December 2021].

Muiderman, Karlijn, Gupta, Aarti, Vervoort, Joost & Biermann, Frank (2020) 'Four Approaches to Anticipatory Climate Governance: Different Conceptions of the Future and Implications for the Present', *Wiley Interdisciplinary Reviews: Climate Change*, 11 (6): e673.

Mukherjee, Shri Pranab (2008) Address by Shri Pranab Mukherjee, External Affairs Minister On 'India And Global Challenges: Climate Change And Energy Security' at The Asia Society, New York. Available at www.mea.gov.in/Speeches-Statements. htm?dtl/1603/Address_by_Shri_Pranab_Mukherjee_External_Affairs_Minister_On

_India_And_Global_Challenges_Climate_Change_And_Energy_Securityat_The_A sia_Society_New_Yo.

Mukherjee, Shri Pranab (2015) Address to Parliament – 23 February 2015. New Delhi. Available at https://eparlib.nic.in/bitstream/123456789/4024/1/mukherjee_23_02_2015.pdf.

Natarajan, Jayanthi (2011) Statement by Ms Jayanthi Natarajan, Minister of Environment & Forests, Government of India. Durban. Available at https://unfccc.int/files/m eetings/durban_nov_2011/statements/application/pdf/111207_cop17_hls_india.pdf.

Oomen, Jeroen, Hoffman, Jesse & Hajer, Maarten A. (2021) 'Techniques of Futuring: On How Imagined Futures Become Socially Performative', *European Journal of Social Theory*, online first. doi:10.1177/1368431020988826.

Pant, Harsh V. (2019) *New Directions in India's Foreign Policy: Theory and Praxis* (Cambridge: Cambridge University Press).

Patil, Pratibha Devisingh (2012) Address to Parliament – 12 March 2012. New Delhi. Available at https://eparlib.nic.in/bitstream/123456789/4022/1/patil_12_03_2012.pdf

Pillai, Aditya Valiathan & Dubash, Navroz K. (2021) 'The Limits of Opportunism: The Uneven Emergence of Climate Institutions in India', *Environmental Politics* 30 (sup1): 1–25.

Prys-Hansen, Miriam (2022) 'Politics of Responsibility: India in Global Climate Governance', in Robert Falkner and Barry Buzan (eds), *Great Powers, Climate Change and Global Environmental Responsibilities* (Oxford: Oxford University Press), pp. 139–163.

Ramesh, Jairam (2010) Minister of Environment and Forests at the COP-16 in Cancun, December 8. Available at https://unfccc.int/files/meetings/cop_16/statem ents/application/pdf/101209_cop16_hls_india.pdf.

Saran, Shri Shyam (2008) Talk by Special Envoy of Prime Minister, Shri Shyam Saran in Mumbai on Climate Change. Mumbai. Available at https://mea.gov.in/in-focus-a rticle.htm?18821/Talk+by+Special+Envoy+of+Prime+Minister+Shri+Shyam+Sara n+in+Mumbai+on+Climate+Change.

Saran, Samir & Jones, Aled (2017) *India's Climate Change Identity* (Cham: Springer International Publishing).

Singh, Manmohan (2009a) Intervention by Prime Minister on Climate Change at CHOGM. Port of Spain. Available at https://mea.gov.in/Speeches-Statements.htm? dtl/1290/Intervention+by+Prime+Minister+on+Climate+Change+at+CHOGM.

Singh, Manmohan (2009b) PM's Remarks at the CNN-IBN Indian of the Year Awards – 2009. New Delhi. Available at https://archivepmo.nic.in/drmanmoha nsingh/content_print.php?nodeid=838&nodetype=2.

Singh, Manmohan (2013) Excerpts of Address by the PM at the Combined Commanders Conference. New Delhi. Available at https://archivepmo.nic.in/drmanm ohansingh/speech-details.php?nodeid=1396.

Swaraj, Sushma (2018) Remarks by External Affairs Minister at the 'EU High Level Event on Climate Change'. Brussels, 22 June 22. Available at www.mea.gov.in/Sp eeches-Statements.htm?dtl/29996/Remarks_by_External_Affairs_Minister_at_the_ EU_High_Level_Event_on_Climate_Change.

Tomar, Vinod Kumar, Sati, Akhilesh & Powell, Lydia (2021) 'India's COP26 Pledges: Ambitious, but Ambiguous', 10 November. Available at www.orfonline.org/expert-spea k/indias-cop26-pledges-ambitious-but-ambiguous/ (last accessed 21 December 2021).

11 India's Foreign Aid to the Pacific

A Strategic Tool of Cooperation?

Teesta Prakash

Since 2014, there has been a dramatic increase in India's aid to the Pacific Island countries. Between 2013 and 2014 there was an increase of 142% of Indian aid (spent) to the Pacific Island countries. What explains this marked increase in India's aid to the Pacific? This is a puzzling development in India's foreign policy, and by extension, its aid programme. India's aid has predominantly been focused on its immediate neighbourhood in South Asia where it has emerged as a significant aid donor, historically as well as presently.

Primarily driven by New Delhi's strategic interests, most literature on India's aid to its neighbours agrees that India's aid is largely given to protect its strategic sphere of influence. India's chief aid recipients – Nepal, Afghanistan and Bhutan – are all landlocked countries in its neighbourhood where India is traditionally competing for influence with its strategic rivals, and neighbours, China and Pakistan. Specifically for India's aid to Nepal, Adhikari argues that 'Indian aid seeks to bolster broader political objectives of assertion of a 'sphere of influence', continuation of the policy of 'special relations', a coordinated foreign policy approach, (and) support of regimes that protect Indian vital security interests' (Adhikari, 2014: 330–331). Concerning Afghanistan, D'Souza highlights that India adopted a 'soft power approach' by concentrating on developmental aid as it was trying 'for the longer term, to position its relationship with Afghanistan in the context of its energy and trade interests in Central Asia' (D'Souza, 2014: 383). Overall, Indian aid is driven by New Delhi's desire to sustain its strategic sphere to influence by protecting and promoting its political and economic interests in the region.

In 2014, newly elected Prime Minister Narendra Modi launched his flagship 'neighbourhood first' policy which would integrate the South Asian region using 'development cooperation'. Following this policy, Modi in 2015 launched the SAGAR initiative ('Security and Growth for All in the Region'), which 'appropriated the idea of a rules-based order and wrapped it into a broader story about India's maritime past, ancient civilisational linkages and the economic ambition of his "New India"' (Hall, 2019: 133). He also relabelled India's previous 'Look East' policy to 'Act East' as New Delhi

DOI: 10.4324/9781003305132-15

now looked to re-engage with its eastern neighbours. Crucially, these policies still, only included India's neighbourhood where New Delhi could look to strengthen capacity building and infrastructure (Ministry of External Affairs, 2015). Yet, these policies reflected India's wider desire to advance South–South cooperation and underline the strategic importance of the Indo-Pacific for India, especially as a way to balance China.

These observations lead us with the question – what are the drivers of Indian aid to the Pacific Island countries and what explains the sudden increase in India's aid to these countries? It is unexplained in terms of India's geopolitical strategy – these Pacific Island countries are located much further away from their landlocked neighbours who are India's main recipients. It is also unexplained in terms of Modi governments' seemingly 'new' policy directives of Neighbourhood First, Act East or SAGAR initiatives as he took office in the same year where we see the dramatic increase in India's aid to this region. To answer these questions, this chapter is structured in three broad sections. Section one looks at the history of India-South Pacific political relations. Section two then provides an assessment of the strategic competition in the South Pacific region arguing that China's increasing assertiveness through aid and strategic presence has concerned the Western, or 'traditional' partners, or powers, of the region. Section three finally looks at India's aid and aid related diplomacy in the region as well as the agency and 'security needs' of PICs as outlined by the Boe Declaration.

Overall, this article argues that there is a growing strategic congruence that is driving India's aid to PICs as it looks to balance China's rise and relatedly, its quest for a multipolar Indo-Pacific. Specifically, setting up regional dialogue forums and summits for cooperation India has made room to understand and respond to the needs of the PICs. This is strategically advantageous for the PICs as well as they are looking for more economic and political choices because they are wary of the instability and possible loss of sovereignty caused by increased dependence on China, while the more traditional partners do not fully understand the 'non-traditional' security threats faced by the PICs and its needs for sustainable aid. Thus, there is a strategic congruence, between the donor, India and the recipients, PICs in this aid relationship that questions the traditional donor-recipient relationships and sets up an example of a South–South cooperation. Through its aid, especially in the Pacific region, New Delhi is practising its vision of a more equitable world – a world wherein both India and the PICs benefit from this strategic relationship. Geographically, the PICs may be far away from India's immediate sphere of influence but they are still within the sphere of *Global India*.

India–South Pacific Relations

Historically, India's relationship with the Pacific Island countries have been fair but without much 'material' substance due to the geographical, and often political, distance between the two regions. In particular, India's has had the strongest ties with Fiji largely due to the Indian diaspora present in Fiji who were brought in as indentured labourers during the Colonial era. The first Indian Prime Minister to visit the region was Indira Gandhi in 1981 where she visited Fiji and Tonga on her way back from Canberra where she attended the Commonwealth Heads of Government Meeting (CHOGM). Ramesh Thakur wrote in 1985 on the India-Fiji bilateral ties that 'at the diplomatic level, India maintains correct yet warm relations with the government of Fiji and through the government with all the peoples of Fiji' (Thakur, 1985: 370).

Thakur was writing before the three coups in Fiji in 1987, 2000 and 2006 respectively, during which India acted quite cautiously and never actively called out Fiji on their 'internal matters'. In the most recent coup of 2006, Fiji's near neighbours Australia and New Zealand condemned the attacks as the 'big brothers' of the Pacific island country (Hill, 2010: 113). Both states reacted negatively by imposing travel bans on coup-related individuals which greatly frustrated the regime as many within the elite had personal ties with both Australia and New Zealand. India however acted cautiously. Indian media noted that New Delhi's 'tepid' response to the crisis was based on this being the first coup not directed against the Indian community in Fiji (Choudhury, 2005). India, unlike Australia and New Zealand was at the time a reluctant 'democracy promoter', as Indian Foreign Secretary, Shyam Saran, during a speech in 2005 emphasized that although 'democracy remains India's abiding conviction, the importance of our neighbourhood requires that we remain engaged with whichever government is exercising authority in any country' (Saran, 2005). Overall, India's reluctance to be wedded to the international liberal order has only strengthened its ties with other developing countries, like Fiji, who see a like-minded ally and a potential aid donor and trade partner.

India's 'Look East' policy employed in the post-Cold War years of 1990s was perhaps New Delhi's first attempt to engage with its east as India liberalized it economy and looked for newer economic partners, though initially this policy was mainly aimed at engaging Association of East Asian Nations (ASEAN). However, in 2003, 'Look East Phase-2' was launched by then External Affairs Minister Yashwant Sinha as 'characterised by an expanded definition of 'East', extending [it] from Australia to East Asia' (Sinha, 2003). As India pushed into East Asia, it also brought in the West Pacific, as 'Look East Phase-3' was launched in 2004. Since then, India's relationship with the South Pacific has been based on strengthening an economic-development partnership, however the strategic undertones of India's foreign policy in the region cannot be ignored. In 2006 at the Pacific Island Forum (PIF), India's representative the Minister for State for External Affairs, E. Ahmed, unveiled India's Pacific Island Country Assistance Initiative, to be made up of an annual grant of US$ 100,000 to each of the 14 island states. This was subsequently increased to US$ 125,000 in 2009. Between 2005 and 2012, Indian development assistance to this region totalled over US$ 50 million in the form of Lines of Credit and over US$ 11 million in grants. This expansion of concerns for India was also reflected in naval outreach in August 2006 when INS Tabar carrying out cooperative naval exercises in Australia, New Zealand, Papua New Guinea, Tonga, and Fiji.

The next big impetus for the India-South Pacific Relations came in 2014 when Prime Minister Modi visited Fiji after announcing the launch of the reinvigorated 'Act East' Policy as India looked to expand its strategic ambitions beyond its neighbourhood. Modi in a speech made at East Asia Summit in Myanmar in November 2014 said, 'since entering office six months ago, my government has moved with a great sense of priority and speed to turn our 'Look East Policy' into 'Act East Policy' (Modi, 2014). A week after this speech, Modi visited Fiji, the first Indian Prime Minister to do so in 33 years. Only two days later, Xi Jinping, President of China also visited Fiji after the G20 Summit in Brisbane, Australia. The strategic undertones of these close visits by Modi and Xi were hard to ignore especially in a region that was fast emerging as a strategically valuable part of what has now been termed as the 'Indo-Pacific'. Medcalf describes the Indo-Pacific as 'a term [that] recognises that both economic ties and strategic competition now encompass an expansive two ocean region, due in large part to China's ascent, and that other countries must protect their interests through new partnerships across the blurring of old geographic boundaries' (Medcalf, 2020: 4). To understand the drivers of India's aid to the South Pacific, in particular the dramatic rise of the aid post 2014, will have to be viewed within the context of strategic competition now emerging in the region.

The Strategic Value of the South Pacific – From 'Arc of Instability' to 'Arc of Strategic Competition'

The strategic competition in the Pacific Islands, has so far, primarily been between the United States (US), including its allies and China. Wallis notes that the latter has been slowly building diplomatic and economic presence in the last forty years (Wallis, 2021: 119). Mainly, this has been because China has been competing with Taiwan for diplomatic recognition. While the competition cooled after the 2008 'truce', it has reignited after Taiwan's 2016 election where the Nationalist Democratic Progressive Party took office (Wallis, 2021: 119). However, China's ambitions are bigger than just diplomatic recognition in the region. China talked about building a 'military base' in Vanuatu in April 2018, and in September 2019 it was reported that a Chinese company had sought to lease a former Japanese naval base in Solomon Islands (AFP, 2019). China's interests in the region are increasingly becoming strategic in nature and this causing substantial tensions especially for the long-established powers.

Reasonably, these activities have concerned Western governments that this region could potentially prove the testing grounds for China's strategic power against the US (Dobell, 2007b). Lanteigne has further argued that China's increased presence in the region has 'accelerated the erosion of the United States as a unipolar power' (Lanteigne, 2012: 23). Long-established external powers in the region may now stand a possibility of losing their influence in the region as Pacific Islands may be encouraged to shift their allegiance (Crocombe, 2007). Scholars have noted the geostrategic importance of the Pacific Ocean as the 'only sea route between China on the one hand and South America, Antarctica, Australia and New Zealand on the other, as well as what China sees as its "second and third island chains of defence"' (Sen Yu, 2015). Chinese academics have also stated that 'it would be helpful to have military basis in the region to break the 'encirclement' of China' (Wallis, 2021: 120).

China has established dense economic linkages in the region, Chinese state-owned corporations have undertaken major logging projects and developed fisheries enterprises across the region and have also began operating Nickel and Cobalt mines in Papua New Guinea. Additionally, it has also increased its aid to the region although it is still dwarfed by Australia's aid in the region (Lowy Institute, 2019). So far, nine Pacific Island states have signed up to the Belt and Road Initiative (BRI), which has seen China invest in infrastructural construction around the world, especially in ports (Rajah, Dayant and Pryke, 2019). It is important to note that the International Monetary Fund and Asian Development Bank have classified the Pacific Islands as being at high risk of debt distress. Wallis notes that China is the region's largest bilateral lender (except for Tonga) and the significant size of Chinese lending raises questions about debt sustainability in the Pacific Islands (Wallis, 2021: 120).

China's increasing diplomatic and economic presence in the region has definitely upped the strategic stakes between the players, and the results have not always been to the benefit of Pacific Islanders. One of the ramifications of the increased flow of money and resources into the region has been growing corruption of local politicians. This was also the chief cause of the riots in Solomon Islands and Tonga in 2006. The competition between Beijing and Taiwan became quite heated as there were reports of physical altercations between Chinese and Taiwanese diplomats in Fiji in October 2020 (Doherty et al., 2020). To counter growing Chinese strategic influence, in October 2019 Taiwan and the US organized a 'Pacific Islands Dialogue' in Taipei involving representatives of Pacific Island states that recognize Taiwan. At this meeting the Taiwanese foreign minister warned that Taiwan doesn't 'want to see the Pacific turned into another South China Sea' (quoted in Chung, 2020) while US diplomats at the forum spoke in support of Taiwan's regional role, as a 'force for good in the Pacific' (quoted in Chung, 2020).

The US has now reinvigorated its strategic presence in the region as tensions have intensified in the last decade. Post-Cold War, Wallis notes that the US was only really focused on the Micronesian sub-region where it had a range of constitutional relations, and also because it saw the region as a valuable security frontier from which to conduct defensive and offensive security operations (Wallis, 2021: 122). She argues that there two key strategic reasons for the US to intensify its presence in the region: one, the region is vital to maintaining sea lines of communication with Australia, New Zealand and Southeast Asia and two, its islands are critical to potential US adversaries' capacity to project naval power in the Pacific Ocean as was demonstrated during the Second World War (Wallis, 2021: 122). Thus, the US has articulated a 'Pacific Pledge of the Indo-Pacific Strategy' to enhance its relationship with the Pacific Island states. However even before this pledge was made, in 2012 the US ended its post-Cold War 'neglect' of the islands and months after Washington announced its pivot to Asia, then Secretary of State Hilary Clinton showed up at the annual meetings of the Pacific Islands Forum. More recently though, US Vice President Mike Pence's attendance at the 2018 Asia Pacific Economic Cooperation summit in PNG and then defence secretary Mark Esper's visit to Palau and Guam are examples of US attempting to re-engage with the region. The US has also expanded its economic cooperation with regional allies and partners as it tries to re-engage more actively through multilateral diplomacy, such as under the 'Trilateral Partnership for Infrastructure and Investment in the Indo-Pacific' agreed with Australia and Japan. The US has also increased its aid, trade and investment ties in an effort to compete with the growing Chinese influence in the region.

'Traditional partners' of the Pacific, most notably Australia and New Zealand, have also stepped up their strategic game. Both Australia and New Zealand have long identified the security of the Pacific Islands as second only in importance to the defence of their own territory, so their strategic interests are determined largely by geography. In its 2016 Defence White Paper, Australia explicitly stated its intent to 'continue to seek to be the principal security partner' for the Pacific Island States (Department of Defence Australia, 2016). Though the common perception is that Australia, due to its size, influence, and geographical proximity, has often dominated decision-making in the region, Wallis has argued that often this influence has been more illusory than real (Wallis, 2017). Reflecting its smaller size, New Zealand has articulated a slightly less ambitious goal- it seeks to 'maintain its position as a trusted and reliable security and economic partner' (Ministry of Foreign Affairs and Trade New Zealand, 2020). Both Australia and New Zealand have strengthened their presence in the region through their 'Pacific Step Up' (announced in 2017) and 'Pacific Reset' (announced in 2018) initiatives.

Australia is also putting a keen focus on strengthening its security relationship with the region. In January 2019, Australia began negotiations on a bilateral security treaty with Vanuatu (Prime Minister of Australia, 2019), and this was quite significant as Vanuatu historically has had chequered relations and much like Fiji and Papua New Guinea, it too is a member of the Non-Aligned Movement. Additionally, Australia has successfully nego-tiated a security treaty with Solomon Islands in 2017 (Department of Foreign Affairs and Trade Australia, 2017) and *vuvale* (friendship) treaty with Fiji in 2019 (Department of Foreign Affairs and Trade Australia, 2019) as well as a strategic and economic partnership with PNG in 2020 (Prime Minister of Australia, 2020). There is now also a focus on advancing the Pacific Island's states own security priorities, particularly those identified by the Boe Declaration to which both Australia and New Zealand are signatories.

France and UK are also regional players due to their colonial links, wherein France controls several Pacific territories while nine Pacific Island states are members of the Commonwealth. French President Emmanuel Macron has claimed that France 'has great power in the Indo-Pacific region through its territories New Caledonia, Wallis and Futuna and French Poly-nesia as well as Mayotte and Reunion which makes France "the second lar-gest maritime power in the world"' (Maclellan, 2018). The emergence of the Australia–France–India 'strategic axis' in the Indo-Pacific is an example of Macron's vision of this Indo-Pacific (Tillett, 2018). Furthermore, France has developed an enhanced security partnership with Australia in 2017 that spe-cifically covers the Pacific Ocean building on their pre-existing agreement on defence cooperation and status of forces (Department of Foreign Affairs and Trade Australia, 2006, 2017). Meanwhile the UK has articulated a 'Pacific Uplift' strategy which has included establishing new diplomatic missions in Samoa, Tonga and Vanuatu and doubling the size of its diplomatic presence in Fiji (UK Government, 2019).

With the rise of the strategic value of the Pacific Island States and the ensuing strategic competition in the region, it would be fair to say that the region has moved from the 'arc of instability' narrative to 'arc of strategic competition' (Dobell, 2007b). The 'arc of instability' narrative was not received positively by the Pacific leaders because of the negative character-ization of their performance and an Australia-centric view of the region (Wallis, 2012: 2). This narrative of instability was also contested by aca-demics, and Hegarty claims that it 'both oversimplifies and overdramatizes a region of vast diversity and complexity' (Hegarty, 2004; Rumley, 2006). These prior narratives and the current one that this section has covered of strategic competition is overlooking an important aspect of the region – the view, and the agency, of the Pacific Islands themselves, and how they view this strategic competition in their region.

India's Aid – Striking a Balance and a Strategic Congruence

The rise of India's aid to the Pacific Islands is largely driven by its strategic interests to balance out growing Chinese influence in the region and its larger foreign policy ambition to seek a multipolar world order. In the previous section, the strategic competition in the region has been established to be growing due to increasing Chinese assertiveness in diplomatic, economic and defence arenas. This growing assertiveness of China, however, is not only limited to the Pacific region. For India this has had strategic consequences not only in its immediate neighbourhood of South Asia but also on its borders as we have seen in the Doklam clashes in 2017 and most recently near the clashes near Ladakh along the Line of Actual Control in May 2020. Thus, the rise of India's aid to the Pacific Islands States where China's strategic influence has been increasing in a staggering manner is directly linked to its strategic interests of balancing out China.

The term 'strategic congruence', particularly here in the aid context, denotes a harmony or agreement between both the donor (India) and the recipient nations (PICs) in the kind of aid that is being delivered by this particular donor. Chiefly, this agreement, or congruence, is mostly due to the strategic interests of both parties involved as India looks to extend its strategic influence in the Indo-Pacific Sphere and as the PICs look to diversify their aid partners in the region too. Focusing more on what is driving India's aid outside its neighbourhood, this chapter finds that it is New Delhi's desire to be a balancer to the growing assertiveness of China more globally than purely regional (restricted to South and perhaps Southeast Asia). This argument of India as a 'balancer' to China, specifically in the Pacific region is not a wholly new one. Raja Mohan has argued previously that 'India's presence offers a prospect of greater regional balance in the South Pacific' (Raja Mohan, 2014). The question then arises can India balance out China with its aid to the region?

Chinese aid far outstrips the Indian aid in the region, consistently. However, India's aid to the region, while much lower than China's in comparison, is still strategically valuable because it meets the strategic needs of both the donor as well as the recipient in the way it is structured and provided. Raja Mohan noted that 'they [Pacific Island states] know that India cannot match the Chinese, dollar to dollar, in providing economic assistance. The islanders, however, would like to have some insurance against over-dependence on Chinese assistance' (Raja Mohan, 2014). Chinese aid in the region has been a destabilizing force as noted in the previous section, as Chinese assistance comes in the form of 'soft loans' that has the Island states engaged in 'debt-trap diplomacy' (Parker and Chefitz, 2018). This has lasting implications for the sovereignty of the Pacific Island states, where if the states fail to repay their loans China could seek to swap the debt for infrastructure with dual use facilities such commercial ports potentially converted into military bases (Wallis, 2020: 49; Wroe, 2018).

In contrast, India's aid to the region has largely been in grant form and in congruence with the strategic needs of the Island as outlined by the 'Boe Declaration on Regional Security'. The Boe Declaration was signed in 2018 by all the members of the Pacific Islands Forum, which is the peak political decision-making body in the region. The main thrust of the Boe Declaration was towards expanding the definition of 'security' that reflected the concerns and priorities of Pacific peoples. Cain has noted that the declaration 'recognises there are issues of geostrategic concern at play, and they have an impact of what happens in the region. However, when it comes to security priorities, the main focus is on issues of human security... that climate changes poses the single greatest security threat to the countries of the Pacific Island region' (Cain, 2020: 33–35). Additionally, the Boe Declaration has advocated a 'Blue Pacific' identity to 'drive collective action in support of our vision under the Framework of Pacific Regionalism' (Pacific Islands Forum Secretariat, 2018). The Pacific Islands states, specifically, the PIF has advocated that the states act as a 'Blue Continent' so that 'they can exercise stronger strategic autonomy ... [and] maintain solidarity in the face of those who seek to divide us' (Taylor, 2018). The Pacific Island states are now asserting their strategic interests through regionalism to underline that their biggest threat is a 'non-traditional' security concern, that of climate change.

Complimentarily, India set up the Forum for India–Pacific Islands Cooperation (FIPIC) with its aid programme in 2014 to enhance its regional approach. India's President, Ram Nath Kovind stated on the Constitution day of Marshall Islands in 2017 that the FIPIC has not only institutionalized the relationship between India and the Pacific Island countries but also strengthened the scope of cooperation and dialogue, and has offered a formal context to expedite exchanges between the two sides: a clear objective put forward by the Indian leadership (Press Information Bureau India, 2017). The inaugural FIPIC summit was held in Suva, Fiji in November 2014 while the second was held in Jaipur, India in 2015.

These summits have underlined India's support for regionalism and development, as outlined by the Boe Doctrine. In his opening remarks for the second FIPIC summit, Prime Minister Modi noted 'India will support the realisation of your vision of Pacific Regionalism. It is a shining example of cooperative regionalism that should inspire others around the world' (Modi, 2015b). Diplomacy through regionalism and aid and development, especially in the arena of South–South cooperation is one of Indian foreign policy's agenda to gain influence against, what India's External Affairs Minister terms, 'stronger opponents' (Jaishankar, 2020). Through FIPIC, India intends to give greater agency to the recipient Pacific Island nations in its aid programme. Modi, in the closing remarks of the second FIPIC summit stated 'let me assure you that we [India] will remain very sensitive to your concerns in international forums. We would also to shape our bilateral cooperation in accordance with your needs and priorities' (Modi, 2015a). This is in stark contrast to China's BRI, as Jaishankar argues 'as a rising China seeks to shape the world to its architectural vision. Many of its key plans are unilateral enterprises. The BRI appears to serve its national objectives and conscious collaboration is naturally for those who envisage convergence with those goals' (Jaishankar, 2020: 78). There is a distinct difference between India's aid and diplomacy in the region that becomes clearer once the kind of aid that is being delivered is analysed further.

India's 'development partnership' focused aid to the Pacific Island states is driven by its principles of harmony and equity that has become a mainstay of the 'Modi Doctrine' in India's foreign policy since 2014. In his closing remarks of the second FIPIC summit Modi stated 'your support to this partnership means a lot to India. We see thus partnership of equals, driven by similar aspirations, in which we will all be more successful by being together. It stems from our belief in *Vasudhaiva Kutumbakam* – the world is one' (Modi, 2015b). This ancient Vedic concept of *Vasudhaiva Kutumbakam*, which is Sanskrit for 'the world is one family', was underlined as a core value of India's foreign policy when Modi and his party, the Bharatiya Janata Party (BJP) were campaigning in 2014. The BJP's election manifesto of 2014 stated that India would continue 'dialogue, engagement and cooperation' and promised a 'proactive diplomacy' that would utilize India's soft power – the appeal of its philosophy and religion, in particular its 'principles of harmony and equity' (Bharatiya Janata Party, 2014: 39). India's aid to the Pacific Island states is driven by 'a sense of "enlightened self-interest"' (Hall, 2015: 102). By raising its strategic profile in the Pacific Islands region through aid, such actions underpinned shifts in perceptions in New Delhi of its 'strategic geography' (Hall, 2019: 132).

India's aid to the Pacific Islands was heavily focused on mitigating climate change impacts, which has been argued as the main security threat for this region underlining the 'development partnership' model of Indian aid. In conjunction, India also inaugurated the India–Pacific Islands Sustainable Development Conference in 2017 in Fiji. This conference addressed issues such as health, disaster management, climate change, International Solar Alliance (ISA), and blue economy (Ministry of External Affairs, 2017a). This conference held in Fiji in 2017 reflected India's commitment to creating 'sustainable partnerships'. India announced here that it would be allotting US$ 1 million to Fiji's trust fund for the presidency of COP-23 which was to be held in November 2017 (Ministry of External Affairs, 2017b). Further, India signed several memorandums of understanding (MoUs) to promote sustainable development and scientific and economic cooperation with the PICs (Ministry of External Affairs, 2017b). This further underlined the congruence between India as an aid donor and the Pacific Island's recipient needs. The Boe Declaration, as Cain argues 'is premised on an affirmation that climate change remains the biggest threat to the signatory countries' (Cain, 2020: 32). Under Modi's leadership, India has paid a special attention to combating climate change especially as he launched the ISA initiative at the Paris Climate Summit in 2015. By creating partnerships through dialogue and recipient-focused cooperation, India's aid model of 'development cooperation' has been welcomed by the PICs despite India not being able to provide the same amount of aid as China.

The common perception of China's aid, not just to the Pacific Island states but globally has been of a 'no strings attached' approach which sits in stark contrast with India's aid 'development partnership' model of recipient focused aid through cooperation and dialogue. However, given the growing strategic competition and China's assertiveness in the south Pacific region –

can China's aid be considered 'no strings attached'? Some scholars vehemently defend the 'no strings attached' argument of Chinese aid and even go as far as to say that 'there is no clear evidence to suggest that China's deepening involvement in the South Pacific is a calculated strategic move for its military security' (Yang, 2009: 154). Wallis has objected to this 'no strings attached' argument very clearly as she states 'of course, there are strings, as for many years this aid was primarily aimed at competing with Taiwan for diplomatic recognition. It now seems to have an additional aim of acquiring influence over regional governments' (Wallis, 2020: 50).

Furthermore, instead of helping out the recipient, Chinese aid has exacerbated political tensions in this region. Wallis adds that '[Chinese] aid has contributed to official corruption and political instability, exemplified by the post-election riots in Solomon Islands and Tonga in 2006 which were incited in part by local resentment about the perceived influence of Chinese and Taiwanese interests on certain political leaders' (Wallis, 2020: 50). Given the tense geostrategic atmosphere, created by Chinese influence, India's aid, no doubt driven by its own growing strategic interests, is seen as a strategic balancer in the region. As such, there is a strategic mutual benefit in India's aid to the PICs, where both donor and recipient get to fulfil their strategic objectives.

India's aid to the PICs, especially its capacity building initiatives, underlines its own strategic imperatives of balancing the growing Chinese assertiveness as it also paves the way for more security and defence ties with the region. In this way, Fiji in particular is seen as the 'heart of the Pacific Ocean' who is also India's strongest link in the region, setting an example for other countries to view India as a strong developmental partner (Chand, 2014). India has also initiated a defence partnership with Fiji, and an MoU with Fiji in areas such as defence, disaster management, military training and humanitarian assistance has been signed that his strengthened India–Fiji cooperation in security areas (Press Information Bureau India, 2017). Fiji has been the loudest appreciator of Indian aid, as Minister for Industry, Trade and Tourism, Lands and Mineral Resources of Fiji Faiyaz Koya stated that 'Fiji is appreciative of the many forms of assistance that we have received from the Government of India and the goodwill India has shown Fiji' (quoted in Kate, 2017). Since 2017, India has markedly increased its ministerial visits to other Pacific countries (namely Nauru, Marshall Islands, Palau, Samoa and Tuvalu) as its Pacific bonding grows as both sides support a shared vision of an 'inclusive Indo-Pacific'.

Theoretically there is also an argument to be made on how India, post 2014, is striving for a multipolar world order, and that this way of shaping the regional economic through aid and even security architecture is one way to do so. Its recipient friendly aid, which stands in congruence with the Boe Declaration, highlights more India's own vision of the Indo-Pacific, as put forth by Modi in the 2018 Shangri La speech as India seeks an order that is grounded in 'sovereignty and territorial integrity, as well as equality of all nations, irrespective of size and strength … [in which] rules and norms should be based on the consent of all, not the power of the few' (quoted in Hall, 2021: 56). As Hall highlights, this vision of multipolarity is more in rhythm with that of US, who it sees as playing a complimentary role in the region, and he writes that India 'now supports a continued US role as a security provider and as a leader in global governance' (Hall, 2021, 56). India's increased aid to the Pacific highlights that India is willing to do more to support its vision of a global multipolar world order and using strategic foreign aid as a way to stabilize the region's balance of power in terms of economic architecture.

Conclusion: Expanding India's Vision of Strategic Influence

India's aid to the PICs has increased because India's strategic interest in the region, in response to growing Chinese's assertiveness as well its own global ambitions of being a *Vishwa guru* (world leader). Most importantly, there is a strategic congruence between the drivers of India's aid to the Pacific Island states and the recipient's growing need for strategic balance in its region. India's increasing aid to the Pacific is further driven by its strategic foreign policy of a 'multipolar' Indo-Pacific, whereby 'in Modi's India, multipolarity has thus emerged as a useful device for pushing back against Chinese assertiveness as Beijing seeks to establish some kind of hegemony over its immediate neighbourhood and the wider Indo-Pacific' (Hall, 2021: 56). Its aid to the PICs is an example of India's desire to strategically challenge the increasingly hegemonic influence of China in its far-neighbourhood. The way India has also differentiated its aid from that of China through Modi's policy of *samvad* (dialogue and cooperation), *samman* (dignity and honour) and *samridhhi* (prosperity) that has led to the creation of cooperative dialogues at FIPIC and the India–Pacific Sustainable Development Conference also underlines that India wants to, normatively at least, highlight its distinct way of thinking about international relations.

Both, India's postcolonial history and its strategic ambitions in the Indo-Pacific have arguably shaped New Delhi's new approach towards gaining global influence as a great power. Though primarily driven by its strategic rivalry with China, India's aid programme in the Pacific points towards a more Global India that values influence even in distant shores. New Delhi's pursuit of influence and status should be recognized not only as a normative concept but one that is aiming to have a tangible and material impact as its Pacific aid agenda highlights, and which is designed to drive India's strategic ambitions to balance China in the wider Indo-Pacific.

The focus of India's aid on the immediate needs of the PICs on issues such as climate change has recast the intense strategic competition to some extent into a strategic cooperation. The growing strategic competition in the Pacific region has somewhat eroded the agency of the Pacific Island states, or at least deemed it of low priority in the larger 'great power competition' in the region. Leaders of the region have claimed this competition as a 'form of strategic manipulation' because 'the big powers are doggedly pursuing strategies to widen and extend their reach and inculcating a far-reaching sense of insecurity' (Lowy Institute, 2018). Wallis also notes that a related risk is that strategic competition creates divisions within Pacific Island states, and as the great powers compete for influence there is a 'race to the bottom' with regard to aid and assistance. However, India's aid and in conjunction regional diplomacy in the region has emphasized the need for addressing climate change through its development partnership initiatives. There is also an explicit mention in the Boe Declaration that the PIF members need to 'respect and assert the sovereign right of every Member to conduct its national affairs free of external interference and coercion' (Pacific Islands Forum Secretariat, 2018). This aligns with India's aid projects in the region, and the strategic interests driving Indian aid to the PICs, therefore, is reciprocal between the donor as well as recipients.

Finally, there is a growing strategic convergence between India and the 'traditional' partners in the region as well – US, Australia and France. India's 'Act East' policy has been strategically congruent with the established powers in the region, and its subsequent participation in the Rim of the Pacific naval exercises held by the US at Hawaii was also a sign India's naval operational capability in the Pacific basin. This congruence further bolstered India's strategic intentions to stay in the region as it emerges as a key donor, and as the 'Indo' connects to the larger 'Pacific' to become the Indo-Pacific.

References

Adhikari, Monalisa (2014) 'Politics and Perceptions of Indian Aid to Nepal', *Strategic Analysis*, 38 (2): 330–331.

AFP (2019), 'Solomons' Government Vetoes Chinese Attempt to Lease an Island', *The Guardian*, 29 October. Available at www.theguardian.com/world/2019/oct/25/solomons-government-vetoes-chinese-attempt-to-lease-an-island [last accessed 9 May 2022].

Bharatiya Janata Party (2014) *Ek Bharat, Shreshtha Bharat: Sabka Saath, Sabka Vikas – Election Manifesto 2014* (New Delhi: BJP). Available at www.thehinducentre.com/multimedia/archive/01831/BJP_Manifesto_1831221a.pdf [last accessed 9 May 2022].

Cain, Tess Newton (2020) 'Let's Hear It for the Boe', *Security Challenges*, 16 (1): 32–36.

Chand, Manish (2014) 'India & Fiji: A Pacific Bonding', 18 November. Available at https://mea.gov.in/outgoing-visit-detail.htm?24560/In+Focus+India+amp+Fiji+A+Pacific+Bonding [last accessed 9 May 2022].

Choudhury, Nilova Roy (2005) 'India Reacts Cautiously to Fiji Coup', *Hindustan Times*, 5 December.

Chung, Lawrence (2019) 'US and Taiwan Hold to Shore Up Support for Taipei in Pacific', *South China Morning Post*, 7 October. Available at www.scmp.com/news/china/diplomacy/article/3031891/us-and-taiwan-hold-forum-shore-support-taipei-pacific [last accessed 9 May 2022].

Crocombe, Ron (2007) *Asia in the Pacific Islands: Replacing the West* (Suva: University of the South Pacific).

Department of Defence Australia (2016) '2016 Defence White Paper', 25 February. Available at www.defence.gov.au/whitepaper/ [last accessed 9 May 2022].

Department of Foreign Affairs and Trade Australia (2006) 'Agreement between the Government of Australia and the Government of the French Republic regarding Defence Co-operation and Status of Forces', 14 December. Available at www.aph. gov.au/Parliamentary_Business/Committees/House_of_representatives_Committee s?url=/jsct/26august2008/treaties/defence_france_text.pdf.

Department of Foreign Affairs and Trade Australia (2017) 'Joint Statement of Enhanced Strategic Partnership between Australia and France'. Available at www. dfat.gov.au/geo/france/joint-statement-of-enhanced-strategic-partnership-between-a ustralia-and-france [last accessed 9 May 2022].

Department of Foreign Affairs and Trade Australia (2019) 'Fiji-Australia Vuvale Partnership', 16 September. Available at www.dfat.gov.au/geo/fiji/fiji-australia-vuva le-partnership#:~:text='Vuvale'%20is%20the%20word%20in,friendship%20betwee n%20our%20two%20nations [last accessed 9 May 2022].

Dobell, Graeme (2007a) *China and Taiwan in the South Pacific: Diplomatic Chess versus Pacific Political Rugby*, Chinese Southern Diaspora Studies Occasional Paper, No. 1, (Australian National University).

Dobell, Graeme (2007b) 'The Arc of Instability: History of an Idea', in Ron Huisken and Meredith Thatcher (eds), *History as Policy: Framing the Debate on the Future of Australia's Defence Policy* (Canberra: ANU E-Press).

Doherty, Ben, Sheldon Chanel, Helend Davidson and Lily Kuo (2020) 'Taiwan Official in Hospital; After Alleged "Violent Attack" by Chinese Diplomats in Fiji', *The Guardian*, 19 October. Available at www.theguardian.com/world/2020/oct/19/taiwa n-official-in-hospital-after-alleged-violent-attack-by-chinese-diplomats-in-fiji   [last accessed 9 May 2022].

D'Souza, Shanthie Mariet (2014) India in Post 2014 Afghanistan: Challenges and Opportunities. Available at https://asiancenturyinstitute.com/international/535-india -in-post-2014-afghanistan.

Hall, Ian (2015) 'Normative Power India?', in Jamie Gaskarth (ed.), *China, India and the Future of International Society* (London: Rowman & Littlefield).

Hall, Ian (2019) *Modi and the Reinvention of Indian Foreign Policy* (Bristol: Bristol University Press).

Hall, Ian (2021) 'India: Seeking Multipolarity, Favouring Multilateralism, Pursuing Multialignment', in Benjamin Zala (ed.), *National Perspectives on a Multipolar Order: Interrogating the Global Power Transition* (Manchester: Manchester University Press).

Hegarty, David (2004) 'Through and Beyond the "Arc of Instability"', in Ivan Molloy (ed.), *The Eye of the Cyclone: Issues in the Pacific Security* (Sippy Downs: Pacific Island Political Studies Association and University of the Sunshine Coast, 2004).

Hill, Matthew (2010) 'A Velvet Glove? Coercion and the Australasian Response to the 2006 Fijian Coup', *Security Challenges*, 6 (2): 105–122.

Jaishankar, Subrahmanyam (2020) *The India Way: Strategies for an Uncertain World* (New Delhi: HarperCollins Publishers India).

Kate, Talebula (2017) 'Fiji Values Relations with India: Koya', *The Fiji Times*, 30 November. Available at www.fijitimes.com/fiji-values-relations-with-india-koya/ [last accessed 9 May 2022].

Lanteigne, Marc (2012) 'Water Dragon? China, Power Shifts and Soft Balancing in the South Pacific', *Political Science*, 64 (1): 21–38.

Lowy Institute (2018) 'Speech by the Hon Prime Minister Tuilaepa Sailele Malielegaoi on Pacific Perspectives on the New Geostrategic Landscape', 30 August. Available at www.lowyinstitute.org/publications/speech-hon-prime-minister-tuilaepa-sailele-malielegaoi-pacific-perspectives-new [last accessed 9 May 2022].

Lowy Institute (2019) 'Pacific Aid Map', 24 June. Available at www.pacificaidmap.lowyinstitute.org [last accessed 24 April 2022].

Maclellan, Nic (2018) '"Macron-ising" the Pacific', *Islands Business*, 14 June. Available at https://islandsbusiness.com/2018/2018-june/macron-ising-the-pacific/ [last accessed 9 May 2022].

Medcalf, Rory (2020) *Contest For The Indo-Pacific: Why China Won't Map The Future* (Carleton, Victoria: La Trobe University Press).

Ministry of Defence India (2017) 'India and Fiji Sign MoU on Defence Cooperation', 29 May. Available at www.indiandiplomacy.org/2017/05/29/india-and-fiji-sign-mou-on-defence-cooperation.

Ministry of External Affairs (2015) 'Breakthrough Diplomacy: New Vision, New Vigour', 2 January. Available at www.mea.gov.in/in-focus-article.htm?24635/EBook+Breakthrough+Diplomacy+New+Vision+New+Vigour [last accessed 24 April 2022].

Ministry of External Affairs India (2017a) 'India-Pacific Sustainable Development Conference to enhance cooperation between India and Island Countries', 12 May. Available at https://mea.gov.in/press-releases.htm?dtl/28460/IndiaPacific_Islands_Sustainable_Development_Conference_to_enhance_cooperation_between_India_and_Pacific_Island_Countries [last accessed 9 May 2022].

Ministry of External Affairs India (2017b) 'Inauguration of India-Pacific Sustainable Development Conference', 25 May. Available at www.mea.gov.in/press-releases.htm?dtl/28488/Inauguration_of_IndiaPacific_Islands_Sustainable_Development_Conference [last accessed 9 May 2022].

Ministry of Foreign Affairs and Trade New Zealand (2020) 'Briefing for Incoming Minister of Foreign Affairs', 1 December. Available at www.mfat.govt.nz/assets/About-us-Corporate/MFAT-corporate-publications/Briefings-to-incoming-Ministers/Briefing-for-incoming-Minister-of-Foreign-Affairs-2020.pdf [last accessed 9 May 2022].

Modi, Narendra (2015a) 'Opening Remarks at Forum for India Pacific Island Countries (FIPIC) Summit', 21 August. Available at www.narendramodi.in/pm-s-opening-remarks-at-forum-for-india-pacific-island-countries-fipic-summit-jaipur-282251 [last accessed 9 May 2022].

Modi, Narendra (2015b) 'Closing Remarks at Forum for India Pacific Island Countries (FIPIC) Summit', 21 August. Available at www.pmindia.gov.in/en/news_updates/text-of-pms-closing-remarks-at-forum-for-india-pacific-island-countries-fipic-summit-jaipur/ [last accessed 9 May 2022].

Modi, Narendra (2014) 'Prime Minister's Remarks at the 9th East Asia Summit', 13 November. Available at http://mea.gov.in/Speeches-Statements.htm?dtl/24238/ [last accessed 18 June 2021].

Pacific Islands Forum Secretariat (2018) 'Boe Declaration on Regional Security', 5 September. Available at www.forumsec.org/2018/09/05/boe-declaration-on-regional-security/ [last accessed 9 May 2022].

Parker, Sam and Gabrielle Chefitz (2018) 'Debtbook Diplomacy: China's Strategic Leveraging of its Newfound Economic Influence and the Consequence for US

Foreign Policy', 24 May. Available at www.belfercenter.org/publication/debt book-diplomacy.

Press Information Bureau India (2017) 'President of India's Message on the Occasion of Constitution Day of Marshall Islands', 1 May. Available at https://pib.gov.in/ newsite/PrintRelease.aspx?relid=161413 [last accessed 9 May 2022].

Prime Minister of Australia (2019) 'Joint Statement with the Prime Minister of Vanuatu', 16 January. Available at www.pm.gov.au/media/joint-statement-prime-m inister-vanuatu [last accessed 9 May 2022].

Prime Minister of Australia (2020) 'Papua New Guinea-Australia Comprehensive Strategic and Economic Partnership', 5 August. Available at www.dfat.gov.au/ geo/papua-new-guinea/papua-new-guinea-australia-comprehensive-strategic-and-ec onomic-partnership [last accessed 9 May 2022].

Raja Mohan, Chilamkuri (2014) 'PM Modi in Fiji: India's Strategic Foray in the South Pacific', 24 November. Available at www.rsis.edu.sg/wp-content/uploads/ 2014/11/CO14233.pdf [last accessed 9 May 2022].

Rajah, Roland, Alexandre Dayant and Jonathan Pryke (2019) 'Ocean of Debt? Belt and Road and dept diplomacy in the Pacific', 21 October. Available at www.low yinstitute.org/publications/ocean-debt-belt-and-road-and-debt-diplomacy-pacific#s ec41161 [last accessed 9 May 2022].

Rumley, Dennis (2006) 'The Emergence of Australia's Arc of Instability', in Dennis Rumley, Vivian Louis Forbes and Christopher Griffin (eds), *Australia's Arc of Instability: The Political and Cultural Dynamics of Regional Security* (Dordrecht: Springer).

Saran, Shyam (2005) 'India and Its Neighbours', 14 February. Available at www.mea. gov.in.

Sen Yu, Chang (2015) 'The Pacific Islands in China's Strategy for the 21st Century', in Chang Sen Yu (ed.), *2014–2015 Dayangzhou lanpi shu* [2014–2015 Blue Book of Oceania], 2nd edition (Beijing: Social Sciences Academic Press).

Sinha, Yashwant (2003) 'Resurgent India in Asia', 29 September. Available at www. mea.gov.in/Speeches-Statements.htm?drl/4744/ [last accessed 18 June 2021].

Taylor, MegDame (2018) 'Keynote Address: 2018 State of the Pacific Conference', 8 September. Available at www.forumsec.org/2018/09/10/keynote-address-by-secreta ry-general-meg-taylor-to-the-2018-state-of-the-pacific-conference/ [last accessed 9 May 2022].

Thakur, Ramesh (1985) 'India and Overseas Indians: The Case of Fiji', *Asian Survey*, 25 (3): 356–370.

Tillett, Andrew (2018) 'Emmanuel Macron's Australia-France-India "Strategic Axis" a Bit of a Stretch', *Australian Financial Review*, 3 May. Available at www.afr.com/p olitics/emmanuel-macrons-australiafranceindia-strategic-axis-a-bit-of-a-stretch-201 80503-h0zkxy [last accessed 9 May 2022].

UK Government (2019) 'UK-Pacific Partnerships and Shared Values: Address by Laura Clarke', 3 July. Available at www.gov.uk/government/speeches/oceans-apa rt-the-uk-the-pacific-partnerships-shared-values [last accessed 9 May 2022].

Wallis, Joanne (2012) 'The Pacific: from "Arc of Instability" to "Arc of Responsibility" and then to "Arc of Opportunity"', *Security Challenges*, 8 (4): 1–12.

Wallis, Joanne (2017) *Pacific Power? Australia's Strategy in the Pacific Islands* (Melbourne: Melbourne University Press).

Wallis, Joanne (2020) 'How Should Australia Respond to China's Increased Presence in the Pacific Islands?', *Security Challenges*, 16 (3): 47–52.

Wallis, Joanne (2021) 'Strategic Competition and the Pacific Islands', in *Asia-Pacific Regional Security Assessment 2021* (Abingdon: Routledge).

Wroe, David (2018) 'Australia Will Compete with China to Save Pacific Sovereignty, Says Bishop', *Sydney Morning Herald*, 18 June. Available at www.smh.com.au/p olitics/federal/australia-will-compete-with-china-to-save-pacific-sovereignty-says-bi shop-20180617-p4zm1h.html [last accessed 9 May 2022].

Yang, Jian (2009) 'China in the South Pacific: Hegemon on the Horizon', *The Pacific Review*, 22 (2): 139–158.

12 Attitudes of the Indian-American Diaspora towards Politics in India

Shubha Kamala Prasad, Maneesh Arora and Sara Sadhwani

Headlines like 'Are Cuban American Voters Really a 'Special' Case?' (Pertierra, 2020) and 'How Indian Americans Got the President's Ear' (Rani, 2021) are not uncommon in media analyses of diasporas' political preferences and/or participation. Many academic political analyses of diasporas also treat them as singular communities whose preferences need to be understood as a whole (Haney & Vanderbush, 1999; Paul & Paul, 2009; Shain, 1994). However, does a diaspora community have a coherent and homogeneous identity with common political preferences? In this chapter, we argue that we need to investigate the internal variation in political preferences of diaspora communities. We posit that internal divisions are often overlooked for the sake of analytical convenience. Using a nationally representative survey of the Indian-American community that we created (see Arora & Sadhwani, forthcoming), we show how political identity, religion, age, and state of origin in India relate to different political preferences with regards to politics in India.

Our assertion for disaggregating diaspora communities is not unique. It follows from work that has unpacked the political preferences of immigrant communities and analyses of diaspora identity politics. Recent work has found major cleavages based on national origin, generation, education level, gender, and other demographic traits in policy preferences among Asian Americans (Arora et al., 2021). Similar results have been found for the Latinx community (e.g. Beltrán, 2010; Castro et al., 2015). Diaspora studies have explored how internal demographic variation like education, generational differences, and relationship to homelands can result in different identity preferences (Benton & Gomez, 2014; Martínez & Gonzalez, 2021; Panossian, 1998). We select the Indian-American community to further break down its internal political differences based on demographic factors that have been identified as relevant for such groups.

Why focus on the Indian-American community? A subset of Asian-Americans, it has been often overlooked, which is a particularly important oversight given that Indian-Americans are the fastest growing racial or ethnic subgroup in the US. Members of this community are also concentrated in electorally important states such as California, Texas, Georgia, Florida, and

DOI: 10.4324/9781003305132-16

Pennsylvania, and have increasingly been more politically active in recent years with voting rates almost doubling from 2014 to 2018 (Ramakrishnan et al., 2019). Indian-Americans have also risen to political prominence as highlighted by the election of Vice President Kamala Harris, with growing numbers in Congress, and their strong presence in the Biden administration that came to power in 2021. Their increased political importance in the US thus merits further investigation of the community's political preferences, and it is important to understand whether the community is cohesive and homogeneous when it comes to politics or if there are variations.

We assert that diaspora communities are not homogeneous entities even if they are characterized as such for the sake of analytical convenience. This is true of the Indian-American community as well. We test its internal variation based on individual opinions of contemporary political developments in India based on novel data we gathered on a nationally representative sample of Indian-Americans. Indian-American perspectives on India matter because diasporas can have both political (Paarlberg, 2019) and economic (Kapur, 2004) impacts on their countries of origin. Remittances, charitable donations, religious donations, political donations, investments, property ownership, and familial connections are just some of the ways in which the Indian diaspora maintain their linkages to India from around the world. A nuanced approach to understanding internal divisions within a diaspora's construction of its identity and preferences allows us to be more sensitive to assessing the variation in support or opposition to politics in the country of origin. We, therefore, test how the Indian-American community's internal divisions based on identity play out in terms of their political preferences for politics in India.

The Indian state's engagement with India's diaspora around the world has been based on its understanding of its own identity. India's attitude towards its diaspora has not been steady since the time of its independence. Pre-independence, the Indian political elite was willing to engage with Indian diaspora organizations in the US and the UK in order to lobby for the cause of independence from British rule (Prasad & Savatic, 2021). At that point, an Indian identity was transnational and encompassed Indian allies who lived around the world. However, from the 1950s onwards, India disengaged from its diaspora. The idea of India was one of self-reliance and a deliberate move away from foreign influence (Miller, 2013). Economic liberalization in the early 1990s though changed India's attitude wherein India now wanted to project itself as a booming economy willing to open up to the world. In order to attract more foreign investments, India began to reach out to its diaspora again. A spike in remittances and other economic linkages between Indians and their homeland began in the late 1990s and continues until today (Naujoks, 2013). Given these variations in the Indian state's shaping of its own identity and its subsequent foreign policy engagement with its diaspora, it is also important to understand the variation in the Indian diaspora's preferences.

In the following section, we argue for deconstructing homogeneous inter-pretations of diaspora identities in order to nuance our understanding of diasporas' political preferences *vis-à-vis* their countries of origin. Using the case of the Indian-American diaspora, we provide some background on contemporary Indian politics and the Indian-American community. We out-line four hypotheses about the variation in political preferences of the Indian-American community based on different factors like political identity, religion, age, and state of origin in India. We test our hypotheses using data gathered from an original nationally representative survey of Indian-Amer-icans. We conclude with the implications of our findings for understanding the role of identity when disentangling political divisions within diaspora communities.

Diaspora Communities and Politics: Diversity from Within

When the country of origin is used as an identifier for a diaspora group, it 'deploys a notion of ethnicity that privileges the point of origin in con-structing identity and thus tends to homogenize the population' (Moghissi et al., 2009: 4). Such homogenization misses out on the intersectionality of identities based on class, gender, and trans-ethnic alliances that exist in dia-sporic communities (Anthias, 1998). The analytical utility of clubbing toge-ther diverse individuals within a diaspora is understandable, especially when studying small groups located within much bigger majority populations. However, delving into the internal variation of a diaspora community can help nuance our assumptions about their political preferences and behaviour. For example, Singh and Singh (2014) critique a homogeneous understanding of diasporic subjects by showing heterogeneity within diasporas based on diverse political activities. Inter-generational identity variation across the Chinese diaspora results in different political and economic networks for newer generations (Benton and Gomez, 2014). The reproduction of home-land socioeconomic status, religion, and time of settlements have been mar-kers of internal diversity for the Iranian diaspora in Australia, UK, and Canada (McAuliffe, 2008). The 'high segmentation and internal disparities of Turkish society' (Bruneau, 2010) are more apparent in the diaspora where minorities can assert their own identities in contrast to being suppressed in Turkey. These studies point out that 'the limits of diaspora lie precisely in its own assumed boundedness, its inevitable tendency to stress its internal coherence and unity, logically set apart from "others"' (Ang, 2003: 142). Thus, diasporas are not homogeneous bodies.

A diaspora's heterogeneity potentially affects its relationships with the country of origin. Links between diasporas and their country of origin matter not only because of their economic impact in terms of remittances, but also because of their political influence (Paarlberg, 2019). Diaspora political preferences can affect political outcomes in their countries of origin. Diaspora communities can engage in politics directly in their countries of origin or indirectly by lobbying the governments in their countries of residence. Diaspora voting in origin country elections is the most significant example of direct participation (Brand, 2014), especially when incumbent parties extend such rights based on perceptions of diaspora support (Wellman, 2021). As for indirect influence, the success of many diasporic lobby groups in the US at influencing US foreign policy outcomes to their advantage is worth noting in this context (Bermeo & Leblang, 2015; Paul & Paul, 2009). Even when they are not actively engaged in influencing politics, diasporas can help activate or reinforce the political convictions of their relatives in countries of origin (Paarlberg, 2017).

Given the myriad ways in which diasporas remain connected politically to their countries of origin, the aim of this chapter is to understand the internal cleavages of the Indian-American community in terms of their political preferences with regards to politics in India. The Indian diaspora has primarily received scrutiny for their economic impact in both their countries of residence and India. Their remittance, investment, and migration patterns based on the Indian government's citizenship policies have been assessed (Naujoks, 2013) and their role in contributing to development in India has been thoroughly examined (Agrawal et al., 2011; Agarwala, 2015; Azeez & Begum, 2009; Kapur, 2004; Prakash, 1998; Sahay, 2009). Their impact in the countries Indians migrate to has also been analysed (Kapur, 2010; Naujoks, 2017). The Indian diaspora's political participation has further been examined in terms of their mobilization for foreign policy lobbying in the US (Kirk, 2008; Mistry, 2013; Prasad & Savatic, 2021) and the role of descriptive representation in voting (Arora & Sadhwani, forthcoming). However, most of these studies examining the Indian diaspora in different countries often treat them as homogeneous entities even when acknowledging the potential fissures within the community (Hathaway, 2001). Scholars though have also been unpacking their internal variation in terms of their partisan preferences (Badrinathan et al., 2020; Raychaudhuri, 2020) and identity politics in the US (Biswas, 2010; Kurien, 2004). These internal divisions matter since we know that the South Asian diaspora has a history of lending political support to causes like the Khalistani movement and Tamil nationalism (Fair, 2005).

In line with the studies that disaggregate diaspora communities, we outline the dimensions along which the Indian-American community is divided when it comes to political preferences for politics in India.

Contemporary Indian Politics and the Indian-American Community

India's political system is a strong multi-party parliamentary federal democracy. At the national level, two political parties are the most prominent – the Indian National Congress (Congress) and the Bharatiya Janata Party (BJP). The primary difference between the two parties is that the former presents itself as secular while the latter carries a Hindu right-wing identity.

Numerous powerful regional parties exist across the 28 states of India that are linguistically and ethnically diverse. From 1989 to 2014, neither the Congress nor the BJP was able to achieve a majority in the Lok Sabha on their own, so coalition governments had become the norm. However, the BJP was elected to power in 2014 and 2019 with majority mandates. What has this swing towards a Hindu right-wing government meant for politics in India?

Narendra Modi, the Prime Minister of India leading the BJP government, has been a pivotal figure in garnering support for the BJP. A populist and charismatic leader, he has won elections with strategies similar to other right-wing populist leaders around the world – playing on the fears of the majority to malign minority groups. In this regard, his policies around *Hindutva* ideology has been crucial. *Hindutva* ideology is the predominant form of Hindu nationalism first articulated by V. D. Savarkar in 1923 wherein India is articulated as the holy land of the Hindus. Therefore, the 'people' constitute Hindu Indians while Muslims are the 'other' (McDonnell & Cabrera, 2019). Modi's promises of economic development while simultaneously promoting Islamophobia have been a winning formula for elections (Palshikar, 2015). Modi has successfully channelled public support towards BJP's Hindu majoritarian policies.

We want to highlight two of the Modi's government's most controversial policies – the abolition of Article 370 and the Citizenship Amendment Act (CAA). We choose to focus on these two policies because they were not only hotly contested domestically[1] in India but also made global headlines. Article 370 of the Indian Constitution conferred special status to the state of Jammu and Kashmir (J&K) in India, wherein the Indian constitution could not be applied in its entirety to the state. For instance, it allowed J&K's residents the ability to own property and access government jobs within the state and prevented the same for Indians living in other states. The BJP government passed a bill in parliament to abolish this article on 5 August 2019. Its abolition was accompanied by a bill in parliament that dissolved J&K's status as a state and divided it into two union territories of Jammu & Kashmir and Ladakh. The dissolution removed the state legislature and, therefore, the power of the people to govern themselves in India's federal structure. Instead, union territories are controlled directly by the central government. BJP and its supporters claim that this move will result in J&K becoming more integrated with India while its opponents assert that this will alienate the population of an already conflict-ridden territory. The aftermath of these legislative moves involved the detention of leading politicians in Kashmir, cutting off the internet in Kashmir for seven months, and a virtual lockdown of the region.

The CAA was also a similarly momentous legislation passed in parliament on 11 December 2019. For the first time in India's independent history, religion became a basis for eligibility for Indian citizenship. The amendment introduced to India's citizenship laws now allows undocumented migrants from Afghanistan, Bangladesh and Pakistan to apply for a fast-tracked citizenship process if they are from a minority religion in these Muslim-majority states. Non-Muslim majority states neighbouring India like Sri Lanka, Nepal and Myanmar were noticeably left out from this list since their minorities would include Muslims. Furthermore, in conjunction with the National Register of Citizens, the potential of targeting Indian Muslims who do not have legal paperwork to prove their birth becomes higher. The BJP's agenda is to implement an India-wide registry of citizens. However, most Indians have no legal documents that prove their birth, so Muslims who cannot show that they were born in India are more likely to face discrimination and potentially be accused of not being Indian, while non-Muslims from neighbouring states can seek citizenship.

The rise of a populist leader in India whose government has been implementing majoritarian policies has not gone unnoticed amongst the Indian-American diaspora (Rao, 2020). Indian-American attention on Indian politics is not surprising given the deep familial and economic ties between Indian-Americans and India. Familial linkages have enabled setting up global transnational networks with issues like familial responsibilities also influencing the migration of Indian-Americans to India (Ray, 2013). Not only do Indian-Americans contribute economically via remittances, they also participate in the Indian economy through promoting the Information Technology sector (Kapur, 2001), endorsing new economic ideas for innovation (Kapur, 2004), and setting up institutionalized transnational networks for development in sectors like health and education (Agarwala, 2015).

The Indian government has also been actively engaging the Indian diaspora since the 1990s in an attempt to foster a 'global Indian' identity (Varadarajan, 2010: 150–151). Since India's implementation of economic liberalization policies in the 1990s, the Indian government has looked to its diaspora to invest in the Indian economy (Naujoks, 2013). Despite India's reluctance to allow dual citizenship, it created an alternative Overseas Citizen of India (OCI) status, which extends almost every citizen privilege to non-resident Indians with the exception of the right to vote in elections or stand for political office. The OCI was the Indian government's response to 'demands for 'dual citizenship' particularly from the Diaspora in North America and other developed countries and keeping in view the Government's deep commitment towards fulfilling the aspirations and expectations of Overseas Indians' (MEA, 2019).

In the light of the close ties between Indian-Americans and India, the diaspora's opinions on political developments in India are worth investigating. Given Modi's unprecedented popularity, we analyse what drives Indian-American support (or lack thereof) for him and his government's policies on Article 370 and CAA.[2]

The Political Preferences of Indian-Americans

Based on the history of strongly contested political elections in India, in addition to India's demographic diversity, we posit that the Indian-American community should also display variation in political preferences, especially based on different demographic factors. We propose that internal divisions can be along multiple dimensions for the Indian-American diaspora and focus on four factors - political identity, religion, age, and state of origin in India.

Political Identity

First, we assert that political identity in the American context might overlap with political preferences in the Indian context. While the type of political regime (Just, 2019) and welfare system (Giuliano & Tabellini, 2020) in the country of origin might influence partisan preferences in the country of residence, it should follow that the political context in the country of residence can correlate with political preferences in the homeland. In the contemporary political climate, we test whether support for a populist leader in the US and India correlates positively, i.e. whether support for Donald Trump means greater support for Modi.

While Indian-Americans might be divided over their support for Modi (Biswas, 2010), we posit that those who support Trump are more likely to support Modi because of the similar appeal of a populist leader. Despite Indian-Americans historical lean towards Democrats, there has been strong support for Trump within the community. Social media support for Trump amongst the Indian diaspora in the West showed the deliberate attempt to embed themselves in a transnational 'populist radical right agenda' (Leidig, 2019). Shalabh Kumar, the founder of the Republican Hindu Coalition, raised nearly US$900,000 for Trump's 2016 presidential campaign (Swan, 2016). The Texas India Forum organized the 'Howdy Modi' event in September 2019 where Donald Trump and Narendra Modi appeared together on stage in a show of US-India solidarity, but more significantly, as an endorsement of each other. Thus, backing a populist figure may travel across political contexts.

However, this support might not just be about the individual leaders. Self-identifying Republicans might be more inclined to align with the conservative cultural ideals of the BJP as well as approve strongly of BJP's neoliberal policies that aim at reducing the welfare capacity of the state. Thus, Indian-Americans who support the Republicans might also support Modi because of their belief in the BJP's political and economic agenda. These observations lead to two of our hypotheses, which are:

H1a   Indian-Americans who support Trump are more likely to
           support Modi.
H1b   Self-identifying Republicans in the Indian-American commu-
           nity are more likely to support Modi.

Religion

Religions provide migrants a conduit to continue participating in the affairs of their country of origin (Levitt, 2004; Menjívar, 1999). It also keeps alive links between the diaspora and the country of origin. For instance, 'the politicization of Hinduism in the United States draws on Hindu nationalist ideologies and networks first articulated in India' (Kurien, 2007: 2). In turn, fundraising for *Hindutva* organizations in the US is common wherein money raised for relief work in India is often used only for Hindus with the exclusion of other religions (Sabrang, 2002). Some of the most powerful Hindu right-wing organizations are active in the US. The Rashtriya Swayamsevak Sangh, the parent body of the current ruling party in India, the BJP, is the main *Hindutva* organization and has an organizational presence in about 150 countries (Bhatt, 2000) under the title of the Hindu Swayamsevak Sangh. The Vishwa Hindu Parishad (World Hindu Council) is also active in 29 countries, including the US. Numerous *Hindutva* organizations and websites have proliferated online, further extending the reach of this movement across the globe (Rajagopal, 2000).

Such organizations reveal the organized mobilization of Hindus outside India (Jaffrelot & Therwath, 2007). It has been argued that diaspora Hindu nationalist movements have shaped anti-secular and anti-minority orientations both within the diaspora and in India (Bhatt & Mukta, 2000). Strong tones of Islamophobia amongst Indian-American lobby groups have also been observed (Therwath, 2007). Thus, we expect to see Hindu Americans be more sympathetic towards *Hindutva* politics in India. We must state at the outset that all Hindus do not subscribe to *Hindutva* ideology. However, we do expect religious variation in terms of more support for Modi amongst Hindus as compared to other religious backgrounds given the robust evidence of a strong Hindu right-wing presence in the US. These observations lead to our next hypothesis:

H2   Hindu Indian-Americans are more likely to support Modi.

Age

Are older Indian-Americans more likely to support Modi due to nostalgia politics? Age has consistently been found to be correlated with partisanship in many election studies (Tilley, 2002) with the common finding that partisanship preferences solidify with age while younger voters are more flexible (Lisi, 2015). In the case of Indian-Americans, they cannot exercise political franchise in India unless they are Indian citizens, so the dynamics of age on partisan preferences may not apply neatly. Instead we draw upon theories of nostalgia in diaspora communities. Older generations of immigrants had to undergo prolonged absences from the country of origin since inter-continental travel was not as commonplace in the 1960s and 1970s. In contrast, 'for contemporary Indian migrants, the concept of home is present in their lives through routine visits to India, Bollywood films, the internet' (Bhatia, 2007: 221) so cultural connections are more dynamic. Thus, nostalgia amongst older generations involved holding onto and preserving memories and customs from the time they left India while younger generations have the option of updating cultural identity. Given this difference, we expect BJP's reification of Hindu cultural purity as a symbol of true Indianness to appeal more to older generations who have tried to hold on to their versions of 'pure' Indian identities. From this basis, our hypothesis is:

H3   Indian-American support for Modi increases with age.

State of Origin in India

There is considerable variation in terms of the number of Indian migrants that move to the US from the different states of India (Bhagat et al., 2013). There is also political variation across India in terms of states leaning left or right. Thus, depending on the states that Indian migrants originate from, one might see potential differences in political preferences. Political cleavages and conflicts within a country often transfer to its diaspora (Baser, 2015; Demmers, 2007). Evidence of diasporas carrying over regional political partisan preferences from their homelands has been demonstrated for Poles and Ukrainians (Ahmadov & Sasse, 2015). We expect the same regional political preferences to map onto the Indian-American diaspora.

Are immigrants from Gujarat, a BJP stronghold, more likely to approve of Modi than immigrants from Kerala, a non-BJP state? We hypothesize that the answer to this question should be 'yes'. India has 28 states of which 14 states have BJP in power in the state legislature and 4 states have BJP in the coalition ruling the state as of 2021. We assert that immigrants from states that voted for BJP in the national elections will be more likely to approve of Modi and his government's policies due to carrying over local political preferences as well as the influence of linkages with family and friends in the state of origin. Thus, we expect Indian-Americans who originate from BJP-supporting states to be more likely to support Modi, the CAA, and the revocation of Article 370. As such, our final hypothesis is:

H4   Indian-Americans are more likely to support Modi/CAA/
             revocation of Article 370 if their state of origin voted for the
             BJP (as of 2021).

Methods

To test our hypotheses we collected a survey sample of 1,003 Indian-Americans using the firm Lucid.[3] The sample includes Hindus, Muslims, Christians and respondents of other religious backgrounds. About 59% were born overseas, mostly in India. Respondents or their families hail from 25 of India's 28 states and the Delhi region. The survey was conducted from 13 to

30 October 2020. The sample was census-matched for age, gender, education level, political party and geographic region. Recent tests of the Lucid platform indicate that demographic and experimental findings from this platform are similar to findings from nationally representative probability samples (Coppock & McClellan, 2019). Lucid can construct samples that are similar to high quality survey panels like Pew's American Trends Panel (Tausanovitch et al., 2019). Respondents were asked a series of questions that gauged demographic characteristics; political attitudes including partisanship, policy preferences in the US and India, and evaluations of US and India-based politicians; as well as media engagement, perceptions of intergroup commonality, and experiences with discrimination. We then used correlation tests, logistic regression models, and difference of means tests to analyse the data.

Results

Hypotheses H1a and H1b

To test our first hypothesis, we look at the correlation between support for former president Donald Trump and support for Prime Minister Narendra Modi. Table 12.1 shows that there is some evidence of an association between Trump support and support for Modi. Trump approval, having voted for Donald Trump, and identification as Republican are all moderately correlated with approval of Modi.

We next tested the effect of Trump approval, having voted for Donald Trump, and identification as Republican on Modi approval using ordered logistic regression analysis. The coefficient for each variable is positive and statistically significant. The models include controls for party identification, ideology, age, education, gender, and Hinduism.[4] These results are shown in Table 12.2.

For ease of interpretation, we look at the predicted probabilities of voting for Trump on Modi approval holding each of the control variables at their means. The probability of strongly approving of Modi is 25 percentage points higher among those who voted for Trump (0.4 out of 1) than among those who did not vote for Trump (0.15 out of 1). On the other end of the scale, those who voted for Trump (0.04) are ten points *less* likely to express strong disapproval of Modi than those who did not vote for Trump (0.14).

Table 12.1 Correlation between Trump support and Modi support.

Variable 1	*Variable 2*	*Correlation coefficient*
Trump approval	Modi approval	0.4145
Trump vote	Modi approval	0.1859
Republican	Modi approval	0.1889

Table 12.2 Ordered logistic regression models testing support for Trump on support for Modi.

	(1)	(2)	(3)
Variables	Model 1	Model 2	Model 2
Trump vote	1.287***		
	(0.186)		
Trump approve		2.430***	
		(0.199)	
Republican			0.976***
			(0.152)
Female	-0.429***	-0.394***	-0.449***
	(0.116)	(0.117)	(0.116)
College degree	-0.193	-0.221	-0.172
	(0.144)	(0.145)	(0.144)
Party ID	0.259	-0.0265	
	(0.180)	(0.174)	
Ideology	0.0715	-0.0385	0.203
	(0.256)	(0.256)	(0.249)
Hindu	1.418***	1.342***	1.420***
	(0.124)	(0.124)	(0.123)
Age	0.0224***	0.0290***	0.0216***
	(0.00523)	(0.00533)	(0.00520)
/cut1	-0.474**	0.120	-0.519**
	(0.221)	(0.227)	(0.219)
/cut2	0.353	1.010***	0.300
	(0.218)	(0.227)	(0.216)
/cut3	1.696***	2.480***	1.612***
	(0.225)	(0.239)	(0.221)
/cut4	3.012***	3.888***	2.881***
	(0.237)	(0.256)	(0.233)
Observations	999	999	999

Standard errors in parentheses
*** $p < 0.01$, ** $p < 0.05$, * $p < 0.1$

Hypothesis H2

For hypothesis 2, we looked at the relationship between Modi approval and identification as Hindu. Mean approval of Modi is 0.67 among Hindus which is a full 24 points higher than mean approval among non-Hindus in the sample.[5] Mean support of Modi is only 0.47 among Christians and 0.41 among Muslims. There are many other religions represented in our sample but no other group has a large enough sample size to be included in this analysis. Moreover, the models in Table 12.2 indicate a strong, positive association between Hindu identification and support for Modi. Thus, Hindu Americans are much more likely to support Modi than non-Hindu Americans. Our findings lend support to the evidence of a strong Hindu right-wing identity being cultivated in the Indian-American diaspora.

Hypothesis H3

In each of the regression models shown in Table 12.2, age has a positive effect on support for Modi. For example, in model 1, each one year increase in a respondent's age is associated with a 0.03 increase in Modi approval on a 0 to 1 scale.[6] Our findings imply that nostalgia politics merit further investigation within the Indian-American community. Conservative identity politics might appeal more to older generations.

Hypothesis H4

Finally, H4 posits a relationship between the political character of respondents' state of origin and respondents' evaluations of Modi and policies that Modi has championed. To test this, we look at mean support for Modi, the Citizenship Amendment Act, and the revocation of Article 370 from the Indian constitution. There are five states from which we have a large enough sample size to analyse separately: Andhra Pradesh, Delhi, Gujarat, Punjab, and Tamil Nadu. We find that mean approval of Modi is between 0.61 and 0.64 among respondents who hail from, or whose families hail from, Andhra Pradesh, Delhi, or Gujarat. But mean approval is only 0.41 among Punjabis and 0.47 among those from Tamil Nadu.[7]

We find similar patterns when examining support for CAA and the revocation of Article 370. Mean support for the CAA is between 0.6 and 0.63 among those from Andhra, Delhi, and Gujarat. Among those from Punjab, mean support is 0.53 and among those from Tamil Nadu, mean support is 0.48. Similarly, mean support for the revocation of Article 370 is between 0.59 and 0.61 among the first three states, but is 0.44 and 0.51 among those from Punjab and Tamil Nadu, respectively. Delhi and Gujarat both elected BJP to power in the *Lok Sabha* while Punjab and Tamil Nadu did not, so the evidence for people originating from these states supports our hypothesis. However, the majority in Andhra Pradesh did not vote for BJP. The anomaly in our findings can possibly be explained by the dimension of caste. Most Andhra immigrants to the US are upper caste, which happens to be the support base of the BJP and its coalition partner within the state (IANS, 2019). Thus, intersectionality of identity is also an important factor to account for in future analyses and the role of caste in Indian-American political preferences requires more unpacking.

Conclusion: Locating Indian-American Identities

In this chapter we provided a more nuanced analysis of a diaspora community's political preferences as opposed to sweeping the preferences of a large and diverse community into a single box. We showed how different identity and demographic factors can affect the political beliefs of diaspora communities *vis-a-vis* their country of origin. Within the Indian-American community we found strong evidence that those who supported Donald Trump are also inclined to support Narendra Modi. Self-identifying Republicans are also more inclined to support Modi. Our findings show that to a certain degree, political preferences can overlap across countries based on support for right-wing populists and conservative political inclinations. Our analyses also show how despite their experiences as immigrants and minorities in the US, some Indian-Americans support majoritarian policies in India. We found strong evidence for the impact of Hindu right-wing identity politics on Indian-Americans with Hindu Americans being far more likely to endorse Modi than non-Hindus. It would be fruitful for future research to unpack the cognitive dissonance between lived experience as a minority and policy support for majoritarianism within diasporas. Additionally, we tested whether the state of origin in India matters for diaspora political preferences. We find that Indian-Americans hailing from states that are pro-BJP tend to approve of Modi more than those who originate from states that did not vote BJP to power.

Finally, while the findings in this paper are specific to the Indian-American community, we provide a framework for understanding the dimensions along which other diaspora communities might display internal divisions. Additionally, this framework can also be tested on a sizable Indian diaspora in other Western democratic contexts like Canada, the UK, Australia, and the EU, which would help us understand the Indian diaspora's political preferences around the world. Disaggregating diaspora preferences is crucial for understanding India's foreign policy orientation towards its diaspora. India's level of engagement with its diaspora is dependent on whether the diaspora's preferences align with the politics within India. India's projection of its identity globally also benefits from its diaspora reinforcing that identity. Thus, moving forward, analysing the variation in diaspora support or opposition for BJP's *Hindutva* vision of India will give us a clearer picture of political preferences based on different identity constellations within diasporas.

Notes

1 We must note that BJP's policies have not been universally accepted by the Indian public. Opposition to the abolition of Article 370 and the CAA have been strong but with little impact due to BJP's control of the parliament.
2 We want to add the caveat that the survey captures the moment after Modi's first Covid-19 lockdown policy but before the catastrophic second wave, so support for Modi might look very different in 2021.
3 Lucid screened potential respondents to ensure that our sample consists only of adult, U.S. residents of Indian ancestry.
4 Alternative models using OLS regression are similar.
5 This difference is significant at the $p < 0.001$ level according to a two-sample t-test.
6 The coefficient in each model is statistically significant to the $p < 0.05$ level.
7 These differences are statistically significant at the $p<.05$ level according to two-sample t-tests.

References

Agarwala, Rina (2015). 'Tapping the Indian Diaspora for Indian Development.' In Alejandro Portes and Patricia Fernandez-Kelly (eds), *The State and the Grassroots: Immigrant Transnational Organizations in Four Continents* (Oxford: Berghahn Books), pp. 84–110.

Agrawal, Ajay, Devesh Kapur, John McHale and Alexander Oettl (2011). 'Brain Drain or Brain Bank? The Impact of Skilled Emigration on Poor-Country Innovation.' *Journal of Urban Economics* 69 (1): 43–55.

Ahmadov, Anar K., and Gwendolyn Sasse (2015). 'Migrants' regional allegiances in homeland elections: evidence on voting by Poles and Ukrainians.' *Journal of Ethnic and Migration Studies* 41 (11): 1769–1793.

Ang, Ien (2003). 'Together-in-Difference: Beyond Diaspora, into Hybridity.' *Asian Studies Review* 27 (2): 141–154.

Anthias, Floya (1998). 'Evaluating "Diaspora": Beyond Ethnicity?' *Sociology* 32 (3): 557–580.

Arora, Maneesh, Sara Sadhwani and Sono Shah (2021). 'Unpacking Identity: Opportunities and Constraints for Cross-Racial Collaboration.' *RSF: The Russell Sage Foundation Journal of the Social Sciences* 7 (2): 93–110.

Arora, Maneesh, and Sara Sadhwani (Forthcoming). Namaste USA: Kamala Harris and Indian American Descriptive Representation. Working Paper.

Azeez, Abdul, and Mustiary Begum (2009). 'Gulf Migration, Remittances and Economic Impact.' *Journal of Social Sciences* 20 (1): 55–60.

Badrinathan, Sumitra, Devesh Kapur and Milan Vaishnav (2020). *How Will Indian Americans Vote? Results From the 2020 Indian American Attitudes Survey* (Carnegie Endowment for International Peace).

Baser, Bahar (2015). *Diasporas and Homeland Conflicts: A Comparative Perspective* (Abingdon: Routledge).

Beltrán, Cristina (2010). *The Trouble with Unity: Latino Politics and the Creation of Identity* (Oxford: Oxford University Press).

Benton, Gregor, and Edmund Terence Gomez (2014). 'Belonging to the Nation: Generational Change, Identity and the Chinese Diaspora.' *Ethnic and Racial Studies* 37 (7): 1157–1171.

Bermeo, Sarah Blodgett, and David Leblang (2015). 'Migration and Foreign Aid.' *International Organization* 69 (3): 627–657.

Bhagat, R. B., Kunal Keshri and Imtiyaz Ali (2013). 'Emigration and Flow of Remittances in India.' *Migration and Development* 2 (1): 93–105.

Bhatia, Sunil (2007). *American Karma: Race, Culture, and Identity in the Indian Diaspora* (New York: NYU Press).

Bhatt, Chetan (2000). 'Dharmo Rakshati Rakshitah: Hindutva Movements in the UK.' *Ethnic and Racial Studies* 23 (3): 559–593.

Bhatt, Chetan, and Parita Mukta (2000). 'Hindutva in the West: Mapping the Antinomies of Diaspora Nationalism.' *Ethnic and Racial Studies* 23 (3): 407–441. http s://doi.org/10.1080/014198700328935.

Biswas, Bidisha (2010). 'Negotiating the Nation: Diaspora Contestations in the USA about Hindu Nationalism in India.' *Nations and Nationalism* 16 (4): 696–714.

Brand, Laurie A. (2014). 'Arab Uprisings and the Changing Frontiers of Transnational Citizenship: Voting from Abroad in Political Transitions.' *Political Geography* 41 (July): 54–63.

Bruneau, Michel (2010). 'Diasporas, Transnational Spaces and Communities.' In Rainer Bauböck and Thomas Faist (eds), *Diaspora and Transnationalism: Concepts, Theories and Methods* (Amsterdam: Amsterdam University Press).

Castro, Lorena, Adrian Felix and Ricardo Ramirez (2015). 'The Limits of Latinidad? Immigration Attitudes Across Latino National Origin Groups.' In Kyle L. Kreider and Thomas J. Baldino (eds), *Minority Voting in the United States* (Santa Barbara, CA: Praeger Publishers).

Coppock, Alexander, and Oliver A. McClellan (2019). 'Validating the Demographic, Political, Psychological, and Experimental Results Obtained from a New Source of Online Survey Respondents.' *Research & Politics* 6 (1): 1–14.

Demmers, Jolle (2007). 'New Wars and Diasporas: Suggestions for Research and Policy.' *Peace, Conflict and Development* 11: 1–26.

Fair, C. Christine (2005). 'Diaspora Involvement in Insurgencies: Insights from the Khalistan and Tamil Eelam Movements.' *Nationalism and Ethnic Politics* 11 (1): 125–156.

Giuliano, Paola, and Marco Tabellini (2020). *The Seeds of Ideology: Historical Immigration and Political Preferences in the United States* (National Bureau of Economic Research).

Haney, Patrick J., and Walt Vanderbush (1999). 'The Role of Ethnic Interest Groups in US Foreign Policy: The Case of the Cuban American National Foundation.' *International Studies Quarterly* 43 (2): 341–361.

Hathaway, Robert M. (2001). 'Unfinished Passage: India, Indian Americans, and the U.S. Congress.' *The Washington Quarterly* 24 (2): 21–34.

IANS (2019). 'Caste Dynamics May Change Poll Equation in AP.' Available at www. business-standard.com/article/news-ians/caste-dynamics-may-change-poll-equation-in-ap-ians-exclusive-119041000243_1.html (accessed 11 June 2021).

Jaffrelot, Christophe, and Ingrid Therwath (2007). 'The Sangh Parivar and the Hindu Diaspora in the West: What Kind of 'Long-Distance Nationalism'?' *International Political Sociology* 1 (3): 278–295.

Just, Aida (2019). 'Political Regimes and Immigrant Party Preferences.' *Comparative Political Studies* 52 (5): 651–686.

Kapur, Devesh (2001).' Diasporas and Technology Transfer.' *Journal of Human Development* 2(2): 265–286.

Kapur, Devesh (2004). 'Ideas and Economic Reforms in India: The Role of International Migration and the Indian Diaspora.' *India Review* 3 (4): 364–384.

Kapur, Devesh (2010). *Diaspora, Development, and Democracy: The Domestic Impact of International Migration from India*. (Princeton, NJ: Princeton University Press).

Kirk, Jason A. (2008). 'Indian-Americans and the US–India Nuclear Agreement: Consolidation of an Ethnic Lobby?' *Foreign Policy Analysis* 4 (3): 275–300.

Kurien, Prema (2004). 'Opposing Constructions and Agendas: The Politics of Hindu and Muslim Indian-American Organizations.' In Rey Koslowski (ed.), *International Migration and Globalization of Domestic Politics* (Abingdon: Routledge), pp. 162–186.

Kurien, Prema (2007). *A Place at the Multicultural Table: The Development of an American Hinduism* (New Brunswick, NJ: Rutgers University Press).

Leidig, Eviane Cheng (2019). 'Immigrant, Nationalist and Proud: A Twitter Analysis of Indian Diaspora Supporters for Brexit and Trump.' *Media and Communication* 7 (1): 77–89.

Levitt, Peggy (2004). 'Redefining the Boundaries of Belonging: The Institutional Character of Transnational Religious Life.' *Sociology of Religion* 65 (1): 1–18.

Lisi, Marco (2015). 'Partisanship and Age Effects in Recent Democracies: Southern Europe from a Comparative Perspective.' *Comparative European Politics* 13 (4): 493–513.

Martínez, Daniel E., and Kelsey E. Gonzalez (2021). '"Latino" or "Hispanic"? The Sociodemographic Correlates of Panethnic Label Preferences among US Latinos/ Hispanics.' *Sociological Perspectives* 64 (3): 365–386.

McAuliffe, Cameron (2008). 'Transnationalism Within: Internal Diversity in the Iranian Diaspora.' *Australian Geographer* 39 (1): 63–80.

McDonnell, Duncan, and Luis Cabrera (2019). 'The Right-Wing Populism of India's Bharatiya Janata Party (and Why Comparativists Should Care).' *Democratization* 26 (3): 484–501.

MEA (2019). 'Overseas Citizenship of India Scheme.' Available at www.mea.gov.in/ overseas-citizenship-of-india-scheme.htm (accessed 8 June 2021).

Menjívar, Cecilia (1999). 'Religious Institutions and Transnationalism: A Case Study of Catholic and Evangelical Salvadoran Immigrants.' *International Journal of Politics, Culture, and Society* 12 (4): 589–612.

Miller, Manjari Chatterjee (2013). *Wronged by Empire* (Stanford, CA: Stanford University Press).

Mistry, Dinshaw (2013). 'The India Lobby and the Nuclear Agreement with India.' *Political Science Quarterly* 128 (4): 717–746.

Moghissi, Haideh, Saeed Rahnema and Mark J. Goodman (2009). *Diaspora by Design: Muslims in Canada and Beyond* (Toronto: University of Toronto Press).

Naujoks, Daniel (2013). *Migration, Citizenship and Development: Diasporic Membership Policies and Overseas Indians in the United States* (Oxford: Oxford University Press).

Naujoks, Daniel (2017). 'The Transnational Political Effects of Diasporic Citizenship in Countries of Destination: Overseas Citizenship of India and Political Participation in the United States.' In David Carment and Ariane Sadjed (eds), *Diaspora as Cultures of Cooperation: Global and Local Perspectives* (Cham: Springer), pp. 199–221.

Paarlberg, Michael Ahn (2017). 'Transnational Militancy: Diaspora Influence over Electoral Activity in Latin America.' *Comparative Politics* 49 (4): 541–562.

Paarlberg, Michael Ahn (2019). 'Competing for the Diaspora's Influence at Home: Party Structure and Transnational Campaign Activity in El Salvador.' *Journal of Ethnic and Migration Studies* 45 (4): 539–560.

Palshikar, Suhas (2015). 'The BJP and Hindu Nationalism: Centrist Politics and Majoritarian Impulses.' *South Asia: Journal of South Asian Studies* 38 (4): 719–735.

Panossian, Razmik (1998). 'The Armenians: Conflicting Identities and the Politics of Division.' In Charles King and Neil J. Melvin (eds), *Nations Abroad* (Abingdon: Routledge), pp. 79–102.

Paul, David M., and Rachel Anderson Paul (2009). *Ethnic Lobbies and US Foreign Policy* (Boulder, CO: Lynne Rienner Publishers).

Pertierra, Andrés (2020). 'Are Cuban American Voters Really a "Special" Case?' Available at www.thenation.com/article/politics/gop-cuban-american-voters/ (accessed 1 June 2021).

Prakash, B.A. (1998). 'Gulf Migration and Its Economic Impact: The Kerala Experience.' *Economic and Political Weekly* 33 (50): 3209–3213.

Prasad, Shubha Kamala, and Filip Savatic (2021). 'Diasporic Foreign Policy Interest Groups in the US: Democracy, Conflict, and Political Entrepreneurship.' *Perspectives on Politics* online ahead of print. doi:10.1017/S1537592721000979.

Rajagopal, Arvind (2000). 'Hindu Nationalism in the US: Changing Configurations of Political Practice.' *Ethnic and Racial Studies* 23 (3): 467–496.

Ramakrishnan, Karthik, Sono Shah and Sunny Shao (2019). 'Record Gains in AAPI Voting Likely to Continue Through 2020.' Available at http://aapidata.com/blog/voting-gains/ (accessed 14 December 2021).

Rani, Rikha Sharma (2021). 'How Indian Americans Got the President's Ear.' Available at www.politico.com/news/magazine/2021/05/04/indian-americans-biden-485382 (accessed 1 June 2021).

Ray, Manashi (2013). 'The Global Circulation of Skill and Capital – Pathways of Return Migration of Indian Entrepreneurs from the United States to India.' In T. T. Yong and M. M. Rahman (eds), *Diaspora Engagement and Development in South Asia* (London: Palgrave Macmillan), pp.75–102.

Raychaudhuri, Tanika (2020). 'Socializing Democrats: Examining Asian American Vote Choice with Evidence from a National Survey.' *Electoral Studies*, 63: 102114.

Rao, Meghna (2020). 'When Parents Love Modi.' Available at www.thejuggernaut.com/when-parents-love-modi (accessed 8 June 2021).

Ruparelia, Sanjay (2015). *Divided We Govern: Coalition Politics in Modern India* (Oxford: Oxford University Press).

Sabrang (2002). 'The Foreign Exchange of Hate: IDRF and the American Funding of Hindutva.' Available at www.sacw.net/2002/FEHi/FEH/ (accessed 8 June 2021).

Sahay, Anjali (2009). *Indian Diaspora in the United States: Brain Drain or Gain?* (Lexington Books).

Shain, Yossi (1994). 'Ethnic Diasporas and US Foreign Policy.' *Political Science Quarterly* 109 (5): 811–841.

Singh, Milan, and Anita Singh (2014). 'Diaspora, Political Action, and Identity: A Case Study of Canada's Indian Diaspora.' *Diaspora: A Journal of Transnational Studies* 17 (2): 149–171.

Swan, Jonathan (2016). 'Hindu-American Emerges as Trump Mega-donor.' Available at https://thehill.com/homenews/campaign/288377-hindu-american-emerges-as-trump-mega-donor (accessed 9 May 2021).

Tausanovitch, Chris, Lynn Vavreck, Tyler Reny, Alex Rossell Hayes and Aaron Rudkin (2019). 'Democracy Fund + UCLA Nationscape Methodology and Representativeness Assessment.' Available at www.voterstudygroup.org/uploads/reports/Data/Nationscape-Methodology-RepresentativenessAssessment.pdf.

Therwath, Ingrid (2007). 'Working for India or against Islam? Islamophobia in Indian American Lobbies.' *South Asia Multidisciplinary Academic Journal*, 1 (October). Available at wwwhttps://doi.org/10.4000/samaj.262.

Tilley, James (2002). 'Political Generations and Partisanship in the UK, 1964–1997.' *Journal of the Royal Statistical Society: Series A (Statistics in Society)* 165 (1): 121–135.

Varadarajan, Latha (2010). *The Domestic Abroad: Diasporas in International Relations* (Oxford: Oxford University Press).

Wellman, Elizabeth Iams (2021). 'Emigrant Inclusion in Home Country Elections: Theory and Evidence from Sub-Saharan Africa.' *American Political Science Review* 115 (1): 82–96.

13 India's Response to Covid-19

A Soft Power Perspective

Aleksandra Jaskólska

The main aim of the chapter is to analyse India's respond to the Covid-19 pandemic as a tool to leverage its image and reputation as a trusted and credible international partner, and to get greater regional and global influence. To explain and understand the dynamics of this process it is important to analyse:

- how India has dealt with the Covid-19 pandemic internally;
- how India is using health diplomacy in South Asia and beyond; and
- how regional and international organizations/forums are used by India to prove its capacity to be a responsible actor in global politics.

The theoretical approach used to analyse India's response to the Covid-19 pandemic is that of soft power. According to Joseph S. Nye (1990, 2002), soft power grows out of a state's culture, domestic values and foreign policies. Nye extended his definition into 'the ability to affect others through the cooperative means of framing the agenda, persuading, and eliciting positive attraction in order to obtain preferred outcomes' (Nye, 2011: 20–21). Soft power can be also defined as 'anything outside of the military and security realm, including not only popular culture and public diplomacy, but also more coercive economic and diplomatic levers, like aid and investment and participation in multilateral organizations' (Kurlantzick, 2007: 6). It is also important to mention that according to Nye, it is a mistake to rely on hard power or soft power alone (Nye, 2002). The best strategy is when two are effectively combined – soft power only becomes credible when there is hard power behind it.

The chapter's primary analytical emphasis is upon the role of India's national identity on its respond to the Covid-19 pandemic. For this reason, it is crucial to analyse the impact of India's history, values, identity on the framing of foreign policy and to designate the fluid elements of continuity and change within India. We can also use soft power to analyse the domestic political actors guiding the formation and delivery during the Covid-19 pandemic in India and the impact that this had upon its foreign policy. Components of a state's soft power can be very diverse. In case of India, these include Bollywood, yoga, meditation, cuisine, Ayurveda, political

DOI: 10.4324/9781003305132-17

pluralism, religious diversity, democratic values and health diplomacy. The efficient use of health diplomacy by India, especially during the Covid-19 pandemic, also relies upon overcoming some of domestic challenges which will be analysed later in the chapter.

Furthermore, it is important to notice that since assuming office in 2014, Prime Minister Narendra Modi, who represents the Bharatiya Janata Party (BJP), has slightly reimagined the tools of India's diplomatic engagement by using, to a larger extent than his predecessors, aspects relating to cultural and spiritual heritage in order to achieve the goals of India's foreign policy (Mazumdar, 2018; Pradhan & Mohapatra, 2020; Tandon, 2016). Narendra Modi's vision of an expanded role for India by using Covid-19 pandemic is no different in that it also seeks to enhance India's global standing and great power ambitions.

India's Internal Anti-Covid-19 Policy

India is a parliamentary republic with a federal system, with health being a state subject. But pandemics also come under the concurrent list in the division of powers on which legislation can be made by the central government but also by state governments, with the proviso that the central rules prevail in the event of a conflict between the two. As an immediate response to the pandemic, central government decided to invoke the 'Colonial Epidemic Diseases Act' of 1897 and the 'Disaster Management Act' of 2005, which enabled it to impose its will on the whole country (Purushothaman & Moolakkattu, 2021). Although state governments had to accept the decision of the central government, there was hardly any cooperation between them. The Indian Council of Medical Research, a central institute, also provided the cues and health advice to be followed by all the states.

The World Health Organization (WHO) declared a Public Health Emergency of International Concern on 30 January 2020. India then had its first officially confirmed coronavirus case in late January 2020, and the infection rate began rising rapidly at the end of March 2020 and in 2020 its reached peak with nearly 100 thousand new daily cases in September.

WHO then declared the Covid-19 outbreak to be a pandemic on 11 March 2020. Soon after this, India was witnessing a strict national lockdown announced in five phases, from 23 March till 31 May 2020. The Indian government decided to announce the first phase with official number standing at only 108 new cases and 2 deaths daily India organized Vande Bharat Mission, to bring back home Indian from all around a world. More than 250 thousand Indians from 53 countries were brought back to India, and India evacuated foreign nationals from ground zero in Wuhan, China, as well as from Bangladesh, Myanmar and Maldives. The Indian Government decided to use C-17 Hercules transport aircraft and were a sign to the international community that India has to take on the responsibility of regional leadership (Talukdar, 2020).

The Indian government decided to impose such a long and strict lockdown for a few key reasons. Firstly because of its high population density, with the Indian population being about 1.3 billion people within a territorial area of 3,28 million km^2, what results in more than 450 people per km^2 (compared to the European Union, which has 446 million people and over 4 million km^2 of land resulting in a population density of 177 people per km^2). In cities like New Delhi, the population density reaches more than 7,400 people and in Mumbai it can reach more than 30,000 people (Census, 2020). The Government of India underlined that without the lockdown it would be impossible to maintain social distancing in public spaces. However, images of empty landmarks in India's cities did not show the real situation in the country, and strict lockdown rules were mostly not implemented in slums, rural areas and the least developed parts of India.

The second reason for the government's policy was unequal the development of Indian states, and GDP per capita, levels of education and access to medical care, medication, clean water and reliable information differ widely from state to state. Indian policy makers from the very beginning were also implementing regulations to stop spread of fake news. In March 2020, National Disaster Management Authority informed the population that spreading fake news will be punished by fine or jail (up to 6 months). Government also decided to use digital tool for education and information. Indian Scientists' Response to Covid-19, a voluntary group comprising scientists from eminent Indian institutes to support evidence-based action, provides scientific data and resources to local administrations and groups fighting on the ground (Dore, 2020). India also has only 0.7 doctors and 0.55 hospital beds per 1,000 people (compared to the EU, which has 3.7 doctors and 5 hospital beds per 1,000 people). These shortcomings mean that in less developed parts of India it is almost impossible to get access to medical care. As such, the Indian government was aware that deteriorating health care system would not be able to deal with the Covid-19 pandemic. According to the Global Health Security Index 2019, out of 195 countries, India is ranked 57th (against a global average score of 46.5) which is the highest among South Asian countries (Global Health Index, 2019) and in 2021 India was reduced to 66th (Global Health Index, 2019). The third reason was that the Indian government wanted to give an example to neighbouring states and to show the international community that India is capable of implementing a strict national lockdown. Modi even underlined though the lockdown caused a slowdown of the Indian economy, India was a responsible actor and had to act in this way. On 12 May 2020, Modi announced a US$260 billion financial stimulus package to the India economy, which was badly hit by the lockdown.

At the beginning, the perception of the Indian lockdown among international actors was very positive as India had set an example to be followed but other developing states. But very soon it became clear that the Indian lockdown had also had a negative side, as the overnight imposition of travel restrictions and the closure of factories and businesses had caused a mass exodus of millions of migrant workers out of Indian cities. Most of them were left stranded with no income for survival and no means of transport to go home, and had to walk to their villages even if they were more than two thousand kilometres away. Lockdown also exposed fundamental social and economic inequalities, as it became clear that because of poor social protection millions of poorest Indians were left alone without any support (Surie, 2020). In the aftermath of the lockdown, many Indian states also sealed their borders, which led to cases of smuggling of homebound people trapped in other states. On the Haryana–Uttar Pradesh border, for example, migrants even attempted to cross the Yamuna River using rubber tubes, as state borders became securitized (Purushothaman & Moolakkattu, 2021).

The unlocking process started from 1 June 2020 and was divided into five phases. Unlock 1.0: 1 June 2020–30 June 2020, Unlock 2.0: 1 July 2020–31 July 2020, Unlock 3.0: 1 August 2020–31 August 2020, Unlock 4.0: 1 September 2020–30 September 2020, Unlock 5.0: 1 October 2020–31 October 2020. When the fifth phase of the lockdown was over, India had 8,380 new cases and 193 deaths daily. But as the government announced a cautious relaxation of lockdown restrictions, India witnessed a spike in case and deaths numbers, with the highest numbers happening in the middle of September 2020 and then starting to decrease. As such, Prime Minister Modi in his speeches stated that Covid-19 is still a serious threat and it should be not ignored (India Today, 2020). It is also worth underlining that one of reasons why the national lockdown was ended was that it had a negative impact on the economy. In this regard, during first quarter of fiscal year 2020/2021, the Indian economy shrunk for 23.9% (Kuszewska, 2020). It is furthermore important to underline that the state governments were not consulted concerning the decision to implement lockdown, and thus the burden of complying with the lockdown regulations or the attendant responsibilities had to be borne solely by them.

India started its mass vaccination program in January 2021. By February 2021, India recorded an average of 11,000 new cases and 90 deaths daily. It was the lowest score since the beginning of the first wave. On 7 March 2021, Harsh Vardhan, India's Health Minister, declared that India was in the 'endgame' of the pandemic (Press Information Bureau, 2021) but this victory was announced too early as by the beginning of April 2021 India was recording more than 90,000 new cases per day. This number was higher than during the first wave of Covid-19. Three weeks later, the number of infections had reached 350,000 per day and continued to rise to more than 400,000 per day in March 2021 and more than 4000 deaths daily, which India's health sector was not prepared for (Rokicka, 2021). As a result, a chaotic situation existed for two weeks in late April and early May 2021 as hospitals in New Delhi and parts of North India were flooded with Covid-19 patients, with many of them dying without any medical attention and support. There was also an acute shortage of oxygen supply and India's crematoriums were overwhelmed (Safi, 2021). It is also important to notice that both during the first and second waves, Maharashtra and the southern states of Kerala, Karnataka, Tamil Nadu, and Andhra Pradesh had the highest number of cases. The northern states had fewer caseloads, except in Delhi. The north-eastern states were also less severely affected and had considerably lower fatality rates (Purushothaman & Moolakkattu, 2021).

The main reason for such a high number of infections was that the central government decided to lift most of the restrictions implemented during the lockdown of 2020. Central government and state governments also did not adopt a common policy against the second wave of Covid-19. Indeed, the Indian Prime Minister announced on 20 April 2021 that there would not be another national lockdown and left the decision to the state governments (Iwanek, 2021), which meant that life went back to normal as exemplified by the holding of weddings and family celebrations, and people returning to their workplaces (Rokicka, 2021).

Prominent among these was the Kumbha Mela religious festival that is celebrated four times over the course of 12 years, rotating between four pilgrimage places on four sacred rivers – at Haridwar on the Ganges River, at Ujjain on the Shipra, at Nashik on the Godavari, and at Prayag (modern Prayagraj) at the confluence of the Ganges, the Jamuna, and the mythical Sarasvati. The Kumbh Mela was organized in Haridwar at the beginning of April 2021 ahead of schedule after astrologers pointed out that 2021 would be more auspicious than the original timing in 2022. As a result, millions of pilgrims came to Haridwar (Jaffrelot, 2021), and later Narendra Modi called on the organizers of the festival to end it on 17 April, as the number of Covid-19 cases was by then growing rapidly. Moreover, political parties also did not stop organizing election rallies in the states where elections were taking place, which included West Bengal (with a population of around 100 million people), Tamil Nadu (72 million), Kerala (34 million) and Assam (30 million). Only at the end of April 2021 was the decision made to not organize more rallies, yet still the government decides to go ahead with the various state elections.

India's Health Diplomacy in the Time of the Pandemic

It was not obvious that India would be so active in regional and global forums concerning dealing with the Covid-19 pandemic. However, India's government decided to promote its response to Covid-19 and to do so through the lens of Indian culture and values, such as the principle of development assistance known as *vasudhaiva kutumbakam* (the world is one family) taken from the Maha Upanishad. This concept promotes an understanding that the whole of humanity is one family and puts stress on global responsibility. It has been used by previous Indian Prime Ministers, such as Rajiv Gandhi who challenged the concept of first, second and third worlds, and instead proposed the idea of 'One World'. In turn, Atal Bihari Vajpayee used *vasudhaiva kutumbakam* in this speech at a meeting on the national human rights institutions of the Asia Pacific Forum, stating that 'India's understanding and advocacy of human rights are as universal as they are ancient' (quoted in Sidhu, 2017). Manmohan Singh also referred to it at G8 summit in 2007 to present India's approach to climate change, and Modi used it even before the pandemic to support India's idea of reforming the Security Council of the United Nations.

Another frequently used phrase as India's response to Covid-19 pandemic, relates to a 'culture of service' known as *seva paramo dharma* (service is the greatest virtue) (Barbato, 2020). It refers to sacrificing one's values for the sake of others and proponents claim that it should be the mantra of civil services. Narendra Modi, during the United Nations General Assembly in 2021, underlined that all Indians live according to *seva paramo dharma* and because of it, and despite limited resources, India is able to be engaged in vaccination development and manufacturing. As such, 'corona warriors' have to live via the mantra of *seva parmo sharma* and serve the people in India and outside India (India Today, 2021b). *Vasudhaiva kutumbakam* and *seva parmo sharma* were implemented into India's global response to the pandemic, and became important aspects of India's foreign policy in this regard, as explained in next sections of the chapter.

Concepts of global health diplomacy, including vaccine diplomacy, have also become an important part of India's soft power. India is the largest provider of generic drugs globally. In terms of volume of pharmaceutical production, it is ranked third highest globally, supplying drugs to more than 200 countries. Overall, India accounts for 20% of the world's drug production while meeting 62% of the global demand for coronavirus vaccines (Pattanaik, 2021). For this reason, India is often called the 'pharmacy of the world'. This concept was also promoted by Indian government, especially during the pandemic as part of India's soft power. In this context, in April 2020, Modi decided to revoke the partial ban on exporting some of the generic medicines produced in India, including hydroxychloroquine (an anti-malaria drug), which once thought to help to lower death rate of Covid-19. The decision was made not only upon requests made by the US and Brazil but also as the Indian government wanted to underline its desire to be seen to the support international community.

With the pandemic bringing Modi's focus back to India's 'Neighbourhood First' policy designed to strengthen India's economic and security relations particularly with the other states surrounding it, it also embraced the spirit of being a 'first responder to a pandemic' (Pattanaik, 2021). As such, India sent Covid-19 medical assistance mostly to South Asia, with Bangladesh being the single largest beneficiary. India also sent Rapid Response Forces Teams, which functions under the Ministry of Defence, to the Maldives and Kuwait, Mauritius, Comoros. Notably, information about these Indian Army medical teams provoked sharp responses from Bangladesh, Sri Lanka, and Afghanistan who argued that Indian troops were not required, and showed that there are limits of India's military presence in the region even during the pandemic. For this reason, India had to change its strategy and decided to send medical teams of civilians and medical supplies to states in need. Furthermore, Indian medical experts were providing online health training, as well as sharing and exchanging valuable information to contain the virus. India was also promoting, especially among the world's least developed and developing countries, low-cost indigenous testing kits, using bandanas as protection masks, sidewalk chalks to maintain social-distancing, hand stamps to mark the quarantine period of individuals and turning railways trains into isolation wards (Pattanaik, 2021).

Aiding these efforts, India launched 'Vaccine Maitri' or 'Vaccine Friendship' in January 2021. Already in November 2020, 18 companies from South Africa, China, Bangladesh and 7 companies from India agreed to accelerate the production of vaccines for the lower- and middle-income countries under the umbrella of the non-profit Medicines Patent Pool. It was initially designed to repair India's strained relations with its South Asian neighbours. In January 2021 the first consignment of 150,000 doses reached Bhutan. Similarly in the first phase, Bangladesh received 2 million doses; Nepal 1 million doses; 100,000 doses to the Maldives; 1.5 million doses to Myanmar and 500,000 doses to Sri Lanka. These vaccines were supplied as part of grant-in-aid, as the External Affairs Minister of India tweeted, 'putting neighbours first, putting people first!' (Pattanaik 2021). India also leveraged its pharmaceutical power and quickly expanded 'Vaccine Maitri' to different parts of the world (Pattanaik, 2021), and Foreign Minister S. Jaishankar tweeted on 19 January 2021 that 'India fulfils commitment to give vaccines to humanity. The Pharmacy of the World will deliver to overcome the Covid challenge. #VaccineMaitri' (Jaishankar, 2021). Prime Minister Modi also tweeted the same day: 'India is deeply honored to be a long-trusted partner in meeting the healthcare needs of the global community. Supplies of Covid vaccines to several countries will commence tomorrow, and more will follow in the days ahead. #VaccineMaitri' (Modi, 2021). Foreign Minister S. Jaishankar further declared that 'Vaccine Maitri' has 'raised India's standing and generated great international goodwill' (quoted in Singh, 2021). In response, Nepal's Premier, Mr. Oli, thanked Prime Minister Modi and the Indian people for the 'generous' supply of the vaccine at a 'critical time' (Bhattacherjee, 2021), and Myanmar's State Counsellor Aung San Suu Kyi, in her New Year address, furthermore mentioned that there was wide appreciation in her country for India's willingness to provide Covid-19 vaccines (Sibal, 2021).

Up until April 2021, India exported 65 million AstraZeneca vaccines to over 80 states in Asia, Africa and South America, some of which was carried out under the WHO programme called COVAX (Mantesso, 2021). In fact, during the current Covid-19 pandemic, India became the first country to give its home-grown vaccine to the WHO for distribution in poorer parts of the world, free of cost. India's medical diplomacy thus caught the world's attention and won praise from several quarters including the WHO, the United

Nations and India's closest strategic partners (Hazarika 2020). WHO Director-General Ghebreyesus appreciated India's vaccine efforts against COVID-19 and praised Prime Minister Modi for 'supporting vaccine equity' (Bharti & Bharti 2021). On 7 March 2021, Harsh Vardhan, Minister of Health and Family Welfare, tweeted that 'we are in the end game of the Covid-19 pandemic in India, and to succeed at this stage, we need to follow 3 steps: Keep politics out of the Covid-19 vaccination drive, trust the science behind Covid-19 vaccines, and ensure our near and dear ones get vaccinated on time' (quoted in Upadhyay, 2021). At the beginning of March 2021, he had also said that 'at a time of global crisis, under the leadership of Modi Ji, India has emerged as an example to the world in international cooperation' (quoted in India Today, 2021a).

But the challenge to make these declarations come true was not only a lack of sufficient number of vaccines but also lack of infrastructure to vaccine India's own citizens with around 900 million people being eligible for vaccination. Bharat Biotech and Serum Institute of India (SII) are in control of production of vaccines in India. SII had agreements with AstraZeneca to produce a billion doses, half to be used in India and half to be exported to 68 countries at US$3 per dose, and to produce a billion doses of the Novavax vaccine to supply to 92 countries. This quantity was later doubled. When SII agreements were signed its production capacity was only for 60–70 million doses per month. Its capacity is expected to increase to 100 million doses a month only by July 2021. India is using Covishield, the Indian version of the AstraZeneca vaccine, manufactured by Serum Institute, and Bharat Biotech's Covaxin, developed along with the Indian Council of Medical Research. In mid-April 2021, during the second wave of the pandemic in India, Bharat Biotech and Serum Institute of India announced that they would be not able to produce as many vaccines as was planned. SII admitted that from now onwards it would only sell the vaccine to India (Iwanek, 2021). As such, Bharat Biotech and Serum Institute of India ask government for financial support to develop extra production lines (Rokicka, 2021), which stopped exports, eliciting a strong response from international institutions.

The WHO called the delay in supplies from India to the African continent 'quite devastating for everybody' (Sanghi 2021). AstraZeneca sent a legal notice to Serum Institute over supply delays to countries against orders placed by the Covax alliance (Sanghi, 2021). At the same time, Moderna Therapeutics and Pfizer/BioNTech declared that they would manufacture more than 3 billion doses till end of 2021, with both companies are also working on new vaccines (Sanghi 2021). In these ways, although India had earned its reputation as the world's pharmacy by reliably supplying affordable medicines in large quantities for over two decades, because of the consequences of second wave domestically, India lost some of this reputation internationally (Sanghi, 2021). SII would resume exports of coronavirus vaccines to the UN-backed COVAX distribution programme in November 2021 (Aljazeera, 2021).

India's Response to Covid-19 in Regional and International Organizations

Besides using health diplomacy in South Asia and beyond, the Indian government was also using regional and international organizations and forums such as the South Asian Association for Regional Cooperation (SAARC), the Non-Alignment Movement (NAM), the G-20, the BRICS (Brazil-Russia-India-China-South Africa grouping), the India-EU Summit, the UN General Assembly, the Quad (the strategic grouping between India, the US, Japan and Australia) and the G-7 to leverage its image and reputation as a trusted, neutral and credible development partner during the time of Covid-19 pandemic.

In this way, India sensed another opportunity in the pandemic to integrate South Asia and reaffirm its status as a leader capable and willing to rise to the grim global and regional situation. Modi announced his invitation for the virtual summit on his Twitter account, stating that 'I would like to propose that the leadership of SAARC nations chalk out a strong strategy to fight Coronavirus. We could discuss, via video conferencing, ways to keep our citizens healthy. Together, we can set an example to the world, and contribute to a healthier planet' (Modi, 2020). All the leaders of the member states supported the idea and announced their participation, except for the Prime Minister of Pakistan, Imran Khan, who delegated his Special Assistant on Health, Zafar Mirza, to attend. A video conference was held on 15 March 2020, which was called 'SAARC Leaders on Combating Covid-19. Setting an Example for the world'.

During the summit Modi proposed to create a SAARC Covid-19 emergency fund. Each member country could pledged an amount of money to the fund, and India offered US\$ 10 million, which was more than half of the total contribution (SAARC, 2020). India also initiated the 'SAARC Covid-19 Information Exchange Platform (COINEX)' to serve as a multipurpose vehicle to further discuss and conduct activities such as online training for emergency response personnel, knowledge partnerships, the sharing of expertise in disease surveillance, including the corresponding software, and joint research for new diagnostic and therapeutic interventions for epidemic diseases (Pattanaik, 2021). To further enhance cooperation through development projects, India launched an 'e-Indian Technical and Economic Cooperation Programme' for all SAARC, as well as non-SAARC, states in March 2020.

SAARC was not the only forum where India wanted to demonstrate its care for fighting the Covid-19 pandemic. During the virtual summit of the G20 on 26 March 2020, Modi stated that there was a need for a more effective global response to the pandemic and called for a new concept of globalization based on principles of fairness, equality and humanity. As such, he called for the multilateral forum to 'focus on promoting the shared interests of humanity' (Nair, 2020), called upon other world leaders to take up India's helps to combat the pandemic and augment international cooperation. During the G20 Summit in Rome in 30–31 October 2021, while addressing the first session on the 'Global Economy and Global Health', Modi spoke about the need for a collaborative approach to fight the Covid-19 pandemic via the scientific communities and governments of multiple states. He also informed the G20 leaders about India's medical diplomacy that had taken place during the Covid-19 pandemic that had covered at least 150 states, and presented a vision of 'One Earth, One Health', which would cover future pandemics and require comprehensive global solutions.

The next forum which was used by India was the BRICS Ministers of Foreign Affairs / International Relations video conference, which was organized on 28 April 2020. India's Minister of External Affairs S. Jaishankar underlined that India had declared a public health emergency much before the outbreak of the pandemic, and he also mentioned that India had offered assistance to more than 120 states in the world. What is more, he pointed out that the BRICS forum needed to be used as platform which would offer solutions and support for the global community (Ministry of External Affairs, 2020). On 9 September 2021 India hosted the online BRICS meeting. The theme of the summit was 'BRICS@15: Intra-BRICS Cooperation for Continuity, Consolidation and Consensus'. At this event, Modi mentioned the leading role that BRICS states could play in the post-Covid global recovery, as the Prime Minister called for enhanced BRICS cooperation under the motto of 'Build-Back Resiliently, Innovatively, Credibly and Sustainably'.

Another platform that was used by Modi to project India's diplomatic outreach and humanitarian response was the NAM. It is important to mention that Prime Minister of India had refused to attend these summits in 2016 and 2019, but he joined an online summit titled 'United Against Covid-19' which was held on 4 May 2020. Here, Modi highlighted how India had promoted coordination in the immediate neighbourhood, had organized online training to share India's medical expertise with its smaller neighbours and had ensured that they received medical supplies. The next important opportunity for India to present itself as responsible partner was at the India-EU virtual summit which was organized on 15 July 2020. The last such summit was held in 2017 and there had been a few unsuccessful attempts to organize the next summit. At the 2020 summit, representatives from the EU and Modi discussed global cooperation and solidarity in order to protect lives and to develop a vaccine. There was also a strong emphasis on how to mitigate the socio-economic consequences of the pandemic and to strengthen preparedness and response capacities. During their next online meeting on 8 May 2021 in Porto (Portugal), a different narrative emerged from the Indian side. The EU in the beginning of May 2021 had sent to India oxygen, medical equipment and drugs worth US$120 million. India was also counting on the EU supporting a temporary patent waiver for Covid-19 vaccines, which had been proposed by India and South Africa at the WTO. The US decided to support this idea but the EU was not willing to do the same. The summit was also dominated by the decision of both parties to re-start negotiations on a Free Trade Agreement, which had been initiated in 2007 and frozen in 2013 (Sachdeva, 2021). In a tweet, Prime Minister Modi wrote that 'our collaboration is essential to stopping the Covid-19 pandemic and ensuring a sustainable and inclusive recovery in a more digital and greener world' (quoted in Malhotra, 2021). As such, India's government narrative was that India stands with an international community in respect of established rules, norms and principles of multilateralism (Bharti & Bharti 2021).

The Prime Minister of India also used the United Nations General Assembly (UNGA) of 15–30 September 2020 to reassure the international community that India is a responsible partner, who is eager to help to combat Covid-19. Modi underlined this position by stated that 'as the largest vaccine-producing country of the world, I want to give one more assurance to the global community today, ... India's vaccine production and delivery capacity will be used to help all humanity in fighting this crisis' (quoted in Hindu, 2020). During the next UNGA (14–21 September 2021), Modi also announced that India has developed the world's first DNA vaccine, which can be administered to anyone above the age of 12, and an mRNA vaccine that is in the final stages of development (UN News, 2021). Despite limited resources, India is completely invested in the development and manufacture of vaccines. Modi also mentioned that India is becoming a democratic and reliable partner for global industrial diversification.

During first meeting of heads of the Quadrilateral Security Dialogue (known as the Quad) on 12 March 2021, key challenges concerning the pandemic were further identified concerning the 'economic and health impacts of Covid-19', (Rej, 2021), as well as climate change, and 'shared challenges, including in cyber space, critical technologies, counterterrorism, quality infrastructure investment, and humanitarian-assistance and disaster-relief as well as maritime domains'. (Rej, 2021). The heads of the Quad states also reached financing agreements to support ramping up the production of vaccines in India to be used in Southeast Asian countries. As such, India would be manufacturing up to 1 billion single-dose of the Johnson & Johnson vaccines, with the US and Japan providing financial support and Australia taking care of logistics (Rej, 2021). The high-level Quad summit further agreed to finance, distribute, and manufacture vaccines.

From 11–13 June 2021, the G7 forum also took place. The Prime Minister of Britain, Boris Johnson had invited Modi to the G7 Summit as a Special Invitee. It was only second time that Modi had been invited to join the G7 Summit, following on from 2019 when he was invited by the French President as a 'Goodwill Partner'. Although Modi decided not to travel to the UK because of the Covid-19 situation, he participated virtually on the 12 and 13 of June. Modi was also a lead speaker in the session entitled 'Open Societies and Open Economies', where he underlined India's civilizational commitment to democracy, freedom of thought and liberty. Modi also emphasized that it is a necessity to waive the patent for Covid-19 vaccines as a way for India to ramp up vaccine production. G-7 countries all supported all 'text-based negotiations' on the Trade-Related Aspects of Intellectual Property Rights waiver proposal, although the EU is yet to endorse it (Haidar, 2021).

Conclusion: The Mixed Effects of India's Response to Covid-19

How successful was India's respond to Covid-19 crisis in building up its soft power, so as to present itself as a trusted, neutral and credible partner? During the pandemic, India has seen an opportunity to bolster its credentials as a responsible stakeholder contributing to global governance, primarily riding on the back of the success of its pharmaceutical industry. As mentioned, soft power grows out of a state's culture, domestic values and foreign policies. For India, specific notions of a culture of service (*seva paramo dharma*) and the world as one family (principles of *vasudhaiva kutumbakam*) played an important role in India's response to Covid-19. Further policies adopted by India such as *Vande Bharat Mission* (bringing back home Indians and neighbouring nationalities), sending financial and logistic support to states in need, and revoking the partial ban on exporting generic medicines were also policies widely appreciated by the international community. India's active role in regional and international organizations/forums acted as proof of New Delhi's ability to affect other states through cooperative means, whereby an ability to persuade and elicit positive attraction from others, in order to obtain preferred outcomes, also harnessed the belief that India is a reliable partner and should have a significant role in global politics. These actions played into India's self-image of being a civilizational power, and its aspiration to be a global power that contributes to global governance that has long demanded a greater voice in international affairs.

The Covid-19 pandemic also showed the importance of cooperation in delivering for essential health products and public goods, which also acted as an important pillar in India's regional diplomacy and was another important cog in India's regional diplomacy. Vaccine diplomacy – 'Vaccine Maitri' – was a valued addition to India's health diplomacy, and provided an opportunity for India to strengthen relations with neighbouring countries. As such, New Delhi has been heavily involved in the distribution of vaccines and is the largest supplier to the global vaccine scheme COVAX. Before the second wave of Covid-19 in India, India also sold 35.7 million doses of vaccines to other countries (Iwanek, 2021). These actions initially helped India claim to be the 'pharmacy of the world' and a source of cheap, reliable vaccines, medicines, and medical equipment, thus increasing its soft power during the first wave. India also used virtual meetings of the G-20, the NAM, the BRICS, the India-EU summit, the UNGA, the G-7, and the Quad so as to boost India's international stature. Regionally, New Delhi used the SAARC Summit to emphasize India role as a regional power and to respond to Chinese influence in South Asia. Regardless of India's true intentions in the region, the state's image as a hegemon adversely affected regional security, political relations and economic cooperation. If India could have effectively improved its attractiveness and built more trust in relations with its smaller neighbours, it would have found it much easier to promote its interests and achieve regional stability, although such gains were not always so apparent. For similar reasons,

Furthermore, as India continues to build its soft power to be seen as a regional power with the ability to act globally, there is growing scrutiny of how it handles the pandemic internally. The Covid-19 pandemic has brought the attention of global community to the weaknesses of India's medical care, welfare and social protection systems, and the social and economic inequities that keep millions of people in poverty. India's coronavirus crisis has thus had international implications. The government's vaccine export reductions have also frequently left intended recipients in the lurch, including many developing countries relying on the Covid-19 Vaccines Global Access initiative. In addition, because of the consequences of the second wave of Covid-19, India lost some of its credibility as India failed to secure its own citizens during the time of pandemic. As such, on 9 May 2021, Yamini Aiyar, President of the Delhi-based think tank Centre for Policy Research wrote in the *Hindustan Times* that 'India has transitioned to a failed state'. The UK-based *Economist* magazine held that the 'state has melted away in India'. *India Today* magazine ran a hard-hitting cover for its 17 May edition calling India 'the failed state'. Ruchir Sharma, chief global strategist at the investment firm Morgan Stanley, wrote in the *Financial Times* that the pandemic had illustrated that the state was 'broken', with India looking mediocre on healthcare compared even to countries such as Pakistan or Bangladesh. In the *Indian Express*, economist Ashok Gulati wrote 'the government seemed to have lost control and many declared India a failed state'. Former bureaucrat Harsh Mander delivered the second JB D'Souza Memorial Lecture on 3 June with the pithy title: 'The Collapse of the Republic' (Daniyal, 2021), as health system in most states, particularly in the North were exposed as showing major vulnerabilities and a lack of preparedness.

What is more, the second wave forced India to stop supplying vaccines globally due to domestic opposition, which exposed the glaring gap between India's domestic capabilities and its global ambitions. China was again able to make inroads into India's neighbourhood by supplying vaccines when India had to stop sending vaccines abroad. India health diplomacy has also not yet led to high increases in its economic cooperation with other states in the Asian region and beyond, underscoring how soft power can be more difficult to use than hard power to build or orchestrate meaningful international relationships (Mullen 2021). As such, the pandemic has had a mixed effect on India's image and reputation as a trusted and credible international partner, and the leverage that New Delhi could use to gain greater regional and global influence. In many ways, through India's domestic and international failures, India's soft power may actually have been diminished.

References

Aljazeera (2021), 'India's Serum Institute Resumes Vaccine Exports to COVAX', 26 November. Available at www.aljazeera.com/news/2021/11/26/indias-serum-institu te-resumes-vaccine-exports-to-covax [last accessed 12 January 2022].

Barbato, Melanic (2020), '"Dear Hindu Friends": Official Diwali Greetings as a Medium for Diplomatic Dialogue', *Religion*, 50 (3): 353–371.

Bharti, Simant Shankar and Bharti, Sushant Shankar (2021) 'India's Vaccine Diplomacy: Role in New Order and Challenges', *Torun International Studies*, 1 (14): 93–104.

Bhattacherjee, Kallol (2021) Nepal, Bangladesh Receive Covishield Consignments. Available at www.thehindu.com/news/national/coronavirus-india-hands-over-2-m illion-vaccine-doses-to-bangladesh/article33626332.ece

Nair, Sangeeta (2020) G20 Virtual Summit 2020: The G20 Leaders Pledged to Inject $5 Trillion into the Global Economy to Reduce the Economic Impact of the Coronavirus Pandemic. Available at www.jagranjosh.com/current-affairs/pm-narendra -modi-virtual-g20-summit-coronavirus-pandemic-1585197217-1

Sibal, Sidhant (2021) In New Year speech, Myanmar's Aung San Suu Kyi Announces Contract to Get COVID-19 Vaccine from India. Available at www.wionews.com/ south-asia/in-new-year-speech-myanmars-aung-san-suu-kyi-announces-contract-to-get-covid-19-vaccine-from-india-354644

Census (2020), 'Census'. Available at https://censusindia.gov.in/ [last accessed 11 August 2020].

Daniyal, Shoaib (2021), '"Emerging Superpower" to "Failed State": How Perceptions of India Changed Drastically under Modi', *Scroll.in*, 6 June. Available at https:// scroll.in/article/996356/emerging-superpower-to-failed-state-how-perceptions-of-ind ia-changed-drastically-under-modi?fbclid=IwAR3FDrJ3kT_W009abtUPsgSSJi22o MMuM2iSYNGHIAnP1sP10J7LH_KaPEw [last accessed 13 June 2021].

Dore, Bhavya (2020), 'How 300 Indian Scientists Are Fighting Fake News about COVID-19', *We forum*, 14 April. Available at www.weforum.org/agenda/2020/04/ ndze-scientists-Covid19-false-I-coronavirus/ [last accessed 14 August 2020].

Frazier, Mark (2021), 'How India and China Are Using Covid-19 'Vaccine Diplomacy' to Compete Globally', *Scroll.in*, 15 April. Available at https://scroll.in/a rticle/992020/how-india-and-china-are-using-Covid-19-vaccine-diplomacy-to-comp ete-globally [last accessed 12 May 2021].

Global Health Index (2019), 'India'. Available at www.ghsindex.org/country/india/ [last accessed 10 August 2020].

Global Health Index (2021) 'India'. Available at www.ghsindex.org/country/india/ [last accessed 21 January 2022].

Gosh, Abantika (2020), 'Explained: How Agra, 'Bhilwara and Pathanamthitta Coronavirus Models Differ', *Indian Express*, 19 April. Available at https://indianexp ress.com/article/explained/pathanamthitta-bhilwara-agra-model-on-coronavirus-ind ia-lockdown-Covid-19-hotspots-6359654/ [last accessed 10 August 2020].

Haidar, Suhasini (2021), 'Fight against Authoritarianism, Extremism, says PM Modi at G7 Meet', *The Hindu*, 14 June. Available at www.thehindu.com/news/national/ india-a-natural-ally-of-g7-narendra-modi/article34805604.ece [last accessed 15 June 2021].

Hazarika, Obja Borah (2020), 'India's Drug Diplomacy: Decoding the HCQ Export Decision', 19 April. Available at www.kiips.in/research/indias-drug-diplomacy-deco

ding-the-hcq-export-decision/?utm_source=Kalinga+Institute+of+Indo-Pacific +Studies+%28KIIPS%29&utm_campaign=5d2b9f0e01-KIIPS+Quarterly+e-News letter+Volume+2%2C+No.2&utm_medium=email&utm_term=0_20bf18b38b-5d2 b9f0e01-65200839 [last accessed 14 August 2020].

Hindu (2020), 'PM Modi Delivers Virtual Speech at United Nations General Assembly', 26 September. Available at www.thehindu.com/news/national/live-upda tes-pm-modi-addresses-un-general-assembly/article32703504.ece [last accessed 20 September 2020].

India Today (2020), 'PM Narendra Modi on Coronavirus: Read Prime Minister's Full Speech on Covid-19 Outbreak', 20 March. Available at www.indiatoday.in/india/ story/pm-narendra-modi-on-coronavirus-read-prime-minister-full-speech-on-covid-19-outbreak-1657677-2020-03-20.

India Today (2021a), 'We Are in the Endgame of Covid-19 Pandemic in India: Health Minister Harsh Vardhan', 7 March. Available at www.indiatoday.in/coronavir us-outbreak/story/we-are-in-the-endgame-of-Covid-19-pandemic-in-india-vardhan-1776697-2021-03-07 [last accessed 13 June 2021].

India Today (2021b), 'PM Modi Invites World's Vaccine Makers to "Make in India" during Address at UN General Assembly', 25 September. Available at www.india today.in/india/story/pm-modi-invites-world-vaccine-makers-to-make-in-india-durin g-address-at-un-general-assembly-1857206-2021-09-25 [last accessed 13 March 2022].

Iwanek, Krzysztof (2021), 'Wzrost zachorowań na COVID-19 w Indiach', *Komentarz Ośrodka Badań Azji Centnd Badań nad Bezpieczeństwem Akademii Sztuki Wojennej Komentarz*, 20.

Iwanek, Krzysztof (2021) 'Don't Write Off Indian Vaccine Diplomacy Yet', *The Diplomat*, 24 May. Available at https://thediplomat.coI21/05/dont-write-off-indian-va ccine-diplomacy-yet/ [last accessed 13 June 2021].

Jaffrelot, Christophe (2021), 'India's Second Wave: A Man-Made Disaster?', *Institute Montaigne*, 28 April. Available at www.institutmontaigne.org/en/blog/indias-sec ond-wave-man-made-disaster [last accessed 5 May 2021].

Jaishankar, Subrahmanyam (2021), [Tweet]. Available at https://twitter.com/DrSJaisha nkar/status/1351528890070564864 [last accessed 12 June 2021].

Kurlantzick, Joshua (2007) *Charm Offensive: How China's Soft Power Is Transforming the World* (New Haven: Yale University Press).

Kuszewska, Agnieszka (2020), 'Iolityka Chin i Indii w czasie pandemii', *Infos, Biuro Analiz Sejmowych*, 15 (281).

Malhotra, Jyoti (2021), 'India's Vaccine Diplomacy is Falling Apart. Why PM Modi Can't Convince EU to Waive Patents', *The Print*, 11 May. Available at https://thep rint.in/opinion/global-print/indias-vaccine-diplomacy-is-falling-apart-why-pm-mod i-cant-convince-eu-to-waive-patents/656410/ [last accessed 4 April 2021].

Mantesso, Sean (2021), 'China and India Spruik their COVID-19 Vaccines in a Soft-Power Push across the World', *ABC*, 25 February. Available at www.abc.net.au/ news/2021-02-25/Covid-vaccine-rivalry-china-and-india-world-influence-in-asia/131 80290 [last accessed 12 May 2021].

Mazumdar A. (2018), 'India's Soft Power Diplomacy under the Modi Administration: Buddhism, Diaspora and Yoga', *Asian Affairs*, 49 (3), p. 468–491.

Ministry of External Affairs (2020), 'Video Conference of the BRICS Ministers of Foreign Affairs/International Relations'. Available at https://mea.gov.in/press-relea

ses.htm?dtl/32652/Video_conference_of_the_BRICS_Ministers_of_Foreign_Affairs International_Relations [last accessed 10 August 2020].

Modi, Narendra (2020), [Tweet]. Available at https://twitter.com/narendramodi/status/ 1238371182094639104 [last accessed 12 March 2022].

Modi, Narendra (2021), [Tweet]. Available at https://twitter.com/narendramodi/status/ 1351524570021441537 [last accessed 12 June 2021].

Mukherjee, Rahul (2020) 'Chaos as Opportunity: the United States and World Order in India's Grand Strategy', *Contemporary Politics*, 26 (4): 420–438.

Mullen, Rani D. (2021), 'Covid's Impact on India's Soft Power in the Indo-Pacific', *Asia Pacific Bulletin*, 29 June. Available at www.eastwestcenter.org/publications/ Covid%E2%80%99s-impact-india%E2%80%99s-soft-power-in-the-indo-pacific [last accessed 9 July 2021].

Nye, Joseph S. (1990), 'Soft Power', *Foreign Policy*, 80: 153–171.

Nye, Joseph S. (2002), *The Paradox of American Power: Why the World's Only Superpower Go It Alone* (Oxford: Oxford University Press).

Nye, Joseph S. (2011), *The Future of Power* (New York: Public Affairs).

Pant, Harsh V., Tirkey, Aarshi (2021), 'India's Vaccine Diplomacy, 'Observer Research Foundation', *Observer Research Foundation*, 23 January. Available at www.orfonline.org/research/indias-vaccine-diplomacy/ [last accessed 15 May 2021].

Pattanaik, Smruti S. (2021), 'COVID-19 Pandemic and India's Regional Diplomacy', *South Asian Survey*, 28 (1): 92–110.

Pradhan, Ramakrushna and Mohapatra, Atanu (2020) 'India's Diaspora Policy: Evidence of Soft Power Diplomacy under Modi', *South Asian Diaspora*, 12 (2): 145–161.

Press Information Bureau (2021), 'Delhi Medical Association (DMA) Honors Dr Harsh Vardhan for Outstanding Service & Exemplary Work during COVID-19 Pandemic'. Available at https://pib.gov.in/Pressreleaseshare.aspx?PRID=1703017 [last accessed 12 June 2021].

Purushothaman, Uma and Moolakkattu, John S. (2021), 'The Politics of the COVID-19 Pandemic in India', *Social Sciences* 10 (10).

Rej, Abijnan (2021), 'In "Historic" Summit Quad Commits to Meeting Key Indo-Pacific Challenges', *The Diplomat*, 13 March. Available at https://thediplomat.com/ 2021/03/in-historic-summit-quad-commits-to-meeting-key-indo-pacific-challenges/ [last accessed 14 June 2021].

Rokicka, Weronika (2021), 'Indie: Druga fala COVID-19 dewastuje kraj', *Krytyka polityczna*, 26 April. Available at https://krytykapolityczna.pl/swiat/indie-korona wirus-druga-fala-pandemii-rokicka/ [last accessed 10 June 2021].

SAARC (2020), 'Covid-19 Emergency Fund'. Available at http://Covid19-sdmc.org/ Covid19-emergency-fund [last accessed 15 November 2020].

Sachdeva, Gulshan (2021), 'India-EU leaders' Meeting Gives New Momentum to Ties', 10 May. Available at www.moneycontrol.com/news/opinion/india-eu-lea ders-meeting-gives-new-momentum-to-ties-6875651.html [last accessed 20 May 2021].

Safi, Michael (2021) '"We Are Not Special": How Triumphalism Led India to Covid-19 Disaster', *The Guardian*, 29 April. Available at online: www.theguardian.com/ world/2021/apr/29/we-are-not-special-how-triumphalism-led-india-to-Covid-19-disa ster [last accessed 25 May 2021].

Sanghi, Neeta (2021), 'A Pandemic Came Calling – and India Was No Longer the World's Pharmacy', *The Wire*, 15 May. Available at https://science.thewire.in/hea

lth/india-pharmacy-of-the-world-Covid-19-vaccines-modi-government/ [last acces-sed 12 June 2021].

Sidhu, Waheguru Pal Singh (2017), 'Vasudhaiva kutumbakam' for the 21st Century', *Brookings*, 22 May. Available at www.brookings.edu/opinions/vasudhaiva-kutumba kam-for-the-21st-century__trashed/ [last accessed 10 March 2022].

Singh, Bhavna (2021), 'Vaccine Nationalism and the India–China Race for Neighbour-hood Diplomacy', 2 April. Available at online: www.orfonline.org/expert-speak/vacci ne-nationalism-and-the-india-china-race-for-neighbourhood-diplomacy/ [last accessed 24 March 2022].

Surie, Mandakini D. (2020), 'India's COVID Diplomacy', 3 June. Available at https:// devpolicy.org/indias-Covid-diplomacy-20200603-2/ [last accessed 10 August 2020].

Talukdar, Sreemoy (2020), 'India's Walked a Fine Foreign Policy Line during COVID-19 Crisis; Test Ahead Lies in How Modi Handles Big Powers', 8 May. Available at www.firstpost.com/india/indias-walked-a-fine-foreign-policy-line-dur ing-Covid-19-crisis-test-ahead-lies-in-how-modi-handles-big-powers-8348031.html [last accessed 13 August 2020].

Tandon, Aakriti (2016), 'India's Foreign Policy Priorities and the Emergence of a Modi Doctrine', *Strategic Analysis*, 40 (5): 349–356.

UN News (2021), 'Prime Minister Modi Spotlights India's Role as a "Reliable, Democratic Global Partner"', 25 September. Available at https://news.un.org/en/ story/2021/09/1101302 [last accessed 15 March 2022].

Upadhyay, Deepak (2021), 'We Are in the Endgame of Covid-19 Pandemic in India, Says Harsh Vardhan', *Mint*7 March. Available at www.livemint.com/science/health/ we-are-in-the-endgame-of-covid-19-pandemic-in-india-harsh-vardhan-11615121893 097.html [last accessed 15 March 2022].

World Health Organization (2020), 'WHO Coronavirus Disease (COVID-19) Dashboard'. Available at https://Covid19.who.int/ [last accessed 15 August 2020].

Conclusions

India's Global Reconfiguration

Chris Ogden

Encapsulating the major research findings of this edited volume, three distinct threads – '*The Shadow of China*', '*An Indo-Pacific Great Power*' and '*Generation Modi*' – became unambiguous throughout its various sections and chapters. Collectively, these threads are crucial reference points for enhancing our appreciation and understanding of *Global India*'s persistent, often tenacious and hastening pursuit of influence and status. As set out in the volume's Introduction, and as reflected throughout the collection's various chapters, the several key themes were integral to analysing these findings, namely:

a   the role of history, memory and experience formed via interaction between states;
b   the intersubjectivity and co-constitution of identity based upon conceptions of 'self' and 'other'; and
c   the designation of fluid elements of continuity and change within both Indian foreign policy and the domestic political actors guiding its formation and delivery.

Moreover, we can highlight a further theme of *evolution*, whereby the nature and delivery – although not the fundamental objectives – of Indian foreign policy continue to reflect Jawaharlal Nehru's assertion at the dawning of India's independence in 1947 that; 'the past clings to us still in some measure, ... yet the turning point is past, and history begins anew for us, the history which we shall live and act and others will write about' (Nehru, 2007). It is now firmly Narendra Modi's BJP who are the driving force making this new history, which is forming the bedrock of India's economic, strategic, political and cultural interests.

The Shadow of China

As the chapters in this volume have shown, the South Asian region is dependent upon *the interaction of internal and external factors* in determining regional power balances and, by extension, the global power balances that

DOI: 10.4324/9781003305132-18

are progressively involving India. Most prominent among such main external factors is China, and in particular the use of Beijing's economic clout to attempt to craft deep seated interdependencies between itself and those states in South Asia. The main mechanisms for such an intertwining is the Belt and Road Initiative (BRI) and one of its major capillaries in the guise of the China–Pakistan Economic Corridor (CPEC). The physical infrastructure of the CPEC especially appears to be eroding the idea of South Asia as a geo-graphically distinct region, and challenges regional architectures that had traditionally been more India-centric. Together with the economic succour of the BRI, it is increasingly pulling more states from the region into Beijing's orbit, and hence China's overall sphere of inter-dependent influence, which now reaches out across most of Asia. The BRI's claims to be a benevolent force for good, based upon win-win cooperation and common prosperity, bolstered by norms of maintaining peace, enhancing stability and heighten-ing development vitally underpin this attraction. They also succeed in juxta-posing relative levels of material prowess between China and India, while China's increasing regional presence appears to be gradually undermining India's status and influence in the region. It is thus altering perceptions concerning New Delhi's claim to be South Asia's undisputed – and natural – hegemon, while underlining how both Islamabad and Beijing remain as obstacles to India augmenting its influence.

This India–China rivalry, which in many ways has now superseded the India–Pakistan rivalry, is becoming a crucial inflection point in terms of New Delhi's identity, and is the most significant contemporary self/other dyad that determines Indian policy norms. As has been shown concerning their terri-torial disputes, 'national prestige', respect, recognition and maintaining face have all become crucial elements within India–China relations. Such senti-ments are arguably detrimental to resolving long standing issues, which underlines the role of identity, psychology and experience as indispensable forces demarcating the India's international affairs. Such apparent obstinacy also points to the role that competition plays within India–China relations, and innate hierarchies of status and influence that are palpable between them, either in South Asia or the Indo-Pacific. Standing up to China also shows how India wants to be taken seriously by its key rival, even if doing so is a 'stumbling block' that seems to negatively affect is overall standing.

China's encroachment in the region is also acting as a stimulus for greater proactivity within Indian diplomacy, whereby India must craft its own alter-native and transparent pathway, with its own specific narratives, lest it allow South Asia to be seen through a dominant Chinese prism. Amassing greater economic strength and appealing to regional states through the associated largess that such financial clout can bring, will thus become a future neces-sity. During the Covid-19 pandemic, Indian leaders have also tried to assert the primacy of Indian diplomacy as New Delhi has searched for a leadership role, especially concerning rolling out vaccines in South Asia. Again however, such efforts have frequently been outshone regionally by a more rapacious, visible and successful Beijing. Furthermore, in an almost compulsive strategic reaction, New Delhi is moreover pushing itself – and is being pulled by other prominent actors – towards the Indo-Pacific zone. Nowhere is this plainer in this volume than concerning relations with Japan and the US, but also regarding significant increases in Indian aid towards states in the Pacific, which are now part of an explicit embryonic push to provide a diplomatic alterative to Beijing.

An Indo-Pacific Great Power

The shadow of China bleeds into India's dealings in the wider Indo-Pacific zone, and significantly impacts upon a range of relations as other states attempt to use New Delhi to balance against Beijing. In this way, both the US and Japan share China as a common 'other' in their regional and global perceptions (and deeper identity constructions), which highlights a now common threat perception between New Delhi and these states. A push-pull effect is also unmistakable, whereby India's amassing of influence with these actors (plus others such as Russia and France) is carried out to essentially *offset the loss of power* that China's increasing influence on South Asia appears to be resulting in. Arguably, gaining greater prominence in the Indo-Pacific is also a way for New Delhi to escape the confines of South Asia and to find a stage more befitting of a would-be great power (Ogden, 2017). The Indo-Pacific thus acts as a region in which we can observe a wider strategic confluence between India's ongoing search for status to be a great power and the proliferation of its strategic relations with key actors such as the US and Japan. They also aid attaining the economic and trade means essential to fulfilling Modi's major development mantra of *sabka saath, sabka vikas, sabka vishwa, sabka prayaas* ('together, for everyone's growth, with everyone's trust, with everyone's effort') (Times of Oman, 2021).

Such interactions further show how India has become an indispensable component within the foreign policy calculations of the international system's major actors. As several chapters in this collection have attested, numerous states are vying for closer India relations, which as a result – purely through association, if not the accompanying benefits – is significantly amplifying New Delhi's global status and influence. For France and Russia, India offers mutual gains relating to the sale of military equipment, nuclear energy and collaboration on space technology, while providing India with support (although not equally by Paris and Moscow) concerning its territorial claims in Kashmir. For Japan, trade, military, common US ties, the Quad and a complementary agreement on India's SAGAR ('Security and Growth for All in the Region') vision for the Indo-Pacific, have also driven their burgeoning strategic partnership. In turn, Washington is having ever closer relations with New Delhi and, as shown in this volume, has accommodated significant divergences with India at the United Nations (UN) primarily due to the US's need to keep India resolutely onside so as to balance against China in the Indo-Pacific and beyond. Taken together, and perhaps with the exception of China, it is apparent that the international system's foremost actors are all conferring increased status on India, which is accelerating New Delhi's global influence as their mutual interests evermore converge.

All of these relations are also a testament to New Delhi's well-established doctrine of multi-alignment (Hall, 2016) that seeks strategic advantage from any and all diplomatic relations. This approach confirms India 'to be a wily chameleon on the world stage that is able to foster positive relations with a range of countries that are often in competition with each other' (Ogden, 2022a). Such an observation notes a growing degree of complexity and sophistication in India's foreign affairs that befits a great power. New Delhi further maximizes its apparent 'status inconsistency' – itself seen as a weakness that prevents, say, an all-weather alliance from emerging with the US – so as to maintain its autonomy and overall strategic flexibility in international relations. As Modi noted in his 2020 Independence Day Speech, such an aim is deeply embedded within India's historical experience whereby 'India faced centuries of foreign rule. All efforts were made to destroy our nation, our culture, our traditions, but they underestimated our self-belief and determination' (quoted in NDTV, 2020). Building upon these tropes, what India's wider global interactions deeply unveil is the dawning of a truly multipolar age in international affairs, with India being one of the indisputable poles – and a truly 'independent centre' – within such a system. Achieving such a new era is a fundamental policy aim of the Modi regime (Ogden, 2018). Moreover, such a largely Indo-Pacific-centric multipolar architecture – within which China, Japan, the US, India and arguably Russia are located – heralds a new world order that is not based upon US dominance.

Generation Modi

The foremost driving influence upon Indian foreign policy – and the major source of their underlying norms and narratives forming India's identity –is that of the BJP under the aegis of Narendra Modi. As the BJP have extended their grip on power in India through successive majority-garnering general election victories, the well-established *Hindutva* norms of the party (Ogden, 2014) and their supporters has been firmly injected into Indian foreign policy. After their triumphs in 2014 and 2019 – and appearing odds-on to repeat such a performance in 2024 and even 2029 – the BJP have become *the centrifugal force of Indian politics*. Shifting and evolving the normative basis of India's dominant identity in the international sphere, within these dynamics the 'othering' of Pakistan, and to an increasing degree China, is acting as a fundamental reference point to amplify the credibility of a *Hindutva*-centred approach. Moreover, anti-Muslim sentiments (buoyed in some cases by increasing Hinduphobia, as is evident in India–Bangladesh relations) are now the mainstay of its increasingly intolerant and incendiary narratives, which are affecting both internal and external politics. Often heightened through social media, the role of history and memory impact upon such nationalist discourses, including Partition, and is currently influencing the ways in which New Delhi conducts its public diplomacy.

As part of its articulation of a narrative of a 'new India', such norms are leading to new conceptions – for instance, of the Indian Ocean region, whereby New Delhi's policies are producing and re-producing a *Global India* identity that is more *Hindutva*-orientated. Underscoring the linkage between the domestic and international spheres concerning the delineation – and nature – of present-day India's foreign policy proclivities, the BJP is now framing New Delhi's strategic preferences through its own image. This process is culminating in what can be referred to as the 'Hinduization of foreign policy'. A sense of threat permeates these preferences, be it against an India-centric hierarchy in South Asia or the potential loss of territory vis-à-vis China, which menace its overall status and wider influence among New Delhi's great power peer group, and which acts as a vital emotional touchstone for Indian diplomacy under the leadership of Narendra Modi. The shadow of China further drives the doubling down of the Modi government upon their *Hindutva* foundations as a way to define, project and ultimately preserve India's national identity.

We have also seen the manifestation of other influences permeating the values and norms central to India's identity. In the domestic sphere, these have related to a range of sub-national actors whose paradiplomacy is adding ever-greater complexity in Indian foreign policy and amalgamating the interests of India's states and the central government. Externally, we also observed how *Hindutva* is resulting in a 'global India brand' within the Indian diaspora in the US that is interlinking with other political identities, most clearly the populist outlook of supporters of former US President Donald Trump. This export sustains core *Hindutva* tropes of othering minorities and Indian exceptionalism. It also points to the wider *global magnetism* of the BJP beyond India's borders – and their resultant impact upon India's international identity –which is acting as a significant emboldening influence upon India's wider international status and influence. It is further evident concerning narratives of the future, be it India becoming a 'proactive global leader' or the way in which the government conceptualizes – for instance – climate change via a BJP orientated framework that is resulting in a '*Hindutva* foreign policy'. In these regards, the identity and normative proclivities of the BJP and Modi are combining with India's strategy towards its international relations and characterize *Global India*.

Conclusions: Essential India

There is little doubt that the bandwidth of India's international relations has never been as deep as it currently is. Across all spheres of her regional and global interaction – and in the economic, military and diplomatic domains –

New Delhi's presence in world affairs is more visible and more influential than it ever has been in the modern era. In many ways, this enhanced status is testimony to the core residual strengths of India – its large population and landmass, its important geo-strategic positioning and its democratic basis – and the associated value that these strengths have in attracting other states towards her, especially within a deeply globalized economy that seeks new markets, investment opportunities and resources. Moreover, the importance of India in terms of prevailing geo-political power balances and power shifts – most clearly shown in this volume concerning the rapid rise of China and the consolidation of the Indo-Pacific region as the fulcrum of international relations – combined with the ever-greater strategic value that New Delhi offers, is only serving to exponentially boost these strengths. The need to capitalize on such a confluence is not lost on prominent leaders in India, leading External Affairs Minister S. Jaishankar to remark; 'this is the time for us to engage America, manage China, cultivate Europe, reassure Russia, bring Japan into play, draw neighbours in, extend the neighbourhood and expand traditional constituencies of support' (Jaishankar, 2020: 10).

As a result, New Delhi's potency and importance within international affairs, and its overall influence and status, is also being significantly augmented. Moreover, India is now a clear variable within the strategic calculations of other major states, which again serves to enhance India's international standing, prominence and overall importance. Indeed, especially in consideration of (mainly) western states (and Japan) to actively balance against China in the Indo-Pacific region, India has become an indispensable and essential part of the strategic calculus underpinning contemporary great power politics. This new role as a core element of twenty-first century international relations is in many ways characteristic of a 'new India' under the BJP but also of a 'new era' for both Indian foreign policy and geo-politics more generally. The peer behaviour of other great powers towards New Delhi is also conferring legitimacy, status and recognition on India, and thus appears to be 'anointing' India as a present or future member of the great power club. Such an observation underscores how international relations is being 'constructed by the participants themselves' via the building blocks of identity, experience and interaction. It also confirms the *inter-national* aspect of global affairs, and how India's self-definition against other states interplays with how other states define themselves, most obviously in relation to China, with the overlap in these identities informing their mutual interests.

Finally, what is also evident is that India will not relent in its pursuit of influence and status, and that such a quest will be done in line with preserving and augmenting New Delhi's autonomy in international relations. Although shared by all previous Prime Ministers, Modi has recast this aim – calling it *atmanirbhar Bharat abhiyan* ('self-reliant India Mission') that rests upon the five pillars of 'economy, infrastructure, technology-driven system, vibrant demography and demand' (Panda, 2020). The key observation here is that India – despite a range of ever closer strategic partnerships, as evidenced at length in numerous chapters of this edited volume – can, and should, never be expected to become a full, unquestionable ally of any state. As such, India will continue to maximize what it can gain bilaterally and multilaterally, and will do so in a way that always focuses upon amplifying India's status and influence first.

In light of this observation, politicians and scholars alike could do well to remember the example of China, which in the late 1970s was engaged with by Washington in order to balance against the US's primary competitor, in the guise of the Soviet Union. 30–40 years later, India is performing a similar function for the US but this time to balance against China. Apart from revealing the limits of pursuing short-term interests in international relations, and the unintended consequences (or strategic naivety) that can accompany such policies, New Delhi may well emerge as the US's primary opponent by around 2050. If Beijing's rise ends up plateauing in a similar fashion to Japan (which was also seen as a threat to US hegemony in the 1980s) or if China endures an internal collapse, perhaps provoked by an economic or ecological catastrophe, then it would also confirm such antagonistic possibility. Furthermore, were India's – and indeed South Asia's – authoritarian descent to intensify further (Chowdhury & Keane, 2021; Jaffrelot, 2021), potentially aiding the emergence of an authoritarian world order (Ogden, 2022b), the US and the western bloc could well find itself faced by a highly powerful and not necessarily democratic competitor. Such a future would herald a new epoch for the trajectory of world politics and for that of *Global India*.

References

Chowdhury, Debasish Roy and John Keane (2021) *To Kill a Democracy: India's Passage to Despotism* (Oxford: Oxford University Press).

Hall, Ian (2016) 'Multialignment and Indian Foreign Policy Under Narendra Modi', *The Round Table*, 105 (3): 271–286.

Jaffrelot, Christophe (2021) *Modi's India: Hindu Nationalism and the Rise of Ethnic Democracy* (Princeton, NJ: Princeton University Press).

Jaishankar, S. (2020) *The India Way: Strategies for an Uncertain World* (New Delhi: HarperCollins).

NDTV (2020) '10 Big Quotes from PM Modi's Independence Day Speech', 15 August. Available at www.ndtv.com/india-news/pm-narendra-modis-independence-day-speech-at-red-fort-top-5-quotes-2279770 [last accessed 23 June 2022].

Nehru, Jawaharlal (2007) 'A Tryst with Destiny (14 August 1947)', *The Guardian*, 1 May. Available at www.theguardian.com/theguardian/2007/may/01/greatspeeches [last accessed 23 April 2019].

Ogden, Chris (2014) *Hindu Nationalism and the Evolution of Contemporary Indian Security: Portents of Power* (Delhi: Oxford University Press).

Ogden, Chris (2017) *China and India: Asia's Emergent Great Powers* (Cambridge: Polity).

Ogden, Chris (2018) 'Tone Shift: India's Dominant Foreign Policy Aims Under Modi', *Indian Politics and Policy*, 1 (1): 3–23.

Ogden, Chris (2022a) 'India is Creating a New World Order – Asia's Chameleon: India, Russia and the Ukraine Inflection Point', 3 May. Available at https://iai.tv/articles/india-is-creating-a-new-world-order-auid-2118?_auid=2020 [last accessed 23 June 2022].

Ogden, Chris (2022b) *The Authoritarian Century: China's Rise and the Demise of the Liberal International Order* (Bristol: Bristol University Press).

Panda, Jagannath (2020) 'Modi's "Self-Reliant India" Has Key Foreign Policy Aspects', *Asia Times*, 13 July. Available at https://asiatimes.com/2020/07/modis-self-reliant-india-has-key-foreign-policy-aspects/ [last accessed 23 June 2022].

Times of Oman (2021) 'Sabka Saath, Sabka Vikas, Sabka Vishwas, Sabka Prayaas Will Ensure Creation of New India: PM Modi', *Times of Oman*, 15 August. Available at https://timesofoman.com/article/105417 [last accessed 23 June 2022].

Index

Page numbers in *italics* and **bold** indicate Figures and Tables, respectively.